Joseph Holt Ingraham

The pillar of fire

or, Israel in bondage

Joseph Holt Ingraham

The pillar of fire
or, Israel in bondage

ISBN/EAN: 9783744738385

Printed in Europe, USA, Canada, Australia, Japan

Cover: Foto ©ninafisch / pixelio.de

More available books at **www.hansebooks.com**

RIVER NILE.

THE PILLAR OF FIRE;

OR,

Israel in Bondage.

BY THE REV. J. H. INGRAHAM,

RECTOR OF CHRIST CHURCH, AND OF ST. THOMAS' HALL, HOLLY SPRINGS, MISS.; AUTHOR OF "THE PRINCE OF THE HOUSE OF DAVID."

London:
JAMES BLACKWOOD AND CO., 8, LOVELL'S COURT,
PATERNOSTER ROW.

TABLE OF CONTENTS.

LETTERS OF SESOSTRIS TO QUEEN EPIPHIA.

LETTER I. On, the City of the Sun—Grandeur of Egypt—Emotions at the sight of its wonders of art and scenes of beauty—The Queen of the ancient house of Pharaoh—Her son, Prince Remeses (Moses)—Tyre, and its traffic with distant lands—Damascus—Voyage from Tyre to Pelusium—Scene at the departure of the fleet—The Nile—Its encroachments—First view of Egypt—Meeting with Egyptian war-ship—Invitation to visit the Court of Queen Amense—Description of Egyptian war-ship—Banquet on the Admiral's ship—Singular custom—Panorama of the Nile—pp. 17—24.

LETTER II. Love for native land—Avenue of temples and palaces—Sublime temple of the Sun—Emblem of Osiris—Artificial canal—Gardens and circular lake—Gathering of philosophers and scholars—Obelisks—Message from Queen Amense—Great temple of Osiris—Splendid approach to the City of the Sun—Row of sphinxes—Osiris and Isis—Colossi—An Arabian charger—Magnificent scene—Spectacle of architectural grandeur—Beautiful palace—Religious notions of the Egyptians—Personal appearance of the Lord-prince Remeses, (Moses)—View of the Desert—Hebrew labourers—Interview with Remeses—pp. 24—31.

LETTER III. Climate of Egypt—Eternal sunshine and crystalline atmosphere—Costume of the Egyptian prince—Hieroglyphic writing—Legend of the Obelisk of Mitres—More of the personal appearance of Remeses (Moses)—The Hebrew prince Abram (the patriarch)—His personal appearance—His tomb—Interior of Egyptian palace—Egyptian Mythology—Mnevis, the sacred ox—Legend of Osiris—Pantheism—Apis, or the sacred Bull—Out-of door life at midday—Hebrews, under their task-masters, in the burning sun—Prospect from the terrace of the palace—Isle of Rhoda, in the Nile—pp. 31—38.

LETTER IV. Palace of Remeses—Invitation to meet the Queen—Costume of a prince of Tyre—Egyptian chariots and horses—Nubian charioteer—Escort of the Queen's body-guard—Pleasure chariots—The Queen in her chariot—Beautiful lake—Sphinxes—Royal palace described—The throne-room—The throne-chair of ivory—Its footstool and canopy—Assembly of military princes—Magnificent attire, and splendid appearance of Remeses (Moses)—Ceremony of presentation to the Queen—Queen Amense; her appearance and costume—Termination of the audience—pp. 38—45.

LETTER V. Egyptian magnificence—Egyptian architecture—Osiride pillars—Vastness of objects—Avenue of sphinxes—Temple of the god Horus—The emblem of Hor-hat—Court of Colonnades—Grand hall—Rich colours in architecture—Sculpture—Bas-reliefs—Splendid temple—Chamber of art and beauty—Magnificent review of the army of four thousand chariots of iron—A warrior-prince in his war-chariot—Description of war-chariot—Ethiopian slaves—Bewildering spectacle—Military and civil homage to the Queen—The Lord of Uz (Job) described—Ceremonies preparatory to a royal banquet—The banquet—Costly wine-goblets—Arabian dancing-girls—Jugglers—Guests overcome by wine—pp. 45—54.

LETTER VI. Visit from Prince Remeses (Moses)—Great gate of the city—Phalanx of dark Libyan soldiers—Varied accomplishments of Remeses—Avenue of gardens, villas, and lakes—Temples in circular lakes—Egyptian field-labourers—Hebrew brick-makers—Description of this "mysterious" race—Account of the mode of their toil—Cruelty of their task-masters—Emotions of pity at the sight of their sufferings—The lash!—Beautiful Hebrew girls—Dwellings of brick-makers—Joseph—Scene at the "Fountain of Strangers"—Distant view of the City of the Sun—Of Raamses—Of the pyramids—Of the illimitable desert—Wounded Hebrew youth at the Fountain of Strangers—Majestic old Hebrew beaten by task-masters—Touching scene—pp. 54—62.

LETTER VII. Interview with the venerable Ben Isaac at the Well of the Strangers—Raamses, the Treasure-city—Joseph's granary—Exquisite temple of Apis—Beautiful young Hebrew girl pursued by the task-master—Her rescue and story—The punishment of the task-master—Intolerable burdens of the Hebrews—Garden of flowers for the use of the temple of Apis—Account of the Syrian prince Abram (Abraham)—Of Melchisedec—Of the Hyksos, or Shepherd-Kings—Their conquest of Egypt—The Princess Sara (wife of Abraham)—Prince Jacob (the patriarch) and his twelve sons—Joseph—Pharaoh's dream—Elevation of Joseph—Monuments of his power—pp. 62—69.

LETTER VIII. Eagles of prey—Account of the Hebrews—Imposing funeral of the Patriarch Jacob—His powerful and able government—Overthrow of the dynasty of the Shepherd-Kings—Dynasty of the Thebaïd—Flourishing condition of the Hebrews in the land of Goshen, under the government of Joseph—Aspirations after the ONE GOD—Reduction of the Hebrews to servitude—Their rapid and miraculous increase—The massacre of their male infants—Courageous affection of the Hebrew mothers—Egyptian nurses sympathize with them—Infants hid—Queen Amense's humanity—Courage and wisdom of many of the Hebrews—Exciting ride past Joseph's ruined palace—Jacob's well—The plain of the Hebrew brick-makers—Death of a

Hebrew under his taskmasters—Sculptured obelisk of Queen Amense—Emotions of Syrian painters at sight of their prince—pp.—69—77.

LETTER IX. Reflections on the degradation of the Hebrews—Hebrew pages and maidens in the service of Egyptian nobles—Amram, the palace gardener—Contrast between the physiognomy of the Egyptians and Hebrews—Remarkable likeness of Prince Remeses to the Israelites—Description of the Lord-prince Mœris—He seeks a quarrel with Remeses—Illness of Queen Amense—Filial devotion of Remeses—Magnificent prospect of the Nile, the Plain of the Pyramids, the City of the Sun, Jizeh and Memphis—Myriads of human beings at labour—Naval review and sham battle—Exciting scene of contending thousands—pp. 77—83.

LETTER X. Recovery of Queen Amense—Gropings after the True God—Pleasure-galley of the Nile—Voluptuous ease—River chant—Phœnician Mythology and Learning—Procession of the Dead—Tradition of the universal Deluge and of Noe-menes (Noah)—Myths of Ammon, and of Belus the Warrior-god and Founder of Babylon—Nimrod's temple—Baalbec—Worship of the Sun—Myths of Apis, Horus, Adonis, and Io—Magnificent worship of Osiris and Isis—Mysteries of the temple of Tyre—Baal-phegor—Pillars of the West—Marvels of foreign lands, and islands of wonderful beauty—Men formed like monkeys—The edge of the world—A sea-storm—Gulf down which the full sea plunges—Legends of the form of the Earth; of its foundation; of its motion through space—pp. 83—91.

LETTER XI. The beautiful Isle of Rhoda—Prince Mœris and his favourite lion—Refinement of Egyptians—Polite observances at the reception of visitors—Parting between Queen Amense and Remeses—Military emblems—Magnificent display of the Egyptian "tented hosts"—Striking religious and military display of the army—Columns formed of trophies taken in battle—The chief priest of Mars—His gorgeous attire and imposing ceremonies—Gigantic statue of Mars, in full armour—Offerings of the soldiers—Invocation by the High-priest—Libations for the army—Clouds of incense—Appearance of the beautiful daughters of the priest—The musical sistrum—Sacred offices in the temple filled by women—The Virgins of the Sun—Social position of Egyptian women—Thrilling martial hymn chaunted by the priests, the army, and the maiden—Sacrifice—Remeses reviews the army—Ethiopia—Description of an Egyptian army; its tactics and weapons—The nations composing it—pp. 91—100.

LETTER XII. Immense military force of Egypt—Sublime sunrise—Morning hymn—Gala of the resurrection of Osiris—Festivals to the gods—Visit to the Queen—Glimpse of dark-eyed Egyptian girls—Their tasteful dress—Life, manners, and customs of high-born Egyptian ladies—Their high social estimation—Egyptians can have but one wife—Occupations of ladies—Classifications of Egyptian society—The habitations of the Egyptians—Family customs and gatherings—House of the Admiral Pathromenes—Home-life of the Egyptians—pp. 100—109.

CONTENTS.

LETTER XIII. Ancient worship of the gods on Libanus—Natural temples—Legend of the weeping for Tamuz—Unsatisfactory nature of the worship of idols—More aspirations and gropings after the true God—Where is the Infinite?—There can be but one God!—His nature —Body-guard rowers of Prince Remeses—Their captain—Nubian slaves—Great quay, or landing-mart of Memphis—Merchants from all parts of the world—Street lined with temples—Avenue of statues and columns—Memphis—Gradual change of the true religion into idolatry —The four deified bulls of Egypt—Sacred birds, serpents, scorpions, vegetables, and monsters—pp. 109—117.

LETTER XIV. Majestic temple of the sacred bull, Apis—Tyrian mariner torn to pieces by the Egyptians for ignorantly killing a sacred cat—Imposing worship of the deified bull—Description of the sacred animal—Costly offerings at his shrine—An omen!—Tasteful palace of the hierarch of the temple—Transmigration of souls—Brute incarnation of deity—Tradition concerning Osiris—Foreshadowing of the coming of the Invisible upon earth in human form—Lamentations upon the death of a deified bull—His obsequies—Pomp and rejoicings over a new god, Apis—Mausoleum of the Serapis—Sarcophagi—The Serapeum—The Lady Nelisa—Beautiful daughter of the priest of Mars—The lake of the Dead—Embalmers and their art—Customs attending death and embalment—Funeral procession of Rathmes, "lord of the Royal gardens"—The venerable head-gardener, Amram—The baris, or sacred boat—pp. 117—127.

LETTER XV. Conclusion of funeral ceremonies of the lord of the royal gardens—The Sacred Way—Processions of mourners—Avenue to the tombs—The "dead-life" of the Egyptians—Awful ceremony of the judgment of the dead—Burial of the unworthy dead prohibited—False accusers stoned away—Myth as to the state of the soul after death—Metempsychosis—The mystery of the tribunal of Osiris—Reception of the justified soul into the celestial kingdom—Doom of the reprobate soul—Monkeys, emblems of the god Thoth—The gate of the pyramids—Colossal Andro-sphinx, or Watcher before the pyramids—Beautiful temple of Osiris—The twin pyramids, Cheops and Chephres—pp. 127—135.

LETTER XVI. Continuation of description of the Pyramids—Colossal monolith of Horus—Perilous ascent of Cheops—Prospect from a resting place upon the pyramid, four hundred feet in air—A prince of Midian falls from Chephres—Magnificent view from the top of Cheops, six hundred feet in air—Tombs of Kings—The Giants before the Flood founders of the great pyramids—Ancient appearance of pyramids—Greater duration of human life—The third pyramid built by Amun, son of Noah—Egyptian Tradition of Noah and his sons—Entombment of Noah in Cheops, and the mourning of the Nations—Verdant plain of the Nile—The desolation of the Desert—Jizeh—Raamses and Pythom, the treasure-cities—The smiling land of Goshen—Prophecy of an Unknown World, in the West—The sacred papyri—Descent of the pyramid—Luxora, the beautiful daughter of the high-priest—Her legend of the Emerald Table of Hermes—Osiria—pp. 135—142.

LETTER XVII. The lovely Osiria's legend of King Saurid—Stately Hebrew woman—Tradition of the construction of the large pyramid—Its foundations—Its gates—Its covering of silk—Its **treasure-chambers and magical guardians of stone and agate**—Miriam, **the papyrus-copier**—Her striking resemblance to Prince Remeses—The pyramid penetrated by a Phœnician conqueror—Discovery of treasures—Mighty **sarcophagus** of the dead monarch **of two worlds**, NOAH—Chamber **of the precession** of the equinoxes—Hall of the Universe—Pyramids built **before the** Deluge—Configuration of the seven planets as at the Creation—Astrology—Enigma of the Phœnix—The riddle solved—Nelisa—Interview with the stately Miriam in the Hall of Books—pp. 143—151.

LETTER XVIII. Tidings from Prince Remeses and the army—Antediluvian origin of the pyramids—The barbaric King of Ethiopia, Occhoris—His body-guard of Bellardines—His sacrilege in the temple of the sacred bull at Thebes—Pious vengeance of the people—Visit of Remeses to the tomb of his father—Remarkable conversation with Miriam, the papyrus-copier—Description of Miriam—Ben Isaac and the lad Israel—Contempt of the Egyptians for Israel—Religious and political degradation of the Hebrews—Miriam declares the mystery of the God of her fathers—Her denunciation of idol-worship—Miriam's occupation—The winged asps—Interview with the Prince of Uz, Ralub (Job)—Job speaks of the ALMIGHTY!—Seems inspired of God—Tradition of a day's-man, or mediator—Job convinces Sesostris that there is but one God—pp. 151—161.

LETTER XIX. Intelligence from Ethiopia—Remeses a conqueror—Great spoils—He enters Memphis in triumphal array—His filial piety—The captive Ethiopian king—Victorious army of one hundred thousand men in triumphal procession—The Prince of Egypt in his war-chariot—Column of twelve thousand Ethiopian captives—Description of the bands of captives, and their treatment—Invocation of the victors in the great temple of Pthah—Distinction between captives taken in war and the Hebrews—pp. 161—169.

LETTER XX. Delightful climate—Indolence and leisure by day—Spirit of life and enjoyment reigns at night—Galley of a noble designedly runs down a small baris—Handsome Hebrew—Another startling resemblance to Prince Remeses!—The lad Israel again—Miriam, the papyrus-copier, the sister of the handsome Hebrew—What he saw, in boyhood, beside the Nile—His infant brother committed to the river—Subterranean chambers for casting images of the Gods—The Hebrew gives an account of his people and his God—He mourns the oppression of his race—pp. 169—177.

LETTER XXI. Thirty-fifth birth-day of Prince Remeses—Queen Amense proposes to abdicate in his favour—The Hebrew page, Israel

—Melancholy of the Queen—Prince Mœris—Moving interview between the Queen and Remeses—He declines the throne of Egypt—A secret!—Prince Mœris seeks the ruin of Remeses—A bribe!—Suspicion!—Terrible agitation of the Queen—Attempt of Mœris to poison Amense at a banquet—Another bribe—A mystery! Rameses consents to accept the sceptre—pp. 177—186.

LETTER XXII. Remeses prepares for his coronation by an initiation into the mysteries of the temple—Power and influence of Egyptian priesthood—Daily public duties of the Queen—Her attire—Her bathing and dressing rooms—Skilful adornment of their hair by Egyptian ladies—The Queen acts as chief priestess—Her delightful hospitalities—Beautiful trait of character—Proposed succession of Remeses—Solemn vigil, and other ceremonies of initiation—Remeses shut out from the world in the gloom of the mysterious temple—Israelisis with a message from the Queen—The Celestial Sea—A courier from Mœris—Great distress and singular manner of the Queen—A terrible secret—An impatient follower—pp. 186—194.

LETTER XXIII. Revelations—Letter from Mœris—His haughty demand—Is Remeses the son of Pharaoh's Daughter?—Another letter and another haughty demand from Mœris—Still another—A doubt! —An investigation—Amense never a mother!—Her descent to the Nile to bathe—The little ark of basket-work and beautiful child—The princess adopts it—A threat!—The Queen unfolds the terrible secret—Her agony of fear—Her touching story of the discovery of the infant Remeses—She gains resolution and defies Mœris—Remeses a Hebrew! —pp. 194—203.

LETTER XXIV. Mournful reflections—Sacred poem by Remeses, being scenes in the life of Job—Remeses discovers all—A sirocco of the soul—He narrates the mysterious scenes of his initiation—Startling spectacles—Overwhelming displays of enchantment and magic—Mysterious journey beneath the pyramids—Labyrinthine catacomb—March of Time through the heavens—Remeses alone beside the altar —Amense not his mother!—His vision in the dark chamber of the pyramids—The massacre of the Hebrew infants—Scene in the Hebrew hut—The mother and child—The babe committed to the Nile—The little maid—The beautiful lady, Pharaoh's Daughter—The Hebrew nurse—The image-caster—pp. 203—211.

LETTER XXV. Continuation of vision of Remeses—Himself the child of his vision—Mysterious voices in the vaulted chamber of the pyramid —Mocking eyes—He flees—Tender interview between the Queen and Remeses—He narrates his vision—The secret fully unveiled—Discovery of a father, mother, brother, sister—Illness of the Queen—She assembles the council of the nation—Remeses renounces the throne—Amense adopts Mœris—Her death—Amram—The mother of Remeses—Miriam—Aaron—Egypt in mourning—Remeses assumes his Hebrew name, **Moses**—Arts of magicians and sorcerers—pp. 212—220.

CONTENTS. 13

LETTERS BETWEN REMESES (MOSES) AND OTHER PERSONS.

LETTER I. Moses beholds the thousands of his countrymen under the lash of the taskmasters—A prophecy—Visits Tyre and is cordially received by Queen Epiphia—Tyre—Damascus—He meets the venerable Prince of Uz (Job)—Nuptials of Sesostris—pp. 221—222.

LETTER II. Defeat of the King of Cyprus by Sesostris—Moses in Syria—He journeys to sit at the feet of Job—Cruelty of Pharaoh (Mœris)—The Lake Amense—pp. 223—224.

LETTER III. Moses visits Job—The wisdom of Job—His wealth and power—Moses writes his life—Job leads Moses to the knowledge of the true God—pp. 224—225.

LETTER IV. Mœris increases the burdens of the Hebrews—Tradition as to the term of their servitude—Nearly accomplished—Moses, in Syria, yearns to be with his brethren in Egypt—pp. 226—227.

LETTER V. Moses determines to visit Egypt—Receives from Job the history of the Creation—Job's piety and his favour with God—Prayer the path to the throne of God—King Sesostris and Queen Thamonda—Israelisis—pp. 227—229.

LETTER VI. Moses departs for Egypt—The Illimitable Sea—Reflections upon the infinity of God—A storm—Despair of passengers—Their gods unavailing to save—Moses invokes the true God—The storm ceases—The crowd offer divine honours to Moses—His anger at their sacrilege—He arrives in Egypt—Is in the bosom of his family—Oppression of the Hebrews—Their miraculous increase—Tradition of God's revelation of Himself to Abram—A miracle!—God's command to Abraham—His obedience—God's promise—The fulness of time at hand—Woman of salt—City of Salem—Moses strives to arouse the Hebrews—He is doubted and discredited—pp. 229—235.

LETTER VII. Moses, in disguise, sees King Mœris amid his chief captains—Terrible cruelties inflicted upon the Hebrews—Task-master pursues a Hebrew youth, to kill him—Moses slays the task-master—Comes upon two Hebrews in altercation—He rebukes them—They threaten to expose him to Pharaoh for slaying the Egyptian—Prophetic inspiration of Amram, the father of Moses—Moses flees from Egypt—pp. 235—238.

LETTERS OF REMESES OF DAMASCUS TO HIS FATHER, KING SESOSTRIS.

LETTER I. The young prince visits Egypt—The acts of the Egyptian kings—The reign of Mœris—He constructs an immense lake—Inauguration of a temple—Splendid spectacle of idol-worship—Plain of the Mummies—Enlargement of Memphis—Discovery of treasures

CONTENTS.

beneath the Sphinx before Chephres—The captive King Occhoris—Increase of Hebrews—Character of the reigning Pharaoh—His cruelty to the Hebrews—Good feeling between Hebrew and Egyptian women—Intelligence of the long absent Remeses (Moses)—pp. 239—243.

LETTER II. A caravan from Ezion-geber—Its governor a Midianite—Prince Jethro—Abram—Moses in Midian—The young prince determines to accompany the caravan into Mirian, and to seek Moses—pp. 243—245.

LETTER III. Moses to his old friend Sesostris—Account of his mode of life—His meditations upon the oppression of his nation, and upon the character of their predicted deliverer—Is inspired to write a narrative of the Creation of the World—pp. 246—247.

LETTER IV. Journey across the desert—Mount Horeb—Moses standing upon a mountain-rock—Affecting interview—Grotto of Moses—His wife and sons—Story of his rescue of the daughters of Jethro at the well—His sublime teachings—Will he be the Deliverer?—View from Mount Horeb—Aaron—Miriam—pp. 247—250.

LETTER V. Moses leads his flock to a secluded valley—Wonderful appearance of the Burning Bush—Astonishment of the shepherds—The Voice in the midst of the fire—God reveals Himself to Moses, and commissions him to lead forth the people—The humility of Moses—His staff converted into a living serpent—The leprous hand—Moses hesitates—The Lord rebukes him, and the flame in the bush shoots fiery tongues—Aaron to be the mouth-piece of the Lord—Miraculously advised, Aaron comes to Moses—Moses converts his staff into a serpent, before Aaron—He obtains the consent of Jethro to his departure from Midian—Moses in Egypt—Sends messengers to summon the elders of Israel to meet him at Jacob's well—Pharaoh's cruel designs against the Hebrews—pp. 250—256.

LETTER VI. Midnight meeting of the elders of Israel—Jacob's well a source of superstitious dread to the Egyptians—Beautiful moonlight scene—Moses opens his errand from the most High—Aaron unfolds the traditional promises—Unbelieving Hebrews—Terrible means used for their conviction—Korah persists in unbelief—His punishment and horror—The assembly dissolves—pp. 257—259.

LETTER VII. Moses goes before Pharaoh—Amazement of the Egyptian courtiers—Harshness of Pharaoh—Moses delivers God's message—Pharaoh defies the Living God—He is overcome by his emotion, but hardens his heart—New toils devised for the Hebrews—pp. 259—261.

LETTER VIII. The rod! the whip! the cry of the sufferers!—The Hebrews reproach Moses and Aaron—Moses appeals to the Lord—Seeks to comfort his brethren with the words of the Most High—Hope dies in their hearts—Pharaoh redoubles his worship of all manner of idols—He curses God—Sacrifices a living Hebrew child to the Nile—Sacrifices a Nubian slave to Typhon—Invokes his idol-god against the God of Moses—A secret dread—Children of Israel groan under oppression—pp. 261—265.

LETTER IX. Moses and Aaron again seek Pharaoh, and demand the freedom of Israel—He requires a miracle—Miracle of Moses' rod—Jambres and Jannes, the magicians—They convert their rods into serpents—Moses' serpent destroys theirs—The brothers confront the King at the river's side—He defies their God—The Nile runs blood—Goshen, the land of the Hebrews, sparkles with clear water—Jambres again appealed to—The plague of the frogs—Jambres and Jannes produce, but cannot remove them—Pharaoh relents, and the plague is stayed—The plague of lice—Jambres and Jannes disgraced—God speaks to Moses by the well of Jacob—The plague of flies—Pharaoh again relents—He hardens his heart, and God sends a pestilence upon the cattle—God again speaks to Moses beside the well—The plague of boils—Goshen unharmed—God threatens further vengeance upon Pharaoh—pp. 266—273.

LETTER X. Moses denounces the plague of thunder and hail against Egypt—Grand gathering of the storm of God's anger—The storm hangs over Goshen but harms it not—The purpose of God in these judgments—Terror of Pharaoh—Agrees to let Israel go—Scene of desolation and death—Pharaoh seeks to drown his terror in a banquet—In his revels curses God—Again refuses to let the people go—He vacillates—Orders Moses and Aaron to be thrust from the palace—The plague of the locusts—Despair of the Egyptians—Pharaoh acknowledges his sin—The plague ceases—Character of Pharaoh—The plague of darkness—Description of the plague—Pharaoh unequal to the combat with God—His rage against Moses—Moses denounces upon Pharaoh God's last and terrible judgment—The Egyptians defy him—pp. 274—283.

LETTER XI. Moses and Aaron call the elders of Israel together—The Passover instituted—The Hebrews cease work—They all flock to Goshen—Moses deified by priests in the temples—Hopefulness of the Hebrews—The sprinkling—Egyptians seek refuge with the Hebrews—Silence of expectation—Awful vision of the Angel of the Lord in the Pillar of Fire—A cry from Egypt—Messengers from Pharaoh to Moses—Amunophis, the son of Pharaoh, slain by the Angel of the Lord—Egyptians implore Moses to depart—Israel marshalled—Guided by the Pillar of Fire, the Hebrew host leave Egypt—The Lamb of God prefigured—Moses explains the lessons of God's judgments—pp. 283—292.

LETTER XII. The departure—Sarcophagus containing the embalmed body of Joseph—The Shekinah—Succoth—Etham—Pihahiroth—Migdol—Hebrews inclosed between the mountains and the sea—Calm confidence of Moses—Fulfilment of prophecy—Pharaoh determines to destroy the entangled Hebrews—Gathers a mighty host and follows in pursuit—Dismay of the Hebrews—The Egyptian army comes in sight—The elders reproach Moses—He calls upon God—The Voice of the Lord—The Pillar of Cloud and the Pillar of Fire—The sea—Israel in the midst of the sea—The procession—The pursuit—Frantic terror of Pharaoh and his army—Their destruction—Israel filled with awe and gratitude—They go into the wilderness—The bitter waters—Journey abounding in miracles—The rock in Horeb—God's awful presence on Horeb—Moses disappears in the mount of God—The people murmur—They demand a god—They sacrifice to a molten calf—An indignant God!—Terrible vengeance upon the offenders—Joshua—pp. 292—302.

APPENDIX.

The author to the scholar and critic—pp. 303—307.

THE PILLAR OF FIRE:

OR,

ISRAEL IN BONDAGE.

PRINCE SESOSTRIS
    TO HIS ROYAL MOTHER, EPIPHIA,
        QUEEN OF PHŒNICIA.

AT length, my dear mother, I have reached the "Land of the Seven Rivers," and do now write to you from her gorgeous capital, ON, The City of the Sun.

How shall I describe to you the grand and solemn magnificence of this city of divine temples, and convey to you a just idea of its palaces that seem rather to have been erected for the abodes of gods than of men!

Wheresoever I turn my eyes, I realize that I am in mighty Egypt; for everywhere I behold grandeur and glory, excellency and perfection. Every object illustrates the power, munificence, and taste of the imperial princess who now sits on the throne of the Pharaohs, and the splendour of whose reign has raised Egypt above the mightiest empires of the earth.

And all that I behold recalls the ancient glory, my dear mother, of our own land, the once princely Palestina and Phœnicia,—twin kingdoms which of old gave conquerors, and rulers, and laws to Egypt, under the short but brilliant dynasty of her Shepherd Kings! But, though fading with age, Phœnicia still lives in the beauty, pride, and power of her daughter Egypt.

I will not lament over the waning glory of my own dear land, my royal mother, while I can see it revived here with increased magnificence. Phœnicia is not dead while Egypt lives. Every ruin in my own kingdom is restored with augmented beauty and splendour on the green plains of this land of the shining River, whose fountain-head is underneath the throne of Thoth, far in the southern sky.

How shall I describe what I behold? Every new object enchants me, and moves my soul with a fresh pleasure. I am intoxicated, not with wine, but with the splendour of art and scenes of beauty, and with manifestations of human glory and power hitherto inconceivable. I have heard my royal father describe the glory of Salem in Palestine, under the princes of the dynasty of Melchisedec, with its gorgeous temples to the Sun, and its palaces of marble, its hanging gardens, and noble terraces overlooking its flower-enamelled valleys; but the cities of Egypt surpass this Syriac magnificence.

In coming hither, across the Levantine seas, from Syria, I seem to have crossed to the shores of that mystic world where dwell the sacred divinities, rather than only to another land of the plane of the earth; for Egypt, compared with the kingdom of Phœnicia seems truly the land of the blessed. What far-famed warriors! what stately priests, clothed with power from the gods! what superb princes! what a majestic queen! what grace and dignity in the virgins of the Sun! what a stupendous system of worship! what mighty mausoleums, both tomb and temple, rising like mountains hewn into solid triangles everywhere over the illimitable plain! What a land of verdure and of flowers!—land of gardens and palaces, obelisks and fountains, fanes and altars, sphinxes and gigantic statues!—land, comprising all that can delight the heart or take captive the sense!

I ask myself—Am I, indeed, in Egypt, the "Land shadowing with wings," as those proud Pharaohs, Thothmeses I. and II., termed it, upon their winged globe-carved shields?—am I in Egypt, the glory of the earth, the kingdom above all kingdoms, whose queen is above all the monarchs that reign, and before the elevation of whose golden sceptre all sceptres fall?

I have not yet, my dearest mother, seen, save at a distance, as she was ascending the steps of her palace, this mighty queen of the ancient house of the Pharaohs: but the third day hence I shall be formally presented to her in the throne-room, where she receives the ambassadors and princes of the nations who come into Egypt either to learn arts, or arms, or to behold the magnificence of her empire, or to study the religion, laws, and government of a nation, the fame of which has filled the earth.

Upon my arrival with my galleys off the mouths of the Nile, I forwarded to her, by a private messenger in my gilded barge, the letters written by your loving hand and sealed with the regal signet of your kingdom, commending me to her personal favour and royal consideration.

Although I have not yet been presented to the court, I have seen and must describe to you, the royal son of Queen Amense—this proud daughter of the Pharaohs—Prince Remeses. Never did the gods set their seal upon a nobler and truer prince. Every movement of his stately and graceful person, his rich voice, his superb height, his lordly eyes, his majestic yet winning carriage, all bespeak a youth born to empire—created for dominion over men.

He is now in his thirty-fourth year, and is in the full glory of manhood. He is skilled in all the arts of war, and not less celebrated for his learning in all the wisdom of the Egyptians. Sages and philosophers listen to his words when he converses, not so much with the deference that is the homage due to rank, as with the attention which intelligence lends to superior wisdom.

He received me with kindness and embraced me with affection, inquiring after the welfare of my royal mother, and welcoming me to his country with gracious and courteous words. Notwithstanding there is a difference of six years in our ages, I feel that I shall be regarded by him on terms of equal friendship, and that to his companionship I shall owe the happiest hours I may pass in the land of Egypt.

But, dear mother, as I promised to write you an account of my voyage hither, with the adventures and scenes thereof worthy of your notice, I will devote the remainder of my letter to this subject.

When I took leave of you on the marble steps of the stately pier which extends along the front of our palace, and had stepped upon the deck of my galley, I felt that a twofold cord had parted at my heart,—one which bound me to thee, O mother, from whom I had never before been separated, and one which tied me to my native land. Although for the first time in command of a beautiful fleet, numbering a score and ten galleys, and about to visit the fairest of all realms under the sunny skies of Afric, yet the pang of this twofold separation deeply grieved my soul. It was with tears glittering upon my eyelids that I gazed upon you, as you waved your adieux and called on the god of our race to bless me! It was with a voice thick with emotion that I gave orders to the admiral to spread the purple sails of my golden galley to the favouring breezes which seemed to be sent in answer to your prayers.

Long I stood upon the lofty poop of my ship, gazing towards the receding city, with its noble lines of palaces, its crowning temples, its familiar groves, and pleasant gardens. (Even now I am moved as I recall the sweet emotions of that time.) As I surveyed the fleets of merchantmen from all lands gathered about her piers and anchored in the haven, I felt my sorrow at parting, yielding gradually to a feeling of pride that I was the prince of the great city to which these argosies came bearing the merchants of all the earth. Indeed it was a noble and stirring sight, dear mother, and calculated to divert my thoughts, to see these ships, as my galley passed through them, lower their banners, or elevate their rows of shining oars high in the air, both in homage and farewell to the departing lord of the port. There were vessels for bringing the merchandise of gold, and silver, and precious stones from unknown seas; galleys from Tarsus and the isles of the West, bearing pearls, and coral, and precious woods, and thyme-wood; gaily decked barges, that carry fine linen, and purple, and silk, and scarlet down to Egypt from Syria; painted ships from the Nile, that receive by caravans from Ind and the East cinnamon and odours, and ointments, and frankincense, and ivory, and diamonds; the low dark galleys from Afric, that bring Ethiopian slaves; and the broad heavier vessels from the Delta, laden with meat and fine flour! There were also the strong craft from Colchis and the North, with iron, and brass, and marble; and oaken argosies from further Britannia, bringing tin; tall ships from Græcia with horses and chariots; while from the south shores of the summery seas were light, graceful vessels laden with dainty and goodly fruits, and birds of gorgeous plumes and of ravishing songs! All these annually lay their treasures at thy feet!

As I moved slowly in my galley through the rich fleet of ships which filled your haven, I felt my heart beat quicker, and I returned the salutations of the ship-masters and of the foreign merchants on their decks, with smiles of gratification at the prosperity still at least of our port of Tyre; though the half our realm has been lost by invasion and our interior cities are decaying. So long as Damascus and Tyre remain, dear mother, those two eyes of your kingdom, your power, and throne will stand. The decadence of our sister city Sidon will not affect our prosperity, since her ships will flock to Tyre. Yet Sidon will rise again, if in my power to restore it.

I remained upon the poop of my ship until we had passed, not only the fleet of merchant galleys, but the four-score war-ships with their hundred banks of oars, that ever guard the entrance to the port with vigilant eyes and arms. The sun was gilding with his setting beams the battlements of the temple of Hercules; and the columns of the graceful temple of Io were richly roseate in the blushing glory of his radiance. The last object on which my eye rested was the gilded gate of the gorgeous Fane of Nyeth on Lebanon; and I sent from my lips a prayer to the fair and kind-hearted goddess to guard thee, mother, and me for thy sake.

We soon passed the bright red Pharos, from the lofty lantern of which, as the shades of evening rapidly fell around us, streamed forth like a new-born star its cheering splendour for the haven-bound mariner. Soon in the heavens over us other lights were kindled by the gods; and the moon, rising over the lofty mountain-range of Libanus, made far out upon the sea a path of light, that seemed like a band of silver with which she would bind me still to the shores I was leaving! But in Egypt I yet behold the same moon shine down upon me with familiar radiance; and as I gaze upon her I can feel, that even here she is a link to bind me to my native land—that upon her winged beams I can send a thought to my dear mother, on whom also she shines.

My whole fleet got well out of the port before the star Aldebaran rose; and as the breeze was light, the governors of the rowers commanded them to ply their oars. Thus with the fall of a thousand sweeps into the blue sea at one motion, keeping time to the voice of a singer who stood upon the bridge across the mid-ship, we kept our course down the coast of Palestine. We would have steered directly for the Delta of the Nile, but had knowledge, by a vessel that met us, of a fleet of Rhodian pirates, which lay wait, in that vicinity, for the Egyptian merchant-ships; and, as my galleys were rather an escort of honour than a war-fleet, I did not wish to measure my strength with them, but dispatched one of my ships, the same night, back to Tyre, to the admiral of your Tyrian fleet, who, no doubt, has gone out ere this in pursuit of these sea-rovers and enemies of our commerce.

Nevertheless, after we had passed Jaffa, and the next day Ascalon in lower Philistia, we beheld half a score of ships of doubtful appearance, and, by my orders, six galleys were detached from the fleet and gave chase. They proved to be fast-sailing Ionian pirates, for one of them, being crippled, was overtaken. They had been many weeks on the sea, and were returning to their own distant and barbarous islands, richly laden. The captain of the galley took out her merchandise, and precious stones, and spices, of which she had robbed other ships, and burned her on the sea, with all the wretches who appertained to her.

The shores of Egypt were reached by us on the seventh day, without any accident to my fleet. It was two hours after the sun rose that we came in view of the low line of land which marks the entrance to the "Garden of the World," and from which open the seven gates of the Nile into the great blue sea.

Upon ascending to the castle for bowmen on the highest mast of the ship, I could discern the tall columns erected by King Menes at the chief entrance of the river, from the summit of each of which at night blazes a wonderful flame, said to have been invented by the Magi of Egypt. As our galley rowed nearer the faint line of coast, I could see numerous ships coming out and entering the Pelusian branch of the Nile,—some of them in the interior so far, that only their tops could be seen above the level land. I was now suddenly surprised with a change in the colour of the sea, which, from an emerald green, became clouded with an intermixture of tawny water, thick with mud, that seemed to flow upon the surface of the sea, as if lighter than itself. I soon perceived that this was the outrush of the river against the sea, with which it refused wholly to intermingle and lose itself,—as if the proud Father Nilus reluctantly yielded his power, so long wielded for a thousand miles, to the sceptre and dominion of the god of the Mediterranean. Yet the latter—so vast was the volume of the yellow waves of the former—was forced a league from the shore before the conquered Nile ceased to resist his fate.

The sun shone upon the battlements of the great city of Pelusium— the oldest fortified place in Egypt, and called "the Key of Egypt," and also "the Strength of Egypt"—and lighted up the terraces of its gardens and temples; but the admiral told me that every year the deposit of the Nile is covering them, and that ere many centuries no trace will be left of a city, which is older than On or Memphis. We saw, from the deck, palaces and obelisks and groves in the suburbs, and further inland a country of wonderful beauty and of the highest cultivation, but as level as the sea, from which it is elevated but a few feet. The muddy and wonderful Nile is overflowing annually these pleasant maritime plains; and as the plane of the Delta is steadily raised, these ancient cities and palaces and this fair land will become a fen for the stork and the sea-mew! How different the site of Tyre, my dear mother! Built upon the firm coast, and defended by nature, it will stand for ever as the key of Syria and of the East; and to the end of time the commerce of the world will flow into the palace-like warehouses of its opulent merchants!

As we drew near the port, one of the large fishing eagles which have their home in the Delta soared above our heads, scanning our deck with his piercing glances : and snow-white birds with black tipped wings skimmed past from wave to wave; while others, resting upon the crest of a shining billow, rocked gracefully with the motion of its undulations. An ibis stalked upon the shore, and numerous aquatic birds, unknown to us, soared about our galleys with sharp and strange outcries.

The atmosphere of the morning was slightly hazy, and, suffused by the sunbeams, cast a soft veil over the land, investing galley, pharos, and fane with the hues of gold. It was a scene of novel beauty, and I hailed the very first view of Egypt with delight. It was a happy omen of the future.

As my galley advanced before the fleet, a large war-ship with a triple poop-deck, and propelled by three hundred oars, swept like a swift dark cloud out of the mouth of the river and bore down towards me in hostile attitude. I displayed the insignia of my kingdom at the top of the chief mast, and awaited the Egyptian guard-ship. The vessel was brought-to a bow-shot from my own, and I was asked by the governor thereof, who I was, whence I came, and my destination? To these inquiries I gave satisfactory replies through my admiral; whereupon the Egyptian captain, commanding an elegant barge to be made ready, came on board, attended by his suite, to pay his respects to me as Prince of Tyre. I came forth from my state-room to receive him, my dear mother, attired as became my rank. In the most courteous language, and with an elegance of manners unsurpassed save in the polite land of Egypt, he assured me of the pleasure it would give his royal mistress, Queen Amense, "The Support of Worlds," as he termed her, to have me visit her court. He said she was just then returning from a visit to the temple of Isis and Nephthys, at Philæ, with a vast retinue of state and sacred galleys, and by the time I arrived at Memphis she would be either there or at her private palace at On.

By his advice, I dispatched, in our handsomest galley, my secretary, Acherres, with a copy of the letter to the queen, which you gave to me, sealed with my own signet. This done, I entertained the Egyptian officer with a magnificence becoming my position and his own. He was much pleased with the elegance of my ship, and the complete appointment of my fleet. He said he had never seen a Tyrian squadron before, but had heard much of our luxury and perfection in maritime affairs.

His ship was stately in height, and terrible with its warlike aspect. The poop bristled with armed warriors in polished helms of brass. It had four short masts, and upon each top thereof a huge castle containing a score of Libyan bowmen with steel-headed arrows. Upon the prow was a sort of fortress, on which stood a group of soldiers armed with long spears and with large oval shields, on which were painted hieroglyphic devices in brilliant colours. Arranged on the sides above the rowers were black Ethiopians, gigantic men in steel cuirasses, with long swords held before them. The captains of these warriors were stationed at various points, arrayed in rich armour of varied fashion, according to the class of soldiers that were under them.

The prow of this mighty battle-ship, which carried one thousand fighting men, besides three hundred rowers, was ornamented with a lion's head and shoulders of colossal size; while across the stern stretched the broad, gilded wings of the feathered globe of the Sun, which is the emblem of the kingdom of Egypt. Besides this gorgeous and majestic galley, there were many lesser ones near, having but a single mast and fifty oars. This fleet ever kept guard at the mouth of the Nile, and thus defended the gates of Egypt on the sea against foes.

When I had sufficiently admired his ship from my own, the admiral, whose name is Pathromenes, invited me to go on board. After viewing all the parts of the ship, and especially the noble apartments devoted to him and his officers, I was entertained with musical instruments by players of infinite skill. Then I was amused with the performances of jugglers and the wonderful antics of grotesque deformed dwarfs, who seemed kept on board only for the entertainment of these Egyptian nobles. Towards evening, a banquet was offered me. Among other rare dishes were gazelles. Before the feast, the admiral made a signal to a priest of Osiris, who presided over the sacred rites on board, and inaugurated it by a prayer to the god for the welfare of the queen and the prosperity of the kingdom. This custom recalled our own, of offering first a libation of wine to the gods. During the banquet, sweet strains of music floated around us. After we had closed the feast, and were drinking wine, an attendant entered, bearing a miniature mummy, elaborately painted and gilded. Holding this emblem of mortality before me and the admiral, he said solemnly:

"Behold this, and drink and be happy; for such thou shalt be when thou art dead!"

I was not a little surprised at this unwelcome, and, as it seemed to me, unseasonable intrusion. Pathromenes, observing my looks, said with a smile: "This introduction of a memorial of death to our feasts, O prince, is not unseasonable. It is designed to exhort us to enjoy life while we possess it, for when we are no more, enjoyment will be past." Thus saying, he poured out a vase of wine into our golden cups, and pledged me "Thy health, my mother!" So I drank to thee, and the glory of thy reign. Nevertheless, I do not agree with the admiral, but think, rather, that the intention of this exhibition of Death to guests, is to warn them that, while life is so short, it ought not to be spent wholly in pleasure and festivities.

At length, night coming on, I returned to my ship, and the next day, with a light wind and aided by but one bank of rowers, entered the mighty Nile, and slowly ascended its powerful but sluggish stream. The courtly Pathromenes escorted me past Pelusium, and then took leave of me, embracing me more like a father than a friend. I left my fleet at the Pelusian Delta, to return to Tyre after it shall have received fresh water on board from the Nile. The only galleys I took with me are the one I came in, and that on board of which I sent my secretary to the capital in advance of me. I trust the remainder will safely reach Syria.

The shores of the Eastern Nile, as we ascended, presented an unchanging scene of gardens, verdant fields of corn, villages, temples, and tombs, all united in one unbroken belt for leagues. The river was dotted with fishers in their slender boats, and we constantly met vessels descending, bound to the open sea : some for Afric, for gold-dust and ivory ; others to Philistia, for copper and iron ; others to Colchis, for silver, or to the Isle of Thasos. The evening of the day we entered the river, we beheld the sacred crocodile. It was a vast scaly monster, basking on the shore. I gazed upon him with wonder and fear. If he be a god, his votaries worship him rather through terror than from love. But to my senses all the minor deities of Egypt are gross and revolting. Yet I must not dare to be impious while in the very land of these gods.

The next day, after sailing for hours between gardens, we drew near the City of On, on the east bank. Our approach to it was marked by the increased size and grandeur of the palaces and temples, and the life and activity on the shores. Before reaching the city, I caught view of Memphis on the west side of the river, and far beyond towered the apex of one of those mighty pyramids whose age is lost in the oblivion of the past.

Farewell, dear mother. In my next letter I will describe my arrival and debarking at the terrace of the City of the Sun, and my gratifying reception by the Prince Remeses.

Your affectionate son,
SESOSTRIS.

LETTER II.

CITY OF THE SUN.

MY DEAR AND ROYAL MOTHER:

THINK not that the splendours of the Court of " Pharaoh's Daughter," as the Egyptians still love to call their queen, will lead me to forget my own royal home and the dear scenes in which I have passed my life—scenes that memory will ever cherish, as they are associated with the love and care of a mother, such as a prince was never before blessed with by the gods. Think not, my queenly mother, that while I describe with pleasure the magnificence of Queen Amense's realm, I think less of your own kingdom; but, rather, all I behold only causes me to love my native land the more ; for the glory of Tyre, my home, is my mother's presence—and my mother is not here ! Queen Amense may have the homage of my intellect, but that of my heart is reserved only for thee !

I have prefaced my letter in this manner, dear mother, lest you should jealously read the glowing descriptions I give of what I behold, and may fear that the luxuries and grandeur of Egypt will make me dissatisfied with the lesser splendour of the Court of Phœnicia. Fear not. I shall bring back to thee a son's faithful love, and to my people the loyal affection due to them from their prince.

I closed my letter to you in sight, as I thought, of the City of the Sun. But what I believed to be the capital of the gods, was but the colossal gateway leading from the river to the city, which is half an hour's ride inland. Yet from the Nile to the city there is a continuous avenue of temples, such as earth has never beheld—not even Nineveh or Babylon, in all their glory. For a mile fronting the river extends a row of palaces, which, stupendous as they are, form but wings to a central temple of vaster dimensions. The palaces that guard it, as it were, are adorned with sculptured columns of the most elegant description. They are three hundred in number, covered with gorgeous paintings in the richest tints, and carved with the most finished art. The beautiful capitals of these columns are shaped alternately like a flower-bud, not yet expanded, or like the open flower of the lotus, and the sides formed of imitations, by the wonderful artist, of leaves and flowers indigenous to Egypt. The columns and capitals, thus exquisitely fashioned, are gigantic in size, and of the grandest altitude.

The central temple is a lofty and wonderful edifice of brilliant red sandstone, with sixty columns of marble enriching its façades; these, with the three hundred, representing the three hundred and sixty days of the ancient Egyptian year. The front of this sublime temple is pierced by three colossal gateways, broad enough for four chariots to pass abreast. These gateways are adorned with paintings, in the brightest tints, representing processions of priests, sacrifices, offering of incense, and all the imposing religious ceremonies appertaining to the worship of the Sun.

Above the centre gateway, between the noble wings of the propyla which flank it, is a representative emblem of Osiris, in the shape of a splendid shield of the sun, a half-sphere of gold, from which extend wings for many yards, each feather glittering with precious stones. Around the globe are entwined two brazen asps, emblems of which I have not yet learned the signification.

Imagine, my dear mother, this stupendous and noble temple, with its vast wings facing the river, and reflected upon its sunny surface. Fancy the river itself, flowing laterally through these gateways into an artificial canal, lined with trees, and bordered by lesser temples, which recede in long lines of diminishing columns. Behold oranges swinging in clusters from branches bending over the water, while scarlet pomegranates, figs, and olives fill trees innumerable that shade the terraces; and vines, either gorgeous with flowers of wonderful beauty and form, or pendent with purple grapes, entwine the columns, and depend from the carved abacus of the capitals.

Into this canal my beautiful galley was received, in the sight of thousands of admiring gazers standing upon the steps of the terrace which led down to the entrance, and on which I had landed to pay my homage to the chief captain at the propylon, who, magnificently attired, waited, by the queen's command, to receive me and conduct me to the city.

Returning with me on board my galley, he gave orders for it to be taken in charge by two royal barges, with prows of silver, and golden banners waving above the heads of the rowers, who were Nubian slaves clothed in scarlet tunics. Thus, in state, my dear mother, as became a prince, was I borne along this avenue of palaces and fanes, and fragrant gardens. The vanishing line of columns was, at short intervals, interrupted by gateways, above which were statues of Osiris and Isis.

I was almost bewildered by the novelty and splendour of these varied scenes, and was thinking that nothing could surpass in magnificence this mighty avenue to a city, when all at once the canal expanded into a circular lake completely enclosed by columns, forming majestic colonnades on all sides, in which were walking and conversing innumerable richly dressed persons, while others were grouped around noble-looking ancient men, listening to their discourses. The chief captain, who was with me in my galley, informed me that these columned halls were the favourite resort of the eminent philosophers and scholars of all lands, who came hither to be taught in the learning and wisdom of the Egyptians. I then looked a little closer, when he was pleased to point out to me several great philosophers, who, called wise men in their own kingdom, yet had come hither to learn at the feet of these masters of the world's wisdom, the wise men of Egypt. As we were rowed past and around this majestic circle of columns, I saw two noble youths from Damascus, who came last year to Tyre, in order to embark for Memphis. I beheld also Prince Melchor of the City of Salem, in Syria, the descendant of the great King Melchisedec, whose wise reign, about three centuries ago, is still remembered with glory and honour to his name. The prince recognized me, and returned my salutation, and leaving the group with which he stood, hastened around the terrace to meet me at the place of debarkation ; for this delightful lake, dear mother, terminated the noble canal which united it with the river. Beyond it, the galleys and barges did not go. Instead of water, this mighty avenue to On was now to be continued by land. At the place opposite the inlet rose two lofty obelisks a hundred feet in the air, of incomparable elegance and beauty. They were dedicated to Osiris and Isis. Elevated upon pedestals of porphyry, they formed the graceful entrance to a semicircular flight of marble steps which led from the lake to a broad terrace interlaid with parti-coloured marbles, in every variety of device which taste could conceive, or art execute. Landing upon these steps, I ascended to the terrace, and was there met and embraced by the Prince of Salem. Here the chief captain took leave of me, and immediately there advanced towards me a noble person, wearing a chain of gold about his neck, and clothed in purple silk, richly embroidered, and who carried in his right hand a long silver wand, with the head of an ibis, cut out of a precious stone, upon it. He said that he was an officer of the court of the queen, and had come to conduct me on my way to the city.

"Her majesty," he said, with dignity becoming one who served so mighty a monarch, "has received your letter, royal prince, and has directed her servants to pay you all honour !"

I acknowledged the grace of the queenly Amense in this courteous reception of a stranger, and followed him across the terrace, which I perceived was encircled by statues of all the divinities of the earth; and I was gratified to see that Io, and Hercules, and the favoured deity of Phœnicia, Athyris, had conspicuous pedestals allotted to their sacred images, near the Theban god Amun.

Indeed, dear mother, this fact, and the manner of my reception, shows that the present dynasty has graciously forgotten the conquest of Egypt by the warlike hosts of Phœnicia. But when we recollect that the first Amosis of the present house of Pharaohs had for his queen the beautiful Ephtha, daughter of the last Phœnician Pharaoh, taking her captive when he expelled the father from the throne of Memphis, we need not be surprised at the favour shown us by the noble Queen Amense, for, fourth only in descent from the fair Phœnician, who was of our own blood, she is our cousin by just hereditary lineage.

When I had traversed the "Hall of the Gods," we came to a lofty two-leaved gate of brass, which stood between two sculptured propyla of Libyan stone. At a wave of the wand of my escorter, they flew wide open, and revealed the most magnificent and awe-inspiring spectacle that it was possible to conceive the world could present.

Before me was revealed an avenue, more than a mile in length to the eye, leading straight to the City of the Sun, which rose, temple rising beyond temple, shining like gold in the sunbeams, a mountain of architecture, fashioned as if by the hands of gods rather than of men. In the midst stood, elevated above all surrounding edifices, the great temple of Osiris itself, encircled by a belt of twelve glittering obelisks, representing the twelve months. In the centre of this wonderful girdle, upon the apex of a pyramid rising within the walls of the temple, two hundred feet high, blazed that sacred gold shield of the sun—the shield of Osiris—the fame of which has filled the world. It was like the sun itself for glory and splendour! Oh, how can I describe all this! My pen refuses to find language to record what I wish to write.

But I will be brief, lest I overpower you with gorgeousness, and blind you with glory. Verily, the Egyptians seem resolved to rob the heavens of their celestial architecture, and set up a rival heaven on earth!

From the open gateway of brass I beheld the city thus described, with its temple, obelisks, pyramid, and countless palaces, while the whole was encircled by a green belt of gardens, which shut it in from the desert, like a setting of Indian diamonds in a bed of Assyrian emeralds.

The avenue itself was paved with red-coloured Syene stones from the isles of the Cataracts, and on each side was a gigantic row of sphinxes, reposing on broad, elevated dromoi. Some of these represented lions, leopards, and other beasts of the African and Nubian deserts. Some of them had the head of a ram, with the body of a lion, the fore-paws extended upon the terrace, the vast body resting upon the hind-paws, all presenting aspects of majestic repose. There were one hundred of these stone effigies, in a double row twenty feet apart, facing the avenue, and fastening upon the passer-by their stony eyes in immovable watchfulness. This avenue I walked up, preceded by the queen's officer, and escorted by a retinue, which fell in behind me.

Having passed this row of crio-sphinxes we ascended three broad steps, on each side of which towered a lofty pylon, elaborately adorned with costly paintings of colossal size, representing sacred scenes. Another dromo bordered with four-score andro-sphinxes, having alternate faces of Osiris and Isis, the one stamped with majesty, the other with beauty, now began, and passing this solemn and awful range of gigantic faces we came to another ascent of marble steps, flanked by obelisks: four lofty pylones, and three spacious courts were at the end of the dromos of sphinxes, also a vast arena enclosed by palaces. Crossing this noble square, we came to two colossi of granite, representing Cheops and Nilus, their shields covered with hieroglyphics wrought with the highest degree of perfection, each cartouch recording their titles and deeds.

At this point there met me a superbly caparisoned Arabian charger, held by two pages; while a young noble, bearing upon his breast the insignia of a prince of the queen's palace, addressed me, and invited me to mount the beautiful and fiery animal.

I obeyed, leaping into the saddle with delight at once more being upon horseback. Scarcely had I pressed the bit with the gilded bridle, ere a score of horsemen, in splendid armour, issued from the propylon on my left, in two columns, and, enclosing me between them, escorted me through several magnificent courts, in which I caught glimpses of obelisks, monoliths of kings, pylones sixty feet in height with pyramidal wings, giving entrance to courts each more magnificent than the last.

At length I saw before me the great and splendid pylon which gives admission to the city. In front of it, raised upon a throne of crimson stone, stood, with his ibis head fifty feet in the air, a monolith statue of Thoth. In his outstretched right hand he held a pair of scales, and in his left a tablet.

At this gate, the city is entered in its central point. Two obelisks, ninety feet in height, towered on each side of the entrance. Here I was received by a venerable noble, who was mounted upon a snow-white horse, and attended by a brilliant retinue, all superbly mounted. This personage extended to me the same hospitable and courteous welcome from his queen, which had been presented to me from the others. He rode by my side, and we took our way at a rapid trot along an avenue of alternate obelisks and sphinxes, until we passed through a pylon which opened into the streets of the city. The splendour around bewildered me. Palaces with gorgeous façades and triple stories of colonnades, composed street after street, while fountains and statues and propyla, temples, monoliths, andro-sphinxes and crio-sphinxes presented, as I rode along through this superb "City of the Sun," an endless spectacle of architectural grandeur and marble magnificence. The streets were thronged with handsomely attired citizens, either in the pursuit of pleasure or buisness, while priestly processions, festival parties crowned with flowers and attended by musicians, and bodies of horse, were met by us. Gilded chariots, palanquins, and vehicles of rare and graceful forms, were numerous. The whole city wore an air of pleasure and life, and impressed me with the idea that the Egyptians are not only master-builders in architecture, but know how to enjoy the splendid cities they erect with such costly care.

My senses sated with luxury, I was not unwilling to alight at the entrance of a beautiful palace, which the venerable horseman said the queen had placed at my service. Upon its portico I was met by my private secretary, Acherres, who, in his joy at beholding me again forgot for a moment my rank, and embraced me with tears of delight; for, in this foreign land, he saw in me alone the link which bound him to his native country.

I have now been two days in this palace, wherein is furnished me, by the queen, the attendance of slaves; and every luxury of Egypt is at my command. As I said to you, dear mother, in my first letter, I have yet only seen the Queen of Egypt at a distance, as she was ascending the steps of her palace, but to-morrow I am formally to be presented to her, for on that day of the week alone she receives princes and ambassadors. She had returned four days before to Memphis, from Philæ, with a great retinue of the lords and officers of her realm, and yesterday, crossing the Nile in her barge of state, she entered this sacred city, which she visits for three days every month to perform in the great temple the sacred rites of her gorgeous religion. Of this worship I will soon write you more fully. It is an error, however, to suppose that these enlightened Egyptians worship the sun, or any other objects, as such, of mere matter. Their fundamental doctrine is the unity of the deity, whose attributes are represented under positive and material forms. The common people perhaps never go beyond these forms, and their minds never are admitted to a knowledge of the truth of the mysteries; but the priests, and the high in rank, look upon the sun, and moon, and animals, and the fecund Nile, only as so many attributes of a one infinite deity. The sun—believed to possess much of the divine influence in its vivifying power and its various other effects—is regarded as one of the grandest agents of the one deity. The moon is another direct manifestation of the invisible author, and as the regulator of time, say their sacred books, is figured in painting and sculpture as the ibis-headed Thoth, and the deity who records, as time flies, the actions of men's lives. Osiris, if I understand their mythology, is this supreme god (symbolized here by the sun), who is also the judge of the souls of the dead, rewarding or punishing hereafter the creatures he has created, according to their lives. But when I learn more fully their system of religion, I will explain it to you, dear mother.

Although I have not seen, to speak with her, the august lady who reigns over Egypt, I have been visited by her son, the lord Prince Remeses. I have already written of him. He is in his thirty-fourth year, and the noblest appearing man my eyes ever beheld. Upon his brow the gods have set the seal and impress of command. I will narrate the manner of our first intercourse.

I was standing by the window of the stately apartment, which overlooks one of the squares of the city, interested in watching the toils of several hundred men, coarsely attired in blue aprons or loin-cloths, and grey breeches reaching only to the knee, the upper part of their bodies being naked, who were at work constructing a wall which was to enclose a new lake before the temple of Apis, in the midst of the square ; for On is a city of alternate lakes (all of great beauty and adorned with trees), temples, squares, and palaces, interspersed with dromos of sphinxes connecting court after court, through lofty pylones ; while obelisks, statues, and fountains fill up the interspaces.

My window not only commanded a view of these labourers with their heavy burdens of bricks, borne on their shoulders to the top of the wall they were building, but also, beyond the wall and distant temples, a glimpse of the yellow expanse of the desert. How mighty, and grand, and solemn it looked in its loneliness and ocean-like vastness ! A faint dark line that I at length perceived in motion, was, doubtless, a caravan coming from the haven of the Red Sea, where the galleys from Farther Ind land their precious freights of untold wealth. This caravan seeks the port of On, six miles below on the Nile, whence sail ships, laden with the treasures of the caravan, to all parts of the known earth. Sesostris, Thothmes, Menes, all planned a canal from the Nile to this sea ; but the camels are the only ships, to this day, that cross this desert waste. Again my eyes rested upon the labourers, seeing that they were sorely pressed by cruel task-masters, who, with long rods, urged them to their ceaseless toil. I perceived, then, that they were men with Syrian features, arched eagle noses, long black beards, and narrow but fine eyes, which seemed to have a strange expression of tears in them. There were among them noble and manly men, handsome youths, though pale with toil, and bent forms of aged men. I marvelled to see so fine a race thus in bondage, as slaves under task-masters, for in the day of the Phœnican Pharaohs, there were no such bondmen in the land of Egypt. From their remarkable likeness to some natives of Mesopotamia I had seen in Tyre, I judged that they must be captives of that ancient Orient people, taken in the wars of Amunoph.

While I was regarding them, and especially an interesting youth, whose dark eyes, as he staggered under a heavy burden of bricks, were turned up to me as if seeking sympathy, Acherres entered and said :

"My lord Sesostris, the mighty Prince Remeses is alighting from his chariot upon the steps of your palace !"

Upon hearing this news I hastened to the portico, wondering if I were to be honoured with a personal visit from the lord of Egypt, ere the queen mother should receive me in state.

Upon reaching the circular peristyle hall within the portico, the ædile of my palace opened the gilded doors, and there stood before me the Prince of Egypt. I have already described his noble presence and personal appearance. Upon seeing me he advanced, waving his attendants to withdraw, and with mingled dignity and sweetness, that at once won my heart, said :

"I welcome you, noble Prince of Tyre, to Egypt ! I have been engaged in reviewing the army of the Nile, a day's march hence, and neard but yesterday of your arrival. I hail you, not as a stranger, but as cousin, dear Sesostris ; for are we not allied by blood ? "

"You, my lord prince," I said, "are descended from two lines of kings—the Syrian and Theban—I from but one. But by that one we are indeed of the same blood. But what is a prince of Tyre, compared with the heir to the throne of Egypt ? "

"We are to be friends and equals," he said, smiling, as he pressed my hands. I accepted this pledge of friendship with grateful emotion, my dear mother ; and from that moment we became as brothers,—he the elder, I the younger, and looking up to him with admiration and pride, as henceforth my model of what a prince should be.

He remained with me three hours. We discoursed of you, of Tyre, of the beautiful city of Damascus,—my sword of Damascene steel attracting his notice (for he is a famous soldier), and leading to the mention of this city. We talked also of Egypt, and her glory, and her power ; of the queen, his mother, and the manners, religion, and policy of the kingdom.

But, my dear mother, I will here close this letter, and in another relate to you what passed at our interview, and the most interesting portion of his conversation.

Your devoted son,
SESOSTRIS.

LETTER III.

THE CITY OF THE SUN.

MY DEAR MOTHER :

THE climate of this land of the Sun is so delightful to the senses that one feels a constant buoyancy of the heart, and experiences in the consciousness of mere existence, an undefinable and delicious joy ; and herein I discover the key to the cheerful gaiety of the Egyptians. The skies are blue with eternal sunshine. The atmosphere, free from moisture, is so transparent and crystalline, that distant objects lose one half their distance to the eye. The sun rises ever with cloudless splendour, and sets in a sea of golden glory, without a shadow of a cloud falling upon his fiery disk. The moon sails by night across the starry ocean of the heavens, with a brilliancy unknown in other lands ; while the stars burn with an increased intensity, and seem enlarged by means of the purity of the upper air through which we behold them. It is no marvel that the dwellers in this happy land are wise, and love art, and delight in forms of beauty, and build palaces for gods !

But I promised in my last letter, dear mother, to describe what particularly passed in the long and interesting interview which the Prince Remeses had with me on his first visit to my palace. I have already described his personal appearance; but, as ladies are always interested in costume, I will relate to you how he was attired.

The Egyptians, you are aware, always shave the head and beard closely, save when in mourning. They have nevertheless a plaited lock of hair on the height of the forehead, which falls down over the ear. Such is the fashion with which the youthful god Horus is represented in paintings and statues, though the beautiful locks of this deity are not so closely removed but that a crest of golden tresses covers the top of his head like the plume of a helmet. Something in this manner Prince Remeses wore the lock of jet-black hair which remained. But upon his head he had a rich cap or kaftan of green silk, the front of which was shaped like the beak of an eagle, while behind, it fell to the shoulders in a sort of cape, fashioned like drooping wings—the whole most becoming and striking. In the eyes of the eagle, blazed diamonds, and his plumage was studded with precious stones, beryls, sardine gems, and the onyx-stone. This head-costume, in varied forms, is worn by all the nobles and men of high rank. With some the ibis or the vulture, with others the lion or the hawk, form the insignia. I have seen him since in his chariot, in a close-fitting helmet-cap of burnished gold, resembling that of the Egyptian god of war, which, with his martial form and commanding glance, lent to him the aspect of the god himself!

His vesture was of fine linen, worn in numerous folds about his form; and a surcoat embroidered with gold in royal devices, left open in front, displayed a girdle of links of steel and gold, exquisitely and cunningly woven, to which hung his jewelled sword. About his neck was fastened, by a pearl of price, a collar of the red-hued gold of Ophir, massive and large; and upon his manly chest glittered a breast-plate, sparkling with the enamelled *cartouch* of the god Athothis, the deity who presided at his birth, and who is the same as our Taut, the inventor of letters.

And here let me remark, that writing by letters is scarcely yet known in Egypt, the hieroglyphic form being still in current use; but Remeses has cultivated the Phœnician art, and writes with a character of his own construction, with the facility and beauty of one of our own men of letters. Ere long, through his influence, this form of writing will supersede wholly the hieroglyph, which is cumbersome and difficult to be understood, save by a native-born Egyptian; yet I have commenced the study of it, and can read already the cartouch of Mitres, on his obelisk over against the portico of my residence. Of this obelisk, which is ninety-nine feet high, it is said that when it was about to be elevated to its position, he employed 20,000 workmen, and apprehensive that the engineer would not raise it with sufficient care, he bound the prince his son to the apex while it lay on the ground, and thus effectually guaranteed the safety of his monument. This was many centuries ago; but, as I gazed to-day upon the towering apex, I could not but think, with a tremor of the nerves, of the hapless young prince as he mounted into the sky, on that slow and perilous journey!

Have I not been digressing, dear mother? But you must not, in familiar letters, look for artistic continuity of narrative. I shall digress, or go from subject to subject, as collateral objects suggest themselves in passing them; but, nevertheless, I shall not leave your curiosity unsatisfied upon any matter which I have commenced, but in due time, from every digression, shall return to it. I will, therefore, this apology once for all, return to the princely Remeses.

He wore upon his right hand a signet-ring of silver, once belonging to his ancestor, Amosis, the leader of the XVIIIth dynasty; and also a large ring of pure gold, set with a chrysoprasus, and bearing the shield of Osirtasen I., or Sesostris—for he has both names in history—for whom I am named.

In all respects he was attired with magnificence, and yet with simplicity, as became a man of taste and a prince. The profuse ornaments of jewellery, with which I perceive the nobles about the court load themselves, his good sense disdains. He retains only the insignia belonging to his high rank.

I have said that his hair is raven-black, and may add that his eyes are large, expressive, heavily-lidded, and with a peculiar expression of mingled softness and brilliancy. Unlike the Egyptians, his features are truly Syriac, with the high arched nose and full red lips of the inhabitants of the city of Damascus. Do you remember when we last year visited Damascus, seeing, in the painted chamber of the adytum of the mausoleum of Eliezer, a representation of the Hebrew prince Abram, of Syria? To that venerable prince, whose virtues and wisdom tradition would have preserved, even if he had not erected this tomb to his own and his master's memory, Eliezer was chamberlain or steward for many years. Returning to Damascus with great wealth, which Abram had bestowed upon him, he brought with him from Egypt, where he had once been, a cunning artist in colours, who decorated the tomb he erected for himself, in that wonderful manner which has excited the admiration of all beholders. But, dear mother, beautiful as that is, and well preserved as it has been for four hundred years, it is not to be compared with art in Egypt at the present day. You remember you were struck with the majesty and almost celestial sublimity of the old shepherd prince's face, which the affection of his steward has preserved. You spoke of the eagle-like nose, the dark yet tearful-looking eyes, with the drooping lid just casting into shadow the depth of its inner light. You remember the nobly shaped head and commanding brow. Such a head and profile is that of Remeses, the Prince of Egypt. My first look at his face recalled the portrait in the tomb, which its founder has so beautifully and modestly inscribed:

"ELIEZER OF DAMASCUS,

THE STEWARD OF ABRAM,

PRINCE

BELOVED OF THE GODS."

After I had received Remeses into my house, I conducted him through a two-valved door, opened before us by my chief butler, into the superb apartment allotted for recreation and repose. My mansion consisted of a court encircled by columns, and from it extended corridors to various chambers. The court is crossed by avenues of trees while fountains and flowering plants refresh the eye in every direction.

The apartment into which Remeses came with me, was divided into tall panels, upon which were executed in the most brilliant colours, the fairest pictures. These panels were intercolumnar, each column adorned with carvings of leaves and flowers, and terminating in a capital in imitation of an open lotus. This room was open to the air but shielded from the sun by a purple awning that extended to its four sides, and was a little raised above the walls upon the columns, so that the breezes, which were wafted over the gardens of flowers, might freely enter.

This was my reception-room, or *mándara*, as it is termed. A beautiful cornice surrounds the whole room. The furniture is of the most tasteful and luxurious description, and of forms and uses unknown to our severer Syrians. There are tables of Arabian wood, inlaid with ivory; sofas of ebony and other rare materials, covered with silken cushions ; a chair ornamented with the skin of a leopard ; another, of still more graceful outline, embroidered with silk and threads of gold; another, the frame of which recedes gradually, terminating at its summit in a graceful curve, and supported by resting upon the back of a swan with feathers of ivory. A chair for repose is covered with gilded leather, and arched by a rich canopy of painted flowers, birds, and fancy devices. The legs of all these chairs were in imitation of some wild beast, while the arms represented in ivory or ebony the beaks of birds,—that of the ibis, sacred as it is, being the favourite. There are couches, too, which are nothing more nor less than crouching lions gilded, upon the backs of which the sleeper reposes on gorgeous housings stuffed with the softest down. The shapes of the furniture exhaust all forms. There are, in some of my rooms, chairs shaped like harps, others like leaves of the fig-tree, others like birds. Tables of ebony are supported on the heads of naked Nubian slaves two feet high, carved in ebony, while the bronze lamps are uplifted upon the palm of a dancing girl cast in bronze, who seems to hold the light for you while you read or write. Carpets and foot-stools, covered with embroidery, are not wanting; and I have three round tables—one of metal, one of ivory, one of ebony—polished like mirrors of steel. These are covered with ornaments of the most exquisite finish and beauty ; and before my window where I write is a sort of bureau ornamented with hieroglyphics, carved in intaglio, inlaid with sycamore, tamarisk, and palm woods, and enriched with bosses of solid gold.

In this apartment I received Remeses. Placing a seat by the window, I sat near him. For a moment he surveyed me with a close but courteous scrutiny, such as strangers irresistibly cast upon each other after a first meeting.

" I hope you are at home here, noble Sesostris," he said. " This is one of my palaces, but I have more than I can make use of, such is the bounty and affection of my mother."

"I have every comfort and luxury—more than I desire," I answered. "I was not prepared to find in Egypt such splendour and magnificence. The half, my noble prince, has not been told the world."

"And yet you have seen but a small portion of this kingdom," he said, with a smile of pardonable pride. "Although On is the city of palaces and temples, for there is a temple to each of the three hundred and sixty gods of our calendar year, yet Memphis is the true seat of our empire. We rule Egypt from Memphis: we worship the gods from On."

"But is not the great god Apis the peculiar deity of Memphis?" I asked; "and is not his worship the most magnificent and imposing on earth?"

"Yet here in the City of the Sun is the temple of Mnevis, the sacred ox of On, honoured with a worship as profound and universal as that of Apis."

"But do the more polished Egyptians indeed worship the ox, either here or in Memphis?" I asked with some hesitation, for, as prince, Remeses is first priest of the realm, next to the high-priest of Osiris.

"Do not fear to ask freely any questions, my dear Sesostris," he said. "We do not worship these animals. They are but the embodiment of attributes. Under both of these gods, at On and at Memphis, Osiris the great Judge of men is veiled. They are but the living images of Osiris. The origin of their introduction is unknown save to the priests, whose office it is to keep the records of all things appertaining to religion."

"What is revealed concerning the history of Osiris?" I asked; "for I am at a loss to understand the exact relation a deity known over the world by name, but of whose worship little is understood, holds to Egypt and to the other gods. At home, in Syria, I have marvelled how the Egyptian mythology could stand, when made up of such contradictory elements,—a part directing the worship of an invisible divinity, and a part directing the adoration of the hosts of heaven and beasts of the earth. In Phœnicia we worship the Invisible through the sun, as his representative. We worship nothing earthly. In Palestine, south of us, Ashteroth, Belus, and images of stone and brass are adored, but not with us."

"The Egyptians, through all their forms, and by all their gods, adore the Supreme Infinite, my Sesostris," said the prince. "The history of our faith is briefly this, according to common tradition: Osiris was in the beginning the one lord of worlds; the sun of truth and the glory of his universe. He came upon earth for the benefit of mankind. Before his coming, the ox and all other animals were wild, and of no service to man. The Nile was a terror to Egypt. Vegetation had perished. He came as a 'manifester of good and truth,' as saith the great golden book in the Hall of Books. He entered into all things, and infused his life, and good, and uses into all. He bound the Nile to its banks, by breasting its flood and subduing it. His spirit passed into the bull, and all cattle. He tempered the heat of the sun, and drew the poison from the moon. The earth became his bride, under the name of Isis; and brought forth Horus, and the order of equal times, and thus man was benefited and the earth made habitable. Upon this, his brother Sethis, who represented 'evil,' as Osiris did 'good,' sought his destruction, and caused him to be hated and put to death. He was buried, and rose again, and became the judge of the dead. And this legend or fable is the foundation, noble Sesostris, of our mythology. The sun, moon, Nile, animals, and vegetables even, are regarded as sacred, therefore, because the spirit or soul of Osiris had been infused into them, to change them from evil to good. Thus one god is worshipped through visible objects, which he has consecrated,—objects once his temples and abodes; for, says the sacred record, he had to enter into everything which he restored to the use of man."

"The mythology of Egypt," I said, "is at once relieved, O prince, from the charge of grossness and superstition which has been attached to it. I can now understand more clearly your system of religion."

"The mysteries of our religion are still unfathomable," answered Remeses. "It is doubtful if they are fully comprehended by the priests. In the multiplicity and diversity of objects of worship I am often confounded, and it is a relief to me to pass by all material forms of Osiris, and send my mind upward only to himself!"

"That is a noble conception, great prince," I said, admiring the lofty and almost divine expression with which this pure sentiment lighted up his fine countenance.

"But the people of Egypt are not able to comprehend Deity except through visible forms; and, in order to convey an impression of the abstract notions men form of the attributes of Deity, it will always be necessary, perhaps, to distinguish them by some fixed representation; hence the figures of Osiris under the various forms in which he is worshipped, of Pthah, of Amun, Neith, and other gods and goddesses, were invented by the ancient priests as the signs of the various attributes of the Deity. And as the subtlety of speculation expanded the simple principles of our mythology, the divine nature was divided and subdivided, until anything which seemed to bear any analogy to it was deified, received a figure or form as a god, and was admitted into the Pantheon of the kingdom, to a share of the worship of the people."

"And this nicety of philosophical speculation," I said, "must have given rise to the several grades of deities in Egypt."

"Yes; the gods of the first, second, and third orders: each with its system of priesthood and rituals."

"In all this, I see you give no divine honours to departed heroes," I remarked.

"No. Our gods are none of them deified men. They are not like Bacchus, and Hercules, and other of the ancient and Syriac deities, who were human heroes. Our mythology is a pure spiritualism: its object, Divinity, worshipped by emblems, symbols, signs, figures, and representative attributes."

"It is a pantheism, then, rather than a polytheism," I remarked.

"You speak justly, Sesostris," he said. "The figures of our gods, which you see hewn in marble, painted on temples, standing colossal monoliths in the entrance of the city, are but vicarious forms, not intended to be looked upon as real divine personages. Not a child in Egypt believes that a being exists, with the head of a bird joined to the human form—as the statue of Thoth, with the ibis head, in front of the temple; or under the form of a Cynocephalus, having the horns of the moon upon his head; or as the goddess Justice, without a head; or a bird with the head of a woman; or a god with a ram-headed vulture's head; or that of a hawk, like the deity Horus; or Anubis, with the head of a dog. Why these unnatural forms were chosen as emblems of these gods, the priests fancifully explain, and perhaps in many cases truly. They are all, simply personifications of divine attributes."

"Abuses," I remarked, when he had thus eloquently spoken, "must naturally flow from such representations, and these emblems, among the people, soon assume the importance of the divine personages to which they appertain. The mass of the population must be idolaters."

"You speak truly. They are. The distinction between the image and the idea which it represents is too subtle for the ignorant; they lose sight of the attribute, by filling the whole horizon of their minds with its image. Thus the Egyptian mind is clearly more and more being drawn away from its ancient spiritual worship, to a superstitious veneration for images, which originally were intended only to control and fix attention, or to represent some religious tradition or idea of divinity."

"Are not Apis, the sacred bull, at Memphis, and Mnevis at On, regarded as gods?" I asked.

"Only as the soul of Osiris. The bull is the most powerful animal in all Egypt, and hence a type of the Deity. But this subject, my dear Sesostris," added the prince, with a fine look of friendship, "you will know more of by and by, as you dwell among us. I will command that you shall have every facility from the priests, and also from the philosophers and wise men, in your further studies of our people. I am happy to have given you your first lesson in Egyptian lore."

"You have done me infinite honour, noble Remeses," I replied, returning with gratitude his looks of kindness. "I hope ere long so to profit by your information as to understand your ancient system of religion. From what you have said, I perceive that it stands above all others on earth, rightly interpreted; and before its spiritual essence our worship in Phœnicia—which is chiefly a union of idolatry and Sabæanism—is pure materialism."

At this moment we rose, as by one impulse, and walked out upon the terrace to enjoy the breeze which was waving refreshingly, to our eyes, the branches of a palm that stood before the door. The day was intensely hot. In the shade of the columns on the square, many of the citizens had gathered for shelter from the sun's beams. But still in its burning heat the bondmen of whom I have spoken, toiled on, with their burdens of brick. Not far off were a score under one task-master, who stood by with a long staff with which he severely beat an old man, who had sunk to the earth under the combined heat of the sun and the weight he was compelled to bear. My heart was touched at once with pity and indignation.

"What unhappy people are these, O prince," I said, "who endure such heavy labour?"

"Hebrews!" he answered, haughtily and indifferently. "Hast thou not heard of these bond-slaves of our land? They have been in Egypt several generations. They build our cities, our walls, our canals. They number two millions, and are the hereditary slaves of the Pharaohs."

"To what circumstances do they owe their captivity?" I asked.

"If it will interest you, my Sesostris," he said, "I will at another time relate their history."

"It will gratify me to listen to it," I answered. "I am struck with the Syriac cast of their features."

"Indeed! They originally came from Syria. Do they preserve still the lineaments of their country?"

"Strikingly so," I answered.

We now walked the noble terrace together, while he pointed out to me the prospect from it. In view was one half the city, and the dark "Lake of the Dead," of which I will speak hereafter; the avenues of sphinxes; the gigantic gateways or pylones and obelisks on the river; and the mighty Nile itself, flowing like an ever-lengthening sea amid the fairest scenery of earth. Reposing upon its bosom, like a gigantic floating garden, was visible the noble isle of Rhoda, decked with gorgeous palaces,—one of which, said Remeses, is the favourite home of his royal mother. Still beyond this lovely island rose from the water the gardens, villas, palaces, temples, and propyla which lay between Memphis and the river; while the city of Apis, "the diadem of Egypt," in all the glory of architectural majesty and beauty, reposed on the plain beyond; the mighty pyramids, with their winged temples and colossal dromos of sphinxes, filling the background of this matchless scene.

Your affectionate son,
SESOSTRIS.

LETTER IV.

CITY OF ON.

DEAR AND ROYAL MOTHER:

I AM still in the City of the Sun, or RE, as I find it is often called by the Egyptians, and I write to you from the palace of Remeses, not the abode which was first allotted me, but in apartments in his own imperial residence, an honoured sharer of his table and society.

Here, in a sumptuous chamber, the walls of which are intercolumnar panels, enriched by paintings on gold and blue grounds, tastefully bordered by flowers and fruit, I once more resume my pen to write to you about this wonderful land.

The day after I closed my last letter, dear mother, a high officer from the Queen Amense alighted from his chariot at my palace, and placed in my hands the signet of his royal mistress, with a message that she desired me to be presented to her.

I had already received an intimation from the prince of this intended honour, and had made myself ready, being attired, when the messenger came, in the full costume of a prince of Tyre, save the golden crown, instead of which I wore the helmet-shaped cap of Tyrian gold-thread, which was presented to me by your own loved hands. Over my shoulders I clasped the cloak of Tyrian purple, embroidered by the hands of the fair princess Thamonda ; and instead of my sword I held a gold-tipped wand, as no one is permitted to appear before the queen with arms. These wands or rods are carried by all Egyptians, of every rank, as constant companions; but their value and beauty are regulated by the position and wealth of the person,—those of nobles being tipped with gold, while ivory, ebony, palm-wood, and common woods, are the materials of which others are made. The rod borne by me was a present from Remeses, and near the burnished gold head of it was a massive ring of great price, bearing his royal cartouch, in which he is called "Remeses-Moses, Son of Pharaoh's Daughter, and Prince of Re Memphis, and Thebes, Son of the god Nilus, and Leader of the Sacred Hosts."

There stood in front of my palace three chariots, two of them drawn by a pair of beautifully spotted horses, while to the third, and most elegant, were harnessed four snow-white steeds. A burnished shield rising above the gracefully curved back, showed that it was a royal chariot. The charioteer was a Nubian, wearing bracelets of gold, as well as otherwise richly attired. The chariot was gorgeously ornamented at the sides with ornaments of light open-work. It was lined with crimson silk, which was visible through the interstices of the open carvings. These chariots had two wheels; the pole projected from the middle of the axle, and was bent upwards at a short distance from the body of the carriage. At the end of the pole the yoke was fastened, and each horse attached to the car by a single trace, extending on his inner side from the base of the pole to the saddle. I noticed, too, that the heads of the spirited horses were borne up tight by a rein made fast to a hook in front of the saddle, and the long reins passed through a loop or ring at the side. Also, that the heads of the horses were adorned with lofty plumes; that the harness was ornamented with silver and gold, or burnished brass, while upon their bodies were housings of the most elaborate and beautiful workmanship, representing royal devices.

One of these superb chariots was that in which the queen's officer came. In the other sat the grand-chamberlain, behind his charioteer. The third, I found, was for my use. Drawn up, hard by, there were not less than three-score footmen of the queen's guard, who, ranging themselves from the door, paid me the lowest obeisance as I passed to my chariot, at the side of which stood the venerable and stately grand-chamberlain, to assist me to enter it.

There was no seat ; for the Egyptians stand in their chariots, as a more dignified and commanding attitude,—a custom probably derived from the necessity of doing so in their war-chariots, in order to combat. I have, however, seen three or four very light and elegant pleasure-chariots, in which ladies of high rank were seated, but one only in each. But when the queen rides, she stands upon a daïs in her chariot, and, as she is borne at speed by six horses harnessed abreast, she has the air and port of a flying goddess. The eyes of her subjects follow her as if she were a meteor, and gaze after her with admiration and awe.

The day was bright, as it always is in Egypt, with a cloudless sun. It lighted up the long lines of palaces where dwelt priests and nobles, illumined the propyla of the temples, burnished the lakes, gilded the obelisks, and flooded the whole City of the Sun with magnificence;— for there is a splendour and glory in the sunshine of Egypt unknown in other lands, the result of the purity of the crystalline atmosphere.

My charioteer dashed onward as if great speed was a royal pace. Before me ran footmen with wands clearing the avenue, and behind came the swift-footed retainers, while on each side of me rolled the two chariots. Acherres, my secretary, rode near upon an Arabian courser; and his superb seat in the saddle and his masterly horsemanship drew the applause of the Egyptians, who are better charioteers than horsemen.

After a dashing ride of a mile, we entered a vast square which I had not before seen. It extended two thousand feet each way. In the centre was a calm lake basking in the sunshine. Around this lake was a border of palm-trees, then a border of orange-trees filled with singing birds, while in their shade walked groups of handsomely attired people, and children enjoyed themselves in play. Upon the lake, ornamented pleasure galleys were moving in various directions, and a spirit of enjoyment pervaded the whole scene. Around this grand square with its central lake were arranged as follows : on the north side a superb colonnade of sculptured columns, forming the façade of the Temple of Mnevis, the sacred ox of On, at the gate or propyla of which crouched two sphinxes, with majestic human heads. On the west side was a vast paved area, in the centre of which towered the obelisk of Thothmes the Great. This area is inclosed by the royal armoury, an edifice expressive of strength and grandeur in its massive and warlike proportions. On the east is a pyramid two hundred feet high, in front of which two sphinxes with heads of women and bodies of birds repose, while on each side extends a range of noble pylones opening into avenues that lead to interior courts. This singular edifice is the temple of Re, and sometimes gives its name to the city. Re being also another name for the sun. On the fourth side of this stupendous area rises a grand palace, which occupies the whole space of the breadth of the square. I can only describe the front of this royal palace by representing it as a city of columns, interspaced at regular intervals by noble propyla, which, in their turn, are sculptured and adorned in such profusion as to bewilder the eye with forms of beauty. Two sphinxes of colossal proportions, with the bodies of lions and the heads of beautiful women wearing double crowns, guard the entrance to this august palace. Upon the terrace, to which a flight of broad steps ascended, stood the royal guard of the palace like statues, each of the one hundred Theban soldiers leaning upon his spear, with his oval shield resting against his side.

We drove up in front, and between the heads of the sphinxes I alighted. The moment I did so, the Theban guard stood to their arms, and their captain, with a glittering helmet upon his head and holding his sword in his hand reversed, descended to receive me. Escorted by him, and followed by the grand-chamberlain, I ascended to the terrace saluted by the guard with the honours paid to royalty. The terrace was surrounded with the statues of the kings of this dynasty, and of the Theban Pharaohs; but the Phœnician Pharaohs are not now numbered among the kings of Egypt. The terrace led into a circular hall which was richly carved, gilded, and painted with historic scenes, battle-pieces and naval combats. Conspicuous upon a panel, directly in front of the entrance, was the representation of the expulsion of the Shepherd Kings from Memphis. In the faces of the monarchs Amosis and Amunophis, the immediate ancestors of Prince Remeses, I see no resemblance to him. His style of face is wholly different from the heroes of the dynasty to which he belongs. His features have a nobler cast, and seem to belong to a man of a higher intellectual development, and no doubt he is superior to all other Egyptians: for, young as he is, his name is already associated with all that is wise, and great, and true.

The entablature of the next hall we entered was a wonderful sculpture. It represented a circle of beautiful girls chained together by wreaths of flowers, and with interlaced arms, bending over and smiling down upon those in the hall, each extending a hand holding a vase. There was a unity of design in the whole of the interior of this adytum or presence-chamber, with the distribution of light and the groups of figures shown by it on the walls, that surpassed any apartment I had yet seen. As I entered this enchanted hall, the martial music which had hailed me as I came into the outer vestibule ceased, and was succeeded by the most ravishing sounds of instrumental music from an unseen source. I would have lingered, but there advanced a beautiful youth, all clad in gold and purple, it seemed to me, so richly was he attired, who said

"The queen desires me to conduct the noble Prince of Tyre to her presence."

I followed, and before him opened, as if by their own volition, a pair of two-leaved doors of ivory, inlaid with emeralds. The throne-room stood before me—if an apartment a thousand feet across may be termed a room. I stood at the threshold of a chamber surrounded by columns ninety feet high. A guard of soldiers, in silver cuirasses and helmets covered with silken scarfs, enclosed the space. An avenue of statues of the gods, in the centre, led for eight hundred feet to the throne. Along this avenue was arranged a brilliant array of officers in armour and uniforms of the most dazzling description, to which every colour and every precious metal contributed, while helm and cuirass, of those highest in rank, blazed with jewels. I advanced, led by the beautiful page, in whose fine black eyes and long lashes, arched brow and aquiline nose, I recognized the now well-known lineaments of the Hebrew race. He moved with his eyes cast down. I experienced, my dear mother, at a public reception so august, not a little embarrassment ; but I repressed it, and endeavoured to receive these honours, at the greatest court on earth, with the ease and self-command that became my rank. As I drew near the throne the scene increased in magnificence. At length two statues of Osiris and Isis terminated the vista I had traversed ; and I saw before me the throne of Egypt, one hundred feet in front, in the centre of a space one half a stadium in diameter, and elevated upon a daïs or platform of variegated marble, twelve feet from the floor. This noble platform was square, and at each of the four corners crouched a lion, respectively with the head of an eagle, a sea-dragon, (no doubt, a fabulous monster), a bull, and a man—all, figures representing the four kingdoms of the air, the sea, the earth, and the intellect or soul. These four colossal beasts faced inward, towards the throne, to signify that they beheld in its occupant their mistress and sovereign. Upon their heads were crowns, namley, of Thebes, Memphis, Re, and Ethiopia.

The platform, upon the angles of which crouched these majestic figures, was ascended by four flights of steps of red Syene stone, inlaid with precious stones. There were seven steps to each ascent, representing the seven mouths of the Nile by which the land of Egypt is approached. These symbols were subsequently explained to me by Remeses ; but I describe them now, as I may not again have an opportunity of so doing in the varied scenes and subjects that challenge my attention.

In the midst of this elevation, rising island-like in the centre of the " Hall of the Pharaohs," stood the throne itself. It was separated from every object in solitary splendour, a space of many yards being left on all sides of the polished floor, in the brilliancy of which not only the throne itself but the heads of the four sphinxes, were reflected. How shall I give you, dear mother, a just conception of the throne-chair ? It was of the purest ivory, carved with wonderful beauty. The simple grandeur of its form and material was more impressive than the most gorgeous display of gilding and precious stones. Its shape was not unlike that of a chariot ; the back curving gracefully over the head of the occupant, and terminating in an expanded canopy of feathers, all of ivory, yet so thin and delicately executed that they waved in the south breeze that stirred through the hall. This chariot-shaped throne rested upon the bodies of two Nigritian lion-leopards of Rhodian marble, between which three steps ascended to the seat of the chair. The seat was a single pearl, a gift from the Queen of Ind to Amunophis the Great, the father of Amense.

The footstool of this beautiful throne was a single onyx stone in a border of gold, standing upon does' feet, each of which was a ruby. The carpet before the throne was woven of the plumage of the bird-of-paradise intermingled with that of birds of India and Arabia, of divers colours. Skins of lions and leopards, fringed with gold-thread, lay upon the mirror-like floor of the daïs, from the footstool to the steps which descended from the platform, or no footstep could have crossed it, so high was the polish of the marble surface.

High above the throne was a canopy of blue silk extending over the whole daïs, and representing the signs of the heavens when Amense was born, with the presiding constellation delineated in its vertical position. Imagine this court of the throne, a peristyle of aqua-marine and white columns, with capitals carved in imitation of flowers, and the shafts enriched by painting and sculpture; surround it with gorgeously attired courtiers, their eyes fixed upon the queen; behold at the steps of the daïs the highest officers of her court, awaiting with looks of homage. On each side of the throne itself stand the two military princes of her realm, one who commands her armies, the other her navies. They are in the full costume of their high rank, and glitter with jewels. Behind the throne, near two stately figures representing Truth and Justice, is a brilliant guard of honour, called "pages of the throne-room," who are sons of nobles, and whose place in public is always near the person of the queen. Their hands are so laden with rings that they appear rather like a chain of gold and jewels held therein. They wear orange-coloured jewelled bonnets and necklaces, and carry blue wands tipped with pearls.

I have now described, dear mother, all the externals of the scene into which I was presented, in order that you may form some idea of the glory and majesty of this court, and the style of its magnificent monarchs. I will now come to the central person, around whom is gathered all this courtly splendour and architectural grandeur.

As I advanced towards the steps of the daïs, two chief officers in flowing linen robes, and wearing chains of gold about their necks, drew near, when my Hebrew page fell back, giving them place.

One of these dignified personages said to me in pure Syriac, for the Egyptians are learned in all polite tongues,—

"We are sent to lead you to the foot of the stairs of the four kingdoms."

They placed themselves one on each side of me, and as I came to the seven steps, to my great joy I beheld prince Remeses descending them to welcome and receive me; for the majesty, and glory, and magnificence, and novelty of the whole scene had nearly overwhelmed me with awe: indeed, I felt as if verily advancing into the presence of the enthroned OSIRIS himself.

The prince looked more strikingly noble than in my first interview. He was attired with the utmost richness, and looked the personification of kingly dignity. He was now distinguished by the amplitude of his robes, and their fineness, and a girdle ornamented with the *uræus* or royal serpent. All his garments were of the lightest and finest material, instead of the heavy and costly stuffs which form the robes of State in Phœnicia and Assyria; for, as my own embroidered and heavy mantle showed me, such material would be out of place in this clime of perennial summer. He wore a gorgeous vesture embroidered with leaves, and a silken sash wound about his body, after the fashion of ancient Egyptian princes, which sash was divided into three different folds, over which fell his upper garment of fine Persian cloth, with long sleeves, also embroidered. The distinguishing mark of his rank, as a prince and "son," and which hung down the side of his face, was the badge of the god Horus, terminating in a fringe of gold, of a fashion worn only by this dynasty. With this badge was entwined his braided lock of hair, of which I have before spoken. This costume is arbitrary, and may not be changed, as the laws regulate it for king, priest, and people; therefore do I so particularly describe it.

With grace and dignity he saluted me before the whole court, saying, "Noble prince, with pleasure I present you to my mother the queen. She is already prepossessed in your favour, and welcomes you to her court with distinctions becoming the heir to the throne of Phœnicia, and our royal cousin."

I bowed in recognition of this courtesy, and Remeses, taking my hand, led me up the steps of the daïs. The Queen Amense, seated upon her ivory throne, awaited my approach. Remeses leading me to within three paces of her footstool, said, with a low obeisance of mingled filial reverence and princely homage,—

"Mother and Queen! I introduce to your court, Sesostris, Prince of Tyre!"

I also did profound obeisance to the majesty of the presence near which I stood, and then fixed my eyes upon the mighty potentate about to address me, and presented to her your original letter.

As she opened it, I observed her face. I beheld before me a woman of noble aspect, with rich brown hair, slightly silvered, worn with severe plainess across her temples. Her face was still beautiful, though fifty-three years had passed over her head, but it was marked with lines of thought and care. What her fine features had lost in beauty, they had gained in majesty. They recalled those of the statue of Astarte, in the temple of the Moon at Sidon: and, in truth, her air and port would have become a goddess. Her eyes were the colour of her hair—a rich sunny brown, like that of the Syrian women of Damascus; and is she not, by descent through Ephtha, the daughter of the last Pœnician Pharaoh, allied to the royal line of Syro-Phœnicia? I never beheld a countenance so dignified, yet so benign. Her eyes are piercing, and imperial in their glance; and she carries her superb head with a consciousness of dominion. I did not marvel longer at her vast power over her subjects, and their submission, as well as that of the kingdoms around her, to the rule of her will.

Upon her head she wore the double diadem of the Thebaïd and Memphis, symbol that the sovereignty of Upper and Lower Egypt is vested in her person. The inner crown was a graceful conical bonnet of white silk, sown with pearls and lined with cloth of silver, terminating in a knob, like a pomegranate bud, which is the emblem, I believe, of Upper Egypt. The outer crown, which is similar to that worn by the Phœnician Pharaohs, is a rich band of gold faced with cloth of gold and lined with red silk, red being the special colour of Lower Egypt as white is of Upper. This crown is open at the top, and is put on over the other; and the two worn together form a diadem of beauty and glory.

About her neck the queen wore a necklace of precious stones, the clasp of which was a vulture, his neck encircled by an asp, on which he was trampling—emblem of the goddess Maut, mother of Isis. She was dressed in a vestment of Persian gauze of silk, of the purest whiteness and of the fineness of mist, and a green vesture enriched with gold and blue needlework, reaching below the waist and secured by a girdle blazing with diamonds. Long robes descended to her feet, of those most beautiful patterns and rare colours which the looms of Damascus produce only for royal wearers, and in the manufacture of which years are consumed. Carelessly over one shoulder was thrown a Persian shawl, one like which is only made in a lifetime, and would buy a king's ransom. The monarchs of Egypt thus can command with their wealth, dear mother, what other kings can only sigh for and envy.

She did not rise to receive me, but when I would have kneeled at her footstool, she bended forward and touched my hand with her jewelled right hand, which I reverently raised to my lips and forehead. She would not suffer me to kneel, but made me stand on one side of her, while Remeses stood on her right, and proceeded to ask me a variety of questions. She uttered her interrogatories with grace and benignity. She expressed her gratification at seeing me at her court—trusted I would find Egypt so agreeable that I should remain a long time her guest—asked after your health and welfare, and desired me to convey to you the expression of her esteem for you, and her desire that the friendly relations now existing between the two courts may be strengthened by my visit. She was also pleased to say, that every opportunity should be afforded me for seeing Egypt, and that if I desired to visit Karnac and Luxor, and the temples and cities of the Thebaïd, she would furnish me with galleys.

To all this exceeding kindness and courtesy, my dear mother, I returned, as you may be sure, appropriate acknowledgments; and after some further conversation, in which Prince Remeses took part, the audience terminated: but only to introduce a spectacle, such as I had no conception was in reserve—the review of her army of chariots and horsemen, on the parade of the palace.

But I must reserve my description of this scene to a subsequent letter. Till then, I remain,

Royal and dear mother,
Your faithful
SESOSTRIS.

LETTER V.

CITY OF THE SUN.

MY EVER BELOVED AND ROYAL MOTHER:

IN my last letter I described to you, as well as the feebleness of language would admit, my presentation to the Queen Amense, and the splendours of her court and palace. In Syria we have no approach to this Egyptian magnificence, unless it is to be found in Tadmor, the city of the Euphrates country, which travellers call a single temple the size of a city! The peculiarity of Egyptian architecture is very striking. It has an air of ponderous majesty—being, in all its proportions, colossal. Yet this massive **aspect is relieved** by shaping the stone and marble in the most **graceful lines, and** enriching with sculpture, either in relief or intaglio, **the immense** surface of their gigantic columns **and enormous** propyla. In all the temples **and palaces I have yet seen here,** two species of column chiefly prevail—one **of which, this being the most** ancient style, is fluted and composed **of a single shaft, with a capital** in the shape of an opening pomegranate, **the reflexed edge being an** imitation of the opened flower of the lotus, **and presenting a graceful object to the** eye. The other column, introduced **by the present dynasty, is always** colossal; but its massiveness **is relieved by being striated, which** gives the mass the appearance **of being composed of united stems,** and increased by horizontal **belts or bands cut in the stone, which seem** to tie them together **under the capital and in the middle.** Just above the square or round plinth, the base of the shaft itself is rounded and adorned with leaves which gives it the appearance of growing up from the plinth. You can judge **of the combined grandeur and grace of** such columns, **dear mother, by imagining several buds of the rose** of Palestine set like cups, **one upon the other, and upon** the top **of all a** lotus-flower, **and the whole magnified to ninety or a** hundred **feet in** height, and converted into Syene stone.

On the abacus of the columns, **which** form **so** prominent and universal a feature in Egyptian architecture, rests a broad but simple architrave, usually sculptured with hieroglyphics illustrating subjects connected with the deity of the temple, or the occupant of the palace which they adorn. The upper edge of it is often occupied by a row of the sacred serpent, *uræus.* The boldness and breadth **of** the cornice supplies the want of a pediment—flat roofs being used in this country, when used at all, where **rain is** scarcely known, and where **snow** was never seen.

The porticos and façades present double and triple rows of columns, but seldom are they found **on the sides or around the temples, as at Damascus and Tadmor.** The circular **arenas in** the city, which I have described **in a former** letter, were **not** temples but colonnades, and these column-enclosed squares are the introduction of Queen Amense, and are only found at **On.** Usually the great lines of Egyptian edifices are straight, and their temples are quadrangles, with avenues of mighty columns extending from pylon to pylon in a succession of inner courts—these series of vast and magnificent vestibules sometimes extending half a mile, their avenues bordered by sphinxes and columns alternately, until the great fane of the temple, to which they are the approach, is reached.

For columns, I have **seen** in the temple of the sacred ox—MNEVIS, colossal figures **of** Osiris, or of sovereigns with the attributes of Osiris. These Osiride pillars are often thirty feet in height. Upon my mind they produce an unpleasing effect. The impression is as if the god was brought into the service of man as a slave, to uphold his temples, though I believe they do not bear any portion of the superincumbent weight. But **one** cannot behold a row of these mighty men of stone without **an emotion of awe.** The general tone of the temples and palaces betrays the pyramid as their type. The walls sloping on the outside as it the lower section of a pyramid, give to the edifices of Egypt that expression of self-reposing and immovable stability which belongs to the pyramidal form. The whole effect is in the highest degree sublime, and at once subdues and elevates my mind as I gaze. The scale of architecture is so vast, that even the innumerable sculptured objects by which walls, columns, and entablatures are covered, do not interfere with the grandeur of the whole effect. Moreover, the heaviness which would adhere to such massive edifices in Syria, disappears when they are seen through the crystalline medium of this Egyptian atmosphere.

There is another peculiarity, my dear mother, of Egyptian architecture, which no one can contemplate without an increasing impression of awe. I allude to the dromos, or double row of sphinxes —figures of which I have already spoken, and of which we have no idea in Syria, though an Assyrian noble whom I met in Sidon, described to me reposing colossi with majestic heads of kings and bodies of lions, as guarding the approach to the temples of the gods of his country. Such mysterious compounds of the human form with a lion or a ram, denoting the union of intellect with strength, are to be encountered here before every temple. These avenues of sphinxes, in profound repose and with a grave and serious aspect, are usually entered through a lofty gateway or pylon, before which are seated gigantic figures of gods, or stand obelisks of granite, placed in pairs, and richly and elaborately sculptured with hieroglyphics. Through such a gateway and avenue, I approached the city of On. A day or two ago I was in a temple dedicated to the god Horus, son of Osiris and Isis. Upon the pylon was inscribed a sun, supported by two asps with outspread wings—the emblem of Hor-hat, the good genius of Egypt—and hence to be found everywhere represented. It is this which is erroneously called, by some travellers, a winged globe. In the entrance, this god was pictured with the head of a hawk (at once his symbol and a type of the sun, from the piercing brightness of its eye), as an actor in various scenes, both celestial and terrestrial, such as hunting, sailing, and engaged in war against Typhon, and others.

Passing these, I entered a spacious court, open to the sky and surrounded by sculptured colonnades. Crossing this court, which inferior priests were traversing or idly lounging in, I came to a second propylon, the magnificent wings of which were divided into numerous compartments, and sculptured ten stories high, with the most exquisite art. This pylon, in the wings of which the priests lodge, led into an open court one hundred paces long, through the centre of which extended an avenue of twenty-four columns, sixty-six feet high and twelve in diameter, and on each side of these were seven rows of lesser columns, forty feet in height and nine in diameter. All these presented sculptured surfaces, and the richest description of capitals. A still more magnificent gateway, at the extremity of this street of columns, conducted me into a vast hall with covered cloisters on the sides, and a double row of colossal pillars running down the centre. All the rest of the space was paved and adorned with fountains, statues, and fruit and flower trees, growing from large alabaster vases. Priests and worshippers moved in all directions through this and the other courts. The walls of this grand hall were decorated with battle-pieces—the triumphs of the Pharaohs in the conquest of neighbouring kingdoms—representations of offerings to the gods, and of captive princes led at the wheels of chariots. I advanced to another pylon, still loftier and more noble than the rest, and as I looked back to the remote outer entrance, two thousand feet off, I discovered that an artifice of architecture had been employed to increase the apparent distance by diminishing the gateways in height, as if by the effect of a lengthened perspective. The effect was all that the architect could have desired.

The Egyptians apply colours freely to their architecture. This peculiarity increases in a wonderful degree the richness and harmony of the general effect. The cloudless sky of Egypt gives brilliancy to all the colours of nature, and these imitated on the walls of temples and palaces, have a beauty and splendour that must be seen to be appreciated. Granite, serpentine stone, breccia, or basalt, whatever be the material, its appearance, however elaborately polished, is by the Egyptians enriched, as they believe, and as I begin to think, by the pencil. The profusion with which they employ colours and sculpture in their temples, palaces, and tombs, has no parallel on earth. In Syria they are subsidiary to architecture. Here they are a part of it. The sloping outer walls, the external surfaces,—ceiling, column, and pylon,—are all covered with sculpture. Their sculptured bas-reliefs unite the qualities of a cameo and an intaglio, the figure itself rising from the broadly cut and deep outline of the design. Thus, though the design is in relief, the figure does not project, and is protected from injury. The colours which are laid on these are softened by their retiring below the surface. Real bas-reliefs, however, exist on the monuments of the age of Sesortasen I.

The adytum of the temple which I am describing so minutely, with descriptions of the peculiarities of the architecture of the Egyptians (knowing your architectural taste and curiosity about all such subjects, my dear mother), was, unlike any of the halls I had traversed, much smaller, and yet far more beautiful than any of them. It was a square chamber, the ceiling of which was painted blue and studded with stars, while the moon shone down, a shield of polished silver, from the zenith point. Figures of vultures, hawks, and other emblems, were placed upon columns around the hall, and separated only by the winged asp-encircled sun. These figures were richly coloured, and the eyes of the birds glittered with diamonds set in them. Upon the entablature around the hall were sculptured the twelve months. All these, and the walls, were beautifully painted, with a harmony of distribution and combination of their gorgeous colours singularly pleasing to the eye. Hieroglyphics, traced in gold on blue panels, recorded the virtues and deeds of Horus. The floor of this sumptuous chamber represented the great circle of the sun through the twelve constellations, and also the images of the seven planetary gods, executed in the pavement with almost every variety of coloured stone, such as the emerald, amethyst, agate, lapis-lazuli, root of emerald, cornelian, greenstone, hæmatite, all interset with gold, silver, and bronze. Nothing could be richer. A sun of pure gold was placed in the centre of this wonderful zodiac, if I may so term it, for I do not know whether it is a true planetary configuration which is represented with a fixed date, or simply arbitrary, and executed as an ornament. The Egyptians are, however, skilful astronomers, and have the skill and learning to interpret and thus record the ages of the past by the procession of the heavens.

On one side of this chamber of art and beauty, stood the monolith which contained the shrine of the god. It was a rock of solid granite, in which a recess was hollowed out, wherein sat the deity. Nothing could be more majestic and simple. The Egyptians seem to delight in contrasts. All the magnificence and architectural glory I have described, directed the footsteps of the votary to a plain block of stone, containing a statue of Syenite marble the size of a man. The face is calm and majestic, and the eyes are fixed upon the worshipper with a supernatural expression which awes him. The genius which had erected the superb edifice of the god, had concentrated its power in the face of the divinity. Though stone, it seemed above humanity; and the soul of the god seemed dwelling in it, and giving its countenance a divine energy.

But, my dear mother, I will not longer occupy your time with temples and architecture. I have written of them sufficiently to give you an idea of the land I sojourn in. But my descriptions will enable you to form a more correct idea of such events as I may hereafter write about, and enable you, when I relate scenes and actions, to conceive, in a measure, the surrrounding features and aspect of places. If I were writing a volume "on Egypt," I would then visit and describe all her magnificent temples, pyramids, obelisks, palaces, canals, lakes, cities and tombs, from Pelusium to the tower of Syene. But I know that these would not interest you, after what I have written, and that what is personal to myself and descriptive of the people, that is, life and action, will be more agreeable for you to read (and for me to write) than gorgeous pictures of architectural results. I shall, therefore, for the future, only incidentally describe edifices (unless, indeed, I give you a letter upon the mighty pyramids), and devote my pen to scenes passing around me.

And in pursuance of this purpose, my dear mother, I will describe to you the review of the army of chariots of iron, which followed my presentation to the queen. I will not be so vain as to suffer you to think that this superb spectacle was arranged purposely in honour of your son; though had it been so, it could hardly have added to the honours which that august and courteous lady has showered upon me; but I feel that the distinction is due rather to the friendship which Remeses entertains for me, than to any merit or claim of my own beyond my simple rank.

The review in question was prepared for this day; and, in order that I might witness it, the queen had graciously appointed the occasion for my presentation to her. Although, in my account of

D

that interview, I spoke only of myself, yet there had been presented, just before I entered the palace, several ambassadors, princes, and philosophers, from various countries, including Arabia, Persia, Sheba, Javan, Iberia, Abyssinia, and the isles of the sea. These had come to Egypt, either to enter the schools of philosophy, to negotiate terms of tribute or alliance, or to study the science of war, for which Egypt has become eminent, even rivalling the mighty Philistine armies in discipline, effect, and valour.

From the throne-room we passed out through a gateway, from which descended steps to the parade, which was a vast square, capable of holding one hundred thousand men; while the colonnades around it would accommodate as many more spectators.

The queen did not descend the steps, but took her seat by a statue of the god of war, upon a sort of throne beneath a canopy, supported by six bearers, to shield her from the sun. But Remeses, leaving me by the side of his royal mother, who was also surrounded by her guard, and near whom stood the ambassadors and princes and philosophers, received from an attendant a helmet of gold, which he put over his silken bonnet, and from another a corselet of steel inlaid, mounted a war-chariot in waiting, and, casting a glance around upon the field, looked all at once the warrior-prince, which the heightened colour of his cheek and proud carriage of his head showed he felt himself to be. Thus, whether a soldier at the head of the hosts of Egypt, a counsellor by the throne of his mother, a courtier among the nobles, a philosopher in the Academies, he is perfect in all things. As a son, he sets an example of devotion and filial respect to the young men of the kingdom; as a man, his private character is pure from every vice or folly—a worthy heir to the throne of the dominant kingdom of the earth. The sight which the square presented surpasses my ability to convey to your mind a just conception of. The vast area was one third occupied by a division of chariots. The chariot corps constitutes a very large and effective portion of the Egyptian army. Each car contained two soldiers—for, from the position I occupied, my eyes could take in the whole splendid scene—besides the charioteer. The car on which Remeses stood was drawn by two horses, but without any charioteer, the reins being fastened to an upright spear. His chariot was inlaid with silver and gold. The sides and back were open, and the base or floor of the car curved upward in front, serving as a safeguard to the charioteer when one was required; but it now supported his quiver of silver and bow-case of gilded leather, richly ornamented with figures of lions. The spear-case, which was of bronze, and fastened by chains of gold, pointed over his shoulder. Close to it was an additional quiver containing Parthian arrows, while a mace of iron and heavy sword, that reflected the sunlight, hung by thongs from the rings of the spear-case. All the other chariots, which were constructed of wood and iron handsomely painted, were similarly accoutred, though less elegant in form and finish, and provided only with a single quiver, bow, and spear. The housings upon the horses were cuirasses of woven links of the finest steel, while gorgeous feathers decked their heads.

No sooner had the prince leaped upon his chariot, than the Ethiopian slaves, who held his two fiery steeds, sprung aside, releasing them in the act, when they bounded into the air and dashed forward over the plain. Remeses, immovable as a statue, let them fly before him until he came in front of the drawn-up phalanx of chariots, when, at a slight signal with his hands, the horses, whose eyes are wholly free from shields or blinders, stopped full. These proved to be his favourite chariot-horses, and had been trained to render perfect obedience.

Now commenced a grand movement of the whole battalion. While Remeses stood in his chariot, the van of the four thousand chariots, which constituted the host, moved forward. In a few moments the whole body was in motion. Dashing forward across the field, they swept round at its extremity in vast curves, and came thundering on, to pass the point were the queen sat. The ground shook with the roll of eight thousand wheels and the fall of twice as many horse hoofs! It was a magnificent sight, as, one hundred abreast, the column came on. The head of it, led by the chief captains, passed our position like a mighty river, the surface of which tossed with helmets, glittering spears, bows, plumed heads of steeds, and gorgeous housings—a dazzling, bewildering spectacle, full of sublimity and terrible power. The splendour of the head-dresses and trappings of the steeds, mingling with the shining cuirasses and steel weapons of the armed charioteers, presented a scene I shall never cease to remember.

In the centre of the field of review stood Remeses, his eagle glance reviewing their movements, with a few of his generals about him, each in his own chariot. When this grand and imposing army had compassed the square, they resumed their former position with a precision and order marvellous to witness. Then followed evolutions by detachments of chariots. Five hundred of them, divided into two equal bodies, took position, one at each end of the parade, and, at a signal, charged upon each other at a speed which, at first slow, increased each moment. My heart leaped with excitement. I looked to see a very battle, and to behold horses and charioteers overturned in tumultuous confusion from the inevitable shock. But so well-drilled were they, that the two lines, deploying as they drew nearer, passed through each other in spaces measured by the eyes of the charioteers so nicely, that in a moment they were rattling away, each to occupy the other's vacated position. There was a general shout of applause from the tens of thousands of spectators at this brilliant manœuvre. Other displays of battle-charioteering took place, during which was exhibited every evolution that war demands on the veritable field of conflict.

This magnificent review occupied three hours, when it terminated by all the generals, and chief captains, and leaders of cohorts and legions, simultaneously detaching themselves from their several commands, and one after another galloping at full speed, first around the prince, saluting him, and then wheeling and turning in front of the queen's pavilion, paying her military homage as they passed her, by placing the left hand upon the breast, lowering the point of the spear, and then raising it above their glittering helmets. The queen rose smiled, and returned the salute by a graceful wave of her hand. This company of warrior chiefs excelled, in richness of armour and apparel, and housings and head-dresses for their steeds, and in the beauty of their war-chariots, all that had gone before. Returning to their post, the trumpets of the whole army sounded, and this martial array of chariots and horsemen moved all together across the parade, at a rapid trot, and, defiling by fifties through a colossal pylon, soon disappeared outside of the walls on their way to their camp. Their retiring trumpets could be still heard dying away beyond the gates, as Remeses rejoined us, alighting from his chariot after loosing the reins of his steeds from about his body, to which he had bound them during one part of the evolutions, in which he took the lead of a charging legion in his own chariot, as ever without a charioteer.

We now retired into the palace, it being past noon, and were conducted towards the reception-rooms of the royal banquet-hall by the grand-chamberlain. At the door we were received by the chief butler, while the other officers of the royal household stood in a line, bending low as the queen and her guests passed in. We consisted, besides her majesty, the prince and myself, of the ambassador from Chaldea, the king's messenger from the Court of Chederlaomer III., in whose country, three hundred years and more ago, the famous battle of Sodom was fought; the ambassador from the kingdom of Assyria; the young Prince of Tarshish; the Duke Chilmed of Sheba, and the Dukes Javan and Tubal; the Lord of Mesech, and the Prince of Midian. Besides these was a great and wise prince from the land of Uz, near the country of Prince Abram, the Mesopotamian. He was accompanied by two friends, philosophers and men of note, Zophar of Naamath, and Lord Eliphaz of Teman. This Lord of Uz came into Egypt with a great retinue and train of servants, for he is a man of vast possessions. He had heard of the wisdom and power of Amense, and had come with his own merchants to visit her court. He is also an eminently wise man, a worshipper of the one Deity, as was the ancient king Abram. He is of venerable and majestic aspect, is learned in all the wisdom of Chaldea and Arabia, and seeks to add thereto the lore of Egypt. Besides this distinguished prince, there are other philosophers of note and name. In such noble company, dear mother, was it my fortunate lot to fall. Truly, to come into Egypt is to see the whole world!

The queen, after entering the ante-room, retired to the right, where her ladies-in-waiting received her and escorted her to her own apartments to prepare for the banquet, which had been delayed by the review. Remeses leading the way, with me by his side, we came to the outer room, where handsomely dressed pages offered us scented water in ewers of gold, to lave our fingers, removed our sandals, and in foot-pans of gold washed our feet, beginning with Remeses. They then dried them with perfumed napkins of the softest linen fringed with threads of gold, and placed upon them sandals of crimson cloth, embroidered with flowers. Our upper garments were removed by Nubian servants, and replaced by a banquet-vesture, more or less rich according to our rank. Thus refreshed, we entered a beautiful reception-room containing the most elegant articles of furniture. Here every one of us was presented by the chief gardener of the palace with a lotus-flower, to be held in the hand during the entertainment. As we moved about, admiring the beauty of the rooms and the furniture, and such objects of luxury and art as were intended to gratify the tastes of guests, there were several arrivals of generals, and officers of the chariot legion, and other divisions of the army of Lower Egypt, who had been summoned to the banquet. Among these I recognized some of the superbly uniformed officers who had lined the avenue of the grand approach to the throne—for you will recollect that I said it was an army of officers, soldiers of this rank alone being permitted to do the honours of the palace on the reception of princes or foreign ambassadors.

There were, also, nobles, and distinguished citizens, Egyptian gentlemen of worth and condition, that entitled them to the honour of dining at the palace. From a window I witnessed the arrival of these. They came in elegant pleasure-chariots, attended by a number of servants. One of these footmen came forward to announce to the chief porter his master's name; others took the reins, for the Egyptian lord prefers to drive himself in the streets; another, who held above his head, standing behind him, a large parasol of gorgeous plumes, alighted, carried it still above him as he crossed to the portico of the palace.

Several aged persons arrived in palanquins exquisitely carved and painted, and borne by slaves. Two or three arrived on foot, an attendant holding a shield or large fan above them. Water was brought also for their feet, but not in golden foot-bowls, and robes and sandals were distributed according to rank.

At length, for these polite Egyptians (as well as ourselves) regard it as a want of good-breeding to sit down to table immediately on arriving, the music, which had played all the while the guests were arriving, ceased, and the chief butler announced the moment of the banquet. At the same instant the queen entered the apartment, and, after receiving the salutations of us all, was escorted by Remeses to the banquet-hall. As we entered, a company of musicians, stationed near the door, struck up one of the favourite airs of the country, playing upon tambourines, cymbals, double-pipes, flutes which rested on the floor, guitars, lyres, and instruments unknown to me. The music was full of harmony, and, to my ear, novel, from the number of strange instruments. This continued until we had been seated according to rank, my place being to the left of the queen, Remeses sitting at her right. There were four ladies of rank also near the queen, along the table, which I may mention was of polished silver.

When we had taken our places the loud music ceased, and seven minstrels, who stood by as many harps behind the queen, commenced playing a beautiful air, accompanying it by their voices. The melody was full of richness and sweetness. While this was performing, servants approached, and from exquisite porcelain vases poured sweet-scented ointment upon our heads. Then entered from the gardens, into which the banquet-room opened on two sides, as many beautiful maidens, bearing necklaces of fresh flowers which they had just gathered, and cast them over our shoulders.

Having received these tokens of welcome, a train of servants presented us wine in one-handled goblets. That of Remeses, and mine own, was of gold and jewelled. The others were of silver or agate. The queen's was presented to her in a single crystal, and that of the ladies in small, delicate vases of some precious metal. The health of the queen, and of the prince, and others present, was drunk, while music regaled our senses. Remeses, who acted as ruler of the feast, pledged me to drink thy health, my dear mother, which was responded to by all the company; the Prince of Uz remarking, that the fame of your virtues and the wisdom of your reign had reached his country. You may judge how my heart swelled with pride and joy at this testimony to your excellencies, O my noble and royal mother, from so dignified a source, in the presence of such a company of witnesses! Until the dinner was served up, various songs and performances were introduced, and at the close of the banquet there were the wonderful dances of Arabian girls, exhibitions of buffoonery, games, and feats of agility by jugglers. I regret to say, that some of the guests retired overcome with wine, and had to be borne on the shoulders of their servants to their homes; while two of the ladies were freer with their little crystal goblets than was seeming for their sex. The queen scarce touched the wine to her lips, while Remeses preserved the severest temperance. After the banquet, Remeses accompanied me to apartments in the palace, which he said were for the future to be my abode. Here, taking leave of him, I commenced this letter, which I now close, assuring you of my filial love and reverence.

SESOSTRIS.

LETTER VI.

PALACE OF THE PHARAOHS, CITY OF ON.

MY DEAR AND HONOURED MOTHER :

THIS morning, as I was about leaving the palace, in order to spend several hours in traversing the city on foot, that I might see the citizens at their pursuits, and observe the manners and customs of this people, the Prince Remeses rode up in his silver-embossed chariot, himself his own charioteer, two footmen, carrying their sandals in their left hand, running by the side of his superb horses. With that absence of form and ceremony which belongs to true friendship, he did not wait for me to order my grand-chamberlain and other chief officers of my retinue to receive him, but came straight to the room "of the alabastron," so called from its alabaster columns, which was my reception-room, and in the window of which he had seen me from the street. I met him at the door of the ante-room, and when I would have saluted him by laying his hand against my heart and then raising it my lips, he embraced me with affection.

"Nay, noble Sesostris, said I not we are friends and cousins, and therefore equals! I have come for you to go with me to Raamses the treasure city, built by Amunophis, my grandfather. I am planning a new palace, to be erected there for the governor of the treasures of the kingdom, and am to meet to-day, the chief architect. Will you accompany me?"

"With pleasure, my prince," I said; "though I had just proposed to walk about the city among the people, and see them in their homes and domestic pursuits."

"You will find time for this always—come with me. You can stand with me in my chariot, or I will give you one to yourself, with a charioteer."

I replied that I would go with him, as I should wish to ask him many questions on the way. In a few moments we were moving rapidly through the superb streets of the city, and, passing through three grand pylones uniting as many courts, we came to the great gate of the city to the south. The towers on each side of it were ninety-nine feet high, and the pylon between them a wonder of beauty, for the elegance of its intaglio adornments.

At this gate stood a phalanx of dark Libyan soldiers, who form, everywhere, the guards of the gates, being noted both for faithfulness and for their gigantic size. They were armed with lances and swords, and as we passed through the gate paid to us the military salutation due to royalty; for though Remeses is not the ruler of Egypt, yet he wields an influence and power, both from his personal popularity and the confidence reposed in him by his queen mother, which is almost equal to the supreme dignity. And when he comes to the throne he will rule wisely, and, if possible, raise Egypt to still greater glory. I have already spoken of the remarkable air of dignity about him, combined with an infinite gracefulness. He has an excellent understanding, and the distinguished Egyptians with whom I have conversed, tell me that "no man ever more perfectly united in his own person the virtues of a philosopher with the talents of a general." Gentle in his manner, he is in temper rather reserved; in his morals irreproachable, and never known (a rare virtue in princes of Egypt) to exceed the bounds of the most rigid temperance. Candour, sincerity, affability, and simplicity, seem to be the striking features of his character; and when occasion offers, he displays, say the officers of his army, the most determined bravery and masterly soldiership.

Having passed the gate, the prince drew rein a little, to relieve the footmen, six of whom ran before and as many behind the chariot, besides the two "pages of the horse," who kept close to the heads of the horses. Once outside of the city, we were in a beautiful avenue, which led through groves and gardens, past villas and ornamental lakes, for half a mile,—the city, for this breadth, being enclosed by such a belt of verdure and rural luxury.

"Here," said Remeses, "dwell the nobles, in the intense heats of summer. The summer palace of my mother is on the island of Rhoda, between On and Memphis, in the Nile. I am yet to conduct you thither, and also to the pyramids. You see pavilions on small islets in these circular lakes. They are temples, or rather shrines for the private devotions of the families.

We left this lovely suburb, and entered upon a broad road, which, after crossing a plain on which stood the ruins of a palace of Osirtasen I., wound through a region of wheat-fields, which extended along the Nile as far as the eye could see. The labourers were chiefly Egyptian, and wore the loin-cloth, and short trowsers reaching half-way to the knee, which I have before described. They sang cheerful songs as they worked, and stopped to gaze after the rolling chariot which was passing across their lands like a meteor, its silver panels flashing in the sun.

About twenty stadia, or nearly four miles, from the city, we came suddenly upon a vast desolate field, upon which thousands of men seemed to be engaged in the occupation of making brick. As we drew near, for the royal road we were traversing passed directly through this busy multitude, I saw by their faces that the toilers were of that mysterious race, the Hebrew people.

I say "mysterious," dear mother; for though I have now been six weeks in Egypt, I have not yet found any of the Egyptians who can tell me whence came this nation, now in bondage to the Pharaohs! Either those whom I questioned were ignorant of their rise, or purposely refrained from talking with a foreigner upon the subject.

You will remember that I once inquired of Remeses as to their origin and present degradation, and he said he would at some other time reply to my question. Since then I have had no opportunity of introducing the subject again to him, other objects wholly absorbing our attention when we met. Yet in the interim I was forced irresistibly to notice these people and their hard tasks; for, though they were never seen in the streets mingling with the citizens (save only in palaces, where handsome Hebrew youths often serve as pages), yet where temples, and granaries, and walls, and arsenals, and treasure-houses were being erected, they were to be found in vast numbers. Old and young men, women, and children, without distinction, were engaged in the plain across which we moved.

"Pardon me, noble prince," I said; "permit me to linger a moment to survey this novel scene."

Remeses drew up his horses, and from the chariot I cast my eyes over the vast level which embraced half a square league.

"These fields, Sesostris," said the prince, "are where the brick are made which are to erect the walls of the treasure-city, one of the towers of which you behold two miles distant. The city itself will take the years of a generation of this people to complete, if the grand design is carried out. On the left of the tower you see the old palace, for this is not a new city we are building so much as an extension of the old on a new site, and with greater magnificence. It is my mother's pride to fill Egypt with monuments of architecture that will mark her reign as an era."

The scene that I beheld from the height of the chariot I will attempt to describe, my dear mother. As far as I could see, the earth was dark with people, some stooping down and with wooden mattocks digging up the clay; others were piling it into heaps; others were chopping straw to mix with the clay; others were treading it with their feet to soften it. Some with moulds were shaping the clay into bricks. Another stood by with the queen's mark, and stamped each brick therewith, or the one which was to be the head of a course when laid. There were also the strongest men employed in raising upon the shoulders of others a load of these bricks, which they bore to a flat open space to be dried in the sun; and a procession of many hundreds were constantly moving, performing this task. Some of the slaves carried yokes, which had cords at each end, to which bricks were fastened; and many of the young men conveyed masses of clay upon their heads to the moulders. Those who carried the brick to the smoothly swept ground where they were to be dried, delivered them to women, who many hundreds in number, placed them side by side on the earth in rows—a lighter task than that of the men. The borders of this busy plain, where it touched the fields of stubble wheat, were thronged with women and children gathering straw for the men who mix the clay. It was an active and busy spectacle. Yet throughout the vast arena not a voice was heard from the thousands of toilers; only the sharp authoritative tones of their task-masters broke the stillness, or the creaking of carts with wooden wheels, as, laden with straw from distant fields, they moved slowly over the plain.

The labourers were divided into companies or parties of from a score to one hundred persons, over whom stood, or was seated, an Egyptian officer. These task-masters were not only distinguishable from the labourers by their linen bonnet or cap with a cape descending to the neck, but by a scarlet or striped tunic, and a rod or whip of a single thong or of small cords. These men watched closely the workmen, who, naked above the waist, with only a loin-cloth upon many of them, worked each moment in fear of the lash. The task-masters showed no mercy; but if the labourer sank under his burden, he was punished on the spot, and left to perish, if he were dying, and his burden transferred to the shoulders of another. So vast was the multitude of these people, that the death of a score a day would not have been regarded. Indeed, their increase already alarms the Egyptians, and their lives, therefore, are held in little estimation.

The vast revenue, however, accruing to the crown from this enslaved nation of brick-makers, leads to regulations which in a great measure check the destructive rigour of the task-masters; for not only are thousands building cities, but tens of thousands are dispersed all over Lower Egypt, who make brick to sell to nobles and citizens, the crown having the monopoly of this branch of labour. Interest alone has not prompted the queen to make laws regulating their treatment, and lessening the rigour of their lot; but also humanity, which is, however, an attribute, in its form of pity, little cultivated in Egypt. Under the preceding Pharaohs, for seventy years, the condition of these Hebrews was far more severe than it has been under the milder reign of the queen. I am assured that she severely punishes all unnecessary cruelty, and has lightened the tasks of the women, who also may not be punished with blows.

I surveyed this interesting and striking scene with emotions of wonder and commiseration. I could not behold, without the deepest pity, venerable and august-looking old men, with grey heads and flowing white beards, smeared with clay, stooping over the wooden moulds, coarsely clad in the blue and grey loin-cloth, which scarcely concealed their nakedness: or fine youths, bareheaded and burned red with the sun, toiling like cattle under heavy burdens, here and there upon a naked shoulder visible a fresh crimson line where the lash or the rod of an angered officer had left its mark! There were young girls, too, whose beautiful faces, though sun-burnt and neglected, would have been the envy of fair ladies in any court. These, as well as the others of their sex, wore a sort of tight gown of coarse material tied at the neck, with short, close sleeves reaching to the elbow. Their black or brown hair was tied in a knot behind, or cut short. And occasionally I saw a plain silver or other metallic ring upon a small hand, showing that even bondage has not destroyed in woman the love of jewels.

As we rode along, those Egyptians who were near the road bowed the knee to the prince, and remained stationary until he passed. We rode for a mile and a half through this brick-field, when at its extremity we came upon a large mean town of huts composed of reeds and covered with straw.

"There," said Remeses, "are the dwellings of the labourers you have seen."

These huts formed long streets or lanes which intersected each other in all directions. There was not a tree to shade them. The streets and doors were crowded with children, and old Hebrew women who were left to watch them while their parents were in the field. There seemed to be a dozen children to every house, and some of five and six years were playing at brick-making, one of their number acting as a task-master, holding a whip which he used with a willingness and frequency that showed how well the Egyptian officers had taught the lesson of severity and cruelty to the children of their victims. In these huts dwelt forty thousand Hebrews, who were engaged either in making brick, or conveying them to Raamses, close at hand, or in placing them in mortar upon the walls.

We passed through the very midst of this wretched village of bondmen, whose only food in their habitations is garlic, and leeks, and fish or flesh, their drink the turbid water of the Nile, unfiltered from its impurities by means of porous stone and paste of almonds—a process of art so well known to the Egyptians. On the skirts of the village was a vast burial-place, without a tomb or stone; for these Hebrews are too poor and miserable to embalm their dead, even if customs of their own did not lead them to place them in the earth. The aspect of this melancholy place of sepulture was gloomy enough. It had the look of a vast ploughed plain; but infinitely desolate and hideous when the imagination pictured the corruption that lay beneath each narrow mound. I felt a sensation of relief when we left this spot behind, and drove upon a green plateau which lay between it and the treasure-city of the king. The place we were crossing had once been the garden of Hermes or Iosepf, the celebrated prince who about one hundred and thirty years ago saved the inhabitants of Egypt from perishing by famine, having received from the god Osiris knowledge of a seven years' famine to befall the kingdom, after seven years of plenty. This Prince Iosepf or Joseph was also called Hermes, though he wrote not all the books attributed to Hermes, as we in Phœnicia understand of that personage.

"Was this Joseph an Egyptian?" I asked of the Prince Remeses, as we dashed past the ruins of a palace in the midst of the gardens.

"No, a Hebrew," he answered. "He was the favourite of the Phœnician Pharaoh who commenced the palaces of this City of Treasure."

"A Hebrew!" I exclaimed. "Not one of the race I behold about me toiling towards the city with sun-dried bricks upon their heads, and whom I have seen at work on the plain of bricks?"

"Of the same," he answered.

"Your reply reminds me, O Remeses, that you have promised to relate to me the history of this remarkable people, who evidently, from their noble physiognomies, belong to a superior race."

"I will redeem my promise, my dear Sesostris," he said, smiling, "as soon as I have left the chariot by yonder ruined well, where I see the architect and his people, whom I have come hither to meet, await me with their drawings and rules."

We soon drove up to the spot, having passed several fallen columns, which had once adorned the baths of the house of this Hebrew prince, who had once been such a benefactor to Egypt; but, as he was the favourite of a Phœnician king, the present dynasty neglect his monuments, as well as deface all those which the Shepherd Kings erected to perpetuate their conquest. Hence it is, dear mother, I find scarcely a trace of the dominion in Lower Egypt of this race of kings.

The ruined well was a massive quadrangle of stone, and was called the "Fountain of the Strangers." It was in ruins, yet the well itself sparkled with clear water as in its ancient days. Grouped upon a stone platform, beneath the shade of three palms, stood the party of artists who awaited the prince. Their horses, and the cars in which they came, or brought their instruments, stood near, held by slaves, who were watering the animals from the fountain.

Upon the approach of the prince these persons, the chief of whom was attired handsomely, as a man of rank (for architects in Egypt are nobles, and are in high place at court), bowed the knee reverently before him. He alighted from his chariot, and at once began to examine their drawings. Leaving him engaged in a business which I perceived would occupy him some time, I walked about, looking at the ancient fountain. In order to obtain a view of the country, I ascended a tower at one of its angles, which elevated me sixty feet above the plain. From this height I beheld the glorious City of the Sun, a league and a half to the north, rising above its girdle of gardens in all its splendour. In the mid-distance lay the plain of brick-workers, covered with its tens of thousands of busy workers in clay. Then, nearer still, stretched their squalid city of huts, and the gloomy burial-place, bordering on the desert at the farther boundary.

Turning to the south, the treasure-city of Raamses lay before me, the one half ancient and ruinous, but the other rising in grand outlines and vast dimensions, stretching even to the Nile, which, shining and majestic, flowed to the west of it. Further still the pyramids of Memphis, the city itself of Apis, and the walls and temples of Jisah towered in noble perspective. The Nile was lively with galleys ascending and descending, and upon the road that followed its banks many people were moving, either on foot, in palanquins, chariots, or upon horseback. Over the whole scene the bright sun shone, giving life and brightness to all I beheld.

To the east the illimitable desert stretched far away, and I could trace the brown line of road along which the caravans travel between the Nile cities and the port of Suez, on the sea of Ezion-Geber, in order to unlade there for ships from Farther Ind that are awaiting them.

Almost beneath the crumbling tower, on which I stood taking in this wide view of a part of the populous valley of the Nile, wound a broad path, well trodden by thousands of naked feet. It was now crowded with Hebrew slaves, some going to the city with burdens of brick slung at the extremities of wooden yokes laid across the shoulder, or borne upon their heads, and others returning to the plain after having deposited their burdens. It was a broad path of tears and sighs, and no loitering step was permitted by the overseers; for even if one would stop to quench his thirst at the fountain, he was beaten forward, and the blows accompanied with execrations. Alas, mother, this cruel bondage of the Hebrews is the only dark spot which I have seen in Egypt,—the only shadow of evil upon the brilliant reign of Queen Amense!

I took one more survey of the wide landscape, which embraces the abodes of one million of souls; for in the valley of Egypt are fourteen thousand villages, towns and cities, and a population of nearly seven millions. Yet the valley of the Nile is a belt of verdure only a few miles wide, bounded by the Libyan and Arabian hills. Every foot of soil seems occupied, and every acre teems with population. In the streets, in the gardens, in the public squares, in temples, and courts of palaces, in the field, or on the river, one can never be alone, for he sees human beings all about him, thronging every place, and engaged either in business or pleasure, or the enjoyment of the luxury of idleness in the shade of a column or a tree.

Descending the tower, and seeing the prince still engaged with his builders, pointing to the unfinished towers of Raamses, and the site of the new palace he proposed erecting near by, I went down the steps to the fountain, to quaff its cool waters. Here I beheld an old and majestic-looking man bending over a youth, a wound in whose temple he was bathing tenderly with water from the well. I perceived at a glance, by the aquiline nose and lash-shaded dark, bright eye, that they were Hebrews.

The old man had one of those Abrahamic faces I have described as extant on the tomb of Eliezer of Damascus: a broad, extensive, and high forehead; a boldly-shaped eagle nose; full lips; and a flowing beard, which would have been white as wool but that it was stained yellow by the sun and soil. He wore the coarse, short trowsers, and body cloth of the bond-slave, and old sandals bound upon his feet with ropes. The young man was similarly dressed. He was pale and nearly lifeless. His beautiful head lay upon the edge of the fountain, and as the old man poured, from the palm of his hand, water upon his face he repeated a name, perhaps the youth's. I stood fixed with interest by the scene. At this moment an Egyptian taskmaster entered, and with his rod struck the venerable man several sharp blows and ordered him to rise and go to his task. He made no reply —regarded not the shower of blows—but bending his eyes tearfully upon the marble face before him, with his fingers softly removed the warm drops of blood that stained the temples.

"Nay," I said, quickly, to the Egyptian, "do not beat him! See, he is old, and is caring for this poor youth!"

The Egyptian looked at me with an angry glance, as if he would also chastise the speaker for interfering; when seeing from my appearance that I was a man of rank, and perceiving, also, the prince through a passage in the ruined wall, he bent his forehead low and said:

"My lord, I did not see you, or I would have taken the idle greybeard out and beaten him."

"But why beat him?" I asked.

"His load awaits him on the road where he dropped it, when my second officer struck down this young fellow, who stopped to gaze at a chariot!"

"What relation do they bear to each other?" said I.

"This is the old man's youngest son. He is a weak fool, my lord, about him, and though, as you see, he can hardly carry a full load for himself, he will try and add to his own, a part of the bricks the boy should bear. Come, old man, leave the boy and on to your work!"

The aged Hebrew raised to my face a look of despair trembling with mute appeal, as if he expected no interposition, yet had no other hope left.

"Leave them here," I said. "I will be responsible for the act."

"But I am under a chief captain who will make me account to him for every brick not delivered. The tale of bricks that leaves the plain and that which is received are taken and compared. I have a certain number of men and boys under me, and they have to make up in their loads a given tale of bricks between sun and sun. If they fail, I lose my wages!" This was spoken sullenly.

"What is thy day's wages?" I demanded.

"A quarter of a scarabæus," he answered. This is the common cheap coin, bearing the sacred beetle cut in stone, copper, lead, and even wood. Higher values are represented by silver, bronze, brass, and gold rings. Money in disk-form I have not yet heard of in Egypt. An Egyptian's purse is a necklace of gold rings of greater or less value. The scarabæus is often broken in four pieces, each fraction containing a hieroglyphic. The value is about equal to a Syrian neffir.

I placed in his hand a copper scarabæus, and said : "Go thy way! This shall justify thee to thy conscience. These Hebrews are too helpless to be of further service to thee this day."

The task-master took the money with a smile of gratification, and at once left the court of the fountain. The old Hebrew looked at me with grateful surprise, caught my hand, pressed it to his heart, and then covered it with kisses. I smiled upon him with friendly sympathy, and, stooping down, raised the head of the young man upon my knee. By our united aid he was soon restored to sensibility.

But, my dear mother, I will, with your permission, continue my narrative in another letter. The trumpets, which from the temple of Osiris proclaim that the last rays of the setting are disappearing from its summit, also warn me to draw my letter to a close. The incense of the altar rises into the blue and golden sky, and typifies prayer. I will receive the lesson it teaches, and retire to my oratory and pray, O mother, for thy health and happiness and the prosperity of thy reign.

Your affectionate son,
SESOSTRIS.

LETTER VII.

CITY OF ON.

MY ROYAL AND BELOVED MOTHER :

I WILL now continue the narrative of my interview with the venerable bond-servant at the fountain or "well of strangers," near the treasure-city Raamses.

After the youth had recovered his senses, I was for a few moments an object of profound surprise to him. He surveyed me with mingled fear and wonder.

"My lord is good, fear him not, Israel," said the old man. The youth looked incredulous, and, had his strength permitted, would have fled away from me. I said,—

"I am not thy task-master! Dread not my presence!" The tone of my voice reassured him. He smiled gently, and an expression of gladness lighted up his eyes. A drop of blood trickled down his forehead and increased the paleness of his skin.

"What is thy name?" I asked the old man, speaking in Syriac, for in that tongue I had heard him murmur the name of his son ; and I have since found that all Hebrews of the older class speak this language, or rather Syro-Chaldaic. They also understand and speak the Egyptian vernacular.

"Ben Isaac, my lord !" he answered.

"Art thou in bondage ?"

"I and my children, as my fathers were !"

"What brought thee and thy people into this servitude?"

"It is a sad history, my lord! Art thou then a stranger in Egypt, that thou art ignorant of the story of the Hebrew?"

"I am a Phœnician. I have been but a few weeks in Egypt."

"Phœnicia! That is beyond Edom; nay, beyond Philistia," he said musingly. "Our fathers came farther, even from Palestine."

"Who were your fathers?"

"Abraham, Isaac, and Jacob."

"I have heard of them, three princes of Syria, many generations past!"

"Yes, my lord of Phœnicia," said the venerable man, his eyes lighting up; "they were princes in their land! But, lo! this day behold their children in bondage! And *such* a servitude!" he cried, raising his withered hands heavenward. "Death, my lord, is preferable to it! How long must we groan in slavery? How long our little ones bear the yoke of Egypt?"

At this moment one of the footmen of Prince Remeses found me and said:

"My lord prince seeks for thee!"

I put money in the hands of the venerable Hebrew and his son, and left them amid their expressions of grateful surprise. When I rejoined Remeses, he was already in his chariot. Having placed myself by his side, he said that he would now drive me around the walls of the new city, and show me its general plan. He had explained all particulars with his builders, and they were to commence the erection of the palace of the governor the following week.

The wide circuit we made along the plain afforded me a commanding view of the treasure-city in its progress. The walls at one part were literally black with slaves, who like ants traversed them, carrying their burdens of bricks to those who laid the courses. A vast pile, built more for strength than beauty, attracted my notice. "That is one of the twelve great granaries of the Prince Joseph, which he built one hundred and fourscore years ago, in the twelve districts of Egypt. It is still in use as such." As we passed the gateway, I perceived that the cartouch was defaced. Remeses said that this was the act of Amunophis, when he came to the throne, whose policy was to remove not only every trace of the rule of the Palestinian kings, but all the memorials which brought their dynasty to remembrance; and these granaries of Pharaoh's prime minister, Iosepf or Joseph, were among the noblest monuments of the reign of the last of the foreign rulers, the father of the Princess Ephtha, from whom Remeses is descended, in the fourth generation only, I believe.

At length we stopped at a beautiful gate of a small temple dedicated to Apis. Every part of it was minutely and exquisitely sculptured. It contained a single shrine, within which was the effigy of the sacred bull, a cubit in length, of solid gold. Boys dressed in the finest white linen were the officiating priests. While I was admiring this miniature edifice and the richness of all its appointments, Remeses said:—

"This is an affectionate tribute of a mother's love. On my twelfth birth-day she had this sacred fane dedicated in honour of the event,

Here she consecrated me as a boy to the youthful god Horus. I remember perfectly, the solemn impression the whole scene made upon my heart and imagination. Once a year I come hither and pass a night watching before its altar and in prayer, rather in filial acquiescence with her wishes, which to me are laws, than from reverence for the god!"

We had already alighted, and were standing on the portico of the temple, which was of crescent shape, and bordered by a row of elegantly veined alabaster columns from Alabastron, rich quarries of the Pharaohs near the Cataracts. After examining the temple, and expressing the admiration which it merited, we were going out, when I saw a young Hebrew girl flying from the pursuit of one of the task-masters. Just as we were entering the temple, I had seen her passing with many other females, some laden with straw, others with bunches of leeks and garlic, which they were taking to the fields for the dinner of the labourers, who were not permitted to go to their huts until dark, having left them at the first blush of dawn to commence their ceaseless toils. Those women who worked not in the brick-fields were the providers of food for the rest. This young girl I had noticed was bending painfully under an intolerable load of garlic and leeks, which she bore upon her head, and yet assisting a tottering woman, who was walking by her side with an equally heavy burden of provisions, in a coarse wicker-basket. I was struck with the elegance of her figure and with the beauty of her face, as well as with her kindness to her companion, when she herself needed aid. We were leaving the temple, as I have said, when I beheld her flying. As she came near, she saw the prince, and cast herself at his feet, embracing them, and exclaiming,—

"O my lord—O great and mighty god! mercy!—save me!"

Remeses regarded her with surprise, and said, sternly yet not cruelly,—

"What dost thou wish? Why dost thou fly from thy task-master?"

"When I cast down my load and took up my mother's, who was ready to die, he struck me because I could not take both together. I would have done it, O lord prince, but had not the strength."

"Go back to thy task, young woman. Thou shalt not be punished for a kind act to thy mother. The gods forbid we should destroy all filial ties, even among our slaves." This last sentence was spoken rather with his own mind than addressed to any one. "What is this I hear?" he continued, speaking to the sub-officer, who, seeing his slave seek the protection of Remeses, had stopped, a short distance off, expecting to have her sent back to him. "Didst thou strike this Hebrew girl?"

"She is wilful and intractable, your highness," answered the man humbly, "and—"

"Is there not a law forbidding blows to be given to the females of this people? You will deliver your rod of office to my chief servant here, and are no longer a task-master. It shall be known, that it is the will of the queen that women shall have light tasks, that they be treated leniently, and not made to suffer the punishment of blows."

The man, with a downcast face, came forward, and placed his rod in the hands of the chief servant, who was the captain of the twelve footmen of the prince's chariot, and who, at a glance from his master, broke it, and cast the pieces upon the ground. "Now go, and bring hither the basket. I will see what are the burdens you place upon the weak, and henceforth they shall be proportioned to the strength of the bearer."

The man returned several hundred yards along the road, and, after several strenuous efforts, with great difficulty lifted the basket, and placed it at the prince's feet. To the amazement of all about him he stooped to raise the wicker-basket of leeks from the ground. Putting forth his strength he lifted it, for he is a man of great vigour, but immediately setting it down again, he said, with indignation flashing from his eyes, as he addressed the disgraced taskmaster,—

"Seest thou what thou wouldst compel this frail child to bear upon her head? Thou art cruel and barbarous! Bind him! He shall go to prison."

"My lord, I am not alone—"

"So much the worse. If the abuse is widespread, it is time to correct it, and see that the law of the realm is observed. Take him away!"

Two of the servants seized him, and, tying his hands behind him with the thong of one of his own sandals, led him away into the citadel of Raamses. The Hebrew girl still kneeled, trembling and wondering. Remeses spoke to her kindly, no doubt moved by her tears and extraordinary beauty, and said,—

"Go in peace, child. Return to thy mother. Fear no more the rod of thy taskmasters. The hand of the first that is laid on a Hebrew woman shall be cut off with a sword."

The young girl kissed the sandaled feet of the prince, and hastened to the spot where she had left her mother seated on the ground. Remeses, with his eyes, followed her, and sighed. Who can tell what heavy thoughts were passing in his mind? When he comes to the throne, I know him not, my mother, if the condition of the Hebrews will not be greatly ameliorated, and their lot rendered far happier. I saw the girl embrace and raise her mother from the earth, and then, supporting her affectionately, lead her away towards a group of huts, not far off, in one of which, probably, was their abode.

"My Sesostris," said the prince, "walk with me along this terrace. I have yet to see the governor of the queen's granaries, and will converse with thee until he arrives."

The terrace ran along the south side of the low pyramidal area on which the temple was elevated. From it there was a lovely view of fields, and gardens, and groves of palm and orange trees, extending over the land of Goshen, which is the most fertile and highly-cultivated portion of Egypt that I have seen. From the terrace, steps of polished porphyry led to a garden fragrant with flowers, which were cultivated alongside of the temple, in order to make of them offerings of chaplets to the god, who was crowned with them every morning by the "flower priest." The office of this dignitary was as sacred as his who offered incense, which indeed is but the fragrance of flowers in another form, purified by fire. In this garden I saw the myrobalanum,

E

with its rich fruit, out of which a rare ointment is extracted for anointing the priests ; the phœnicobalanus, which bears an intoxicating fruit, and gives to the priests who eat of it divining powers ; the graceful palma, or sheath for the palm-flowers ; the almond-tree, brilliant with its flowering branches; the wine-giving myxa ; the ivory palm-fruit, of which censers are made ; the mimosa Nilotica, and the golden olive of Arsinoë. All these grew on one path, which traversed the garden close to the terrace, and I enumerate them, dear mother, as I know your horticultural taste, and that anything about the plants of Egypt will gratify you. I have already selected several of the most beautiful, and intend, by the first ship that sails for Tyre from the Nile, to forward them to you. That they may be cared for, and rightly managed when you receive them, I shall send with them an Egyptian gardener. I have seen no oaks in Egypt, nor does our majestic Libanian cedar grow here. It is a land rather of flowers than of trees. The myrtle is everywhere seen as an ornamental tree, and is highly odoriferous in this climate. Here I saw also the endive, and the Amaracus, from the latter of which the celebrated amaracine ointment, used to anoint the Pharaohs, is expressed. One bed of variegated flowers, at the end of the terrace, attracted my attention from their combined splendour. There were the edthbah, with its proud purple flower ; the ivy-shaped-leaved dulcamara, used by the priests for sacred chaplets ; also the acinos, of which wreaths are made by maidens, to wear intermingled with their braided tresses. Above all towered the heliochrysum, with which the gods are crowned, and by it grew its rival, the sacred palm, the branches of which are borne at the feasts of Isis.

There were many other rare and beautiful plants, but I have enumerated these to show you what a land of flowers is this sunny land of Osiris and Isis.

The prince, after we had once traversed the terrace in silence, turned his thoughtful face towards me and said, betraying what was upon his thoughts,—

" Prince, this is the problem of Egypt. Its solution calls for greater wisdom than belongs to man ! "

" You mean the bondage of the Hebrew people?" I answered, at once perceiving the meaning of his words.

" Yes," he replied, with a sigh and a grave brow. " I have promised to acquaint you with their history. Listen, and as far as I know it you shall have it given to you. Our records, kept and preserved by the priests in the Hall of Books in the Temple of the Sun, give the following account of the origin of this race, which, allowing for the errors that are interwoven in all mere tradition, is, no doubt, worthy of credit.

"' About four hundred years ago,' says the History of the Priests, ' there arrived in the land of Palestine a Syrian prince from Mesopotamia or Assyria, with large flocks and herds ; having formed an alliance with Melchisedec, king of Salem, the two dwelt near one another in peace and friendship,—for not only was the Assyrian wise and upright, but the gods were with him, and blessed and prospered him in all that he did.' "

'This Melchisedec the king," I said, "was also favoured of his god; and his virtues have come down to us fragrant with the beauty of piety and good deeds."

"Tradition has been faithful to him," answered Remeses. "Among the Arabian priests of Petra he is held as a god, who came down on earth to show kings how to reign and benefit mankind. With him the Prince of Assyria, Abram, was on terms of the closest friendship. At length, a famine arising in the land where he dwelt, he came down into Egypt just after the invading hosts of Phœnicia and Palestine had inundated our kingdom, and, conquering On and Memphis, had subdued Lower Egypt, and set up their foreign dynasty, known as that of the Hyksos or Shepherd Kings."

"This history is well known to our archives kept in the temple of Astarte at Tyre," I answered; "and therein we learn that the hero SAITES, who had a warlike spirit which could not find field in Lower Syria, was threatened by famine, and hearing of the abundance in Egypt and the splendour of its cities, combined with the enervating habits which grow out of luxury and unbroken peace, he conceived the idea of its invasion; and at the head of an undisciplined but brave army of one hundred and seventy thousand men, horsemen and footmen, with three hundred chariots of iron, he descended through Arabia Deserta, and entered Egypt by the desert of the sea, capturing and fortifying Ezion-Geber on his march."

"These particulars are not so fully given by our historians," answered Remeses. "This ambitious warrior, having entered the Sethroite country, encamped and founded a city which he made his arsenal of war; and from it he sent out his armies and conquered Memphis and the whole of Lower Egypt. The kings of Egypt, abandoning to him Lower Egypt, retired with their court and army to the Thebaïd, and were content to reign there over half the kingdom, while the haughty conquerors established their foreign throne at Memphis.

"It was," continued Remeses, "during the reign of Bnon, the first Phœnician Pharaoh after the death of the conqueror, that Abram came into Egypt. He had known this prince in Palestine when he was in his youth, and the king gladly welcomed so powerful a lord and warrior, who had in battle overthrown Chedorlaomer, the mighty King of Elam, and whose language was nearly similar to his own. This Prince Abram dwelt in Egypt during the continuance of the famine in Syria, and near the court of the king, who not only took him into his counsels, but lavished upon him great riches. 'But the king,' says the history, 'becoming enamoured of the beautiful Princess Sara, the wife of the Lord of Palestine, Abram removed from his court; and with great riches of gold, silver, cattle, and servants, marched out of Egypt into Arabia of the South, and so to his own city.'"

"It is probably," I said, "from this fact of Prince Abram's coming into Egypt about the time that the Phœnicians came, that some traditions have made him its conqueror and the founder of the dynasty of the Shepherd Kings."

"Yes; for this Abram was not only eminent as a warlike prince, but his usual retinue was an army, wherever he moved; and no doubt Bnon, the king, willingly let him depart when he had offended him, rather than meet the valour of the arm which had already slain five kings of the East, and taken their spoil. At length Prince Abram died and left a son, who succeeded him not only in his riches but his wisdom. After a time he also died and left a son, Prince Jacob, who had twelve sons, all princes of valour—but who, like the Arabians of to-day, lived a nomadic life. One of these brothers was beloved of his father more than the others; and, moved by envy, they seized upon him and sold him to a caravan of the bands of Ishmael, the robber king of Idumea, as it was on its way to Egypt. These barbarians sold the young Prince Joseph to an officer of the king's palace, Potipharis, captain of the guard, whose descendant, Potiphar-Meses, is the general of cavalry you met at the queen's banquet. This officer became the friend of the young Syrian, and raised him to a place of honour in his household. In the course of time the king, who was the eminent Pharaoh-Apophis, dreamed a dream which greatly troubled his mind, and which neither his soothsayers, magicians, nor the priests could interpret. Joseph, who was eminent for his piety, love of truth, and devotion to his God, being in prison—to which, on some false charge of seeking the love of his master's wife, he had been committed—had interpreted the dreams of two prisoners, one of whom, being released and hearing of the king's dream, sent him word that while in prison the Hebrew captive had truly interpreted a dream, which both he and his companion had dreamed. Thereupon Pharaoh sent for the Hebrew, who interpreted his dream, which prophesied seven years of great plenty, such as was never known in Egypt, and seven years to follow them of such scarcity as no kingdom on earth had ever suffered from. And when the Hebrew had recommended the king to appoint an officer to gather in the corn during the years of plenty, and to husband it in treasure-houses against the seven years of scarcity, Apophis at once elevated him to that high position. Removing from his hand his own signet-ring, he placed it upon the finger of Joseph; and, having arrayed him in vestures of fine linen and placed a gold chain about his neck, presented him with the second state-chariot to ride in, and made him ruler over all his realm, commanding all men to bow the knee before him as to a prince of the blood, and second in power only to himself."

"And these," I said, glancing at a group of Hebrew labourers not far off, who were seated upon a ruin eating garlic and coarse bread for their noon-day meal—" and these are of the same blood?"

"Yes, Sesostris! But you shall hear their history. This Joseph reigned in Egypt above threescore years, holding in his hand the supreme power, save only that he wore not the crown of Apophis, who, given up to pleasure or to war, gladly relieved himself of the active cares of state. But while he was early in power, and yet a young man, his father and brothers were driven into Egypt by the seven years' famine, which followed the seven years of plenty."

"Then," I interrupted, "the dream of Pharaoh was rightly read by he Hebrew youth?"

"In all particulars he interpreted it with the wisdom of a god, who sees into the future as into the past! But, to resume my narrative—he recognized his father, Jacob, and his brethren."

"Did he make use of his power to punish the latter for their cruelty in selling him into bondage?"

"On the contrary, he forgave them! At first they did not recognize their shepherd brother in the powerful and splendid prince of Egypt, before whom they came under his name of Hermes-Osiris, which Pharaoh had conferred upon him."

"It must have been both a wonderful surprise and a source of terror to them when they at length found in whose presence they bowed," I said, picturing in my mind the scene when they perceived who he was. I imagined not only the trembling fear of the men, but the joy of the venerable father.

"Doubtless a most touching and interesting interview," answered Remeses. "Instead of avenging their cruelty he entertained them in his palace with a banquet, and afterwards solicited of Pharaoh, who refused him no request, that his father and brethren might dwell in the land."

At this moment a tall Hebrew young man passed, returning with a proud, free step, having carried his burden and placed it by a well, which some workmen were repairing. I gazed upon him with interest, fancying I beheld in his face the lineaments of the prince of whom Remeses was talking. I thought, too, the eyes of my companion followed the youthful bondman, as he went away, with something like a kindred sentiment; for, as he discoursed of the glory and virtues of Prince Joseph, it was impossible that we should not be drawn nearer, as it were, to these hapless captives of his race.

"It was in this part of Egypt where the Syrian patriarch dwelt. This very temple is erected upon the site of his habitation, and from here, as far as you can see, stretched the rich fields and fertile plains occupied by him, his sons, and their descendants. Here they erected cities, most of which were destroyed by the subsequent dynasty, with all the monuments of Joseph's power; and here they dwelt for seventy years in peace and plenty, increasing in numbers, wealth, and intelligence—their best-educated men holding offices in the state, and commanding the respect and confidence not only of the king, but of the Egyptians."

But, my dear mother, it is time I close this letter. Until I again take up my pen to write you, remain assured, I pray you, of my filial reverence and love.

Your affectionate

SESOSTRIS.

LETTER VIII.

PALACE OF AMENSE.

MY HONOURED AND BELOVED MOTHER,—

MY last letter closed with the narration of a history of the Hebrews, from the lips of Prince Remeses, to which I listened as we walked to and fro on the terrace of the temple. I will in this letter continue, or rather conclude, the subject, feeling that it will have interested you quite as deeply as it has engaged my attention.

The governor of the queen's granaries having arrived, mounted upon a handsomely caparisoned horse, and attended by runners, the prince at once gave him the orders for which he came, and then, dismissing him with a wave of his hand, turned to me, as I was watching the majestic flight of several eagles of prey, which, circling above my head at a great height, with seemingly immovable wings, through cutting the air so swiftly, gradually diminished the circles of their flight, and descended upon some object not far distant, on the road leading to another treasure-city, called Pithom, many leagues up the Nile, which the Hebrews had built for Amunophis I., threescore years and more ago.

"I will now resume my history of the Hebrews, my dear Sesostris," said the prince, "and will be brief, as we must return to On. The Prince Joseph, as I have said, obtained for his father and brethren all this fair plain, the heart and beauty of Egypt. Here they dwelt when the old man died, after seventeen years' residence in Egypt; and the Hebrew prime minister of the king made for his father a funeral such as few kings receive. It is said to have been more magnificent than that of Osirtasen I., of which our poets have sung. By Pharaoh's command, as his favourite wished to bury his father in Palestine, a vast army went up with the body—chariots, horsemen, and footmen—so that to this day the splendour and pomp of the funeral is a tradition throughout the lands they traversed. Joseph then returned to Egypt, and ruled sixty-one years, until both he and Apophis the king were waxed in years. At length he died, and was embalmed, and his body placed in the second pyramid, which you behold a little to the right of Memphis. There his body does not now rest, for, after the expulsion of the Phœnician dynasty, the Hebrews secretly removed it, and its place of concealment is known only to themselves. There is a saying among them that the bones of this prince shall rise again, and that he shall go with them forth from Egypt to a new and fair country beyond Arabia."

"Then they have a hope of being one day delivered from their present condition?" I asked.

"It is a part of their faith, and inborn, if I may so speak. It is this hope, I think, which makes them bear up so patiently under their servitude."

"And how, noble Remeses, were they reduced to bondage in the fair land wherein they once dwelt so peacefully, under the benign sway of their mighty brother?"

"The answer to this question, my Sesostris," said the prince, "will involve a history of the overthrow of the dynasty of the Phœnician conquerors, which lasted over two hundred years, with a succession of six kings. Upon the death of the Prince Joseph in his one hundred and tenth year, Apophis the king, being also of great age, became incapable of managing his kingdom, which he had for sixty years entrusted to the hands of his Hebrew prime minister. Ignorant of the true condition of his government—known to but few of his subjects—aged and imbecile, he was incapable of holding the reins of state, left by the Hebrew in his hands. The ever-jealous and watchful king of the Thebaïd, in Upper Egypt, did not delay to take advantage of an opportunity like this to attempt the restoration, in Lower Egypt, of the ancient throne of the native Pharaohs, by the expulsion of the usurping dynasty. But, my Sesostris, you know well the subsequent history—how Pharaoh Amosis, with his Theban hosts, drove them from city to city, and finally pursued them into Arabia, whence they settled in the land of the Philistines, and, capturing Salem, made it their capital city—at least such is one of the traditions."

"They held it for a time," I answered, "but, being driven from it by the King of Elam, they subsequently fortified Askelon. They are still a powerful people, under the name of Philistines ; and, what is singular, retain scarcely a custom derived from the two hundred and twenty-five years' residence and reign in Egypt."

"It is not more remarkable than the fact that their domination here made no impression upon the people of Egypt ; they left no words of their own in our language, and no customs of theirs were adopted by the Egyptians. They simply held military possession of the kingdom, living in fortified cities, and levying tribute upon the people for their support. The few monuments they erected were defaced or overthrown by the victorious Theban king and restorer, Amosis, my great ancestor, or by his successor, Amunophis I.

"When these invaders were expelled from Lower Egypt, then the two crowns of the Thebaïd and Memphitic kingdoms became united in the person of Amunophis, the son of 'the Restorer,' and it is this Thebaïd dynasty which now holds the sceptre of the two kingdoms, and which is represented in the person of my mother, the daughter of Amunophis, who died when she was a young girl. She has ever since reigned with the title of 'the Daughter of Pharaoh,' being so called by the people when she ascended the throne of Memphis and Thebes. But, my dear prince," said Remeses, with a smile, " I have been giving you the history of the dynasty of my race rather than of the Hebrew people."

" I am not the less interested, dear Remeses," I said, "and perceive that the two histories are naturally united."

"Yes. The new king, Amosis, called 'Restorer,' upon the obelisk at Memphis which bears his name, and upon which the scenes of the expulsion of these Philistine soldier-monarchs are depicted with great spirit and fidelity—the new king, I say, upon driving out the invaders, keeping the Phœnician king's fair daughter, Ephtha, as his wife, turned his attention to the other class of strangers, who had the fairest portion of Egypt for their possession. He accordingly visited, in state, the city of Succoth, in the province of Goshen, which they had built and beautified during the seventy years they had dwelt there under Prince Joseph's mild and partial rule. It was without walls, wholly unfortified, and had not even a temple—for the Hebrews of the better class worship only with the intellect, a spiritual Deity in His unity."

"Which, if I dare speak so boldly to you. O Remeses," I said, "appears to me to be the noblest species of worship, and the purest sort of religion for an intellectual being."

"Sayest thou?" quickly demanded the prince, surveying my face with his full bright gaze. "Thou art in advance of the rest of mankind, my Sesostris! The same feeling exists in my own bosom; but I believed myself alone in experiencing it. Some day we will hold discourse together on this high mystery. There seems to come up from my childhood a voice which I can never silence, and which I hear loudest when I am most solemnly engaged in the sacred rites of the altars of our gods, saying,—

"'Son of earth, there is but one GOD, invisible, eternal, uncreated, and whose glory He will not share with another; worship Him with the spirit and with the understanding.'"

"This is remarkable," I said, "for such also is the mystery taught by the priests of Chaldea, of whom Melchisedec was the first high priest. I have read their sacred books in Damascus."

"I have never seen them; yet this voice forces itself upon me everywhere, my Sesostris. All is dark and inscrutable to us mortals. We hang our faith upon a tradition, and our hopes upon a myth. We feel ourselves equal or superior to the deities we worship, and find no repose in the observances our religion demands. Would that I had the power to penetrate the blue heavens above us and find out God, and know what life means, and whence we came and whither we go."

"Once across the Lake of the Dead," I answered, "and all will be revealed. Osiris in his vast judgment-hall will give each soul the key of the past and the future."

"So say the priests, and so we believe. But to return to the Hebrews. Another time we will discourse on these themes. The new king, hearing that two hundred thousand and more foreigners dwelt here, called all the elders and chief men before him: and when he had questioned them and heard their history, and had learned that the Prince Joseph, who had done so much to uphold and consolidate the Phœnician rule, was one of their ancestors, his wrath was presently kindled against them. He saw in them the friends and adherents of the overthrown dynasty; both as allied by blood to the great Hebrew prime minister, and as originating from the same country with the expelled Phœnician king. He, therefore, perceiving they were not a warlike people, and could not be dreaded as an army, instead of declaring war against them and driving them out of Egypt, as he had done the Syrian kings, resolved to reduce them to servitude like captives taken in war. Having come to this resolution, he held as prisoners the chief men before him, and placed the whole people under the yoke of bondage, enrolling them under task-officers, and putting them to work upon the cities, temples, palaces, and canals, which the Phœnicians had either destroyed, or suffered to fall into ruin. This was the beginning, my Sesostris, of the subjugation to perpetual labour of these Syrians or Hebrews in the very land where one of their family had ruled next to the throne. They have been engaged since in building cities, and walls, and in cultivating and irrigating the royal wheat-fields; aiding in hewing stone in the quarries, and in all other works of servitude: but as the making of bricks requires no intelligence, and as it was not the policy of Amunophis-Pharaoh to elevate their intellects, but the contrary, lest they should prove troublesome, they have chiefly been kept to this, the most degrading of all labour."

"How long is it that they have been in this condition?" I asked.

"About one hundred and five or six years have elapsed since the death of Prince Joseph. But they were gradually reduced to their present state. During the latter years only of Amunophis were their tasks increased. They, nevertheless, multiplied in such numbers that the king began to apprehend danger to his crown from their multitude."

"Were there men among them who sought to free their fellows?" I inquired.

"Always, and to this hour. They are a proud, haughty, resolute, and stubborn race. They bend to the yoke, indeed, but with hatred of the oppressor, not with the willing submission of the Libyan or Nubian captive. The king had reason to fear from the increase of their numbers, when he found the census of this people gave more than a million of souls, while the number of his own subjects in both provinces did not exceed six millions; his own Thebans not amounting to as many as the Hebrews numbered. Upon this he became alarmed, for he was about entering into a war with the kings of Syro-Arabia, and apprehended that, being of the same Syrian stock, they might join themselves to his enemies. He, therefore, increased their burdens and taskmasters, in order to keep them in closer subjugation; but the more he oppressed them the more they multiplied. In relating these facts, O prince, do not think I approve of cruelty even in my royal ancestor. It was, no doubt, a great wrong in the beginning inflicted upon them, in making them servants, and the subsequent series of oppressions were but the natural results of the first act. It was one unmixed evil throughout. Having committed the manifest error in the outset, of enslaving them to the crown, it now became a necessary policy to prevent their dangerous increase. He would not send them with his army into Arabia lest they should join his enemies. He, therefore, to keep down their numbers, ordered all the male infants as soon as born to be put to death by the Egyptian women."

"A dreadful alternative!" I exclaimed.

"Yes, and one not to be defended," answered Remeses, in a decided tone. "But Amunophis, having caught the lion by the jaws, was compelled either to destroy him, or be destroyed himself. The result of the edict was, that many perished. The Nile, it is said, was constantly bearing down upon its bosom corpses of new-born Hebrew babes."

"Dreadful!" I ejaculated.

"It became so to the king. But he felt that one or the other must perish, and that these innocent infants must die for the future safety of the kingdom. There were sad and tragic scenes! Many a Hebrew mother fought to save her infant, or perished with it clasped to her heart! Many a desperate father resisted the soldiers who sought his hut for his concealed child, and died on the threshold, in the ineffectual effort to save his son! You perceive, Sesostris, that I speak with emotion. I have heard the scenes of that era described by those who witnessed them. I was an infant at the time, and do not speak of my own knowledge; but many live who then saw tragedies of horror such as few lands have witnessed. Had I been Amunophis I think I should have devised some other way to ward off the anticipated danger from my kingdom. But this sanguinary edict was unsuccessful. The Egyptian nurses were tenderer of heart than the king, and saved many to the tears and entreaties of mothers. Thousands of mothers, stifling every cry of nature, gave birth secretly, and in silence, to their babes, and the fathers or friends stood ready to fly with it to some prepared concealment. Thousands were thus saved, as the innumerable multitudes of men you have beheld this day toiling in the fields, making bricks to build up Raamses, bear witness. The edict continued in force for two years, when Amunophis died. After the seventy days of mourning were ended, his daughter Amense, who had been married to the prince of the Thebaïd, a nephew of Amunophis, but had been left a widow about the time of her father's death, came to the throne as the next in succession to the double crown. With the sceptre was bequeathed to her the iron chain that bound the Hebrews. Young, inexperienced in rule, without advisers, my mother knew not how to solve the problem these enslaved Syrians presented to her. As a woman, she felt that she could originate no new policy. But prompted by humanity, the first act of her power was to repeal the edict commanding the death of the infants. This act alone kindled in the hearts of the whole of the oppressed people a sentiment of gratitude. On the contrary, her lords, generals, chief princes of the nomes, and dukes of cities, with one voice assured her that this act of clemency would destroy her throne. But you see, my Sesostris, that it still stands. For thirty-four years she has reigned over the empire of Egypt, and it has never before reached so high a degree of prosperity, power, and strength. Her armies of the east, and of the south, and of Libya, are superior to those of all nations."

"Yet is the problem more intricate, and farther from solution than ever," I said to the prince. "The Hebrew is still in the land, still increasing in numbers, and now far more formidable than in the reign of your grandsire, Amunophis."

"This is true. My mother and I have talked for hours together upon the theme. She, with her woman's gentler nature, would not oppress them, yet has she been compelled by necessity to hold them in strict subjugation, lest they become a formidable element of insurrection in the kingdom. So far as is consistent with safety to her two crowns, she mitigates the severity of their condition; and, as you have understood, has forbidden the women to be struck with blows, or put to heavy toil. Still it is not easy, among so many thousand taskmasters, and so many myriads of bondmen, to oversee all individual acts of oppression; but when brought to our notice they are severely punished. The condition of the Hebrew is an incubus upon the soul of my noble mother, and if it were in her power, with safety

DAMASCUS.

to her subjects, to release them to-morrow from their bondage, she would do so. But state policy demands imperatively, rigid supervision, severe discipline, and constant labour, lest being idle, and at liberty to go where they choose, they conspire against us. Several times agents from the King of Ethiopia, our natural and hereditary foe, with whom we are almost always at war, have been discovered among them; and arms have been placed in their possession by the spies of the Queen of Arabia. They have, moreover, among them men of courage and talent, who, like their ancestor, Prince Abram, possess warlike fire, and, like the Prime Minister Joseph, have wisdom in council, to advise and rule. Such persons, among slaves, are to be feared, and there is necessary a certain severity, you would call it oppression, to keep down all such spirit."

"The burdens of these Hebrews still seem very heavy, O Remeses," I said.

"They doubtless are; but their condition is far lighter than it has been. They are allotted certain tasks, according to their strength, and if these are done early they have the rest of the day to themselves."

"And if late?"

"They must complete their tale of bricks, unless disabled by sickness. Blows are not given to men unless they are wilful and insubordinate. Once a year the queen visits all the Hebrews in the country of Avaris, of which Goshen forms but a part, and regulates abuses. The Hebrew always has the right of appealing to the governor of the province against his taskmaster, if cruelly treated. All that the queen can do is to execute with severity the laws against oppressing them."

"This Hebrew people, O Remeses," I said, as he ceased speaking, "are the cloud which overshadows Egypt. I foresee danger to the dynasty from it."

"I have in vain tried to settle upon some policy to be pursued—when I come to the throne, if it please Heaven that my mother depart this life before me (I pray the god to keep her to a good old age)—in reference to them. But my wisdom is at fault. When I take the sceptre I shall feel that the bondage of the Hebrew, which I inherit with it, will make it lead in my hand."

While he was speaking, the impatient pawing of his spirited chariot horses, restrained with difficulty by three footmen, reminded him that we were delaying at Raamses when we ought to be on our way back to On.

"Come, Sesostris, let us get upon the chariot and return, for I promised to dine with my mother and the Lord Prince Mœris to-day; and it is already past noon by the shadow of that obelisk."

We stood upon the silver-chased chariot, and, taking the leopard-skin reins in his left hand, he made a sign to his footmen, who, springing away from the heads of the fretting and frothing horses, let them fly. Away, like the wind, we swept the plain in front of the treasure-city; along the plateau where had stood the palace and gardens of Joseph, the lord of Egypt; past the ruined strangers' fountain, where I had talked with the venerable Ben Isaac and his handsome son past a well beside which Jacob had his great house, during the seventeen years he lived in Goshen, the ruins of which were visible a little way off to the east. On we rolled, preceded and followed by the fleet-footed runners, across the plain of the Hebrew brickmakers, who still bent to their labours. Women and children, with dark fine eyes and raven hair, gathering straw by the wayside or in the stubble-fields, were passed in vast numbers. Crossing an open space, I saw before me a black mass on the ground, which, as we advanced, proved to be a crowd of vultures or carrion eagles, that slowly and reluctantly moved aside at our coming; and the next moment our horses shied at the dead body of a man, around which they had been gathered feasting upon the flesh. The long beard and dark hair, the coarse blue loin-cloth, and the pile of bricks at his side, told the whole tale. It was an emaciated Hebrew, who had perished on the road-side under his burden.

I did not look at Remeses. I knew that he saw and felt. He reined up, and sternly commanded two of his footmen to remain and bury the body.

"Sesostris," he said, as we went forward again, "what can be done? Humanity, piety, and every element of the soul call for the deepest commiseration of this unhappy people. I sometimes feel that it would be better to send them in a mass out of Egypt into Arabia, and follow them with an army to see that they went beyond our boundaries, and then establish a cordon of military posts from Ezion-Geber, on the Arabian Sea, to the shores of the Great Sea, north. But how could we provide food for such a host, now amounting to two and a half millions of people? Thousands would perish in the wilderness for want of water and food. Only a miracle of the gods could preserve them, their women and children, from a lingering death. And would not this be more cruel than the edict of Amunophis; only executing it in an indirect way, and on a gigantic scale? I would, were I Pharaoh to-day, give the half of my kingdom to the wise man who could devise a practicable way of freeing Egypt from the Hebrews, without destroying them or suffering them to die in the wilderness. If men are ever deified, such a benefactor would deserve the honour."

These words, my dear mother, were spoken with deep feeling, and showed me that the heart of Remeses is manly and tender, that his sentiments are always elevated and noble, and that the oppression of the Hebrew is not so much the fault of himself or of the queen-mother, as it is the irresistible sequence of causes which were in action before they were born; and to the effects of which they must yield, until the gods in their wisdom and power make known to them the way to remove from the land so great an evil: for none but the Deity Supreme is wise enough to solve this intricate problem of Egypt. Certain it is, that if the Hebrews go on multiplying and growing as they now do, in another generation they will outnumber the Egyptians, and will need only a great leader like their warlike ancestor Prince Abram, or the hero king of Philistia, who established the Phœnician dynasty, to enable them to subvert the kingdom, and upon its ruins establish another Syro-Hebraic dynasty. One of their ancestors has already ruled Egypt, and another may yet sit in the very seat of the Pharaohs.

As we re-entered the City of the Sun, we passed by the base of an obelisk which Queen Amense is erecting to mark the era and acts of her long reign. Upon it were sculptured representations of her battles with the Ethiopians, her wars with Libya, and her conquest of Arabia. The work was executed by Phœnician and Egyptian artists; and I am rejoiced to see that the painters of Tyre and the sculptors of Sidon are greatly esteemed for the delicacy and perfection of their work. When these persons saw me, they dropped their pencils and chisels, and, with their hands upon their bosoms, manifested every sign of delight. You may suppose I responded with more than usual gratification to the homage thus paid me; for in a foreign land the sight of the humblest of one's own countrymen refreshes the eye and warms the heart.

But I have too long occupied your time, dearest mother, with one letter.

Your devoted son,
SESOSTRIS.

LETTER IX.

ISLE OF RHODA, NILE.

ROYAL AND BELOVED MOTHER,—

My preceding letters, dearest mother, have enabled you to form some idea of the Hebrew vassalage, which is one of the peculiarities of Egypt. This subject has deeply interested me. In that oppressed people I behold Syrians and men of my own race, as it were, reduced to such a pitiable and miserable condition. My sympathies are therefore naturally with them. Was not Prince Abram, of Palestine, who conquered the enemy of our ancestor's throne in those days, Chedorlaomer, King of Elam and Tidal, and sovereign of the nations east of the inland sea, the founder of their family; and was not the same Abram the friend of Neathor, the founder or restorer of Tyre upon the Isle? When I recall these facts of past history, and how ably the wise Prince Joseph ruled here, I am deeply moved at their present degradation and suffering.

Since writing to you, I have conversed with the queen upon the subject. I find her ready and willing, with mind and heart and hand, to take any safe steps for putting an end to this bondage. But, as she feelingly says,—

"It is an evil which descended to me with the crown and sceptre of my father; and I know not how to remove it, and yet protect that crown which I am bound to transmit to Remeses!"

Such, then, dear mother, is the present condition of Hebrew servitude. When it will terminate, whether by some bold act of Remeses, when he comes to the throne, or by their own act, or by he intervention of the gods, are questions the solution of which lies hidden in the womb of the future.

Not all the Hebrews are employed in the field. It has of late years been a fashion with the nobles, governors, and chief captains of Egypt to have the young captives of both sexes as servants near their persons; their beauty, activity, and trustfulness rendering these Syrian youths particularly fitted for this domestic employment. Thus, I have seen Hebrew pages attending on lords and ladies in their palaces, and Hebrew maidens acting as personal attendants upon the mistress of the family. These young foreigners soon become favourites, and are rewarded for their devotion and usefulness by rich dresses and jewels, which last they all especially delight in, and wear in great quantities. The Egyptians, also, lavishly display them on their fingers, in their ears, and upon their necks. Every lord wears a large signet, on which is carved his *cartouch*, or shield of arms. To present this to any friend is a mark of the highest confidence and honour. Such an expression of regard, you will remember, the Prince Remeses bestowed upon me. With it I shall seal this letter, that you may see its designs in the hieroglyph representation.

The queen has three Hebrew pages, noble and princely-looking boys, with fine, sparkling, black eyes, and intelligent faces; but there is a fixed air of pensiveness about them all, which is perhaps the result of hereditary oppression. This pensive look I have remarked in Prince Remeses, whose style of face is very strongly Syriac or Hebraic. Indeed, I have seen an old Hebrew bondman, a gardener in the palace garden, by the name of Amram, who is so strikingly like the prince that I can easily see by him, how Remeses himself will look at eighty years of age. But this Syriac countenance of Remeses comes from his grandmother, Ephtha, the daughter of the last Phœnician Pharaoh; yet it is marvellous he has about him nothing of the Egyptian type. The Egyptian or Nilotic race have a sharp and prominent face, in which a long and straight, or gently aquiline, nose forms a principal part. The eye is sometimes oblique; the chin short and retracted; the lips rather full and tumid, so to speak; and the hair, when it is suffered to escape the razor in times of mourning, long and flowing. The head is elongated upward, with a receding forehead. The profile is delicate rather than strong. This style of features and head is strictly Egyptian, and pertains to every class, from Amense on the throne to the priests and people. I see it sculptured on all the tombs and monuments, and carved on the most ancient sarcophagi. The head of Horus is but a sublimer modification of this type.

On the contrary, the head of the Hebrew is large and round, with full brows, a forehead low in front, and high temples. The nose is strongly eagle-like; the eyes set even, but of an almond-shape—yet large, full, and exceedingly black, and soft in expression. The chin is full; the face oval; the hair short, and inclined to curl in the neck and over the brow. The profile is strong and bold—not unlike the Arabian. The Egyptian is slender and light; the Hebrew usually below the medium height, with broad shoulders and full chest. The Egyptian has a pale reddish-copper complexion—save the women, who are bright olive-coloured—while the Hebrew face is a ruddy and finely-toned brown. The Egyptian females, when not exposed to the sun and outer-door labour, are exceedingly fair. The children of the race are all beautiful. Prince Remeses does not share a single characteristic of this Egyptian national head and face; on the contrary, he resembles the highest type of the Hebrew. Is not this remarkable? That is, is it not wonderful that the Syriac blood, derived from the Queen Ephtha, should descend pure to the third generation, unmingled with the Thebaïd characteristics of Amunophis, his grandfather?

I am not aware whether the prince is conscious of his great likeness to this oppressed people, nor would I be so rude as to speak to him of it; for though he has sympathy for them, and tries to improve their condition, yet he possesses that haughty sense of superiority which is natural in a prince and an Egyptian educated to despise them both as foreigners and slaves of the crown.

The father of Remeses, as I have before said, was the Vicegerent or Prince of Upper Egypt, and one of the royal line of the powerful Theban kings. He had been married but a few months to Pharaoh's daughter, when, being called to repulse an invasion of the warlike Ethiopians, he was slain in battle. Remeses was born not long afterwards, and is, therefore, in a twofold degree the heir of the silver crown of the Thebaïd. Had he been willing to leave his mother, she would, when he became thirty years old (which is the age of maturity by the laws of Egypt), have sent him with a splendid retinue to Upper Egypt, and made him Prince of Thebes, as his father had been before him. But he chose to remain with the queen, to whom he appears as much attached as I am to you, my dear mother; and Amense substituted a nephew of her deceased husband, Prince Mœris, and placed him, four years since, on the vicegerent throne of the kingdom of the Upper Nile.

It was this Prince Mœris with whom Remeses was to dine in the palace on the day we drove to the treasure-city of Raamses. I was also present, dear mother, at the dinner. The Lord Mœris is about the age of Remeses, but altogether a very different person. He is thoroughly Egyptian, both in looks and lineage as well as by prejudice and feeling.

He has a slender, elegant person; delicate straight features; a high, retreating forehead; and a nose slightly aquiline. His mouth is full-lipped and sensual. His retreating chin betrays deficiency of firmness, and an undue proportion of obstinacy. The expression of his oblique, Nubian-looking eye, I did not like. It was sinister and restlessly observant. He was reserved, and while he asked questions from time to time, he never replied to any. His complexion is a bright olive, and he is a handsome man; his rich dress increasing the fine effect of his personal appearance. The uniform he wore was that of Admiral of the Nile; the queen having appointed him commander of the great fleet of war-galleys she has collected near Memphis for the subjugation of Ethiopia. He has, therefore, come down within a few days to take charge of his ships. The character of this man for courage is undoubted, but he has the reputation of great cruelty. He tarries long at the wine-cup, and in his private life is a gross sensualist. He professes great piety to the gods, and sacrifices often, with pomp and display. In Memphis yesterday he burned incense with his own hands to Apis, and to-day he worshipped Mnevis, the sacred ox of On.

He was more communicative with me at the dinner than with Remeses. He expressed the greatest admiration of Phœnicia, praised the brilliancy of your reign, and the rich commerce of the Isle of Tyre. He said he had a great reverence for our deities, Astarte, Hercules, Io, and Isis; for he asserted that Isis was quite as much a Phœnician as an Egyptian goddess. "Had he not in Thebes," said he, "instituted a procession and a rite in honour of the return of Isis from Phœnicia? We are one in religion, one in commerce, one in glory," he continued, with fulsome enthusiasm. "Are not our kingdoms both ruled by queens? Let us draw closer the bonds of alliance, and together rule the world! You are a free city, your Tyre! never been conquered! Amunophis would have exacted tribute, but your king replied, 'Since the foundation of the earth, and the great Deluge retired from Libanus, Tyre has been free, and will remain free to the end of days.'"

I answered, that I trusted the words of my noble grandsire would remain prophetic for ever. He then gave as a toast,—

"Phœnicia and Egypt, twin sisters of Isis, and health to their fair queens!"

This was well received. Mœris was, however, evidently deep in his cups, and soon became quarrelsome towards Remeses, to whom he said, with a sneer,—

"You and I, prince, when the queen, my aunt, has departed to the shades of the realm of Osiris, will divide Egypt between us. I will be content with the Thebaïd country, and will defend your borders on that side. Two crowns are too much for one man's head, albeit you have a large one upon your shoulders."

"Prince Mœris," said Remeses, with a look of indignation, "forget not yourself in my mother's palace!"

Thus speaking, the son of Amense rose from the table, and I followed him to the portico which overlooked the gardens.

"That man, Sesostris," said he to me, after a moment's silence, "would not hesitate to conspire to the whole throne and both crowns of Egypt, if he were hopeful of success."

"He is a man of an evil eye," I said.

"And heart! But he must not be incensed. He is powerful, and as wicked as powerful. In a few days he will be on his way to Upper Egypt, and, in this war with Ethiopia, will find an outlet for his restless ambition."

"Suppose (the gods guarding your gracious mother, the queen) you should come to the throne; what, Remeses, would you do with or for your cousin, your father's nephew? Would you suffer so dangerous a man to hold the viceroyalty of Upper Nile?"

"I should wear both crowns, Sesostris," answered Remeses, quietly and steadily.

While we were thus conversing, a Hebrew page came, and said,—

"My lord prince, her majesty is taken ill, and desires to have you come to her."

"My mother ill!" he exclaimed, with deadly pallor covering his face. "Pardon me, prince, I must leave you and go to her." And in a moment he hastened to the wing of the palace occupied by his mother and the ladies of her retinue.

The queen had left the table some time before Prince Mœris began to converse with me, excusing herself on the plea of slight fatigue and indisposition; for she had passed an hour that day in giving directions to the chief architect, to whom was intrusted the erection of her obelisk, outside of the gate of the Temple of the Sun. Remeses had been gone but a few moments, when I beheld Prince Mœris borne across the terrace by his servants to his chariot, in a state of helpless intoxication.

The illness of the queen was not of an alarming nature, and the next day she appeared in the saloon, but was very pale. The result is, the court physicians have advised her to go to her palace on the isle of Rhoda, in the Nile, as a more salubrious spot than the interior of a vast city. Remeses accompanied her thither, and the date of my letter, my dear mother, shows you that I am also still one of the queen's favoured household. Her health continues doubtful, but she is much improved in appearance by the change. Remeses, with beautiful filial devotion, passes with her every hour he can spare from the various pressing duties which demand his personal attention; and preparations for the Ethiopian war call for all his time as general of the armies.

Opposite the palace in which I write to you, the plain between the river and the pyramids is covered with a vast army assembled there within three days, preparatory to their southern march; while the bosom of the Nile, for half a league above this palace-covered island, is almost concealed by war-galleys, which, to the number of one thousand and upward, are at anchor ready to ascend the river.

From the lofty west wing of the propylon of the gate of this island-palace of the Pharaohs, I command not only a prospect of the fleet, but of the plain of the pyramids outside of Memphis. I have but to turn slowly round from that elevation to see On with its three hundred and sixty temples—its gardens and towers; and Raamses, the treasure-city, to the east: to the south, the Nile, studded with barges and gay vessels having silken and coloured sails, filled with citizens, come to look at the fleet of war-ships; the immense squadron itself, gay with the variegated flags of its different divisions and captains; with towers, temples, obelisks, and propyla on the two shores terminating the perspective: and on the west, Jizeh, with its sphinxes and colossi, its terraced gardens and amphitheatre of the gods; and still farther off, Memphis united to the Nile by a magnificent aqueduct; and the pyramids of Cheops and of his daughter. Between the city and these mysterious mausolea, stands alone, amid gardens, the red granite temple of Pthah and Athor, the two chief divinities of Memphis: for Apis, the sacred bull of Memphis, is not a divinity, properly, but only a visible incarnation of Osiris, the emblem and type of the power and strength of the Supreme Creator. Imagine this vast and varied scene of architectural and naval glory, interspersed with verdure

F

of the brightest green, with palm, orange, and fig trees, garden linked to garden, grove to grove, and villas half seen through the foliage; and lastly, the mighty river flowing with shining waves amid the inimitable landscape, and you have before you a scene of grandeur and beauty such as Egypt alone can produce. Add the myriads of human beings, the crowded galleys, the thronged shores, the eighty thousand soldiers encamped on the west plain, the army of chariots drawn up on the east bank, and farther up, opposite the aqueduct of Pharaoh-Apophis, a battalion of twelve thousand cavalry manœuvring, and the scene which I, an hour since, beheld from the top of the gateway is before you.

Since I wrote the last sentence, I have witnessed a naval review, with a sham battle. The Prince Mœris, in a gorgeous galley decorated with all the emblems of the cities and nomes of Egypt, after displaying the skill of his one hundred oarsmen, and the swiftness of his vessel in front of the palace, before the eyes of the queen, moved among his ships, and gave orders for their division into lines of battle. The greater number of these galleys had only a single mast with a long swallow-winged sail, and were propelled by forty rowers. But the ships of the captains were larger and more imposing. All the galleys were handsomely painted, and the whole fleet together made a splendid moving spectacle, which was heightened by the thousand bannerets fluttering in the wind, and the ten thousand shields and spears gleaming in the sun, as they were held in the hands of the soldiers upon their decks.

When the signal was given for the two parties to combat, the air was filled by a loud shout, and a hundred galleys charged each other, just as did the battalions of chariots in the review I have already described. The vessels, set in motion by the rowers, were driven towards each other with terrific velocity. The Abyssinian soldiers upon the bows, and the bowmen in the tops, shot off flights of arrows, which sounded like a storm of wind as they hurtled through the air. The Libyan spearmen, on the lofty poops, brandished their spears with wild cries; while the Nubians, amidships, struck their triangular shields with battle-axes of iron, producing a sound like crashing thunders. The war bugles and hollow drums beaten on board each vessel increased the loud confusion, and added to the terror of the scene. The fall of thousands of oars, the rush of waters from the cleaving bows, the shouts of the captains, the warlike spirit and battle-fierceness of the whole, presented a spectacle of sublimity unequalled. Nor was it without an element of terror. Such was the excited manner of the simulating combatants, I believed that no earthly power could prevent a real collision and hand-to-hand conflict in hot blood, when, at a signal from the Prince Mœris, the rowers of the leading galleys turned suddenly, as they came within touch of each other's sweeps, and so, one after another wheeling in line, both divisions passed down the river, until they moved in parallel columns. The whole manœuvre was one of the most wonderful exhibitions of naval discipline and generalship. Ere the shouts of the people on the shores and in the numerous pleasure barges had died away, the two columns, at a signal from the mast of the ship of their admiral, came side by side, and a **battle** between the soldiers **on** opposite decks commenced—one party attempting to board, the other repelling them. Not less than six thousand combatants were engaged at once, above the heads of the banks of rowers. The clash of swords and spears and battle-axes, and other offensive and defensive weapons, produced a noise so terrible and grand that I believe there is no other sound on earth, as well calculated to quicken the pulse and bring out all the enthusiasm of the soul of a man. I can compare these metallic and iron tones only to what might be the sound of the brazen voice of Mars himself rolling his war-cry along the battle-ranks **of his foes.** Suddenly the iron din of war ceased, and, separating, **one of the** divisions commenced a flight, and the other a pursuit. This scene was the most exciting of all. The chase was in a direction down the east side of the island, opposite the queen's window; for all these exhibitions **were** given in her honour, and, though by no means well, she remained upon the terrace during the whole; and it was, perhaps, the consciousness of their monarch's eye being upon them that caused these demi-barbaric soldiers, gathered from all the provinces and tributary countries of Egypt, to surpass themselves, being ready even, at her nod, to convert the mock battle into a real one.

The two fleets, flying and pursuing, **moved** past the island like a sirocco. Their lion or eagle-headed prows tossed high in the air clouds of white spray. The roar of the waters as the vessels ploughed through them, the dash of the banks of oars, the cries of pursuit, the whizzing and shrieks of arrows cleaving the air, the shouts of the contending thousands, and the velocity with which they moved, brought colour to the queen's cheek, and the light of interest to her eyes. It was now an actual and real trial for mastery in speed; and the contest partook of all the realities of a war-chase. The two divisions, rounding the lower end of the island, were hidden by the Temple of Isis, which crowns it, but soon reappeared on the west arm of the river, ascending. When they came opposite to the queen, having passed entirely round the island, they resumed their former line, two or three with broken banks of oars, and shattered poops or prows from collision.

Prince Mœris came on shore to receive the compliments of the queen, and dined with us. Remeses was not present, being with the cohorts of cavalry; for he is visiting and inspecting every arm of the service, as it is intended this shall be the most formidable host that has ever been sent into Ethiopia.

Adieu, dearest mother, and believe me
Your truly devoted son,
SESOSTRIS.

LETTER X.

ISLAND PALACE OF RHODA.

MY DEAREST MOTHER,—

It is with heartfelt pleasure I assure you of the recovery of the queen. The heart of the noble and devoted Remeses is lightened of a heavy weight of solicitude. Smiles once more revisit his features, and cheerfulness replaces his late depression.

"Sesostris," said he to me this morning, as we were returning in his galley from a visit to the pyramids and vast city of tombs that stretch between Memphis and the Libyan hills, "if my excellent and dear mother had died, I should have been made one of the most unhappy of men. I shall to-morrow, in testimony of my gratitude, offer in the Temple of Osiris a libation and incense to the God of Health and Life, wherever in His illimitable universe such a Being may dwell."

"Then you would not, my dear Remeses, offer it to Osiris himself?" I said.

"You have heard, my friend," he replied, "my views of these mysteries of faith: that I look, through all material and vicarious representatives, onward and upward to the Infinite and Supreme Essence of Life—the Generator, Upholder, and Guide of the worlds and all that dwell upon them. From a child I have never entered, as my dear mother does, into the heart and spirit of our worship. There is something within me which tells me that we consist of a twofold being—a soul within a body. The soul must have had a Soul as its creator; therefore, O Sesostris, do I believe in a Supreme Soul of the universe—the Fountain of all souls—a Being of thought, invisibility, intelligence, and reason, each supreme and eternal; for I can conceive no creator of a SOUL, nor end of its existence. Before all things that actually exist, and before all beings, there is One Being whom I would designate, for want of another term, God of gods, prior to the first god or king of earth, remaining unmoved and unapproachable in the singleness of His own unity. He is greater than, as He was prior to, all material things, of which He is the sole fountain; and He is also the foundation of things conceived by the intellect, and from His intellect spring the spirits of the gods and the souls of men."

"Then," said I to the prince, to whom I had listened with surprise and pleasure—for, mother, similar to these are the deep mysteries taught by our most sacred priest of Io, into which I was initiated when I became twenty-five years of age—"then you believe that God is Intellect conceiving itself, and that the creation of man was but the beginning of an infinite series of resistless conceptions of Himself?"

"Not resistless, but voluntary. Finding Himself existing, He multiplied Himself, for His own glory and delight primarily; and, secondly, for the happiness of the offspring of His Intellect."

"We are, then, His offspring—that is, our souls?"

"Without doubt, if my theories be founded in truth," he answered contemplatively. We were then in mid-river, and the forty-four rowers of our gilded barge were slowly dipping their brazen-mounted oars into the glassy water, while with gentle motion we were borne towards the isle of palaces and terraces. Our heads were shaded from the sun by a silken pavilion stretched above the stern of the galley, under which we reclined upon sumptuous cushions as we conversed. Remeses, however, is by no means a voluntary seeker of luxurious ease; but in Egypt, where splendour and voluptuous furniture everywhere invite to indulgence, one must either deprive himself of all comforts, for the sake of enduring hardship, or yield unchallenging to the countless seductive forms of couches, lounges, chairs, and sofas, which everywhere, on the galleys and in houses, offer themselves to his use.

The air was balmy and soft, and fanned our faces ; while the beautiful shores, lined with villas of the chief men of the court, afforded a grateful picture to the eye. Our rowers let their sweeps fall and rise to the low and harmonious time of a river chant, which, while it inspired conversation between the prince and myself, did not disturb, but rather veiled our subdued voices.

"Do you believe there are lesser gods?" I asked.

"Do you mean, Sesostris, beings higher in rank than men, and so created, to whom the Supreme Intellect of the Universe delegates a part of His authority and power over man and nature? Such, in its purity, is our Egyptian idea of gods."

"Such is not the Phœnician," I answered, hesitatingly ; for I felt how far in advance of the hero demigods of our Assyrio-Median mythology was the Egyptian theological conception of a god, while the still sublimer idea held by Remeses, that they are celestial princes under the Supreme Prince, created as His servants, yet so far above men as to be as gods to us, took fast hold of my imagination, and commended itself to my intellect.

"What, my dear Sesostris, is the mythology of your country?" he asked, with a look of deep interest. "I have read some of your sacred books, and from them I perceive we obtain our myths of Isis, Mars, Hercules, Vulcan, and even Venus, who is your Astarte and our Athor. We **owe** much of our religion and learning to you Tyrians, my Sesostris."

"The recipient has **become** mightier than the giver," I replied. "Without doubt you have received from us the great invention of the phonetic alphabet, which your scholars are already making use of, though I learn the priests oppose it as an invasion upon the sacred writing of the hieroglyphic representations. I have seen here many rolls of papyrus written in our Phœnician letter, in the vernacular Koptic words, and executed with taste and beauty."

"It is not pictorial, and therefore the priests, who are all artists and lovers of colours, reject it. It will be slowly introduced. Upon obelisks and tombs the brilliant and varied hieroglyphic **writing** will continue, even though the records and rolls may by-and-by be written with the Tyrian alphabet. You have seen my Chaldaic letter, which I have formed partly on the model of your great Kadmus, and partly on the sacred characters, reducing forms of things to **outlines** and strokes of the stylus. This I invented, hoping to introduce it into Egypt, if the Tyrian letter is opposed by our priests, on the score of being foreign cabalistic signs ; for such do they see fit to regard them, and speak of them. But, my Sesostris, let me learn of you something of your mythology."

I was about to reply, when my attention was attracted to a "procession of the dead" crossing the river just above us, the body being placed in a gorgeous car which stood in a richly painted and gilded *baris*, with a curved prow carved with the head of Osiris. It was tied to a barge, with twenty rowers, which moved to a slow and solemn strain of music that came wildly floating across the waters to our ears, mingled with the wails of mourners who crowded the deck of the galley; chiefly women with long dishevelled hair and naked breasts, which they beat frantically at times, with piercing cries. Through a small window in the ark or car I could see the painted visage upon the head of the mummy-case.

It soon landed, and we resumed our conversation.

"You are aware, O prince," I said, turning to him, "that Phœnicia was settled among the first of the nations, after Typhon sent the flood of waters to destroy Osiris upon earth. Of course you Egyptians believe in the universal inundation of the earth?"

"The tradition is well-founded," he answered. "We believe that mighty nations existed aforetime, beyond the history of any kingdom, and that for their evils the Divine Creator of men brought upon them as punishment a mighty unknown sea, which drowned the world: that Menes, a great and good king, also called Noe-Menes, was spared by the gods, he with all his family being saved in a ship of the old world, which sailed to the mountains of Arabia Deserta, where, guided by a dove, they landed and sacrificed to the gods. This Menes, descending from the mountain, founded Egypt, first building This, or Thebis, and then Memphthis, dividing Egypt into the Thinite and Memphite provinces; and so from Egypt all the world was repeopled."

"Such is our tradition, O Remeses," I said, smiling, "only instead of a mountain in Arabia, it was Libanus, in Syria, to which his galley was guided, not by a dove, but by a raven; and that his name was Ammon, or Hammun; and that the first city built was Sidon, and the next the city of the Island of Tyre."

Remeses returned my smile and said, "No doubt there was a disposition in all our forefathers to give the honour of being the oldest nation to their own. Ham-mun is also a person in our Egyptian tradition, but is called the son of Menes, who, rebelling against his father, was driven from This or Thebis into Africa, where he founded Libya, and erected to himself, as a god, the ancient temple and worship of Ammon. From him come the Nubians and Ethiopians."

"Then I will claim no traditionary alliance with him," I answered good-humouredly. "*Our* Ammon was called also Hercules, and the first temple of the earth was built to him on the rocky isle of ancient Tyre. Then Belus, the hero and warrior-god, and founder of Babylon, became the patron of Tyre; and a noble temple was also erected to Nimrod, who slew the wild beasts that swarmed in ancient Syria, and who became the protector of shepherds and agriculture. Thus came our first gods, being men deified; while yours are but attributes, or created celestial powers, high above men; or animated forms representing the Deity incarnate and comprehensible to the senses. Baalbec was a city built to Bel or Belus, who, like your Osiris, is the symbol of the sun, which, of burnished gold, he displayed upon his shield in battle. In Phœnicia we call him 'the Lord of the Sun,' and the 'Sun-God.' We pay him divine honours by sacrifices, libations, and offerings of incense. And this recalls a discovery I recently made in On that the true meaning of Re and of On is not 'the City of the Sun,' but the 'Lord of the Sun's' city; that is, the city of Osiris, who is the lord of the sun. This meaning of the name at once removes from On the impression which was at first made upon my mind, that you, and the queen, and your whole court, worshipped the sun as the Persic and Parthian nations do; whereas it is Osiris, the Lord of the Sun, that is the Supreme god, generator, producer, and creator of the sun and all things that are. No sooner had I made this discovery, which I did by conversing with the high priest of On, than I perceived that whatsoever grossness may be found in the religion of the lower castes of the people, who seldom see beyond the symbol, the theology of the wise and great is free from idolatry."

"I am glad you justify us in this matter, dear Sesostris," answered the prince. "We are not idolaters like the Persian and Barbara kings. Our sacred books teach an intellectual and spiritual theology. But, as I have before said to you, the Invisible is so veiled from the people, by the visible forms under which he is offered to them by the priesthood, that while *we* adore the God of power and strength in Apis, *they* worship the bull himself: while *we* in the form of Horus, with his uræus and disk, adore Him who made him a benefactor to men and a pursuer of evil, *they* bow down to the hawk-headed statue of porphyry and worship the sculptured colossus of stone. But I interrupt you. Proceed, if you please, with the account of the origin of your country's religion."

"I have not much more to add of interest," I answered, "save of Adonis and Astarte."

"Are not these your Osiris and Isis?" asked the prince readily.

"I will first explain," said I, not immediately answering his question, "what we in Phœnicia think of Isis. The priests teach that the identity of the goddess Io, who is worshipped with rites unusually imposing at Byblos, is one with Isis."

"What is your opinion, Sesostris?"

"There is," I answered, "a close resemblance between the rites which relate to the death and revival of Adonis at Byblos, and of your divinity Osiris in Egypt. Indeed, the priests at Byblos claim to have the sepulchre of Osiris among them, and maintain that all the rites which are commonly referred to Adonis properly relate to Osiris."

"Then Egypt derives Osiris from Phœnicia?" remarked Remeses, with a slight movement of the brows, and a smile.

"Without doubt," I replied. "In Tyre, we call Egypt the daughter of Phœnicia."

"The daughter has outgrown the mother, dear Sesostris. We are proud of our parentage. We bow to Phœnicia as the mistress of letters and queen of the merchants of the earth. But what think the priests of Baalbec of Osiris and Isis?"

"It is the tradition of those haughty priests that they are distinct persons," I replied. "The ceremonies and rites with which they worship these deities are truly magnificent, and are invested with every form of the beautiful and gorgeous. Ours, as I have said, in some points resemble your **Egyptian rites in** honouring Osiris and Isis ; but while you Egyptians, Remeses, adore only an abstract attribute of the deity, *we* adore the hero and the heroic woman— Adonis and Astarte. We rise not beyond them. We elevate them to the heavens and to the moon, and call them our gods. Truly, in the presence of the sublimer, purer myth which is the element of your faith, O Remeses, I feel that I **am** not far **above** the Barbara kings of Southern Africa, who deify each his predecessor. The priests of Isis, when they were in Phœnicia, attempted **to elevate our** worship ; but **we are** still idolaters—that is, mere men-worshippers. Or, where we **do not pay** them divine honours, we offer them to the sun, and moon, **and stars.** I must be initiated, O Remeses, into the profounder intellectual mysteries of your spiritual myth, now that I am in Egypt."

" You shall have **your** wish gratified. The high priest of On shall **receive** orders to open **to you** (what is closed to all strangers) the sacred **and** mystic rites of our faith."

" I have alluded to the mysteries of the temple at Tyre," I added. " Initiated thereinto, I was taught that religion had a higher object than human heroes, and that in Astarte **is** worshipped the daughter of Heaven and Light, who is LIFE, and **that** Adonis, her son by the Earth, signifies Truth. Thus from heaven **spring** Light, Life, and Truth. These three, say the mystic books **which I** studied, constitute the Trinity **of God,** who consists and subsists **only** in this undivided Trinity **as a** unit ; **not** Light alone, **not** Life alone, nor Truth alone ; but One in Three. That these three are not three deities, just as in geometry the three sides and three angles are not three triangles, **but one** triangle. That **in order to** bring this mystery to a level with **the** minds of men, light was symbolized by the sun, life by **Astarte,** truth by Adonis. In the temple of Bel-Pheor, in Cœle-Syria, the sun itself is worshipped as light, life, and truth in one ; his **rays representing** light, his heat life, his material disk or body truth."

" This is interesting to me, Sesostris," said Remeses. " It explains to me what I did not before understand, why the Syrians worship the sun. To them it is the majestic symbol of the trinity of deity. But I fear that in Egypt he is worshipped as an idol ; for he, doubtless, is worshipped **by** many, and in many cities are temples to him. But this material worship, which separates the symbol from the truth behind it, **was** introduced by the Palestinian dynasty, and it is almost the only trace it has left in Egypt of its presence. The worship of Osiris, rightly understood, is the worship of **the** deity, as revealed in our sacred books. But the mystery of his trinity is unknown to our theology. Have you many temples **of the** sun in Tyre ?"

" One only," was my answer, " but worthy, if I may so say, from its splendour, to stand **in** your city **of** ' the Lord of the Sun,' **as I** must call it."

" **Is** there **not a city of** your kingdom called Baalphegor, **in** which is a famous sun-temple ? "

" You mean Baalbec, the same words, only changed slightly. This city deserves its great fame, so grand are its fanes, so noble its palaces, so imposing the worship of the sun before its altars, so gorgeous the interiors of its temples, so rich the apparel of its priests, so sublime its choral worship. It is in Syrio-Euphrates, and is so shaded by palms that it has the aspect, in approaching it across the desert, of being an oasis filled with temples."

"Is not Phœnicia a lovely land, Sesostris?" he asked, at the same time returning the salutation of the admiral, Pathromenes, who passed in his war-galley, on his way to join the Prince Mœris, whose fleet sails to-morrow on its expedition. I was glad, also, to behold again my courteous friend of the Pelusian coast, and cordially received and answered his polite and pleased recognition of my person.

"It is indeed a lovely land, with its verdant plains, majestic mountains clothed with cedar, and beautiful but narrow rivers. It is covered with fair cities from the peninsula of Tyre to the further limits of Cœle-Syria, and is a rich and lovely kingdom, populous and happy. Its two great cities, Tyre and Sidon, are called the eyes of the world."

"I have so heard," he answered, "and when this Ethiopian war ends, and I find time to be absent, I hope to cross the sea to your kingdom and see 'the mother of Egypt,' as she also calls herself; 'the merchant of the seas,' whose galleys have discovered in unknown oceans, beyond the Pillars of the West, the isles of the blessed."

"So report our bold and venturous mariners," I answered.

"We who stay at home know not, Sesostris, what marvels lie beyond the seas at the extremity of the plane of the earth's vast area. It is possible that islands and lands of wonderful beauty may exist where the sun wheels over the West to return to his rising in the Orient; and if we credit mariners who follow the shores of the Arabian and Indian seas, there are fair shores from whence come off to them breezes laden with fragrance of unknown flowers, while birds of rare melody fill the air with their songs by day; but at night the odorant forests echo with the dread roar of fierce monsters, that guard the shores from the invasion of man!"

"I have sailed along those shores, if I may be so bold as to speak in such a presence, my lord prince," interrupted the captain of the galley, who had stood by listening to our discourse.

"Say on, Rathos," answered the prince courteously. "What have you to tell of marvels on foreign seas?"

"The lands at the earth's end, your excellency, are not like ours of Egypt. I have seen isles where the men are like larger monkeys, and have a language no one understands, and build their houses in the trees. Evil demons I doubt not, or else souls sent back to earth from Amenthe, by Osiris, to atone for crimes in monstrous forms, neither human nor beast!"

"I have heard of these creatures," said I. "How far hast thou sailed, O Rathos?"

"To the very edge of the world, my lord of Tyre," he answered quietly. "I was in a ship going to Farther Ind. In sailing round the end of the earth we lost the shore in a dark storm; and when day came we saw only sky and water. All were in consternation to be thus between heaven and sea, and no land to guide our course. To add to our terror, I perceived that we were borne swiftly upon an ocean-current eastward. It increased in velocity, and I soon saw that we must be approaching the verge of the vast and horrid gulf, over which the full ocean plunges, a thousand leagues in breadth, prone into chaos and the regions of the lost spirits of the unburied souls of men! But by the interposition of the god of winds, to whom I vowed a libation and a bale of the richest spices of Bengal, a great storm swept over the sea against us, and before it we fled as with wings, until we came to a great island, under the shelter of which we anchored, rejoicing in our safety."

"Verily, brave Rathos, thou wert in a great peril," I said. "Thinkest thou it was at the world's end?"

"So said the king of the island, and he congratulated us on our escape, saying that few ships, when once upon that downward tide, ever returned again to the top of the earth."

"Thinkest thou the earth is square, Rathos, from what voyages thou hast made?" I asked of the grey-haired captain, whose silvery locks were braided around his head, and covered by a green embroidered bonnet, with a fringed cape falling to his neck.

"Or a triangle, my lord prince; but some say four square, with a burning mountain at each angle."

"Which is thine own opinion, Rathos?" asked the prince, who had been listening to our conversation.

"That it is irregular and jagged, my lord of Egypt, in shape not unlike this fair Isle of Rhoda, at which we are about to land."

"And what thinkest thou, Rathos, is its foundation?" continued the prince.

"The Indian wise men say it is held up on the back of a huge tortoise; and our priests of Egypt that it floats in a vast ocean; while in Jaffa they teach that it floats on a boundless sea of fire. I know not, my lord prince. I leave knowledge of such wisdom to the great philosophers; and for my part am content to live upon our fair earth as long as the gods will, be it fire, or tortoise, or even though it stand on nothing, as the people in Persia hold that it does. But we are at the terrace-steps, my lord of Memphis!"

Here he bowed low, holding his hand to his heart, and left us to superintend the landing of the galley, at the porphyry staircase of the propylæum of the palace.

"Sesostris," said the prince to me, "has the idea occurred to you that this world may be a globe, suspended in subtle ether, and in diurnal revolution around the *fixed* sun?"

"Never, Remeses!" I cried, with a look of amazement at this bold and original thought. "It is impossible it should be so!"

"Nothing is impossible with the Author of creation!" said Remeses, with great solemnity, And then, after an instant's pause, he added pleasantly—"On what does the sea of fire or the tortoise rest, my dear prince? Which theory is the most difficult to receive? But I have given astrology considerable attention, and if you will examine with me some observations and calculations that I have made, I think you will be with me in my novel opinion that this earth *may prove* to be a sphere and in orbital motion, with its seven planets, about the sun; its annual progress in its circuit giving us seasons, its diurnal motion night and day! But I see you stand perplexed and amazed. By-and-by you shall be initiated into the mysteries of my studies. Let us land!"

Farewell, dear mother. The great length of this letter renders it necessary that I should close it abruptly, but believe me ever

Your dutiful son,
SESOSTRIS.

LETTER XI.

PALACE OF RHODA, ON THE NILE.

MY BELOVED MOTHER,—

In my last letter I narrated a conversation between Prince Remeses and myself, upon the myths of Egypt and Phœnicia, and other subjects, while being borne in his galley from the Memphis bank of the river down to the Island of Rhoda. I have already described this beautiful isle, and spoken of it as the favourite residence of the queen. It is situated nearly midway between her two chief cities, On and Memphis, both of which—one on the west and the other on the east—are in sight from the top of the central pylon of her palace, that divides the "court of fountains and statues" from her gardens.

Also from this point the queen commands, at one view, the noble spectacle of her navy anchored in the river, and her armies encamped, the one on the plain of Memphis, and the other upon that of Raamses.

I wrote you a letter day before yesterday, my dear mother, after my return from a very interesting visit to the plain of Memphis, whither the prince went in his state barge to review the 80,000 soldiers encamped there. I will devote this letter to an account of a second visit, and a description of the scenes I witnessed, and a narration of the events which transpired.

Early this morning, when the queen and Remeses and I were about to be seated at our repast; and, as the pious custom of the Egyptians of all ranks is, Remeses having just asked the blessing of the gods before partaking, lo! Prince Mœris, lord of the Thebaid, came in unannounced, accompanied by his favourite lion, which always follows his steps or stalks by his side, and said, with bluntness unsuited to the presence,—

"Your majesty, I have come to say to you that I am ready to weigh anchor and commence my voyage to the Cataracts! I await your orders and pleasure!"

Thus speaking, he stood with his head-admiral and half a dozen of his chief officers behind him in the entrance, his sword at his side, and his gold helm with its nodding plumes towering proudly. His whole appearance was singularly splendid and martial, and he seemed to be conscious of the effect the striking elegance and brilliancy of his costume produced upon me; for, though brave as Osirtasen the Conqueror, he is as vain as ever was the fair Princess Nitocris.

Queen Amense, who enjoined the strictest etiquette in her court, frowned at this discourteous intrusion; for the nobles of Lower Egypt are remarkable by the grace and refinement of their manners, and the court of the Pharaohs has for ages been distinguished for the high tone of its polite observances. From portico to saloon, from saloon to ante-room, from ante-room to reception-room, and so onward to the deepest recesses of the palace or house, the guest is ushered by successive pages, until the chief steward or grand-chamberlain admits him into the presence of the lord of the mansion, who already, by a swift page, has been informed of the advance of the visitor. In no case are these formalities dispensed with by persons of high breeding. Breaking through all such ancient and social ceremonies, the rude Theban viceroy came before her as I have described. The brow of Remeses darkened, but he preserved silence.

"I am glad, prince, that you have been so diligent," said Amense coldly. "When will you depart?"

"Within the hour, my royal aunt. If Remeses, my warlike cousin, wishes to co-operate with me at Thebes, he will not long delay marching his army forward. I hear, by a swift galley just arrived, that the fierce Ethiopian king, Occhoris, with half his mighty host, has already dared to enter the Thinite province, and menaces Thebes!"

"There is no time for delay, then," cried Remeses, rising from the table, leaving the grapes, figs, and wheaten rolls untouched. "Farewell, my mother!" he said, embracing her. "In a few weeks I shall return to you with tidings that the scourge of your kingdom has perished with his armies!"

I will not describe the tenderness of the parting between the queen and Remeses, whom she would have held, refusing to release him, if he had not gently disengaged himself, taken up his sword and helmet, and hastened from the apartment. Prince Mœris, with a haughty bow to the queen, for whom he seems to entertain bitter dislike, had already taken his departure with his captains at his heels. I followed Remeses, and together we crossed to the shore on the side of On, and there meeting chariots, we were in a short time in the midst of the war-camp of his chariot legions. They were encamped several stadia south of On, on the plain beyond Raamses. Here, in the little Temple of Horus, on the terrace of which we held our conversation about the Hebrews as we paced its long pavement (and which I have already repeated to you), the prince with his chief captains offered libations and burned incense, invoking the favour and aid of Heaven on the expedition. He then gave his orders to his generals of division, chiefs of legions, and captains; and the whole host, forming in column of march, moved forward towards the south, with trumpets sounding and the rumbling thunder of thousands of wheels of iron. Seeing that they were all in motion—each battalion under its own head-captain—the prince took boat to cross the Nile to the plain of Memphis, in order to put in motion the army of horse and foot there encamped. On our way over, we saw the van of the fleet of the Prince of Thebes coming up the broad river in stately style, fifty abreast, propelled by innumerable oars. It was a brave and battle-like front, and what with pennons flying, spears and shields gleaming from their poop-decks and mast-towers, and the brazen or gilt insignia of hawks', eagles', lions', or ibis' heads rising upon a thousand topmasts, and all catching the sunbeams, the spectacle was singularly impressive.

"There comes a prince, my Sesostris," said Remeses to me, as he surveyed the advancing front of war, "who, if I should fall in this Ethiopian expedition, will be Pharaoh of Egypt when my mother dies."

"The gods forbid!" I exclaimed with warmth.

"He is the next of blood. It is true, my mother could, by will, alienate her crown and confer her sceptre upon any one she chose to adopt. Indeed, I now remember that, by our laws, it would be necessary for her publicly and ceremoniously to adopt him as her son before he could reign—since a nephew, by the ancient Memphitic law regulating succession, cannot inherit. Mœris would, therefore, have to be adopted."

"Then he would never reign," I said.

Remeses remained silent a moment. Resuming, he said, with a tone of indignant emotion,—

"Sesostris, my mother fears that evil young prince. He possesses over her an inexplicable power. To this influence he owes his elevation, from being a mere governor of Saïs, to the viceroyalty of Upper Egypt. He would not fail, should I fall, to exert his mysterious power over her mind, and his ambition would prompt him to aim at even the throne of all Egypt. But let us mount!" he added, as we touched the shore.

A score of horsemen, armed with long spears, were in waiting. Remeses and I mounted horses already provided; and, at a wave of his hand, the whole party dashed off along the avenue of the aqueduct, a magnificent thoroughfare, two miles in length, bordered by palm-trees, with, at intervals, a monolith statue of red Syenite granite, or an obelisk, casting its needle-like shadow across the wide, paved road. At the end of this avenue, which leads straight from the river to the pyramids, we turned south, and before us beheld, spread out as far as the eye could reach, the tented field of the vast Egyptian host, cavalry and footmen of all arms, languages, and costumes, belonging to the nations tributary to Egypt. I had visited this vast camp the preceding day. It covered a league of ground, presenting a sea of tents, banners, plumes, spears, and shining helms. As we came in sight, a trumpeter sounded a few loud notes to proclaim the presence of the prince-general. We dashed up to the central pavilion, on the summit of which the winged sun of burnished gold showed that the army was to march under the particular guardianship of the god. From the summit of the staff of other handsome tents, the emblems of generals and chiefs of battalions were displayed in the form of silver hawks' heads, the brazen head of a lion or wolf, or the heads of the ibis, crocodile, and vulture. Each phalanx thus marched under and knew its peculiar emblem, following its lead in the column of advance on the march, and rallying around it in the midst of battle.

Prince Remeses was in a few moments surrounded by his generals and chief warriors, to whom he made known the advance of the Ethiopian king, Occhoris, upon Thebes,—intelligence of which he and the queen had received by a mounted messenger, while Prince Mœris, who had come to announce it also, was in her apartment. In a few words he made known his orders to each general in succession, who, making a low military obeisance, by bowing the head and turning the sword-point to the earth, instantly departed to their divisions. The general-in-chief in immediate command he retained by his side, with his gorgeous staff of officers. In a few minutes all was life and movement throughout the tented field. In four hours the whole army—their tents struck and conveyed to barges, together with all other military impediments not necessary for the soldiers on their march—was formed into a hollow square on the plain, twenty thousand men on each side facing inward to a temple of their war-god, Ranpo-re, which stood on the plain. This was a small but beautiful temple, or marble pavilion, in the form of a peristyle, with brazen columns, dedicated to the Egyptian Mars. It was erected in this martial plain by Amunophis I., for the purpose of sacrifices and oblations, and of offering libations and incense for armies assembled about it before marching on warlike expeditions. The circle of columns was cast from the shields and weapons which he had taken in his Arabian and Asiatic wars.

The chief priest of Mars, who is a prince in rank, and allied to the throne, attended by more than one hundred inferior priests, advanced from the inner shrine upon a marble terrace, in the centre of which stood the iron-columned pavilion that inclosed the shrine of the god. He was attired in a grand and imposing costume, having a tiara, adorned by a winged sun sparkling with jewels, and the sacred uræus, encircling his brows. He wore a flowing robe of the whitest linen, descending to his feet. A loose upper cape of crimson, embroidered with gold, and having flowing sleeves, was put on over the robe. Still above this was a breast-plate of precious stones, in the form of a corselet, while the tiara partook also of the martial form, being shaped like a helmet, with the sacred asp of gold projecting in front as a visor. Above all this, hanging from his left shoulder, was a splendid leopard's skin, heavy with a border of closely-woven rings of gold. As he advanced, he extended in his right hand a short sword, the hilt of which was a crux, or the sacred cross-shaped Tau, surmounted by a ball, the whole being an emblem of life; while in his helmet towered, as symbols of truth and order, two ostrich feathers—the evenness and symmetry with which the feathery filaments grow on each side of their stem having suggested to the Egyptians the adoption of this emblem; for order and truth, according to Egyptian philosophy, are the foundation and preservation of the universe.

Having reached the front of the lofty terrace, upon which was an altar of brass, he raised his left arm by throwing back the superb leopard-skin mantle; and, elevating his commanding form to its full grandeur, he turned slowly round, pointing heavenward with his left hand, and holding his sword, as it were, over the army as he turned until with it he had swept the circle of the horizon. This was an n vocation to all the gods for a blessing upon the assembled hosts. During the act, every general bowed his head as if to reacive it, every soldier lowered his weapon, and, at its conclusion, all the music bands in the army before him simultaneously burst into an overwhelming sound —drums, trumpets, cornets, cymbals, filling the air with their mingled roll! Silence deep as night then succeeded; and the high-priest, facing the shrine, stood while a company of priests rolled out from the door of the temple the statue of the god, clad in full armour of steel, inlaid with gold, a jewelled helmet upon his head, and a spear in his right hand. It was of gigantic size, and standing in an attitude of battle, upon a lofty chariot of burnished brass, with wheels of iron. It was an imposing and splendid figure, and a just image of war. The priests, who wheeled the car out of the temple, having drawn it once all around the terrace, so that the whole army could behold the mailed and helmeted god (whose presence they hailed by striking their swords upon their shields, or swords against swords), stopped in front of the prince-priest. He then prostrated himself before it, the profoundest silence and awe prevailing during the few moments he remained upon his face at the feet of the deity.

When he rose and turned to the west, the Prince Remeses and all his captains advanced to the steps of the pyramidal base on which the temple was elevated. Each captain was followed by a Nubian slave, bearing in a sacred vase the offering of his own phalanx of soldiers. Remeses bore in his hand a costly necklace, dazzling with precious stones, the offering of his mother. The generals and captains came with flowers, chains of gold, the lotus-leaf made of ivory, and sparkling with jewels scattered upon it in imitation of dewdrops. Some bore swords, and spears, and plumes.

Remeses, at the head of his officers, ascended the steps and presented to the priest his mother's offering, which he placed over the head of the god. He then laid a sword, brought for the purpose, at the feet of the statue; but, as he afterwards explained to me, and as I understood, not as an offering to a mythical Mars, but to the Infinite God of armies, whom the statue symbolized; yet I could see that the greater part of his officers paid their homage and made their offerings to the mere material statue. Such is the twofold idea attached, either by one or another class of devotees, dear mother, to all worship in Egypt. They do one thing and mean another; of course I speak of the priests, princes, and philosophers. As for the people, they mean what they do when they offer a libation or an invocation to a statue.

When the chief captains had presented their offerings, and the high-priest had either decorated the god with them, or laid them upon the altar of brass, then came the Nubian slaves, laden with the gifts of the soldiers. There were sixty of these offering-bearers, and in procession they ascended the terrace, each with a painted earthen vase upon his shoulder. One after another they deposited them around the overburdened altar and descended to the plain, not daring to lift their eyes to the god, so near to whose presence they came. It was my privilege to stand always by the side of Remeses, who desired me to witness the scene.

The vases contained every imaginable article that, at the moment, a common soldier might have about his person. There were rings of silver, of copper, of wood, of glass; dried figs, tamarinds, dates, and raisins; garlics, leeks, onions, bits of inscribed papyrus, palm-leaves, flowers innumerable, scarabæi of burnt clay, pebbles, and metal; seeds of the melon and radish, and incense-gum; little clay images of Mars, of various weapons, and of Osiris. There were also myrrh, resin, and small pots of ointment; pieces of iron, fragments of weapons, locks of hair, shreds of linen, and bits of ostrich feathers; beans, sandal-clasps, charms, amulets, and even tiny bottles of wine. Indeed, to enumerate what met my eyes in the vases, which the common soldiers in their piety voted to the god, praying for a successful campaign, would fill the page on which I write, and give you the name of nearly everything to be found in Egypt.

When all these offerings had been received by the high-priest, and while the prince and his officers stood some paces to one side, he stood before the altar: and one article from each vase being brought to him, he laid it upon the altar, and then, in a solemn manner, invoked the god, asking him to accept the offerings of this great army, and of its prince and captains, and to grant them victories over their foes, and a return to their queen crowned with conquest and glory.

In his prayer I could see that he elevated his noble countenance to the heavens, as if, in his mind, mentally overlooking the inanimate statue before him, and directing his thoughts to the Invisible and Supreme Dweller in the secret places of His universe beyond the sun! Remeses stood in a devotional attitude, but with his thoughtful brow bent to the ground. I could perceive, now that we had conversed so much together upon these divine things, that he was worshipping, in the depths of his heart, the God of gods, wherever that Dread and Mighty Power is enthroned on the height of His universe, or the wings of the imagination can go out to Him and find Him.

The great invocatory prayer ended, the high-priest received from Remeses a votive crystal box of the fragrant Ameracine ointment—a gift so costly and precious that only the princes and the priests are permitted to possess it—and broke it upon the breast of the god, anointing him in the name of the people of Egypt. The odour filled all the air. A priest then handed to him a golden cup richly chased with sacred symbols, and another, filling it from a vase of wine, the offering of the chief Archencherses, who is next in military rank to Remeses; he elevated it a moment, and poured it out at the feet of the god as a libation for the hosts. Some other interesting ceremonies followed, such as consecrating and presenting a sword to the prince, and the touching of the altar by all the chiefs with the points of their weapons, as they passed it in descending to the field, the high-priest sprinkling each one of them with sacred water from the Nile. The last act of sacrifice—for, though bloodless, the Egyptians term the whole rite a sacrifice to the god—was by Remeses. The high-priest placed in his hands a censer—for the prince, by virtue of his rank, is a royal priest; and Remeses, accepting it with reverence, cast upon the live coals of palm-wood a quantity of incense. Then approaching the altar, he waved it before it until clouds of smoke rose into the air and enveloped his head.

At this moment, the most sacred one of the whole scene, there appeared advancing from the pavilion-temple a beautiful maiden, the daughter of the high-priest. She was arrayed in a pure white robe, which floated about her in the wind like a cloud. Over her shoulders was thrown a crimson scarf, on which was embroidered the cartouch of the god. Her rich, flowing hair was bound about her stately brow by a crown of flowers, above which rose a silver helm with a crest of emeralds and sapphires, in imitation of the feathery coronet of the bird-of-paradise. Her face was wonderfully beautiful, her dark eyes beamed with love and joy, and her form was the impersonation of grace.

As she advanced, the priests on either side drew back with their hands crossed upon their foreheads, and their heads bent lowly before her presence. Coming forward between the two rows of officials, she shook in the air above her head a small temple bell called the *sistrum*, which emitted the sweetest and clearest melody. This little musical instrument is sacred to the services of the temples, and the sound of it is the signal for the beginning or ending of every rite. That which was now borne by the high-priest's daughter consisted of a cylindrical handle of pearl, surmounted by a double-faced head of ivory, one side being that of Isis, the other of Nephthys. From this twofold head rose a silver almond-shaped bow about five inches high, inlaid with gold and precious stones. In this bended loop of metal were inserted four metallic bars in the shape of asps, upon the body of which were loosely strung several silver rings. As the maiden held this beautiful instrument in the air, and shook it, the rings, moving to and fro upon the bars, produced the clear bell-like sounds I have mentioned. In ancient times so great was the privilege of holding the sacred sistrum in the temple, it was given to the queens; and on great occasions Amense has performed this high office. On an obelisk, now old, the daughter of Cheops is represented holding the sistrum while the king is sacrificing to Thoth. Though I have said little about the Egyptian females, as in truth I have seen but little of them, yet I ought not to omit to tell you that some of the most sacred offices are intrusted to distinguished women, in the services of temples. I have seen not only priests' daughters, but ladies of rank and eminent beauty, holding these places; and in On there is a band of noble young ladies having the distinguished title of "Virgins of the Sun," who devote their lives until they are thirty years of age, to certain principal services of the temples of Osiris and Isis. Indeed, my dear mother, in Egypt woman is singularly free, and regarded as man's companion and equal. She is respected and honoured, both as wife and mother, and her social relations are of the most unrestrained and agreeable kind. In all houses, she is prepared gracefully to do honour to her lord's guests; and while she is devoted to domestic duties, prides herself upon her skill and taste at home; abroad, at banquets and evening festivals, which are frequent, and where there is music and dancing, she shines with all the charms she can borrow from splendour of attire, or derive from inherent loveliness of person; while a profusion of jewels upon her hands and neck reveal her wealth and rank.

When the prince saw her advancing, he approached the statue with his censer, and waving it once in the sight of the army, hung it upon the spear of the god. The sistrum sounded as the incense rose, and every man of that vast host bent his knee for a moment! Then the high-priest commenced a verse of a loud chant in a sonorous voice. The one hundred priests marching in procession around the god, answered antiphonally with one voice in a part; and, the whole army catching up the hymn, the very pyramids seemed to tremble at the thunder of eighty thousand deep voices of men rolling along the air. Then Remeses chanted a few stirring words of this national and sacred war-hymn, the high-priest answered, the maiden's clear voice rose in a melodious solo, the hundred priests caught up the ravishing strain as it melted from her lips in the skies, and again the great army uttered its voice! My heart was oppressed by the sublimity. Tears of emotion filled my eyes. I never was more deeply impressed with the majesty of the human voice, united in a vast multitude, uttered as the voice of one man. The combined voice of the human race—if such a thing could be—must be like the voice of God when He speaks!

The invocation and sacrifice were over. Remeses embraced the priest, and receiving his blessing, in a few minutes every chief captain had joined his battalion, and at the cry of trumpets and cornets, sounded all over the plain, and echoed back from Cheops, the whole host formed in columns of march. Remeses, I being in his company, galloped forward and took a position on an elevation, from which he reviewed the whole army as it tramped by. The fleet was in parallel motion at the same time, and I saw the splendid galley of the Prince Mœris, with its coloured silken sails, and golden beak, gallantly ascending the river. He stood upon the poop; a tame lion crouched by his side, on the tawny shoulders of which he rested one foot as he gazed at us. The division of cavalry was the last in moving, and trotted past us in splendid array. This arm of the service is not large, nor much relied on in Egypt. The chariots of iron, to the hubs of which terrible scythes are sometimes fastened on the eve of battle, and the bowmen and spearmen, have always been the main dependence of the kings in their wars.

Ethiopia, against which this great army is moving by water and land, is in a state of civilization and political power not greatly inferior to Egypt. It has vast cities, noble temples, extensive cultivated regions, adorned with palaces and villas; it has a gorgeous but semi-barbaric court, a well-disciplined army, and skilful generals. It is a race allied by blood and lineage to that of Egpyt, and is not to be confounded with Nubia and the pure Africanic kingdoms. In religion it is idolatrous, and hostile to the worship of Egypt. A supposed title, by a former conquest, to the crown of Thebes, has made Ethiopia for three centuries the hereditary foe of Egypt.

The Egyptian army is divided into sections, formed and distinguished according to the arms they bear. They coasist, like ours, of bowmen, spearmen, swordsmen, macemen, slingers, and other corps. There are captains of thousands, captains of hundreds, fifties, and tens. When in battle-array, the heavy foot-soldiers, or infantry armed with spears, and a falchion, or other similar weapon, are drawn up in the form of an impenetrable phalanx; and once this massive wall of ten thousand men formed, it is fixed and unchangeable; and such is its strength, one hundred men on each front, and one hundred deep, no efforts of any of the enemies of Egypt have been able to break it. Presenting a wall of huge shields lapping and interlocked, resting on the ground, and reaching to their heads, the missiles of the foe rattle against it as against the steel-sheathed side of one of their battle-ships. The bowmen, slingers, javelin-men, and lighter troops act in line, or dispose themselves according to the nature of the ground, or the exigency of the moment. There is a corps armed with battle-axes and pole-axes, having bronze blades ornamented with heads of animals. These wear quilted helmets, without crests, which effectually protect the head. The chariot battalions are drawn up to charge and rout the enemy's line, and the cavalry follow to slay the resisting, and pursue the flying. Each battalion has its particular standard, which represents a sacred subject—either a king's name on his cartouch or painted shield, a sacred baris, a hawk, or a feather. The chief standard-bearer is a man of approved valour, and an officer of the greatest dignity, and stands next to the chief in rank. He is distinguished by a gold necklace collar, on which are represented two lions and an eagle—emblems of courage. The troops are summoned to all movements by the sound of the trumpet and the long drum, with other instruments.

. The offensive weapons of the army are the bow, spear, javelin, sling, a short, straight sword, a dagger, broad knife, falchion, battle-axe, spear-axe, iron-headed mace, and a curved club adopted from the Ethiopians. Their defensive arms consist of the helmet, either of iron, bronze, brass, silver, or plaited gold, according to the rank of the wearer; usually without a crest, and extending to the shoulders, in a collar or hood of chain-mail, protecting the neck; they wear also a cuirass of metal plates, or quilted with bands of polished iron, and an ample shield, of various forms, but usually that of a funeral tablet or a long and narrow horseshoe. This piece of armour is the chief defence. It is a frame covered with bull's or lion's hide, bound with a rim of metal, and studded with iron pins. The archers wear no bucklers, but corselets of scale-armour.

I will now end this long letter, my dear mother, and my description of Egyptian armies, by naming the nations of which it was made up. As I sat upon my horse by the side of the prince, surveying the marching columns as they moved southward, I distinguished the tall, Asiatic-looking Sharetanian by his helmet ornamented with bull's horns, and a red ball for a crest, his round shield, and large ear-rings —a fierce race, once the foes but now the allies of Egypt; the bearded Tokkari from beyond the horns of the Arabian Sea, armed with a pointed knife, and short, straight sword, with arched noses and eagle eyes,—also once enemies of the queen, but now added to her armies;

an unknown people, with tall caps, short kilt and knife-girdle of lion's hide, an amulet of agate on the neck of every man—strangers, with wild, restless eyes, and fierce looks ; the swarthy Rebos, with his naked breast and shoulders, and long two-headed javelin ; the Pouonti, with faces painted with vermilion, and cross-bows with iron-headed arrows, archers that never miss their mark. There marched by, also, the relentless Shari, who neither ask nor give quarter to their enemies, their masses of black hair bound up in fillets of leather, and scull-caps of bull's hide on their heads, whose weapons are clubs and short daggers. Other bands, differing in costume and appearance, continued to pass, until it seemed that the queen's army had in it representatives of all nations tributary to Egypt.

Continuing with Remeses a day's march, I then parted from him to return to the palace, promising, as soon as I had seen Lower Egypt, I would ascend the Nile and meet him at Thebes.

Farewell, dearest mother ; may the gods of our country preserve you in health.

Your devoted son,
SESOSTRIS.

LETTER XII.

PALACE OF THE PHARAOHS, MEMPHIS.

MY HONOURED AND VERY DEAR MOTHER :

In my last letter I was particular in describing to you the armies of Egypt, as I have not forgotten the interest you take in the discipline of your own, nor that once you led in your chariot a battle-charge when your kingdom was invaded by the king of the Elamites. In Egypt, which is truly a warlike country, one cannot but be inspired by the military spirit. Not only is she the school to all the world of astronomy, sculpture, physic, astrology, and magic, but also of arms.

In the army, recently departed for Ethiopia, I saw many young lords and princes and heroes, strangers who accompany the expedition to learn the art of war. The Egyptians are eminent in planning and executing sieges, and few fortified towns can resist their war-engines.

From my description in the last letter, you would suppose that Egypt is now emptied of its soldiers. On the contrary, there is a garrison in every city, and a fortress filled with troops in every one of the thirty or more nomes. Besides, there are all over the country, where the Hebrews are congregated, lesser detachments, who keep vigilant guard over this toiling nation in bondage. The queen is also at war with a prince of Arabia Deserta, and an army of twelve thousand men, four hundred chariots, and a thousand horsemen, have recently marched against him. Egypt is powerful enough to combat the combined world. Her forces are not less than four hundred thousand trained warriors of all arms, besides sixteen thousand chariots of iron. Power, thrift, activity, and energy characterize Egypt. The wise, courageous, firm rule of the queen has contributed to this. What she has brought to such glory and perfection, Remeses, when he comes to the throne, will preserve and perpetuate.

The mention of my noble friend reminds me that he is no longer near me. The army has been in motion southward eight days, and he has written to the queen, and also to me, speaking of the prosperity attending their advance. The fleet had not kept up with the army of foot, while the chariot legion on the east bank has gone far in advance and encamped. Every day incense is burned, and intervention made in all the temples, for the success of the expedition.

In the mean while, my dear mother, I will devote my letters to daily scenes around me.

The queen's health is now firmly established, and she extends to me the kindness and, I may say, affection, which she would to a son; but I am conscious that I am so honoured as the friend of her absent son, who, at parting from me a stadium above Memphis, said:

"My Sesostris, be near my mother, and in the pleasure of your society, let her regrets at my absence find compensation. When you have seen all of Lower Egypt, come to the Thebaïd, and go with me and my army into Ethiopia."

I promised that I would follow him by and by; but now I am engaged in seeing the wonders of Memphis, and those marvels of ages —those "temples of the gods"—the mighty pyramids. I will soon devote a letter to an account of my first visit to Memphis and the pyramids. It was made a day or two after we came to reside in the palace at Rhoda. Remeses, though hourly occupied, had kindly promised he would accompany me to the city of Apis, and there place me in charge of a son of the priest of the temple. I arose the following morning a few minutes before sunrise, in order to be prepared to go early. My window looked forth upon On, a league and a half distant, with its grand avenue of columns, sphinxes, obelisks, and towering propyla clasping it to the shining river. The splendour of that morning, my dear mother, I shall never cease to remember. The atmosphere of Egypt is so crystalline, that light lends to it a peculiar glow. As I looked eastward, the skies had the appearance of sapphire blended with dust of gold; and from the as yet invisible sun, a gorgeous fan of radiant beams, of a pale orange-colour, spread itself over the sky to the zenith. Not a cloud was visible; nor, indeed, have I seen one since I have been in Egypt. This magnificent glory of the Orient steadily grew more and more wonderful for beauty and richness of coloured light, when, all at once, the disk of the bright god of day himself majestically rolled up into sight, filling heaven and earth with his dazzling and overpowering light, while the golden shield on the temple of the sun caught and reflected his rays with almost undiminished brilliancy.

As I regarded with delight this sublime sunrise, there came borne to my ears, from the direction of the temple of Osiris, in Memphis, the sound of music. Walking round the terrace to that side, I heard the voices of a thousand priests chanting the morning hymn to the god of light, the dazzling "Eye of Osiris." Then I recollected that this was the day of the celebration of the revival or resurrection of Osiris, one of the most important days in the sacred calendar. The whole city seemed to be in motion, and boats garlanded with flowers, and filled with gaily attired people, were crossing to the city and temple at every point. Music from a hundred instruments filled the air, which seemed to vibrate with joy and delight. The city of Apis had on its gala apparel, and all the world was abroad to welcome the sunrising and join in the processions.

Remeses joined me while I was watching the scene, and listening to the grand waves of harmony as they rolled away from the temple and sounded along the air in majestic volumes of sound.

"I see you are interested, my Sesostris, in this enlivening scene. It is a day of rejoicing to the worshippers of Osiris."

"It seems, my dear prince," I replied, "as if every day I have passed in Egypt has been a festival to some of its deities."

"Our year is more than two-thirds of it consecrated to the gods; that is, supposing a day given to each, the most of the year is religious. We are a people given to piety, so far as we understand. All our works are consecrated by prayer or sacrifice; and whether we go to war, or engage in merchandise, build a palace or a tomb, prayer and oblation precede all. Are you ready to go to the city and pyramids as soon as we break our fast? My mother has invited us to breakfast with her."

I expressed my readiness, and we left to seek the presence of the queen. As we entered, she was superintending a piece of embroidery of the richest colours, which three maidens were at work upon at one end of the apartment. They remained a few minutes after our entrance, glancing at us timidly, yet curiously and archly. When their royal mistress had received us, she made a slight gesture with her hand, and the dark-eyed girls, disappearing behind a screen, left the apartment. I had time to see that they were very young, of an olive, brunette complexion, with braided and tastefully arranged dark-brown hair, their slender persons habited in neat vestures of mingled colours, fitting the form, but open in front, displaying a soft, fine linen robe, with loose, fringed sleeves. They had ear-rings, and numerous finger-rings, and gilt, red, gazelle-leather sandals, laced with gay ribbons across the small, naked foot. These, as the queen informed me, belonged to families of officers of the palace. One of them, the tallest, and who was most striking in her appearance, had eyes of wonderful beauty, the effect of the expression of which was deepened by painting the lids with a delicate shade of cohol. She was the daughter of the royal scribe, Venephis, and her own name is Venephe; and here, my dear mother, since you asked me in your last letter why I am so silent upon the subject of Egyptian ladies, I will devote a little space to them. But you know that my heart so wholly belongs to the lovely Princess Thamonda, the daughter of the Prince of Chaldea, that it is entirely insensible to any impressions which the high-born Egyptian maids might otherwise make upon it. I will, however, learn more of them by seeking their society, my dear mother, and henceforward will give them all the attention they merit in my letters.

I have seen many ladies of great elegance and ease of manner. The court of Egypt is composed of an immense number of nobles and high officers, whose palaces crowd the cities of On and Memphis, and whose tasteful, garden-environed villas extend far beyond their limits. Some of these nobles have the title of princes, when they govern one of the thirty-six *nomes*, or command armies. They are opulent, fond of display in apparel and architecture, great lovers of flowers and paintings, and their dwellings are profusely decorated with the one and adorned with the other. These men of rank are educated, polished in bearing, courteous and affable. Their wives are their superiors in refinement, being daughters of men of the same rank and social distinction. Nobles and noble ladies by hereditary title there are none in Egypt; for it is the boast of the Egyptians, and it is often inscribed on their monuments, that Egyptians, being all equally "sons of Misr," are all born equal. It is official elevation and position at court, as the reward of talent or services, which create noble rank. Yet there are families here who speak with pride of the glory and fame of ancestors; and I know young Egyptian nobles whose forefathers were lords in the court of the old Pharaohs, of the XVth and XVIth dynasties. I have already alluded to the brave young officer of the chariot battalion, Potipharis, whose ancestor, a lord of the court of Apophis, purchased of the Idumeans the youthful Hebrew who subsequently ruled Egypt as prime minister; and whose family, now grown to a great nation, are held here in hopeless bondage.

The women of Egypt owe their high social rank to the respect shown them by the men, who give them precedence everywhere. The fact that Egypt is ruled by a queen, is testimony that woman is honoured here by the laws of the realm, as well as by the customs of the people, or she would not have succeeded to the throne. It is not a mere influence derived from their personal attractions that women possess here; but their claims to honour and respect are acknowledged by law, in private as well as in public. Said Remeses to me, a day or two since, when I was remarking upon the universal deference paid to the sex, "We know, unless women are treated with respect and made to exercise an influence over the social state, that the standard of private virtue and of public opinion would soon be lowered, and the manners and morals of men would suffer." How differently situated is woman with us! Respected she undoubtedly is, but instead of the liberty she enjoys here, behold her confined to certain apartments, not permitted to go abroad unveiled, and leading a life of indolent repose.

In acknowledging this, dear mother, the laws point out to the favoured women of Egypt the very responsible duties they have to perform. The elevation of woman to be the friend and companion of man, is due to the wisdom of the priesthood. These men have wives whom they love and respect, and I have seen the priest of On seated in his summer parlour, which overlooks the street, by the side of his noble-looking wife (who, it is said, is a descendant of a priest of On, whose daughter was married to Prince Joseph, the Hebrew), surrounded by their children, and manifesting their mutual affection by numberless domestic graces; and I was charmed with the expressions of endearment I heard them use to each other and to their children. What a contrast all this to the priests of Tyre, who regard celibacy as the highest act of piety!

The hand of your sex, my dear mother, is apparent in all the household arrangements, and in the furniture and style of the dwellings. In her contract of marriage it is written, that the lady shall have the whole regulation of domestic affairs and the management of the house, and that the husband shall, in all such matters, defer to the judgment and wishes of the wife. Neither king, priest, nor subject can have more than one wife, a custom differing from our own, and far superior to it. It is owing to this universal honour paid to the sex, that queens have repeatedly, since the ancient reign of Binothris, held the royal authority and had the supreme direction of affairs intrusted to them. It is proper to say, that although the Egyptians have but one wife, they are not forbidden by the laws to have favourites, who are usually slaves, and owe their elevation to talents or beauty. They do not, however, hold any social relation; and the wife, to whom alone is given the title "lady of the house," enjoys an acknowledged superiority over them. But concubinage, though tolerated, is not regarded with favour, and is practised by few.

The Egyptian ladies employ much of their time with the needle; and either with their own hands, or by the agency of their maidens, they embroider, weave, spin, and do needle-work—the last in the most skilful and beautiful manner. They embroider chairs with thread of gold or silver, adorn sofas with embroidery, and ornament coverings for their couches with needle-work of divers colours, so artfully executed as to appear, on both sides, of equal beauty and finish. At the banquets or social festivals, which are very frequent, for the Egyptians are fond of society, the ladies sit at the same table with the men, and no rigid mistrust closes their doors on such occasions to strangers, towards whom they are ever courteous and hospitable, save only in religious ceremonies, from which, and "the mysteries of their theology," they are jealously excluded.

I have already spoken of the services of women in the temples. These do not marry. Although females may make offerings to Isis, they cannot be invested with any sacerdotal office; and a priest must preside at the oblation. They are rarely seen reading, their leisure being occupied chiefly in talking together in social companies. They vie with each other in the display of silver jewels, and jewels set in gold; in the texture of their raiment, the neatness and elegance of the form of their sandals, and the arrangement or beauty of their plaited hair.

If two ladies meet at a banquet or festival, it is considered an amiable courtesy to exchange flowers from the bouquet that Egyptian ladies always carry in the hand when in full costume. They are passionately devoted to dancing, and frequently both ladies and gentlemen dance together; but I think when the former dance in separate parties, their movements are marked by superior grace and elegance. Their dances consist usually of a succession of figures more or less involved; yet I have seen two daughters of the captain of the guard, at a private entertainment given by the queen, perform a dance to a slow air played upon the flute and lyre, with a grace of attitude and harmony of motion delightful to follow with the eye. Grace in posture, elegance of attitude, and ease of movement are their chief objects in the dance.

It is not, however, customary for the nobles and their families to indulge in this amusement in public, where usually the dancing is performed by those who gain a livelihood by attending festive meetings. They look upon it, however, as a recreation in which all classes may partake; and all castes engage in it, either in private festivities or in public. The lower orders delight in exhibiting great spirit in their dances, which often partake of the nature of pantomime; and they aim rather at ludicrous and extravagant dexterity, than displays of elegance and grace. At evening, under the trees of an avenue; at noon, in the shade of a temple, by public fountains, and before the doors of their dwellings, I often see the men and women amusing themselves, dancing to the sound of music, which is indispensable. At the houses of the higher classes, they dance to the harp, pipe, guitar, lyre, and tambourine; but in the streets and other places, the people perform their part to the music of the shrill double-pipe, the crotala or wooden clappers, held in the fingers, and even to the sound of the drum; indeed, I have seen a man dancing a solo on the deck of a galley at anchor in the river, to the sound of the clapping of hands by his companions. Certain wanton dances, consisting of voluptuous and passionate movements, by Arabian and Theban girls, whose profession it was, from the impure tendency of their songs and gestures, have been very properly forbidden by the queen in her dominions. There are certain religious processions in which women take part; they attend the funerals of their deceased relatives, and hired women appear as mourners.

I have devoted, my dear mother, so much of this letter to a description of the ladies of Egypt, in compliance with your expressed wish, and I will appropriate the residue of my papyrus, if the ink fail not, to an account of their homes, that you may see how they live; since, from their private life, great insight is obtained into their manners and customs. The household arrangements, the style of the dwellings, as well as the amusements and occupations of a people, explain their habits.

The style of domestic architecture, in this warm climate, is modified to suit the heat of the weather. The poorer classes (for though all Egyptians are born equal, yet there are poor classes), as well as *castes*, live a great part of their time out of doors, seeking rather the shade of trees than the warmth of habitations. And now that I have alluded to "castes," I will briefly explain the degrees of society in Egypt.

Though a marked line of distinction is maintained between the different ranks of society, they appear to be divided rather into "classes" than "castes," as no man is bound by law to follow the occupation of his father. Sons, indeed, do usually follow the trade of their father, and the rank of each man depends on his occupation. But there are occasional exceptions, as, for instance, the sons of a distinguished priest are in the army with Remeses, and a son of the admiral of the fleet of the Delta is high-priest in Memphis.

Below the crown and royal family, the first class consists of the priests; the second of soldiers; the third of husbandmen, gardeners, huntsmen, and boatmen; the fourth, of tradesmen, shop-keepers, artificers in stone and metals, carpenters, boat-builders, stone-masons, and public weighers; the fifth, of shepherds, poulterers, fowlers, fishermen, labourers, and the common people at large. Many of these, says the record from which I have obtained my information, are again subdivided, as chief shepherds into ox-herds, goat-herds, and swine-herds; which last is the lowest grade of the whole community, since no one of the others will marry their daughters, or establish any family connexion with them; for so degrading is the occupation of tending swine held by the Egyptians, that they are looked upon as impure, and are even forbidden to enter a temple without previously undergoing purification.

Thus you perceive, my mother, that Egypt practically acknowledges many degrees of rank, although she boasts that "every son of Misr is born equal."

These classes keep singularly distinct, and yet live harmoniously and sociably with each other. Out of them the queen's workmen are taken, and the lowest supply the common labourers on the public works,—thousands of whom, clad only in an apron and short trowsers of coarsely woven grass-cloth, are to be found at work all over Egypt, and even mingled with the Hebrews in some parts of their task. "And the Hebrews?" you may ask; for I perceive by your letter that you are interested in the fate and history of this captive nation; "what rank do they hold among all these castes?"

They remain a distinct and separate people, neither regarded as a class or *caste*. They pursue but one occupation, brick-making, with its kindred work of digging the loam, gathering the straw, kneading the clay, and carrying the bricks to the place where the masons need them. They neither associate nor intermarry with any of the Egyptian classes. They are the crown slaves, born in bondage, below the lowest free-born Egyptian in the land of Misraim. Even the swine-herd belongs to a *class*, and is equal by birth, at least, with the Pharaoh who rules; but the Hebrew is a bond-servant, a stranger, despised and oppressed. Yet among them have I seen men worthy to be kings, if dignity of aspect and nobleness of bearing entitle men to that position.

I will now return, and describe to you the habitations of the Egyptians, my dear mother. Houses slightly removed beyond the degree of mere barbarous huts, built of crude brick, and very small, are the habitations of the lower orders. Others, of more pretension, are stuccoed, and have a court: others, still superior, have the stuccoed surface painted, either vermilion and orange, in stripes, or of a pale-brown colour, with green or blue ornaments, fanciful rather than tasteful. Those of merchants, and persons of that grade, are more imposing;—corridors, supported on columns, give access to the different apartments, through a succession of shady avenues and courts, having one side open to the breezes; while currents of fresh air are made to circulate freely through the rooms and halls, by a peculiar arrangement of the passages and courts; for, to have a cool house in this ardent latitude is the aim of all who erect habitations. Even small detached dwellings of artificers and tradesmen, consisting of four walls, with a flat roof of palm-branches, laid on split date-trees as a beam, covered with mats, and plastered with mud of the Nile, having but one door, and wooden shutters,—even such humble habitations have in the centre an open court, however limited, with rooms opening to the air on one side: while around the small court are planted one or more palms, for shade, besides adorning it with plants of their favourite flowers. I have seen some such neat little abodes, not much larger than cages, with a cheerful family in it, who lived out of doors all day, dining under the shade of their tree, and dancing in their open court by moonlight, to the music of clapping hands or the castanets, until bedtime, using their houses only to sleep in; and such is the happy life of half the Egyptians of their grade.

The grander mansions, less than palaces, are not only stuccoed within and without, but painted with artistic and tasteful combinations of brilliant tints. They have numerous paved courts, with fountains and decorated walls, and are adorned with beautiful architectural devices, copied from the sacred emblems and symbols in the temples, and arranged and combined in forms or groups in the most attractive style. Over the doors of many houses are handsome shields or tablets, charged with the hieroglyph of the master, inscribed with some sentence. Over that of the house of the chief weigher of metals, opposite my palace window in On, was written "The House of the Just Balance." Over another "The good house;" and over a third, "The friend of Rathoth, the royal scribe, liveth here." Any distinction, or long journey, or merit, or attribute, gives occasion for an inscription over the entrances.

The beauty of a house depends on the taste, caprice, or wealth of its builders. The priests and lords of Egypt live in luxurious abodes, and a display of wealth is found to be useful in maintaining their power, and securing the respect and obedience of the under classes.

"The worldly possessions of the priest," said an Egyptian scribe of the temple of Apis, "are very great, and as a compensation for imposing upon themselves at times abstemiousness, and occasionally limiting their food to certain things, they are repaid by improved health, and by the influence they acquire thereby. Their superior intelligence enables them," he continued, ironically, "to put their own construction on regulations and injunctions emanating from their sacred body, with the convenient argument, that what suits them does not suit others." The windows of the houses are not large, and freely admit the cool breezes, but are closed at night by shutters. The apartments are usually on the ground-floor, and few houses, except perhaps in Thebes, exceed two stories in height. They are accessible by an entrance court, often having a columnar portico decked with banners or ribbons, while larger porticos have double rows of columns, with statues between them. When there is an additional story, a terrace surmounts it, covered by an awning, or by a light roof supported upon graceful columns. Here the ladies often sit by day : and here all the family gather at the close of the afternoon to enjoy the breeze, and the sight of the thronged streets and surrounding scene,—for it is open on all sides to the air. In the trades' streets the shops are on the ground-floor, and the apartments for families are above. As it scarcely ever rains, the tops of the houses, terraced, and covered with a handsomely fringed awning, are occupied at all hours, and even at night as sleeping-places by the "lord of the house," if the apartments below are sultry and close. Some noble edifices have flights of steps of porphyry or marble leading to a raised platform of Elephantine or Arabic stone, with a doorway between two columns as massive as towers—ambitious imitations of the propyla of the temples. These gateways have three entrances, a smaller one on each side of the principal entrance for servants, who are very numerous in an Egyptian house of the first class. Such is the house of my friend, the Admiral Pathromenes, whom I visited the day I saw him in his galley, and just before he sailed with the fleet for Ethiopia.

On entering the portal, I passed into an open court, on the right side of which was the mandara or receiving-room for visitors, where servants took my sandals, and offered water for my hands in silver ewers, at the same time giving me bouquets of flowers. This room, surrounded by gilt columns, and decorated with banners, was covered by an awning supported by the columns, and was on all sides open to within four feet of the floor, which lower space was closed by intercolumnar panels, exquisitely painted with marine subjects. Above the paneling a stream of cool air was admitted, while the awning afforded protection from the rays of the sun. This elegant reception-hall had two doors—that by which I had entered from the street, and another opposite to it which communicated with the inner apartments. Upon my announcement by the chief usher, the admiral came through the latter door to receive me ; hence the title of "reception-room" given to this column-adorned and paneled hall. He embraced me, and entered with me by his side into a corridor which led into a court of large dimensions, ornamented in the centre with an avenue of trees—palm, olive, orange, and fig trees, the latter being an emblem of the land of Egypt. Here numerous birds filled their leafy coverts with melody. Six apartments faced as many more on two sides of this court—the corridor, or piazza, of pictured columns extending along their entire front ; and before the corridor was a double row of acacia-trees. We did not turn to these rooms, but, advancing along the charming avenue between them, passed around a brazen fountain-statue of Eothos or Neptune, who was pouring water out of a shell upon a marble lotus-leaf, from which it fell into a vase of granite. Passing this figure, we kept the avenue till we came to a beautiful door facing the great court. It was of palm-wood, carved with devices of branches and flowers, and inlaid with ivory and coloured woods, all finely polished. At this door a servant, in neat apparel, met us, and opening it ushered us into the sitting-room of "the lady of the house," who had already received notice of our approach, and who, presenting me with flowers, welcomed me graciously, and with a cordiality that gave me a favourable estimation of the goodness of her heart, and the amiability of her disposition.

Thus, dear mother, have I given you some insight into Egyptian home-life, and introduced you into the inmost private room of one of their houses. I will close my description by saying, that the ceiling of the reception-room was richly and tastefully adorned with the pencil; that gracefully shaped chairs, covered with needle-work; sofas, inlaid tables, couches with crimson and gold embroidery, and elegant vases of flowers, were charmingly disposed about it; and that a lute and two sistra were placed near a window, and a harp stood between two of the columns that inclosed a pictured panel representing the finding of Osiris.

Farewell, dearest mother. You will see that I have now acquitted myself of the charge of indifference to so interesting a subject as the mode of life of the ladies of Egypt, and by hastening to describe it to you in this letter, have evinced my profound filial reverence for your slightest wish.

Your faithful and affectionate son,
SESOSTRIS.

LETTER XIII.

THE CITY OF APIS.

MY DEAR MOTHER:

I THANK you for your long and very welcome letter, written from your palace, at Sidon, whither you went to celebrate the rites of Adonis. It assures me of your continued health, which may the gods guard with jealous care, for not only the stability of your kingdom, but my whole happiness depends on your life, beloved mother and queen. You also allude to your visits to the temples of Astarte and of Tammuz, on Lebanon. What a noble worship was that of our fathers, who, amid its gigantic cedars, old as the earth itself, there first worshipped the gods! How majestic must have appeared their simple rites, with no altar but the mountain rock, no columns but the vast trunks of mighty trees, no roof but the blue heavens by day, and the starry dome by night; while at morning and evening went up the smoke of the sacrifice of bullocks to the gods. These were the first temples of men, not builded by art, but made by the gods themselves as meet places for their own worship. I question, dear mother, if the subsequent descent of religion from its solemn shrines, in the dark forests of Libanus, into the valleys and cities, to be enshrined in temples of marble, however beautiful, has elevated it. Though the Phœnicians built the first temples on the peninsula of Tyre, before any others existed, save in groves; yet in Egypt (which claims also this honour), the "houses of the gods," in their vast and pyramidal aspects, their pillars like palm-trees, their columns like cedars, approach more nearly to the dignity, sublimity, and majesty of the primeval forests and eternal mountains where religion first offered prayer to heaven.

Your visit to the temple of Tammuz, at Sarepta, recalls a legend which, singularly enough, I first hear in Egypt, of the origin of the rites to that deity.

The books of the priests here, relating to Phœnician, Sabæan, Persian, and Chaldean ceremonies (for the learning of the Egyptians seems to embrace a knowledge of books of all countries), relate that Tammuz was a "certain idolatrous prophet of the Sabæan Fire-worshippers, who called upon King Ossynœces, our remote ancestor, and commanded him to worship the Seven Planets and the Twelve Signs of the constellations. The king, in reply, ordered him to be put to death. On the same night on which he was slain," continues the book from which I write, "a great gathering of all the images of the gods of the whole earth was held at the palace, where the huge golden image of the sun was suspended; whereupon this image of the sun related what had happened to his prophet, weeping and mourning as he spoke to them. Then all the lesser gods present likewise commenced weeping and mourning, which they continued until daylight, when they all departed through the air, returning to their respective temples in the most distant regions of the earth." Such, dear mother, is the tradition here of the origin of the weeping for Tammuz, the observance of which now forms so important a feature in our Phœnician worship, although introduced, as it was, from the Sabæans themselves.

But the more I have conversed with the wise and virtuous Prince Remeses, the more I feel the gross nature of our mythology, O mother, and that images and myths, such as form the ground and expression of our national worship, and that rest wholly in the material figure itself, are unworthy the reverence of an intelligent mind. It is true, we can look at them, and honour that which they represent,—as I daily look at your picture, which I wear over my heart, and kissing it from love for thee, do not worship and adore the ivory, and the colours that mark upon its surface a sweet reflection of your beloved and beautiful countenance. Oh, no! It is you far away I think of, kiss, love, and in a manner adore. Yet an Egyptian of the lowest order, seeing me almost worshipping your picture, would believe I was adoring an effigy of my tutelar goddess. And he would be right, so far as my heart and thought, and you are concerned, my mother. In this representative way, I am now sure that Remeses regards all images, looking through and beyond them up to the Supreme Infinite. I also have imbibed his lofty spirit of worship, and have come to adore the statues as I worship your picture. But *where*, O mother, is the Infinite? When I think of you, I can send my soul towards you, on wings that bear me to your feet, either in your private chamber at needle-work, or with your royal scribe as you are dictating laws for the realm, or upon your throne giving judgment. In memory and imagination, I can instantly send my thoughts out to you, and behold you as you are. But the Infinite, whom Remeses calls GOD, in contra-distinction to lesser gods, where does He hide Himself? Why, if He is, does He not reveal himself? Why does He suffer us to grope after Him, and not find Him? If He be good, and loving, and gracious in His nature, He will desire to make known to His creatures these attributes. But how silent—how impenetrable the mystery that environs Him in the habitation of His throne! Will He for ever remain wrapped up in the dark clouds of space? Will He never reveal Himself in His moral nature to man? Will He never of Himself proclaim to the creation His unity—that there is no God but One, and besides Him there is none else? How can He demand obedience and virtue of men when they know not His laws? Yet, consciousness within, visible nature, reason, all demonstrate that there is but one Supreme God, a single First Cause, how numerous soever the inferior deities He may have created to aid in the government of His vast universe; and that to Him an intellectual and spiritual worship should be paid. This is the theory of Remeses, who seems to be infinitely above his people and country in piety and wisdom. Sometimes I fancy that he draws inspiration from this Infinite God whom he worships in his heart, and recognizes through his intellect; for his utterances on these themes are often like the words of a god, so wonderful are the mysteries treated of by him, so elevating to the heart and mind.

But I will repeat part of a conversation we had together, after he had offered in the temple of Apis his sacrifice for the restoration of the queen's health. He said, as we walked away together, along a beautiful and sacred avenue of acacia and delicate, fringe-like ittel or tamarisk trees, alternating with the pomegranate and mimosa:

"Sesostris, doubtless, after all my conversations with you, I seemed an idolater to-day, quite as material and gross, in the offerings and prayers I made, as the galley-rower we saw offering a coarse garland of papyrus-leaves and poppies to the god."

"No, my noble prince," I answered; "I saw in you an intellectual sacrificer, whose bodily eyes indeed beheld the sacred bull, but whose spirit saw the Great Osiris, who once dwelt in the bull when on earth. You honoured the house where anciently a god abode."

"No, Sesostris, the bull is nothing to me in any sense, but as the prince of a realm whose laws ordain the worship of Apis in Memphis, of the ram-headed Ammon at Thebes, or the sacred ox at On, I outwardly conform to customs which I dare not and cannot change. Or if I would, what shall I give the people if I take away their gods? My own religion is spiritual, as I believe yours is becoming; but how shall I present a spiritual faith to the Egyptians? In what form—what visible shape, can I offer it to them? for the priests will demand a visible religion—one tangible and material. The people cannot worship an intellectual abstraction, as we can, Sesostris, and as the more intelligent priests pretend they do and can. Yet if, when I come to the throne, by an imperial edict I remodel the theology of the priesthood and the worship of the people—remove the golden sun from the temple in On, slay the sacred bull Apis, and banish the idols from all the thousand temples of the two Egypts, with *what* shall I replace the religion I depose?"

"With an intellectual and spiritual worship of the Supreme Infinite," I answered.

"But who will enlighten my own ignorance of Him, Sesostris?" he inquired sadly. "What do I know of Him, save from an awakened consciousness within my bosom? How can I make others possess that consciousness which is only intuitive, and so incommunicable? I must first know *where* God is, before I can direct the people whither to look for Him when they pray. I must first cultivate their minds and imaginations, in order to enable them to embrace a purely mental religion, and to worship the Infinite independently of figures, images, and visible mementos or symbols; for, so long as they have these at all, they will rest their faith in them, and will look upon them as their gods. But what do I know of the God I would reveal to them? Absolutely nothing! That there can be but one Supreme God, reason demonstrates; for if there were two equal gods, they would have equal power, equal agency in the creation and upholding of all things, in the government of the world, and in the worship of men! Two equal gods, who in no case differ one from the other, but are in all things one and the same, are virtually but one god. Therefore, as neither two, nor any number of *equal* gods, can exist without acting as a unit (for *otherwise* they cannot act), there can be only one God!"

I at once assented to the conclusiveness of the prince's reasoning.

"God, then, existing as One, all beings in His universe are below Him, even His creatures the 'gods,' if there be such made by Him. It becomes, therefore, all men to worship, not these gods, but the God of gods. That He should be worshipped spiritually is evident, for He must be a spiritual essence; and as we are certainly composed of spirits and material bodies, and as our spirits are no less certainly our superior part, so He who made the spirit of man must be superior to all bodies or forms of matter; that is, He must be that by reason of which He is superior, namely, a SPIRIT."

I then said to this learned and great prince, "Thinkest thou, Remeses, that this Infinite God, whom we believe exists, will ever make a revelation of Himself, so that He may be worshipped as becomes His perfections? Do you think the veil of ignorance which hangs between Him and us will ever be lifted?"

"Without question, my Sesostris," he answered, with animation, the light of hope kindling in his noble eyes, "the Creator of this world must be a benevolent, good, and wise Being."

"Of that there can be no doubt," was my reply.

"Benevolence, goodness, and wisdom, then, will seek the happiness and elevation of man. A knowledge of the true God, whom we are now feeling and groping after in darkness, with only the faint light of our reason to illumine its mysterious gloom,—this knowledge would elevate and render happy the race of men. It would dissipate ignorance, overthrow idolatry, place man near God, and, consequently, lift him higher in the scale of the universe. A God of wisdom, benevolence, and justice will seek to produce this result. The world, therefore, *will* have a revelation from Him, in the fulness of time,—when men are ready to receive it. It may not be while I live, Sesostris, but the time will come when the knowledge of the Infinite God will be revealed by Himself to man, who will then worship Him, and Him alone, with the pure worship due to His majesty, glory and dominion."

As Remeses concluded, his face seemed to shine with a supernatural inspiration, as if he had talked with the Infinite and Spiritual God of whom he spoke, and had learned from Him the mighty mysteries of His being. Then there passed a shadow over his face, and he said, sorrowfully—

"How can I lead the people of Egypt to the true God, when He hath not taught me anything of Himself? No, no, Sesostris, Egypt must wait, I must wait, the world must wait the day of revelation. And that day will come, or there is *no* God! For an ever-silent God —a God who for ever hideth Himself from His creatures—is as if there were no God! But that there is a God the heavens declare in their glory, the ocean hoarsely murmurs His name, the thunders proclaim His power, the lilies of the field speak of His goodness, and we ourselves are living manifestations of His benevolence and love. Let us, therefore, amid all the splendour of the idolatry which fills the earth, lift up *our* hearts, O Sesostris, to the One God! and in secret worship Him, wheresoever our souls can find Him, until He reveals Himself openly to the inhabitants of the earth."

In relating this conversation, my dear mother, I not only am preparing you to see my views of our mythology materially changed, but I unfold to you more of the sublime character of Remeses, and give you some insight into his deep philosophy and wonderful wisdom.

I will, in connexion with this subject, describe to you a religious scene I witnessed in the Temple of Apis on the occasion of an excursion made by me in company with Remeses, from the Island of Rhoda.

I have already spoken of his courtesy in offering to accompany me to Memphis, at which city he left me, immediately after his oblation and thanksgiving, and proceeded to attend to some urgent affairs connected with the proposed movement of the army; with which, since then, he has taken his departure.

The barge in which I left the palace at Rhoda, was rowed by forty-four men, swarthy and muscular to a noticeable degree, who belong to a maritime people, once possessing the Pelusian Delta, but who are now reduced to a servitude to the crown. They have a sort of chief, called Fellac, whom they regard partly as a priest, partly as a patriarch. Under him, by permission of the crown, they are held in discipline. They have a mysterious worship of their own, and are reputed to deal in magic, and to sacrifice to Typhon, the principle of evil.

They were attired in scarlet sashes, bound about the waist, and holding together loose white linen drawers, which terminated at the knee in a fringe. Their shoulders were naked, but upon their heads each wore a sort of turban of green cloth, having one end falling over the ear, and terminating in a silver knob. These were the favourite body-guard rowers of the prince. Their captain was a young man, with glittering teeth, and large oval black eyes. He was mild and serene of aspect, richly attired in a vesture of silver tissue, and had his black hair perfumed with jasmine oil. His baton of office was a long stick—not the long, slender, acacia cane which all Egyptian gentlemen carry, but a staff short and heavy, ornamented with an alligator's head, which, with that of the pelican, seem to be favourite decorations of this singular people.

As we were on the water, moving swiftly towards the quay of the city, amid countless vessels of all nations, a slave-barge passed down from Upper Egypt, laden with Nubian boys and girls, destined to be sold as slaves in the market. Borne with velocity along, we soon landed at the grand terrace-steps of the quay. They were thronged with pilots, shipmen, those who hold the helm and the oar, mariners, and stranger-merchants innumerable. A majestic gateway, at the top of the flight of porphyry stairs, led to an avenue of palm-trees, on each side of which was a vast open colonnade covered with a wide awning, and filled with merchants, buyers, captains, and officers of the customs, dispersed amid bales of goods from all lands of the earth. I lingered here, for a short time, gazing upon these representatives of the wealth and commerce of the world. This is the great landing-mart of Memphis, for the products of the other lands; while Jizeh, lower down, is the point from whence all that goes out of the country is shipped. The strange cry of the foreign seamen, as they hoisted heavy bales, and the wild song of the Egyptian labourers, as they bore away the goods, the confused voices of the owners of the merchandise, the variety and strange fashion of their costumes, the numerous languages which fell upon my ear, produced an effect as novel as it was interesting.

The riches and beauty of what I saw surprised me, familiar as I am with the commerce of Tyre. There were merchants from Sheba, bearded and long-robed men, with gold-dust, spices of all kinds, and precious stones of price; and others from the markets of Javan, with cassia, iron, and calamus; there were wines from the vine-country of Helbona, and honey, oil and balm from Philistia; merchants of Dedan, with embroidered linings and rich cloths for chariots, and costly housings for horses, of lynx and leopard-skins; tall, grave-looking merchants from our own Damascus, with elegant wares, cutlery, and damascened sword-blades of wonderful beauty, and which bring great price here; shrewd-visaged merchants of Tyre, with purple and broidered work and fine linen; and merchants of Sidon, with emeralds, coral, and agate, and the valuable calmine-stone out of which, in combination with copper, brass is molten by the Egyptians.

There were also merchants, in an attire rich and picturesque, from many isles of the sea, with vessels of bronze, vases, and other exquisitely painted wares, and boxes inlaid with ivory, jewels, and ebony. I saw the dark, handsome men of Tarshish and far Gades, with all kinds of riches of silver, iron, tin, lead, and scales of gold. Shields from Arvad, beautifully embossed and inlaid; helmets and shawls from Persia; ivory from Ind, and boxes of precious stones—the jasper, the sapphire, the sardius, the onyx, the beryl, the topaz, the carbuncle, and the diamond—from the south seas, and those lands under the sun, where he casts no shadow. There were, also, wild-looking merchant horsemen from Arabia, with horses and mules to be traded for the fine linen, and gilt wares, and dyes of Egypt; and

TYRE.

proud-looking shepherd chiefs of Khedar, with flocks of lambs, rams, and goats; while beyond these, some merchants of Saïs, men of stern aspects, had bands of slaves, whose shining black skins and glittering teeth showed them to be Nubians from Farther Africa, who had been brought from the Upper Nile to be sold in the mart.

Thus does all the earth lay its riches at the feet of Egypt, even as she pours them into the lap of Tyre. Meet it is that two nations, so equal in commerce, should be allied in friendship. May this friendly alliance, more closely cemented by my visit to this court, never be broken! I am willing to surrender to Egypt the title, "Mistress of the World," which I have seen inscribed on the obelisk that Amense is now erecting, so long as she makes no attempt upon our cherished freedom, nor asks of us other tribute to her greatness than the jewelled necklace it was my pleasure to present to her queen, from your hand.

Having crossed this wonderful mart of the world, we issued upon a broad street, which diverging to the right led towards Jizeh, not far distant, and to the left towards Memphis, the noble pylon of which was in full sight. The street was lined with small temples, six on each side, dedicated to the twelve gods of the months, statues of each of whom stood upon pedestals before its gateway.

This avenue, which was but a succession of columns and statues, and in which we met several pleasure-chariots, terminated at an obelisk one hundred feet in height—a majestic and richly elaborated monument, erected by Amunophis I., whose name it bears upon a cartouch, to the honour of his Syrian queen, Ephtha. Upon its surface is recounted, in exquisitely coloured intaglio hieroglyphs, her virtues and the deeds of his own reign. At each of its four corners crouches a sphinx, with a dog's head, symbolic of ceaseless vigilance. A noble square surrounds the obelisk, and on its west side is the propylon of Memphis. The great wings that inclose the pylon are ninety feet in height, and are resplendent with coloured pictorial designs, done in the most brilliant style of Egyptian art.

Here we found a guard of soldiers, whose captain received the prince with marks of the profoundest military respect. We passed in, through ranks of soldiers, who bent one knee to the ground, and entered the chief street of Memphis—the second city in Egypt, in architectural magnificence, and the first in religious importance, as the city of the sacred bull Apis.

A description of this city would be almost a repetition of that of On, slightly varying the avenues, squares, and forms of temples. You have, therefore, to imagine, or rather recall, the splendour of the "City of the *Lord of the Sun*" (for this is its true Egyptian designation), and apply to Memphis the picture hitherto given of that gorgeous metropolis of Osiris.

After we had passed a few squares through the thronged and handsome street, which was exclusively filled with beautiful and tasteful abodes of priests, adorned with gardens and corridors, we came to a large open space in the city, where was a great fountain, surrounded by lions sculptured in grey porphyry stone. On one side of this square was a lake, bordered with trees; on another, a grove sacred to certain mysteries; on a third, a temple dedicated to all the sacred animals of Egyyt,—images of which surrounded a vast portico in front. An enumeration of them will exhibit to you, how the first departure, in ancient days, from the worship of the One Deity, by personating His attributes in animal forms, has converted religion into a gross and sensual superstition. It is not enough that they have fanciful emblems in all their temples, and on all their sculptured monuments, of Life, Goodness, Power, Purity, Majesty, and Dominion (as in the crook and flail of Osiris), of Authority, of Royalty, of Stability; but they elevate into representatives of the gods, the ape, sacred to Thoth; the monkey; the fox, dog, wolf, and jackal, all four sacred to Anubis; the ichneumon and cat, which last is superstitiously reverenced, and when dead embalmed with divine rites. The ibex, which I once believed to be sacred, is regarded only as an emblem; and so with the horse, ass, panther, and leopard, which are not sacred, but merely used in sculptures as emblems. The hippopotamus is sacred, and also an emblem of Typhon, dedicated to the god of war. The cow is held eminently sacred by the Egyptians, and is dedicated to the deity Athor.

There are four sacred bulls in Egypt,—nor only sacred, but deified. In Middle Egypt, Onuphis and Basis are worshipped in superb temples; and at On, Mnevis, sacred to the Sun. Here in Memphis, is Apis, not only sacred but a god, and type of Osiris, who, in his turn, is the type of the Sun, which is the type of the Infinite Invisible; at least this is the formula, so far as I have learned its mysteries. How much purer the religion, dear mother, which, passing by or overleaping all these intermediate types and incarnations, prostrates the soul before the footstool of the Lord of the Sun Himself, the One Spiritual God of gods!

Of all the sacred animals above named, I beheld images in stone upon the dromos which bordered the portico. There were also figures of the sacred birds,—as the ibis, sacred to the god Thoth; the vulture, the falcon-hawk, sacred to Re, and honoured in the city of On, and the egret, sacred to Osiris. Besides these sacred figures which decorated this pantheonic portico, at each of the four gates was one of the four deified bulls in stone, larger than life-size. There are also to be found, all over Egypt, sculptured sphinxes,—a sort of fabulous monster, represented either with the head of a man, a hawk, or a ram; to these may be added a vulture with a serpent's head, and a tortoise-headed god

The phœnix, sacred to Osiris, I shall by and by speak of, and the white and saffron-coloured cock, sacred to, and sacrificed in the Temple of Anubis. Certain fishes are also held sacred by this extraordinary people, who convert everything into gods. The oxyrhincus, the eel, the lepidotus, and others are sacred, and at Thebes, are embalmed by the priests. The scorpion is an emblem of the goddess Selk, the frog of Pthah, and the unwieldy crocodile sacred to the god Savak—a barbarous deity. Serpents having human heads, and also hawk's and lion's heads, were sculptured along the frieze of this pantheon, intermingled with figures of nearly all the above sacred animals. On the abacus of each column was sculptured the scarabæus—the sacred beetle—consecrated to Pthah, and adopted as an emblem of the world; also the type of the god Hor-hat, the Good Genius of Egypt, whose emblem is a sun supported by two winged asps encircling it. Flies, ichneumons, and bees, with many other insects and animals, are represented in the sculptures, but are not sacred.

Even vegetables do not escape the service of their religion. The persea is sacred to Athor; the ivy to Osiris, and much made use of at his festivals; the feathery tamarisk is also sacred to this deity; and the peach and papyrus are supposed to be sacred, or at least used, for religious purposes. Contrary to the opinion I formed when I first came into Egypt, the onion, leek, and garlic are not sacred. The pomegranate, vine, and acanthus are used for sacred rites, and the sycamore-fig is sacred to Netpe. The lotus, the favourite object of imitation in all temple-sculpture, is sacred to, and the emblem of, the most ancient god of Egypt, whom the priests call Nofiratmoosis—a name wholly new to me among the deities;—but it is also clearly a favourite emblem of Osiris, being found profusely sculptured on all his temples. Lastly, the palm-branch is a symbol of astrology and type of the year, and conspicuous among the offerings made to the gods.

Now, my dear mother, can you wonder at Prince Remeses—that a man of his learning, intellect, sensibility, and sound judgment, should turn away from these thousand contemptible gods of Egypt, to seek a purer faith and worship, and that he should wish to give his people a more elevating and spiritual religion? Divisions and subdivisions have here reached their climax, and the Egyptians who worship God in everything may be said to have ceased to worship Him at all!

What was on the fourth side of the great square, of which the lake, the grove, and the pantheon composed three, was the central and great Temple of Apis in Lower Egypt. In my next letter I will describe my visit to it. I am at present a guest of the high-priest of the temple, and hence the date of my letter at Memphis.

Your affectionate son,
SESOSTRIS.

LETTER XIV.

THE PALACE OF THE PRIEST OF APIS.

MY DEAR MOTHER:

I WILL now describe to you my visit, with the prince, to the most remarkable shrine in Egypt. While the worship of Osiris, at On, is a series of splendid pageantries, but little differing from the gorgeous sun-worship which you witnessed some years ago at Baalbec, the rites of Apis are as solemn and severe as the temple in which they are celebrated is grand and majestic.

The temple itself is a massive and imposing edifice, of reddish Elephantine stone. It is of vast proportions, and the effect produced is that of a mountain of rock hewn into a temple, as travellers say temples are cut out of the face of cliffs in Idumea-Arabia. Its expression is majesty and grandeur. It occupies the whole of one side of the vast square described by me in my last letter.

As we were about to ascend to the gate, I was startled by a loud and menacing cry from many voices, and, looking around, perceived a Tyrian mariner, recognized by me as such by his dress, who was flying across the square with wings of fear. A crowd, which momentarily increased, pursued him swiftly with execrations and cries of vengeance! As he drew near, I noticed that he was as pale as a corpse. Seeing that he was a Phœnician, I felt interested in him, and by a gesture drew him towards me. He fell at my feet, crying—
"Save me, O my prince!"
"What hast thou done?" I demanded.
"Only killed one of their cats, my lord!"
The throng came rushing on, like a stormy wave, uttering fearful cries
"May I try and protect him, O Remeses," I asked, for I knew that if taken, he would be slain for destroying one of their sacred animals
"I will see if I can; but I fear my interposition will not be heeded in a case like this," he replied. At the same time he deprecatingly waved his hand to the infuriated populace, which had in a few moments increased to a thousand people.
"No, not even for the prince! He has killed a sacred animal. By our laws he also must die. We will sacrifice him to the gods!"

In vain I entreated, and Remeses interposed. The wretched man was torn from our presence by as many hands as could seize him, thrown down the steps of the temple, and trampled upon by the furious crowd, until nothing like a human shape remained. The formless mass was then divided into pieces, and carried to a temple where numerous sacred cats are kept, in order to be given to them to devour. Such is the terrible death they inflict upon one who by accident kills a cat or an ibis!

"The power of the State is weak when contending with the mad strength of superstition," remarked Remeses, as we entered the temple between two statues of brazen bulls. Entering through a majestic doorway, we came into an avenue of vast columns, the size of which impressed me with awe. The temple was originally erected to Pthah, anciently the chief deity of Memphis, and dedicated in the present reign to the sacred bull, whose apartment is the original adytum of the temple.

The worship of Apis and Mnevis, the bulls consecrated to Osiris, exhibits the highest point to which the worship of animals in Egypt has reached, and it was with no little interest I felt myself advancing into the presence of this deified animal. We were met, at the entrance of the avenue of columns, by two priests in white linen robes, over which was a crimson scarf, the sacred colour of Apis. They had tall caps on their heads, and each carried a sort of crook. They received the prince with prostrations. Going one before and one behind us, they escorted us along the gloomy and solemn avenue of sculptured columns, until we came to a brazen door. A priest opened it, and we entered a magnificent peristyle court supported by caryatides twelve cubits in height, representing the forms of Egyptian women. We remained in this grand hall a few moments, when a door on the opposite side opened and the sacred bull appeared. He was conducted by a priest, who led him by a gold chain fastened to his horns, which, were garlanded with flowers. The animal was large, noble-looking, and jet-black in colour, with the exception of a square spot of white upon his forehead. Upon his shoulder was the resemblance of a vulture, and the hairs were double in his tail! These being the sacred marks of Apis, I observed them particularly; there should be also the mark of a scarabæus on his tongue.

The deity stalked proudly forth, slowly heaving up and down his huge head and thick neck,—a look of barbaric power and grandeur glancing from his eye.

The curator of the sacred animal led him once around the hall, the Egyptians prostrating themselves as he passed them, and even Remeses, instinctively, from custom, bending his head. When he stopped, the prince advanced to him, and taking a jewelled collar from a casket which he brought with him, he said to the high-priest—who, with a censer of incense, prepared to invoke the god—

"My lord priest of Apis: I, Remeses the prince, as a token of my gratitude to the god, of whom the sacred bull is the emblem, for the restoration of my mother, the queen, do make to the temple an offering of this jewelled collar for the sacred bull."

"His sacred majesty, my lord prince, accepts, with condescension and grace, your offering," answered the gorgeously attired high-priest. He then passed the necklace through the cloud of incense thrice, and going up to the bull, fastened the costly gift about his neck, already decorated with the price of a kingdom, while his forehead glittered like a mass of diamonds. A cool draft of wind passing through the open hall, a priest (at least two hundred attendant priests were assembled there to witness the prince's offering) brought a covering or housing of silver and gold tissue, magnificently embroidered, and threw it over the god.

The prince now, at the request of the queen, proceeded to obtain an omen as to the success of his army. He therefore approached and offered the bull a peculiar cake, of which he is very fond, which the animal took from his palm and ate. At this good omen there was a murmur of satisfaction; for a refusal to eat is accounted a bad omen. Remeses smiled as if gratified. Could it be that he had faith in the omen? I know not. Much must be allowed to the customs of a lifetime! Trained to all these rituals from a child, had the philosophy of his later years wholly destroyed in him *all* faith and confidence in the gods of his mother and his country? The priest now asked a question aloud, addressed to the god:

"Will the Prince of Egypt, O sacred Apis, be a successful king, when he shall come to the throne?"

The reply to the question was to be found in the first words Remeses should hear spoken by any one when he left the temple. He immediately departed from the peristyle, and we returned through the solemn avenue to the portico. As we descended the steps, a seller of small images of the bull called out, in reply to something said by another—

" He will never get there !"

" Mark those words, Sesostris ! " he said, not unimpressed by them; "my mother is to outlive me, or Mœris will seize the throne from me ! "

" Do you put faith in this omen ?"

" I know not what to answer you, my Sesostris. You have, no doubt," he added, " after all I have said, marveiled at my offering to Apis. But it is hard to destroy early impressions, even with philosophy, especially if the mind has no certain revelation to cling to, when it casts off its superstitions. But here I must leave you, at the door of the hierarch's palace. This noble priest is head of the priesthood of Pthah, a part of whose temple, as you have seen, is devoted to Apis,— or rather the two temples subsist side by side. You saw him last week at our palace. He has asked you to be his guest while here. Honour his invitation, and he will not only teach you much that you desire to know, but will visit with you the great pyramidal temple of Cheops."

Having entered the palace, and placed me under the hospitality of the noble Egyptian hierarch therein, the prince took leave of me. I would like to describe to you the taste and elegance of this abode, my dear mother; its gardens, fountains, flower-courts, paintings, and rich furniture. But I must first say a little more about the god Apis, who holds so prominent a place in the mythology of Egypt. In the hieroglyphic legends he is called Hapi, and his figurative sign on the monuments is a bull with a globe of the sun upon his head, and the hieroglyphic cruciform emblem of Life drawn near it. Numerous bronze figures of this bull are cast, whereupon they are consecrated, distributed over Egypt, and placed in the tombs of the priests. The time to which the sacred books limit the life of Apis is twenty-five years, which is a mystic number here ; and if his representative does not die a natural death by that time, he is driven to the great fountain of the temple, where the priests were accustomed to bathe him (for he is fed and tended with the greatest delicacy, luxury, and servility by his priestly curators), and there, with hymns chanted and incense burning, they drown him amid many rites and ceremonies, all of which are written in the forty-two books of papyrus kept in the sacred archives of the oldest temple.

No sooner does the god expire, than certain priests, who are selected for the purpose, go in search of some other bull ; for they believe that the soul of Osiris has migrated into another body of one of these animals, or "Lords of Egypt," as I have heard them called. This belief of the constant transfer of himself by Osiris from the body of one bull to another, is but the expression of a popular notion here, that souls of men transmigrate from body to body ; and my opinion is confirmed by a scene depicted in the judgment-hall of Osiris, where the god is represented as sending a soul, whose evil deeds outweighed his good ones, back to earth, and condemning it to enter the body of a hog, and so begin anew, from the lowest animal condition, to rise by successive transmigrations through other beasts, higher and higher, until he became man again, when, if he had acquired virtue in his probation, he was admitted to the houses of the gods and became immortal.

The prince assures me that the belief in the transmigration of souls is almost universal in the Thebaïd, as well as among the lower orders in the northern nomes; and that the universal reverence for animals is without doubt, in a great measure to be traced to this sentiment. A monstrous doctrine of the perpetual incarnation of deity in the form, not of man, but of the brute, seems to be the groundwork of all religious faith in Egypt. This idea is the key to the mysteries, inconsistencies, and grossness of their outward worship; the interpreter of their animal Pantheon.

"There is a tradition," said to me, to-day, the prince-priest Misrai, with whom I am now remaining, "that when Osiris came down to earth, in order to benefit the human race by teaching them the wisdom of the gods, evil men, the sons of Typhon, pursued to destroy him, when he took refuge in the body of a bull, who protected and concealed him. After his return to the heavens, he ordained that divine honours should be paid to the bull for ever."

This account, my dear mother, is the more satisfactory myth than any other, if any can be so; and recognizes incarnation as the principle of the worship of Apis. This universal idea in the minds of men, that the Creator once dwelt in the body of a creature, would lead one to believe, that in ages past the Infinite had descended from heaven for the good of men, and dwelt in a body; or that, responding to this universal idea, he may yet do it. Perhaps, dear mother, the worship of Osiris under the form of Apis, may be the foreshadowing and type of what is yet really to come—a dispensation, preparing men for the actual coming of the Invisible in a visible form. What a day of glory and splendour for earth, should this prove true! The conception, dear mother, is not my own; it is a thought of the great, and wise, and good Remeses, who, if ever men are deified, deserves a place, after death, among the gods. His vast and earnest mind, enriched with all the stores of knowledge that man can compass, seems as if it derived inspiration from the heavens. His conversation is deeper than the sacred books; the ideas of his soul more wonderful than the mysteries of the temple!

The priests who seek another bull, discover him by certain signs mentioned in their sacred books. These I have already described. In the mean while, a public lamentation is performed, as if Osiris, that is, "the Lord of Heaven," had died, and the mourning lasts until the new Apis is found. This information is proclaimed by swift messengers in all the cities, and is hailed with the wildest rejoicings. The scribes who have found the young calf which is to be the new god, keep it with its mother in a small temple facing the rising sun, and feed it with milk for four months. When that term is expired, a grand procession of priests, scribes, prophets, and interpreters of omens, headed by the high-priest, and often by the king, as hereditary priest of his realm, proceed to the temple or house of the sacred calf, at the time of the new moon—the slender and delicate horns of which symbolize those of the juvenile Apis. With chants and musical instruments playing, they escort him to a gorgeously decorated *baris* or barge, rowed by twelve oars, and place him in a gilded cabin on costly mats. They then convey him in great pomp and with loud rejoicings to Memphis. Here the whole city receives him with trumpets blowing and shouts of welcome; garlands are cast upon his neck by young girls, and flowers strewed before him by the virgins of the temple.

Thus escorted, the "Living Soul of Osiris" is conducted to the temple provided for him, which is now, as I have before observed, an appendage to the Temple of Pthah or Vulcan, an edifice remarkable for its architectural beauty, its extent, and the richness of its decorations; indeed, the most magnificent temple in the city. A festival of many days succeeds, and the young deity is then led in solemn procession throughout the city, that all the people may see him. These come out of their houses to welcome him, with gifts, as he passes. Mothers press their children forward towards the sacred animal that they may receive his breath, which, they believe, conveys the power to them of predicting future events. Returned to his sacred adytum, he henceforth reigns as a god, daintily fed, and reverently served. Pleasure-gardens and rooms for recreation are provided for him when he would exercise.

At the death of Apis, all the priests are immediately excluded from the temple, which is given up to profound solitude and silence, as if it also mourned, in solemn desolation, the loss of its god. His obsequies are celebrated on a scale of grandeur and expenditure hardly conceivable. Sometimes the rich treasury of the temple, though filled with the accumulated gold of a quarter of a century, is exhausted. Upon the death of the last Apis, the priests expended one hundred talents of gold in his obsequies, and Prince Mœris, who seeks every opportunity to make a show of piety, and to please the Egyptians, gave them fifty talents more, to enable them to defray the enormous costs of the funeral of the god.

The burial-place of the Serapis, as the name is on the mausoleum (formed by pronouncing together Osiris-Apis), is outside of the western pylon of the city. We approached it through a paved avenue, with lions ranged on each side of it. It consists of a vast gallery, hewn in a rocky spur of the Libyan cliff, twenty feet in height, and two thousand long. I visited this tomb yesterday, accompanied by the high priest. He showed me the series of chambers on the sides of this sepulchral hall, where each embalmed Apis was deposited in a sarcophagus of granite fifteen feet in length. There were sixty of these sarcophagi, showing the permanency and age of this system of worship. They were adorned with royal ovals, inscribed, or with tablets containing dedications, to Apis. One of these bore the inscription, "To the god Osiris-Apis, the Lord of the Soul of Osiris, and emblem of the Sun, by Amense, Queen and upholder of the two kingdoms."

In front of the sculptured entrance of this hall of the dead god is the Sarapeum, a funeral temple for perpetual obsequies. It has a vestibule of noble proportions, its columns being of the delicately blue-veined alabaster from the quarries in the south. On each side of the doorway is a crouching lion, with a tablet above one, upon which a king is represented making an offering. Within the vestibule stand, in half circle, twelve statues of ancient kings. In a circle above these sit, with altars before each, as many gods. Upon a pedestal in the centre stands the statue of the Pharaoh who erected this beautiful edifice.

Thus, my dear mother, have I endeavoured, as you requested, to present before your mind a clear view of the system of theology, and the forms of worship of the Egyptians. To evolve from the contradictory and vague traditions a reasonable faith; to select from the countless myths a dominating idea; to separate the true from the false, to bring harmony out of what, regarded as a whole, is confusion; to know what is local, what national in rites, and to reconcile all the theories of Osiris with one another, is a task far from easy to perform. At first, I believed I should never be able to arrive at any system in these multifarious traditions and usages, but I think that my researches have given me an insight into the difficulties of their religion, and enabled me, in a great measure, to unravel the tangled thread of their mythology.

I will now resume my pen, which, since writing the above, I laid down to partake of a banquet with the priest, my princely host, at which I met many of the great lords of Memphis, namely, the lord-keeper of the royal signet, the lord of the wardrobe and rings of the queen's palace, and the lord of the treasury. These men of rank I well knew, having met them before at the table of the queen. There were also strangers whom I had not met before—men of elegant address, and in rich apparel, each with the signet of his office on his left hand; among others, the lord of the Nilometer, who reports the progress of the elevation of the river in the annual overflows, and by which all Lower Egypt is governed in its agricultural work; the president of the engravers on hard stones, an officer of trust and high honour; the governors of several nomes, in their gold collars and chains; the lord of the house of silver; the president of architects; the lord of sculptors; the president of the school of art and colour; with other men of dignity. There were also high-priests of several fanes, of Athor, of Pthah, of Horus, of Maut, and of Amun. Besides these gentlemen, there was a large company of noble ladies, their wives and daughters, who came to the banquet by invitation of the Princess Nelisa, the superb and dark-eyed wife of the Prince Hierarch, and one of the most magnificent and queenly women (next to the queen herself) I have seen in this land of beautiful women.

It was a splendid banquet. The Lady Nelisa presided with matchless dignity and grace. But I have already described a banquet to you. This was similar in display and the mode of entertaining the guests.

I was seated opposite the daughter of the Priest of Mars, of whose beauty I have before spoken. She asked many questions in the most captivating way, about Tyre, and yourself, and the Phœnician ladies generally. She smiled, and looked surprised, when I informed her that I was betrothed to the fair Princess Thamonda, and asked me if she were as fair as the women of Egypt. She inquired if Damascus had always been a part of Phœnicia, and how large your kingdom was. When I told her that your kingdom was composed of several lesser kingdoms, once independent, but now united far east of Libanus, under your crown, she inquired if you were a warlike queen to make such conquests. I replied that this union of the free cities of Phœnicia, and of the cities of Cœle-Syria under your sceptre, was a voluntary one, partly for union against the kings of Philistia, partly from a desire to be under so powerful and wise a queen. She said that if the danger were passed, or you were no more, the kings of these independent cities might dissolve the bonds, and so diminish the splendour of the crown which I was to wear. To this I replied, that to be king of Tyre and its peninsula was a glory that would meet my ambition. "Yes," said she, "for Tyre is the key of the riches of the earth."

I repeat this conversation, dear mother, in order to show you that the high-born daughters of Egypt are not only affable and sensible, but that they possess no little knowledge of other lands, and take an interest in countries friendly to their own. The grace and beauty of this maiden, as well as her modesty, rendered her conversation attractive and pleasing. She is to become the wife of a brave young captain of the chariot battalion, when he returns from the Ethiopian war.

My visit to the pyramids I will now describe, dear mother, although in a letter to the Princess Thamonda I have given a very full account of it. Accompanied by the hierarch and a few young lords—his friends and mine—we rode in chariots out of the gate of the city, passed the guards, who made obeisance to the high-priest, and entered upon an avenue (what noble avenues are everywhere!) of trees growing upon a raised and terraced mound which bounded each side of it. The mound was emerald-green with verdancy, and the colour of the foliage of the palms, acacias, and tamarisk trees was enriched by the bright sunshine as seen through the pure atmosphere. At intervals we passed a pair of obelisks, or through a grand pylon of granite. Then we came to a beautiful lake—the Lake of the Dead—where we passed a procession of shrines. Every nome and all large cities have such a lake. I will here state its use, which, like everything in Egypt, is a religious one. It is connected with the passage of the dead from this world to the next; for the Egyptians not only believe in a future state, but that rewards or punishments await the soul. When a person of distinction dies, after the second or third day his body is taken charge of by embalmers, a class of persons whose occupation it is to embalm the dead. They have houses in a quarter of the city set apart for this purpose. Here the friends of the dead are shown three models of as many different modes of embalment, of which they choose one, according to the expense they are willing to incur. "The most honourable and most costly," said the high-priest to me, as we were surveying the Lake of the Dead, towards which a procession was moving from the city, when we came before it "is that in which the body is made to resemble Osiris. And a custom prevails among us, that the operator who first wounds the body with the sharp embalming flint, preparatory to embalming, is odious by the act, and is compelled to take to flight, pursued with execrations and pelted with stones. No doubt the man we saw flying out of a house this morning, as we passed, was one of these incisors."

The body remains seventy days, if that of a person of rank, at the embalmers. It is then either taken to the house, to be detained a longer or shorter time—according to the attachment of relatives, and their reluctance to part with it—or is prepared for entombment. During the interval of seventy days, the mourners continue their signs of lamentation, which often are excessive in degree, such as tearing off raiment, beating the breast, and pouring dust upon the head. The pomp of the burial of the Pharaohs, I am informed, is inconceivably grand and imposing. The whole realm joins in the rites and processions, and every temple is crowded with sacrificers and incense-burners.

We stopped our chariots to witness the funeral procession advance to the shore of the lake, from the wide street leading from Memphis.

First came seven musicians, playing a solemn dirge upon lyres, flutes, and harps with four chords. Then servants carrying vases of flowers; and others followed, bearing baskets containing gilded cakes, fruit, and crystal goblets of wine. Two boys led a red calf for sacrifice in behalf of the dead, and two others carried in a basket three snow-white geese, also for sacrifice. Others bore beautiful chairs, tablets, napkins, and numerous articles of a household description; while others still held little shrines, containing the household gods or effigies of their ancestors. Seven men carrying daggers, fans, sandals, and bows, each having a napkin on his shoulder, followed. Next I saw eight men appear, supporting a table; and lying upon it, as offerings, were embroidered couches and lounges, richly inlaid boxes, and an ivory chariot with silver panels, which, with the foregoing articles, the high-priest informed me had belonged to the deceased, who, from the cartouch on the chariot, was Rathmes, "lord of the royal gardens."

Behind this chariot] came the charioteer, with a pair of horses caparisoned with harness for driving, but which he led on foot out of respect to his late master.

Then came a venerable man, with the features and beard of the Hebrew race. Surprised to see one of these people anywhere, save with an implement of toil in his hand, or bowed down to the earth under a burden, I looked more closely, and recognized the face of the head gardener, Amrami, or Amram, whom I had often seen in the queen's garden, and whom Remeses had taken, as it were, into his service, as he was his foster-father: for it is no uncommon thing with the nobles to have Hebrew nurses for their infants; on the contrary, they are preferred. When Remeses was an infant, it seems, therefore, that the wife of this fine-looking old Hebrew was his foster-mother, or nurse. I have before spoken of the striking resemblance he bears to Remeses. Were he his father (if I may so speak of a prince in connexion with a slave), there could not be a much greater likeness.

This venerable man, who must be full seventy years of age, bore in his hand a bunch of flowers, inverted and trailing, in token that his lord was no more. He was followed by not less than fifty under-gardeners, four or five of whom had Hebrew lineaments, but the rest were Egyptians and Persians,—the latter celebrated for the culture of flowers, which are so lavishly used here in all the ceremonies of society and rites of religion.

After them followed four men, each bearing aloft a vase of gold, upon a sort of canopy, with other offerings; then came a large bronze chest, borne by priests, containing the money left to their temple by the deceased. Then, in succession, one who bore his arms; another, a pruning-hook of silver; another, his fans; a fourth, his signets, jewelled collars, and necklaces, displayed upon a cushion of blue silk, adorned with needle-work; and a fifth, the other insignia peculiar to a noble who had been intrusted with the supervision of all the royal gardens in the Memphite kingdom.

Now came four trumpeters and a cymbal-player, performing a martial air, in which voices of men mingled, called "The Hymn of Heroes."

Next appeared a decorated barge or *baris*,—a small, sacred boat, carried by six men, whom I saw elevate to view the mysterious "Eye of Osiris;" while others carried a tray of blue images, representing the deceased under the form of that god, also of the sacred bird emblematic of the soul. Following these were twelve men, bearing upon yokes balanced across the shoulders, baskets and cases filled with flowers and crystal bottles for libation. Next were a large company of hired females, with fillets upon their brows, beating their bared breasts, and throwing dust upon their heads,—now lamenting the dead, now praising his virtues.

Then came the officiating priest, his sacred leopard-skin cast over his shoulders, bearing in his hand the censer and vase of libation, and accompanied by his attendants holding the various implements required for the occasion. Behind this priest came a car, without wheels, drawn by four white oxen and seven men, yoked to it, while beside them walked a chief officer, who regulated the movements of the procession. Upon this car was the consecrated boat, containing the ark or hearse. The pontiff of the Temple of Horus walked by the sarcophagus, which was decked with flowers, and richly painted with various emblems. A panel, left open on one side, exposed to view the head of the mummy.

Finally came the male relatives of the dead, and his friends. In his honour the queen's grand-chamberlain and the master of horse marched together in silence, and with solemn steps, leaning on their long sticks. Other men followed, whose rich dresses, and long walking canes, which are the peculiar mark of an Egyptian gentleman, showed them to be persons of distinction. A little in the rear of these walked a young man, who dropped a lotus-flower from a basket at every few steps, and closed the long procession.

In no country but this, where rain seldom falls, and it is always pleasant in the open air, could such a procession safely appear bearing wares so delicate and frail. The only danger to be apprehended is from storms of sand from the desert beyond the pyramids, of the approach of which, however, the atmosphere gives a sufficient warning.

This letter is quite long enough, dear mother, and I close it, with wishes for your happiness, and assurances of the filial devotion of

Your son,
SESOSTRIS.

LETTER XV.

CITY OF MEMPHIS.

DEAREST MOTHER:

Your last letter, assuring me of your health, and that of the Princess Thamonda, I received by the chief pilot, Onothis, who, in his new and handsome galley, reached the head of the Delta two days ago. Thence he came here in his boat, his ship being too large, in the present depth of water, to come up to Memphis.

I will now continue the description of the funeral of "the lord of the royal gardens." When the procession reached the steps leading down to the sacred lake, the hearse was borne upon a gilded and carved *baris*, the consecrated boat for the dead. This was secured to a decorated galley with sails and oars and a spacious cabin, richly painted with funeral emblems. The friends and relatives of the deceased embarked in other barges in waiting, and to the strains of wailing music, the procession, reverently joined by the boats of several gentlemen, in gay apparel, who were fishing on the lake, crossed to the other side. Reaching the opposite shore, it formed again, as before, and moved down "the Street of the Tombs," crossed a narrow plain, and entered the gate of the great burial-place of Memphis. We slowly followed the procession; and, alighting from the chariot, I saw them take the mummy from the sarcophagus on the car, and place it upright in a chamber of the tomb. An assistant priest then sprinkled all who were present with sacred water, and the chief-priest burnt incense before an altar of the tomb, and poured libations upon it, with other ceremonies. To close the scene, the mummy was embraced by weeping friends, and a funeral dirge played by the musicians without, which was wildly answered by the mourning wail of woe from within.

Driving around the Acherusis Lake, under the shade of its solemn groves, the priest directed his charioteer to take me in again at the gate of the tombs. Reseating myself by his side—for the chariots of the priests, as well as those of ladies, are provided with a movable curved chair which holds two persons—we proceeded in a direct line towards the greatest of the three pyramids that stand near Memphis. We were upon what is called "The Sacred Way." It commenced at the gate of a temple to the god of the winds, beneath the pylon of which we passed, and extended nearly a league in length over a vast plain crowded with funeral temples, monuments, mausolean porticos, statues and fountains. All the architectural magnificence which is found in other avenues, seemed to be combined here to form a royal road which has no parallel on earth; not even the long column-lined approach to the Temple of the Sun, at the end of the Straight street in Damascus, can be compared with it.

This noble thoroughfare, as we drove slowly along that I might admire its grandeur and beauty, was thronged with people going to and coming from the city. There were processions returning from having deposited their dead in one of the many tombs which covered the vast plain; processions of the humble orders, with but few signs of display and wealth, proceeding, with real mourners, to the tomb. There were groups of children, their hands filled with garlands, going to place them upon the sarcophagus of a departed parent; for the custom of decorating the resting-places of the dead with wreaths often renewed, belongs to Egypt as well as to Syria.

We overtook a rich lady in a gilded palanquin, borne on the shoulders of four slaves. She was opulently and handsomely attired, and carried a blue and green fan, while an attendant walked behind and held over her head a large parasol.

Two chariots, containing young Egyptian lords, dashed by us at full speed in the excitement of a race, each driving his own ornamented car, the charioteers standing a little in the rear.

People selling little images of gods, or of eminent deceased persons, or fruit, or flowers, or scarabæi, and amulets, were seated all along the highway, upon pedestals, or in the shade of statues and tombs; while along the road walked sellers of vegetables, and fowls, and bread. Indeed, the way was crowded with life and activity. With no other people would the avenue to its tombs be the most thronged of any, and the favourite of all in the city; for Memphis, which extends from and includes Jizeh, past the pyramids south for six miles, has noble streets, but none like this leading to the pyramids. The Egyptians say that the house is but the temporary abode of man, but in the tombs his embalmed body dwells for ever. "Let us, therefore, decorate our tombs with paintings and art, and fill them with flowers, and adorn the homes which are to be permanent."

Hence the "dead-life" of the sepulchres is not less a reality to the Egyptian than his life in the city. The poor, however, do not find tombs. They are buried in graves or pits, like the Hebrew people. On the other side of the river lies the most ancient burial-place of Memphis; but since the construction of the Lake of the Dead, it is no longer necessary to cross the Nile (for the dead *must* be ferried across water) for interment.

As we drove on, we came to a stately sepulchre, before which was gathered a large multitude. The coffin had just been removed from a gorgeous hearse and set down upon the steps of the tomb. It was the funeral of a lady. I never saw any painting so rich as that which adorned the mummy-case. It was an Osirian coffin, and covered it in every part with columns of hieroglyphics or emblematical figures, among which were represented the winged serpent, the ibis, the cynocephalus or the genii of Amenthe, and the scarabæus.

"The hieroglyphics," said my companion, "contain the name and qualities of the deceased."

At this moment an official, partly in a priestly dress, advanced in an imposing manner, touched the coffin with a wand, and said aloud:

"Approved! Let the good be entombed, and may their souls dwell in Amenthe with Osiris. Judgment is passed in her favour! Let her be buried!"

Upon hearing this address, I asked the high-priest what it signified. He replied, with that courtesy which has always distinguished his replies to my numerous questions:

"This act has reference to the judgment of Osiris. We did not witness a similar ceremony at the lake, because the deceased was brought from On, and had already been judged at the crossing of the Nile. If we had sooner seen this funeral procession, which came only from the city to the lake, we should have beheld forty-two just persons, chosen as judges, seated upon a semicircular stone bench along the shore."

"I noticed the stone seats," I answered, "and intended to have inquired their use."

"Seated upon them, the forty-two judges await the procession. The baris, or gilded galley, which is to receive the body, is then drawn alongside of the steps. Before it the bearers stop, and turning to the judges, rest their burden on the ground before them. Then, while all the friends stand anxiously around, and hundreds of spectators line the shores, one of the judges rises and asks if any one present can lawfully accuse the deceased of having done wrong to any man. If the dead has done injustice or evil, his enemy, or the one wronged, or their relatives, advance and make the charge. The judges weigh the accusation, and if it be sustained, the rites of sepulchre are commanded not to proceed."

Such a judgment, dear mother, I afterwards witnessed on our return from the pyramids. It was the funeral of a woman of respectability.

The accuser said, advancing into the space before the judges—

"I accuse the deceased of suffering her father to perish in want."

"This is a great crime by our laws," said the judge sternly; "for, though sons are not bound to provide for poor parents, daughters are. This she knew, and was able to do it. Where are the proofs?"

Three persons came forward and bore testimony to the fact.

"The deceased is not worthy to pass the Lake of the Dead. The burial is prohibited."

Hereupon there was a great cry of woe on the part of the mortified relations; and the mummy, without being permitted to enter the sacred baris, was retaken to the city, where in a shrine in the house it will remain above-ground for years; until finally, after certain ceremonies, it is permitted to be ignominiously entombed in "the sepulchre of the evil."

This accusation and judgment, dear mother, is a striking illustration of the veneration and respect children are expected to pay to their parents in Egypt.

If, on the other hand, the accusation is not sustained, the accusers are stoned away by the friends, who then with great joy unite in a eulogy of the dead, and joined by all the people present pray the gods below to receive him to dwell among the pious dead. In the eulogy, they speak only of virtues—praising his learning, his integrity, his justice, his piety, his temperance, and truthfulness; but no mention is made of rank, since all Egyptians are deemed equally noble. Such an ordeal has no doubt a great influence upon the living Egyptian; for he is certain that at his death every act of injustice he has committed will be brought up before the forty-two judges, and if found guilty, he will be denied sepulture, while infamy will be attached to his memory.

"What," I asked of my companion, the high-priest, "is the state of the deceased soul after death?"

"That, O prince," said he, "is one of the mysteries. But as you have been initiated into the knowledge of the mystic books in your own land, I will explain to you what our books of the dead teach. We priests of Apis do not believe with those of Osiris at On."

"What is their faith?" I asked.

"That the soul of man is immortal (which we all believe"), he added positively; "that when the body decays, the soul enters into and is born in the form of a lower animal; and when it has gone the round of the bodies of all terrestrial and marine animals, and of all flying creatures, it enters again into the body of an infant at its birth."

"Possibly in this belief," I remarked, "is found the reason for preserving the human body as long as possible by embalming it, thus keeping off the transmigration of its soul into a brute as long as possible."

"Without doubt," he replied, "embalming the dead grew out of the doctrine of transmigration of souls. The circuit performed by a soul in this series of inhabitations of the forms of animals, is three thousand years in duration. Such is the belief of the priests of the Sun. This transmigration is not connected either with reward or punishment, but it is a necessity of its creation that the soul should accomplish the whole circuit of the kingdom of animated nature ere it again enters a human body. Our doctrine of metempsychosis only so far embodies this, as to make Osiris send back the transgressing soul from Amenthe to earth, to dwell in the body of swine as a punishment; and when its probation is passed, we allow an ultimate return to the Divine Essence."

"What is this tribunal of Osiris?" I asked.

"The dead carry with them to the tomb a papyrus, on which is written their address to the gods, and the deeds which entitle them to admission into Heaven. When the soul leaves the grave, it is received by Horus, son of Osiris, and conducted to the gates of Amenthe, or the regions of the gods. At the entrance, a dog with four heads—of the wolf, lion, serpent, and bear—keeps guard. Near the gate, which is called the gate of Truth, sits the goddess of Justice, with her gigantic scales of gold between her and the gate of Truth. Hard by sits the god Thoth, with a tablet and stylus. The scales are superintended by the deity Anubis. Through the open gate the throne of Osiris is visible with the deity upon it.

"As Horus advances with the soul to the Gate of Truth, as if to enter, the goddess of Justice commands him to stop, that the sum of its deeds, both good and evil, may be weighed and recorded.

"Anubis then places a vase containing all the human virtues in one scale, and the heart of the deceased, or sometimes the soul itself, in the other. Horus repeats the result, which the god Thoth inscribes upon his iron Tablet. The dog watches the issue of the weighing with eyes red with furious longing to devour the soul. If the sum of its good deeds predominates, Horus, taking it by one hand, and the tablet of Thoth in the other, advances into the hall, where his father, Osiris, is seated upon the throne, holding his crook and flagellum, and awaiting the report from the hand of his son. They approach the throne between four genii of Amenthe, and come before three deities who sit in front of the throne. These ask if he has been weighed, and Horus exhibits to each the tablet of Thoth. They then permit him to pass. Horus now stands before Osiris, with the soul by his side, and presents the tablet, which the deity takes from his son's hand. If satisfied by an inspection of the tablet, which records not only the virtues but every error of the soul's life on earth, Osiris presents him with an ostrich feather, the emblem of truth. One of the three deities then gives him a vase containing all the virtues, his few sins being pardoned; a second offers him a jewelled band for the forehead, on which is inscribed in diamonds the word 'justified;' and the third presents him with the emblem of life. He is now received by Isis, and conducted through gates of gold that open with divine music, and enters into scenes of celestial beauty and splendour; palaces of the gods become his abode, he reposes by heavenly rivers of crystal beauty, wanders through fields of delight, and dwells with the Lord of the Sun, and all the immortal gods, in glory ineffable and endless."

The hierarch said all this with great animation, and like a man who believes what he utters. I was deeply interested.

"And what, my lord priest, becomes of the soul which cannot meet the scales of justice with confidence, whose evil deeds outweigh his good ones?"

"Such a soul does not see Osiris, nor the farther heavens where he dwells illumined by the glory of the divine disk of the Lord of the Sun. The reprobate spirit does not behold the Eye of Osiris, nor repose in its pure light. It is not manifested to the sacred deities of the inner heavens, nor does he hear the voice of the great god, saying, 'Thou art justified, O soul! Enter thou the Gate of Truth.'

"If the soul is all wicked, with no virtues, then Horus releases its hand with horror, and the dog devours the wretched being in a moment. But if he has one or two virtues—such as honouring his parents, having saved a human life, or fed the hungry—then he is not given over to the monster; but Horus, with a sad aspect, leads him to the throne of Osiris, who, reading the dark tablet of Thoth, sternly inclines his sceptre in token of condemnation, and pronounces judgment upon him according to his sin, when, Horus leaving him, two evil gods from the realms of Typhon appear and lead him forth."

"What is the punishment ordained?'

"To be led back to the gate of Truth and delivered to Justice, who, without a head, sits thereat. The goddess seals the sentence of Osiris upon the forehead of the unclean soul, and instantly it assumes the form of a pig, or some other base animal. The god Thoth then calls up two monkeys, who take the condemned soul to a boat and ferry it back to the world, while the bridge by which it came from the earth is cut down by Anubis, in the form of a man with an axe."

"As everything in Egyptian mythology is symbolical, what is the signification of these monkeys?"

"Monkeys are emblems of Thoth, the god of time," he answered. "The books of our mysteries teach that the human race began with the monkey, and progressively advanced to man. Osiris, by his judgment, condemns the unclean soul to the level of the monkey again, but first commands it to enter a swine's body, the uncleanest of all beasts, and make its way through the whole circle of animal creation, back to the monkey, and up through the black, barbaric races of men, who have arms like apes, to true man himself. Then, practising virtue and rejecting his former vices, he may after death finally attain to the mansions of the blessed, in the presence of Osiris. But I should add, the souls of bodies unburied can never enter the Gate of Truth."

Here we came in sight of the gigantic pylon that opens to the Temple of the Pyramid of Cheops, and the hierarch ceased speaking. He had, however, but little to add, for his explanations covered all the ground of my inquiries.

Thus, dear mother, have I presented to you the system of worship in this wonderful land. I will now proceed to a description of my visit to the pyramids, which, in sublime majesty, occupied the whole horizon as we advanced beyond the plain of the tombs. At the extremity of the paved causeway of this stately "Avenue of the Dead," leading from the Nile to the pyramids, we beheld the three great triangular mountains of gigantic art obliquely, so that they were grasped by the eye in one grand view. But the lofty mass of Cheops immediately before us, at the end of the avenue, challenged the eye and whole attention of the observer. For a moment, as we dashed onward in our brilliantly painted chariot, our steeds tossing their plumed heads as if proud of their housings of gold and needle-work, we lost sight of the pyramid by the interposition of the gigantic wings of the Gate of the Pyramids. These wings were towers of Syenite rock, one hundred and twenty feet in height, looking down from their twelfth painted and sculptured story upon the tops of the loftiest palms that grew on each side of the entrance. The gate was guarded by priests, who wore a close silver helmet, and held in their hands a short sword, the sheath of which hung to a belt of leopard's skin. They were young men, numbering in all three hundred and sixty, corresponding to the days of the former Egyptian year; while their five captains typify five days added by the gods.

"These young men," said the high-priest, "are all sons of warlike fathers. They desire to become priests, and are now in their noviitiate; but after a year's service as guards to the greatest of temples, they will be advanced to a higher degree, and exchange the sword for the shepherd's crook, and thence they rise to be bearers of libation vases, and assistants in sacrifices."

We passed under the lofty pylon, which was spanned by a bronze winged sun, saluted by sixty of the guard on duty; this being the number of each of the six bodies into which they are divided. As soon as we entered the court of the gate, a sight of inconceivable grandeur burst upon me. Imagine a double colonnade of the most magnificent pillars which art could create, extending on each side of an open way a thousand cubits in length. At the end of the grand vista, behold crouched at full length, on the eastern edge of the elevated table on which the pyramids stand, and in an attitude of eternal repose, with an aspect of majesty and benignity inconceivable in the human lineaments, an andro-sphinx of colossal size, having the face of a warrior. Although stretched on the earth, with its fore-paws extended, the summit of the brow is seventy feet above the earth. This sublime image is emblematical, like all Egyptian sphinxes, and represents strength or power combined with intellect. The face I at once recognized to be that of Chephres, as seen upon his obelisk at Rhoda, aggrandized by the vastness of its proportions to the aspect of a god.

From my companion, the prince-hierarch, I learned it was begun by an ancient Pharaoh of the same name, one of the kings of the oldest dynasty, who conceived the idea of chiselling into these grand proportions a mass of rock, which, projecting from the Libyan hills, nearly obstructed the view of the principal pyramid.

We were here forbidden to advance in our chariot, and the footmen, who had never left the side of the horses, however swiftly our charioteer might drive, caught them by the head, and we alighted.

I had leisure now to contemplate the scene before me. The personation of majesty, the sphinx, fills the breadth of the approach between the massive pillars of the colonnade. Between his fore-paws, which extend fifty feet, while the body is nearly three times this measure, stands a beautiful temple faced with oriental alabaster. His head is crowned with a helmet slightly convex, upon which, like a crest, is affixed the sacred uræus or serpent, shining with gold. The cape or neck-band of the helmet is of scales, coloured blue, red, green, and orange, intermingled with gilding. A great and full beard descends over his breast, immediately under which, and between his feet, is the summit of the temple where sacrifices are daily offered to the god. Above his towering brow soars the mighty pyramid before which this colossus keeps guard.

"The majesty of this image, O prince," said the high-priest, as, leaning at every step upon his slender acacia rod, he walked by my side, " impresses you."

" It is the most majestic of all the gods of Egypt," I answered.

" Yes. Its age is nearly coeval with the pyramid."

" On the pyramidion base of the left obelisk in front of the temple of Osiris, have I not seen reposing four small sphinxes copied from this ?"

" Thou hast seen them. That obelisk is many ages old; yet long before it, was this sphinx-god, as silent, majestic and immovable in eternal repose as you behold him now."

At the termination of the avenue of direct approach, we descended an inclined plane to a platform of marble, on which is an image of Osiris in stone, and were brought nearly opposite the lower part of its face. Then another flight of steps, cased with polished porphyry, brought us on a level with the top of the temple. In the centre of this level platform stands a statue of Horus, cast in bronze. Thence descending another flight of thirty broad steps, we stood in the space between the enormous feet of the sphinx, and directly before the beautiful temple.

Our gradual approach in this descent, during which the sphinx was kept constantly in view, rising above us as we descended, heightened the impressions first made upon me by its colossal size; and I beheld, with new emotions of sublimity, its posture of repose and calm majesty of aspect.

A priest, in the full costume of his sacred office, stood at the door, and preceded by him we entered. As it was the hour of oblation, he held a censer in his hand, and approaching an altar before a granite tablet at the end of the temple, he invoked the mysterious god. The temple has no roof, but is exquisitely decorated and painted with sacred symbols. On each side stands a tablet of limestone. The tablet over the altar is inscribed with the name of the designer of the sphinx, Menes, the first mortal king after the general overflow of the mountains, and also with the destruction of the gigantic gods by the uprising of unknown oceans upon the globe. The tablet holds his shield, and on it is pictured the escape of the son of the ancient gods, in a ship, which is resting upon a mountain peak. In this tradition, mother, we find repeated our Phœnician history of the flood, before the days of the first kings. Without doubt all nations retain a similar tradition. Upon the same tablet is also a representation of a later king offering incense and libations to the god to whom the sphinx is consecrated. The tablets on the side also represent kings offering prayer to the god. The floor is beautifully tesselated with variegated stones; and on all sides are ivory or silver tables, covered with beautifully shaped vases, containing offerings of worshippers. There are, besides, ten shrines before the altar, upon each of which rests a golden crown, gifts of kings of other lands. Without question this temple of the sphinx is the richest in Egypt in gifts, as well as most honoured by its Pharaohs. Is it not the vestibule to the grand pyramidal temple which is the tomb of the first mortal king?

But, my dear mother, I must not linger at the feet of the sphinx. Leaving the temple, we ascended one of two broad stair-cases, and mounting to a succession of terraces, adorned with statues of gods, the vast bulk of the sphinx being on our right, we reached a noble stone platform behind the image, upon which stands an ancient figure, in coarse marble, worn by age, of Chephres the Great. He stamps a sea-dragon under his feet, and upon his capped head is the beak of a galley, with the head and wings of a dove. In this symbol, dear mother, behold again the representation of the deluge, and the dove that guided the ship which held Chephren, or Chephres, and his father, the god Noachis, or Noah.

When we had gained this terrace, we beheld before us both pyramids, and between them the pylon of a vast temple, which, extending its great arms on each side, embraced the twin pyramids in one god-like edifice, of grandeur and dimensions immeasurable to the eye, and overpowering to the imagination. To explain more clearly what I beheld :—between, but in advance of them, towered a colossal pylon, to which each pyramid was a wing, united by a wall of brick, ninety feet high, encased with marble. This central temple, or pylon, was as massive and solemn in its aspect as the pyramids which formed its propyla. For a few moments I stood and gazed with awe. Until the spectator reaches the terrace, the whole effect is not perceived; for, though the central temple is visible, even from the Lake of the Dead, it appears as if merely intervening; it is only on the terrace before which the sphinx, the gigantic watcher before the pyramids, reposes, that the whole grand design is comprehended. Had I been all at once brought in sight of the House of Osiris, in the realm of the gods, I should not have been more overawed and impressed.

This temple, built of brick, with marble casing, has in its outline the ruinous aspect of great age, and is not in as good preservation as the pyramids, although subsequently erected, not as an after-thought, but in keeping with the great design.

But a visitor is announced as in the hall of reception; therefore, at present, dear mother, farewell,

SESOSTRIS.

LETTER XVI.

CITY OF ON.

MY HONOURED AND DEAR MOTHER,—

I HAVE described my chariot ride through the plain of tombs, along the magnificent causeway, which extends from the Lake of the Dead to the feet of the sphinx. All that I beheld of the grandeur of the monuments showed, that the Egyptians of past generations who built them, and lie buried here, were a populous and powerful nation, in advance of all others in the arts of life; since not only do the cities for the living, but the "Homes of the Dead," attest their taste and love for the beautiful and sublime in nature and art. The culmination of all Egyptian marvels in architecture is the sphinx-guarded pyramidal temple.

We approached the central pylon along a paved court, across which two hundred chariots could have driven in a line. This court was entirely surrounded by a double row of majestic columns, with the lotus-leaf capitals I have before described. The vastness of their proportions seemed to be increased by contrast with a group of priests, who looked like pigmies in size as they stood by their bases. The gigantic entablature, which united their summits, was covered with sacred symbols, richly coloured, and crowned with statues of kings, hewn out of the dark gray granite of Ethiopia. But some of these were mutilated by Time, which, indeed, had thrown its mantle of decay over the whole,—pillars, architecture, and sculpture ; for this court is coeval with the sphinx crouched at its entrance, and but a little later than the two pyramids. In a few centuries, decay will have brought the mighty fabric to the earth ; for, massive as it looks, it is built of brick, covered with pictured stucco ; but the pyramids of stone, which have withstood the lapse of ages beyond history, will last as long as the everlasting hills of granite from which their enormous blocks were hewn.

Passing beneath the great portal, we found ourselves in the sacred square of the temple of the Pyramids, and I could now perceive the mighty design. Connected by stupendous columnar wings, the pyramids rose in sublime grandeur on either hand. Their summits shone with the light of the setting sun, which, reflected from the polished casing of the pictured tiles yet remaining near the top, and that once covered the whole surface from base to apex, lent a splendour to them indescribable. On the opposite side of the quadrangle, formed by the temple in front and the bases of the pyramids on the two sides, is a dark grove of palms, intermingled with statues and altars ; and beyond rise the dark hills of Libya—a fitting and solemn background to the scene.

About the summit of the Queen's Pyramid, which is a little smaller than the other, though it appears to be of equal height, from the superior elevation of the platform of rock on which it stands, soared flocks of the white ibis, their snow-white wings flashing like pinions of silver as they wheeled in mid-air. At that immense height they looked no larger than sparrows.

A statue of Horus, whose name I had also seen inscribed on the tablet of the temple of the sphinx, rose a colossal monolith in the centre of the quadrangle, with one of Thoth upon his right, and another of Anubis on his left hand. These figures were symbolical of the funereal use of the pyramids between which they stood.

After walking around the columned avenue of this great mausoleum, we began the ascent of the larger pyramid, known as that of Cheops ; the other bearing the name of Chephres, as the high-priest informs me ; and the third, which towers in its own unaided grandeur farther to the south, being that of Pharaoh-Men-Cherines. We found the ascent extremely difficult—indeed, in ancient times it must have been impossible, when its polished and beautiful casing remained entire ; but this having been removed by time and accident in many places, and purposely in others, a path, if it may be so termed, is made to the summit. We were aided by attendants of the temple, who, from long practice, ascend with ease, assisting also those strangers who would climb the perilous height.

As we reached half-way, a block, which had been removed from its place either by the irresistible force of a sirocco from the desert, or by lightning, gave the high-priest and myself a welcome resting-place.

As we stood here a few moments, I looked down upon the prospect below. The sight at first made me dizzy, for we were elevated four hundred feet above the base. I seemed to be suspended upon wings above an abyss, and a dreadful desire to throw myself out into mid-air seized me; so that to resist it I closed my eyes and clung firmly to the attendant. It soon passed off, and I gazed down upon the vast quadrangle, the persons in which looked no bigger than ants, while the three colossi of the gods, in the centre, were reduced to the natural size of men.

Opposite, not six hundred cubits distant, stood Chephres. From each pyramid swept the avenues of columns and the great wall connecting both with the central temple and its pylon. From the grove of palms, curled up into the pure orange-coloured atmosphere a blue cloud of incense, where some priest offered at one of its shrines.

Again we mounted upwards, and after incredible fatigue, gained the summit—not without peril, for a slip of the foot or the hand, each block being as high as a man's neck, would prove fatal. Indeed, more than one life has been lost in falling down the side of the pyramid. A prince of Midian, a country in Arabia, lost his life last century by losing his hold and falling from Chephres, which is more difficult of ascent than Cheops (or Chuphu), as the priests there call its name.

How shall I describe to you, my dear mother, the scene which burst upon my vision, as I gazed about me from this mountain-like elevation! As I ascended the prospect of the country enlarged at every step, but now I seemed to behold the earth itself spread out beneath me. The place where we stood, which looks from below like a sharp apex, is a platform several cubits across, on which twenty men could stand or move about with ease.

I can give you no adequate conception of the scene I beheld. First the valley of the Nile was visible, extending for many leagues to the right and left, and resembling a green belt a few miles wide, through which the river flowed like a silver band—while upon its borders countless cities were set like precious stones. It was a gorgeous and magnificent assemblage of cities, temples, palaces, obelisks, villas, gardens, monuments, avenues of trees and sphinxes, sepulchres, aqueducts, statue-lined causeways, galleys and pleasure barges, chariots, horses, and multitudes of people. Nor should I omit what now became visible in one field of view, to the north and south. I mean not less than one hundred pyramids, all much smaller than the mighty triad, but each, had not the others been up-builded, would have been a marvel of grandeur.

"Those are all tombs of kings, but of a later age than this one," said the hierarch, looking towards them. "Each monarch, at the commencement of his reign, laid the foundation of a pyramid. He built first a small one, containing his sarcophagus and sepulchral chamber. Then every year he added to the outside a complete layer of stones, which, after many years, extended its base, and increased its elevation in like proportions. Therefore the size of the pyramids marks the age to which the king lived."

"Then," said I, "the kings who built the multitude of lesser pyramids, which we behold in the distance, must have had much shorter lives than the builders of these vast piles."

"You are right, O prince," he said. "When the pyramid, on which we now stand, and its companions were builded, men's lives were of the duration of a thousand years."

"That was before the traditional deluge?" I replied with surprise and interest.

"True, O Prince of Tyre!" he answered. "These two great pyramids, say our sacred books, were the work of the giants who lived in the days before the flood of Noachis, or Noah. They are the tombs of their kings, and were centuries in being built according to our years. And when the gods brought the unknown oceans over the earth, to punish the nations which living so long became as wise as the gods, but at the same time grew as wicked as wise, these vast sepulchres withstood, like the lesser hills, the waters of desolation, and remained in ruinous grandeur, not only as witnesses of the flood, but monuments of a past people, whose towers, as well as tombs, reached unto the heavens. You see these pyramids, and how they are now defaced by the billows that dashed against and over them. Anciently, when they were completed, their whole surfaces were encased with beautiful tiles of the brightest blue and purest white, inlaid alternately in perfect squares. Upon this magnificent encasing was inscribed, in pictorial signs, the history of man; but no person has ever interpreted them. You see, my prince, that here, at the top, are a few strata still remaining of this rich encasement; all the rest having been destroyed by the deluge—by the abrasion of the waves, and the hurling against its sides of mighty ships, driven by the huge and angry billows which rolled like a boiling sea across the earth. Thus you behold these vast structures, as it were in ruins, yet still retaining fragmentary portions of their original glory and beauty. When the waters departed, the gods limited the lives of men to one hundred years; hence the pyramids that the kings this side the flood have erected are comparatively small in magnitude."

"But the third, was it not built before the flood?"

"I did not intend you should so understand," he answered. "It was commenced before the flood by the king who was destroyed thereby. But the son of the wise and good Prince Noah completed it during the several hundred years that he lived—as did his father also —after the flood; for it was only the lives of their descendants that were to be limited. Thus Amun, says tradition, finished the third pyramid, but did not encase it, as the art was lost by the deluge, which had destroyed those who were skilled in it. There are other accounts, my prince, but they either come near this one, or so far differ from it that they are entitled to no credit."

"It is *your* opinion, then, O high-priest, that these two pyramids were built by the giants of the ages before the great deluge?" I asked.

"I have no other one," he replied firmly. "When the age of man was shortened to one hundred years from one thousand, his stature was also lessened. Hence the men of the ages since the flood cannot build a pyramid like one of these. All the power of engines and art cannot uprear such stones six hundred feet into the air. This is giants' work."

"Then you believe that there were giants in the earth in the days before the flood?" I said, doubtingly.

"These pyramids attest the fact," he replied, with an impressive gesture of his right hand towards the opposite one. "Noah himself, says tradition, and his sons, Chephres, Chufu, and Amun or Men-Cherines, were gigantic, and are worshipped as gods, as you know, not only here and in Syria and Ethiopia, but in the Orient, and beyond the seas, under various names. In the third pyramid Amun was entombed. In the second is Chephres, or Chefret, who, when an aged king, was brought from the place where he died, and placed in a sarcophagus above the chamber where lay the king who found sepulture there before the flood. Within the pyramid on which we are, rest the sacred bones of the Prince-god Noah, who, at the age of nine hundred and fifty years, came hither to be buried by the side of his eldest son Chephres. 'Such a mourning of the nations, all of whom sprung from his loins, the earth never knew, and will never witness more,' say the sacred scrolls of the temples. All kings, and queens, and princes, and lords, and nobles of every realm followed the embalmed body of their father and deity; and King Menes, his grandson, went up from Egypt with all the hosts of the land to meet the funeral procession, and to receive the divine body. Cheops is but another name for Noah. Here also is entombed Menes."

Such, my dear mother, is the priestly tradition of the pyramids. We, of Tyre, have a myth that the Father of the Flood is buried in Damascus; but though Egyptians love to concentrate all history around their own land, and make Egypt the cradle of the human race, yet as this tradition seems to be better founded than ours, and as they can point to the grand tombs of these kings of the flood, I am ready to concede to her the honour which she claims of being the place of sepulture of the giants who survived the deluge, And what fitter tombs than these eternal mountains of granite, could the progenitors of the race repose in! Fit sepulchres are these in their grandeur of proportions, for men whose stature was gigantic, and whose lives extended through a thousand years!

But I must return to the prospect from the summit of this mausoleum of giants. The sun was near the horizon, and sent his level and mingled rose, golden, and purple beams aslant across the valley. The air was perfectly clear, and our view unimpeded in all directions.

To the south, along the verdant plain of the Nile, the pyramids shone in the sun as if sheathed with plates of gold. Palms, temples, obelisks in pairs, and pylones were mingled with them in the richest confusion; while as far as the eye could penetrate they receded into ths desert, till their size was diminished by distance to shining mounds.

Turning my eyes to the west, the yellow plain of Libya, with its rocky hills inclosing the verdant valley of the Nile in that direction, rolled away to the edge of the horizon, an arid, undulating, illimitable expanse, which, under the sun, blazed like a lake of fire from the burning reflection of its sands. The contrast of this realm of desolation, and its storm-piled drifts of grey, brown, and dusky sand, lying so near the groves, and green fields, and blooming gardens which surrounded the pyramids and extended to the base of the ridge, was very remarkable. One part looked like the abode of Osiris, full of beauty, and light, and happiness : the other, like that of Typhon, or the spirit of evil, who strove, ever battling with his storms of sand, to invade, overwhelm, and desolate these scenes of beauty ! And, ere many centuries, his arid hosts threaten to sweep past the pyramids, and to overleap the very gates of Memphis ! But at present, all the land within the hills is a region of delight, presenting a pleasing contrast, with its perennial green, to the desolate and savage realm of the desert. Luxuriantly covered with verdure ; bright with golden wheat-fields, charming green meadows, foliage of every variety ; groups of trees rising from a thousand courts ; countless villages everywhere, and myriads of brilliant lakes, it was a scene of unmixed beauty. Jizeh, a little to the east, with its temple-palaces, and gardens, filled the view. Farther east lay, first, the glorious city of Apis, its squares, avenues, lakes, groves, fanes, and monuments, all open to the eye like a magnificent picture. Beyond the glittering Nile, the banks of which were rich with fertility and adorned with villas, I beheld Raamses, and still farther Python, the treasure-cities, in the fair expanse of the land of Goshen,—alas ! beautiful only to the eye, for upon it rests the dark shadow of Hebrew bondage ; and south, a few miles, after a thousand scenes of rural beauty fill the vision, towers, like the throne of the kingdom, the city of the Lord of the Sun, its gorgeous temple and forests of obelisks flinging back the sunbeams with a splendour that fills the soul with wonder and delight !

"O happy, glorious, mighty Egypt ! what a blessed and favoured land art thou ! With one foot upon the seven mouths of thy mighty river, another upon Ethiopia, and thy head in the clouds, all nations bow down to thy might and greatness ! Leader of the kingdoms of the earth ! what a future is thine, if thy kings and rulers are true to thee and to themselves !"

The hierarch heard me utter these words, for I spake aloud in my wonder at the glory of this kingdom and the magnificence of her power.

"The future of Egypt, my prince, no man can foresee. But the sacred books contain a prophecy that during one cycle of a soul, three thousand years, she will be a nation despised and ruled by kings of another race, and all that will remain to her will be her defaced pyramids and temples ; the marvel of which will bring strangers from the ends of the earth, curious to gaze upon these mute witnesses of her ancient power and glory."

"The gods forbid !" I said warmly.

"The gods," he answered, "govern the earth, and do what they will with its kingdoms. These sacred papyri also speak of Tyre and prophecy its desolation, and say that the empire of commerce shall be removed to an unknown world beyond the great sea of the West, and that a race yet unborn shall sway the destinies of the earth, and another religion shall prevail in the hearts of men."

"What are these papyri?" I asked.

"Books which have been handed down from the first kings, who in their turn received them from the ancient gods."

I turned away sorrowfully at the thought of this prediction, my dear mother. The idea that Tyre, which now sits a queen upon the shores of her sea, will ever be desolate, is not possible for me to conceive. May her prosperity and peace be prolonged to the ends of the ages.

We now turned to descend this elevation, from whence the heart of Egypt lay open before us. The sight of the sheer eight hundred feet along the inclined side of the pyramid was fearful. The projections which were to receive our feet were not apparent; and we commenced the descent with the greatest caution, being obliged to lower ourselves from block to block; and where the encasement of tiles remained, we were sustained by the iron heads of short spears with which each of us was provided, a hook being secured at the opposite end.

At length we reached the broad terrace which surrounds the pyramid, and upon which are statues and small sphinxes facing outward. Between two of large size, representing Osiris and Isis, we descended a broad flight of steps to an ancient gate, which, as I was told, led to the entrance of the pyramid. The passage, however, has not been opened for many centuries—the piety of the Pharaohs permitting the mighty dead to rest in their granite tumuli undisturbed by curiosity or cupidity.

When we had crossed the court, the priest ascended with me one of the towers of the pylon. From thence he showed me a mass of rock lying in a position which answered, in reference to the main pyramid, to that which the sphinx occupied.

"Seest thou, O prince," he said, "that isolated rock? The ancients intended to chisel it also into a sphinx to match this one, for they used to place them in pairs, like their obelisks. But the grand conception has never been carried out; and you perceive that our noble queen, Amense, is erecting the pyramid of her years so near, that it in part stands upon it. Two such sphinxes crouched in front of Cheops would have been an entrance to the mausoleum worthy of it, and of him who reposes therein. Instead of carrying out this original design, the great temple and colossal wings have been built, and the avenue from the sphinx so turned aside by a slight angle, as to terminate at the central pylon; thereby making one sphinx answer the purpose of two, but at the sacrifice of proportion; for the twofold grandeur of the combined pyramids lessens the impression of the single sphinx, while the two reposing before Cheops alone, would have been in keeping with its majesty."

As it was now sunset, we hastened to our chariot and drove back to the city, along the magnificent causeway I have before described.

Upon my return to the palace of the high-priest, and after describing to his beautiful daughter, Luxora, the incidents of my visit, she said with an arch smile,—

"You ought not, O Sesostris, to have come away without seeing the emerald table of Hermes!"

"I heard nothing of it, lady," I answered. "I have, moreover, seen splendour enough for one day. What and where is this table?"

"In the central chamber of the great pyramid. The people of Egypt believe the tradition, and so also have some of its kings."

"What is the tradition?" I asked. "But first, do you believe it?"

"With all my heart. I never doubted it since I was a child," she answered, smiling, yet with a tone of sincerity. "My father thinks if it were true, it would have been removed when the god Noachis was placed there."

"It is not in the chamber of the sarcophagus, sister," said Osiria, the sister younger than Luxora—a maiden remarkable for her sprightliness and intelligence; "it is in a vault of crystal *under* the pyramid."

"You are right, my dear sister," replied the elder gracefully, "I will tell the prince the legend."

"Then I will tell him mine," said Osiria, with an arch look. "I know he will like mine the best."

"Because he likes you the best, is it?" her sister replied, playfully. "But have a care, Osiria; our guest is bethrothed to a great princess, in his own country."

"That need not prevent him from being my good friend in this," responded Osiria, pleasantly.

"Your tradition, noble Luxora?" I asked.

"It is this. In the ancient days of the earth, before the deluge of the gods, the thrice great Hermes, who knew all the secrets of alchemy, engraved them upon an emerald table and placed it in a cave, which he sealed up. His motive for doing this was both to preserve them and to conceal them from men—for the race of man had grown so wicked, that they made use of what they knew of alchemy to injure one another and defy the deities, answering back the thunder of heaven with thunders of their own. Over this cave the first pyramid was built, and there the emerald table, with all its secrets, so dear to our sex, has remained to this hour!"

I thanked Luxora for her legend, and assured her that I had quite as much curiosity to see the wonderful emerald as she had.

"But if it were discovered," said Osiria, "who could read and understand the writing upon it? Now, O prince, hear *my* tradition: for, having visited the pyramids, it will be agreeable to you to hear all that is said about them."

"I will listen with the greatest pleasure," I answered.

But, dear mother, I will here close this long letter, and reserve for the commencement of my next, the singular tradition related to me by Osiria.

Your affectionate son,
SESOSTRIS.

LETTER XVII.

Palace of the Hierarch, at Memphis.

My much honoured Mother,—

I have much of interest concerning which to write to you in this letter; but will first redeem my promise to give you the traditional story narrated by the lovely Osiria, daughter of the pontiff of Memphis. Her father came in as she commenced, and smilingly said—

"Daughter, are you about to overthrow the prince's faith in the true history of the pyramids, by a fanciful legend?"

"No, my dear father," she answered; "I only desire him to know all he can about these mighty monuments of a former world, and if he does not believe with me in the legend, it will at least interest him."

I assured the beautiful maiden that it would without doubt interest me, and possibly upon hearing it I might receive it "as the most reliable account of the origin of the pyramids."

"Not in opposition," said the high-priest, with a smile, "to the sacred books."

"Not in opposition," said Luxora, archly, "to my emerald table."

"Let the prince, dear father, and sister, hear and judge," said the youngest daughter; and commenced as follows:—

"A very long time ago—before the time of the vast deluge, when all the oceans that roll around the world's verge met in the centre and overflowed the highest mountains—a king, whose name was Saurida Salhouhis, was informed by his astrologers that seven stars had fallen into the sea, betokening a great overflow thereof. He answered, 'The mountains of my kingdom are higher than the ocean, and will defy its waves.'

"The next year his astrologers again came to him, and said that the sun was covered with dark spots, and that a comet was visible with a crest of fire, and threatened evil to the earth. The same night the king dreamed that the mountains became plains, and that all the stars of heaven were extinguished. On awakening he called his one hundred and forty-four priests, and commanding them to consult the gods, received for answer that the earth was to be drowned. Thereupon he commenced building the two pyramids, and ordered vaults to be made under them, which he filled with the riches and treasures of his kingdom. He prepared seven tables or shields of pure gold, on which he engraved all the sciences of the earth, all the knowledge he had learned from his wise men, the names of the subtle alkalies, and alakakirs, and the uses and hurts of them; and all the mysteries of astrology, physics, geometry, and arithmetic."

"These seven golden tables of my sister's legend," said Luxora, laughing, "are not near so wonderful as my table of emerald."

"Lest," said Osiria, "you should imagine I am drawing upon my fancy, I will read to you the remaider of the tradition from the ancient book in the keeping of the priests of Amun, in the Thebaid, given me by my mother, who was the daughter of the priest of the sacred house there."

Having thus spoken the maiden retired, and, after a few minutes absence, returned, followed by a Hebrew woman carrying a pictured scroll, such as I had never before seen. Aided by her attendant, she unrolled it for several cubits, and having found the legend, commenced to read (a rare art among Egyptian ladies, except daughters of the learned priests) as follows,—the tall and stately Hebrew supporting the roll rather with an air of royal condescension than of submission :—

"After the king, Saurida Salhouhis, had given orders for the building of the pyramids, the workmen cut out gigantic columns, vast stones, and wonderful pillars hewn of single rocks. From the mountains of Ethiopia they fetched enormous masses of granite, and from Nubia of gray porphyry, and made with these the foundations of the pyramids, fastening the stones tegether by bars of lead and bands of iron. They built the gates forty cubits under ground, and made the height of them one hundred royal cubits, each of which is equal to six of ours; and each side also was made a hundred royal cubits in extent. The beginning of this undertaking happened under a fortunate horoscope, and resulted successfully. After he had finished the larger of the pyramids, the king covered it with blue satin from the top to the bottom, and appointed a solemn festival, at which were present all the inhabitants of his kingdom.

"Then in this great pyramid he built thirty treasure-chambers, which he filled with an immense store of riches,—precious vessels, signatures of agates, blood-stones, and cornelian, instruments of iron, earthen vases, arms which rust not, and crystal which might be bended yet not broken, strange shells, and deadly poisons, with many other things besides. He made, in the west pyramid, a subterranean hall with divers spheres and stars in the vaulted roof placed in their celestial houses, as they appear in the sky, each in his own aspect; and he deposited here the perfumes which are burned to them, and the books that treat of their mysteries. He placed, also, in the coloured pyramid the scrolls of the priests, in chests of black marble, every chest having upon it a book with leaves of brass, in which were inscribed the duties and wonders of the priesthood, its nature, and the mode of worship in his time; and in a chest of iron were seven books which revealed what was, and is, and shall be from the beginning to the end of time.

"In every pyramid he placed a treasurer: the treasurer of the western pyramid was a statue of red marble-stone, standing upright by the door of the treasure-house,—a lance in his hand, and about his head a wreathed serpent. Whosoever came near the door, and stood still, the serpent entwined about the throat, and, killing him, returned to its place.

"The treasurer of the coloured pyramid was an idol of black agate, sitting upon the throne, with a lance in its hand, and its eyes open and shining. If any mortal looked upon it, he heard a voice so terrible that his senses fled away from him, and he fell prostrate upon his face and died

"The treasurer of his seven tables of gold was a statue ot stone, called Albutis, in a sitting posture: whosoever looked towards it, was drawn to the statue till he was pressed against it so hard that he died there. Over the portal of each he caused to be written:—

"'I, King Saurid, built the pyramids in six years. He that comes after me, and says he is equal to me, let him destroy them in six hundred years. It is easier to pluck down than to build up. I also covered them, when I had finished them, with satin; and let him cover them with mats of grass.'

"Here ends the record on the scroll," said the maiden. "Miriam, thou wilt roll it up, and place it whence I took it, in the sacred shrine of books."

The Hebrew woman, whose appearance was so remarkable for dignity and a certain air of command, that I could not but regard her with interest, then rolled up the book, and moved quietly, but with a stately step, from the room. As she went out, attracted by my close scrutiny, she fixed upon me a large pair of splendid eyes, dark and beautiful, and lighted up by the inward fire of an earnest spirit. Her age was about eight or nine and forty. I do not know why, in looking at her, I thought of Remeses, now at Thebes, waiting to assemble his vast army; perhaps there was a style of face and shape of the eye that recalled him.

"Who is this Hebrew woman?" I asked; for though I have been several days a guest of the high-priest, I had not before seen her.

"My assistant and copier of the scrolls and papyrus leaves, in the Hall of the Sacred Books," answered Osiria; "for know, O prince, that I am my father's scribe, and have the care of all the rolls of the temple."

"Nor can any temple," interposed the hierarch, "boast so orderly a chamber of books as mine; neither do I see any copies of prayers and rites so beautifully done as those by Osiria."

"I do not deserve all the praise, my father," answered the maiden; "for the rich colouring of the heading cartouches of chapters, as well as the graceful form of the characters, is due to Miriam."

"What the servant does the master is praised for," answered the priest smilingly. "But you have not told the prince the whole of the tradition."

"It is true. I must now state how the pyramid was opened by one of the Phœnician conqueror kings. This Philistine warrior, whose barbaric name I have forgotten, and do not wish to remember, on seeing the pyramids, demanded to know what was within them. He was answered by the priest of the sphinx, who is the guardian of the two pyramids, that 'they contained the embalmed bodies of the ancient gods, and first kings of men, the emerald and golden tablets, and all the treasures of gold, silver, and works of art, and everything which appertained to the world before the deluge,—all of which had been preserved by them from the waters, and were now therein.'

"Hearing this, this king told them he would have them opened. All the priests assured him that it could not be done; but he replied, 'I will have it certainly done.' So the engineers of his army opened a place in the great pyramid by means of fire and vinegar; smiths

K

aided the work with sharpened iron and copper wedges, and huge engines to remove the stones. It was a vast work, as the thickness of the wall was twenty cubits. They were many months reaching an apartment within, where they found a ewer made of bright-green emerald, containing a thousand dinars, very weighty, one hundred chœnixes of gold-dust, twenty blocks of ebony, a hundred tusks of ivory, and a thousand ounces of rings of Arabic gold.

"This was all he found, for beyond this small chamber the workmen could not penetrate, by reason of the three treasure-keepers, namely,—the awful statue, with an enwreathed serpent upon his head; the statue of agate, with the terrible voice; and the statue of stone, with the power to draw every one to him, and press him to death between his arm and his iron breast."

"Then said the king, 'Cast up the cost of making this entrance. So the money expended being computed, lo! it was the same sum which they had found; it neither exceeded nor was defective. So he closed up the opening and went his ways, seeing that the gods were against him.

"Many years afterwards, another king opened the other pyramid, and found a passage which descended far below in the earth, in the direction of the centre of the pyramid. By it he reached a subterranean chamber far beneath the level of the foundation, almost directly under the apex. In it was a square well, on each side of which were doors opening into subterranean passages; these he followed, and at length reached a gate of brass, which he perceived led into the foundations of the greater pyramid. But he could not open it, nor has any power been sufficient to do so to this day. Returning, he found another side passage, leading into the pyramid, and so upward to a vaulted room, containing the mighty sarcophagus of the great Noah. This dead monarch of two worlds, before and after the deluge, was reposing in calm majesty in his colossal mummy-case, which was covered with plates of gold. Upon his head was a crown of emerald olive-leaves, each leaf an emerald; and upon his breast, a white dove, made of one pearl. Leaving with awe the father of the world to his sublime and eternal repose, guarded only by the pure white dove, the king, in retiring, found, to his great joy, a narrow passage, which led upward towards the top of the pyramid. It conducted him and his attendants to a chamber with twelve sides, on each of which was pictured one of the constellations in the path of the procession of the equinoxes, in their motion towards the west. The floor was of polished ivory, inlaid with silver stars, dispersed over it as they appeared in their heavenly places when the pyramid was completed. The seven planets, including the sun and the moon, were represented in the ceiling, each one in a panel of silver, with its deity,—all inlaid with silver and precious stones.

"In the centre of this 'Hall of the Universe,' was a hollow stone: when the king entered the chamber, the stone vanished at the pressure of his feet on the floor, and a statue larger than life, of pure crystal, was displayed to his sight. This statue represented a king upon whom was a breastplate of gold set with jewels; on his breast was a stone of incalculable price, and over his head, a carbuncle of the shape and bigness of the sacred egg of the phœnix, shining like the light of the day. He held upon his left arm a shield formed of one single topaz, upon which were characters written with a pen, that neither the king, nor the wise men, nor astrologers, nor magicians, nor the priests who knew all languages, could interpret. Suddenly, darkness filled the place, their torches were extinguished, and save only the king who had with him his diamond-set signet, which shed light before his steps, no one ever returned to the entrance; nor could he ever find the chamber of the statue again. But the first passage to the subterranean chamber remains open to this day, by which men descend; and others are from time to time discovered; the treasury-chambers, however, remain sealed to eyes of men!"

When the intelligent Osiria had ended her account, I gratefully expressed to her my appreciation of her kindness in giving me such interesting information. She accepted my thanks in the graceful manner which characterizes Egyptian ladies of rank. The magnificent Luxora said, with a charming air of feigned provocation,—

"With your brilliant tradition, sister, you have quite thrown into the shade my poor solitary emerald table!"

"There is no doubt whatever, O Sesostris,' said their father, who had listened to the tradition as he sat in his ivory chair, in the rich undress vestments he wore when not engaged in official acts in the temple; "or rather, we of the priesthood do not doubt, that the pyramids, at least the pair so nearly of a size and so close together, were builded before the deluge, which, according to our astrologers, took place under the dynasty of the demigods, about one thousand five hundred and forty years ago, when the world was nearly two thousand four hundred years old; but our books of mysteries give many more thousands of years! In the most ancient temple of Thoth, at Thebes, which is the true astronomical capital of the kingdom, as well as the ecclesiastical one, there is a tablet in the ceiling of the adytum, representing the configuration of the seven planets as they existed on the first day after the creation. This was the beginning of the world, and since that day the heavenly bodies have not stood thus again! Upon the walls beneath it is a *stele*, portraying their position at the time of the Noachic deluge. The arc of their celestial motion, between the creation and the deluge, being accurately measured in the progress of centuries, by astrologers of the houses of the mysteries, compared with the arc measured for one thousand years since the deluge, shows that the fixed stars, between the creation and the deluge, moved thirty spaces of the thousand years along the zodiac westward. That is, the arc of the zodiac was thirty times as large between the creation and deluge, as between the deluge and the end of a thousand years after it; while the seven planets changed their places in the same proportions of time and change. Hence, guided by the march of the heavenly bodies, they teach that thirty thousand years elapsed between the creation and the deluge; since it would take that time to change the configuration of the stars so greatly as to subtend so vast an arc as their precession drew along the zodiacal path! But, as I have said, the sacred books of the priests, who are governed only by the planetary constellations, aided by tradition, give the number of years I have previously stated."

"Do not the Egyptian astrologers," I asked, "give a period for a year of the heavens to make one revolution through the zodiac?"

"It is one of their mysteries. Finishing upon a chart the arc of precession, which they measure on the zodiac, they measure the whole circle it will sweep, and calculate a cycle or period of thirty-six thousand years, as the duration of one grand year of the universe!"

"As, then, thirty thousand years of this year of the stars passed before the deluge, if the astrologers are correct in their sidereal calculations," I remarked, "there are but four thousand and four hundred and fifty years to the end of the first celestial year of creation!"

"Which," said Luxora, "they teach will terminate time; and the earth will then be recreated, and there will be a new starry world, and the year of the universe will be doubled to seventy-two thousand years; and when twelve of these vast years are completed, the creation will be dissolved and all things return to nothing as before the beginning of time, and the souls of men will be absorbed in the Divine Essence!"

"You are remarkably well versed in astrology," I said to the noble-looking young women.

"We are priest's daughters," she answered; "and from our father we derive all our knowledge."

"Can you then," I asked, "explain to me one thing that has been alluded to in our conversation? I am desirous of knowing something about the phœnix, which I see even now represented, inlaid in ivory, upon this table of vases."

"I fear that I shall not be able, prince, to make you understand, what, I confess, I am not well informed upon. The phœnix has always been a mystery to me."

"I understand the bird," said Osiria, "to be the symbol of a star. But I have never fully comprehended it. I have doubts if there be such an extraordinary bird. Will you, father, gratify us and the Prince of Tyre at the same time?"

The kind and courteous hierarch, before replying, laid down a beautiful fishing-rod which he was arranging—it being a favourite pastime of his leisure to sit in the pavilion before his windows, and amuse himself by fishing in the oval lake that fills one of the areas of his palace, and around which runs a columnar arcade, in whose cool shade we take our walks for exercise in the heat of the day. And this amusement, my dear mother, is not only a favourite one with him, but with all Egyptian gentlemen; who also delight in hunting the gazelle and other animals—keeping for the purpose leashes of trained dogs, some of them very beautiful, and as swift as the winds. They are singularly fond of having dogs accompany them in their walks, and adorn them with gold or silver collars. The ladies also have pet dogs, chosen either for their beauty, or—odd distinction—for their peculiar ugliness. Luxora boasts a little dog, of the rare and admired Osirtasen breed, which is as beautiful and symmetrical as a gazelle, with soft, expressive eyes, and graceful movements; while Osiria prides herself on a pet animal, the ugliness of which, as it seems to me, is its only recommendation. Remeses has a noble, lion-like dog, that he admits into his private sitting-room, and has for his attendant at all times when he walks abroad. Nearly every lord has his hounds; and to own a handsome dog is as much a mark of rank, as is the slender acacia cane.

"The phœnix, according to the ancients," said the priest, "is a bird of which there exists but one specimen in the world. It comes flying from the east once in the course of six hundred and fifty-one years, many other birds with dazzling wings bearing it company. It reaches the City of the Sun about the time of the vernal equinox, where it burns itself upon the roof of the temple, in the fire of the concentrated rays of the sun as they are reflected from the golden shield thereon with consuming radiance. No sooner is it consumed to ashes, than an egg appears in the funeral pyre, which the heat that consumed the parent warms instantly into life, and out of it the same phœnix comes forth, in full plumage, and spreading its wings it flies away again, to return no more until the expiration of six hundred and fifty-one years!"

"This is a very extraordinary story," I said.

"It is," answered the high-priest; "yet it has a simple explanation."

"I should be gratified to hear it," I answered.

"Do you believe, dear father," asked Osiria, "there ever was such a bird?"

"I have seen it," answered the priest mysteriously. "But I will gratify your curiosity. The first recorded appearance of this phœnix was nineteen hundred and two years ago, in the reign of Sesostris, a king of the twelfth Egyptian dynasty."

"The Pharaoh from whom I am named," I said.

"How came you, O prince, to have an Egyptian name?" asked Luxora.

"The memory of Sesostris the Great was highly venerated by my father, and hence his selection of it for me; besides, I am related to the Phœnician kings."

I had no sooner made this unlucky confession, than the two sisters looked at their father, then interchanged glances, and appeared quite embarrassed. I at once reflected that the memory of the Phœnician dynasty is distasteful to the Egyptians; and that, by confessing my alliance with them, I had risked their good-will. But the surprise passed off instantly, for they were too well-bred to show any continued feeling, and the priest resumed,—

"The last appearance was six hundred years ago and in fifty-one years he will reappear, to consume himself in the burning rays of the sun."

"I hope I shall be alive to see it," said Osiria, with animation.

"This singular myth," pursued the hierarch, "signifies to us of the priests who are initiated into these astrological mysteries, nothing more than the transit of the planet Mercury across the disk of the sun. The fabulous bird, the phœnix, is an emblem of Mercury, as Osiris is of the sun, according to the teaching of the books of Isis."

"I perceive the whole truth now," I answered.

"What is it, my lord prince?" asked the sisters.

"There is but one planet Mercury, as there was but one phœnix. The City of the Sun, or the Temple of the Sun, on which the phœnix was said to consume himself, is simply the sun, or the house of the god Sun, in which Mercury, during his passage across the disk, may be said to be consumed by fire. As the phœnix consumes himself once every six hundred and fifty-one years, at the vernal equinox,—so say our Sabæan books, kept in the Temple of Hercules at Tyre,— Mercury once every six hundred and fifty-one years enters the flames of the sun on nearly the same days of the year! As the phœnix flies from the east westward to the City of the Sun, so the course of Mercury is from east to west athwart the sun. While the phœnix in its passage to the City of the Sun is attended by a flight of dazzling birds, so Mercury in its passage across the disk of the sun is accompanied by bright scintillating stars in the heavens around. As the phœnix came forth anew out of the flames which had consumed him to ashes, so Mercury, while in the direct line of the sun, is lost to the vision as if consumed, but, having crossed its disk, reappears and flies away on his course again, resuming all his former splendour! Is not this a full solution, my lord priest?" I asked

"You have well solved the riddle," he answered; "and I must compliment you on your knowledge of astrology, O prince. In Egypt we are acquainted with this science, but it is not expected of strangers. In all the years in which the phœnix, according to the 'Books of the Stars,' is said to have destroyed himself with fire in the City of On, Mercury has likewise performed his transits over the sun, according to the calculations of our hierogrammatists, whose duty it is to keep records of descriptions of the world, the course of the sun, moon, and planets, and the condition of the land of Egypt, and the Nile."

When I had expressed my thanks to the noble and intelligent priest, his wife, Nelisa, who entered a few moments before, said to him playfully,—

"What a beautiful mystery you have destroyed with your science and learning my lord! I have from a child delighted in the mysterious story of the phœnix."

"We have mysteries enough left in our mythology and astrology, my dear wife," he answered. "There is scarcely a deity of the land who is not in his origin a greater mystery than the phœnix. Around them all are clouds and mists, often impenetrable by the limited reason of man; and in many lands, as it was anciently in Egypt, the word for religion is 'mystery.'"

The hierarch was now summoned by the sound of a sistrum to enter the temple, with which his palace communicated—it being the hour of evening prayer and oblation. The young ladies prepared to ride in a beautiful chariot brought to the palace by their brother, a fine specimen of the young Egyptian noble; while the lady of the house left me to return and oversee her numerous servants in their occupation of making confections and pastry, and preparing fruits for a festivity that is to take place in the evening, I believe, in my honour; for, were I a son, I could not be more cordially regarded than beneath the hospitable roof of the hierarch of Memphis.

As I was proceeding along the corridor which leads past the "Hall of Books," I saw through the open door the stately and handsome Hebrew woman, Miriam. She was engaged in colouring, with cakes of the richest tints before her, a heading to a scroll of papyrus. Her noble profile was turned to my view. I started with surprise and a half exclamation, for I beheld in its grand and faultless outline the features of Remeses! How wonderful it is that he so strikingly resembles two, nay three, of this foreign race!—not only this woman, though much older than Remeses, and the venerable under-gardener Amram, but also a third Hebrew whom I have met under singular circumstances. I will defer, however, my dear mother, to another letter, the **account** of it, as well as of my interview with Miriam; for, hearing my exclamation, she looked up and smiled so courteously that I asked permission to enter and examine the work she was so skilfully executing **with** her pencil.

The hierarch, the lady Nelisa, and their daughters, Luxora **and** Osiria, desire to unite with me in my regards to you.

Your affectionate son,
SESOSTRIS.

LETTER XVIII.

CITY OF MEMPHIS, PALACE OF THE HIERARCH.

MY DEAR MOTHER,—

I HAVE received from the Prince Remeses a letter informing me of the arrival of each division of his army, chariots, horse, and footmen, with the fleets under the viceroy Mœris, at the city of the Thebaïd. They entered it, however, as conquerors, for the Ethiopian king had already taken possession of it with his advanced guard.

I will quote to you from the letter of the prince:—

"I trust, my dear Sesostris," he writes, "that you are passing your time both with pleasure and profit, in visiting places of interest in the valley of the Lower Nile, and in studying the manners and usages of the people. You will find the pyramids an exhaustless source of attraction. From the priests, who are the most intelligent and learned class in Egypt, you will **obtain** all the information respecting those mysterious monuments of the past, which is known, besides many legends.

"The idea of their antediluvian origin is by no means an unlikely one. As we travel down the past, at every epoch we find the pyramids uplifting their lofty heads into the skies! Still we move down the path of ages, and see the throne of the first mortal king overshadowed by their hoary tops! Further back, against their bases, beat the receding waves of the deluge; for, between the king of the first dynasty and the flood, there seems to be no interval in which they could have been upreared, even if there were time for a nation to rise and advance in power, civilization, art, and wealth, adequate to the product of such gigantic geometric works. Either our chronology is at fault, or the pyramids must have been constructed by the antediluvian demigods, and have outstood the strength of the surging seas which rolled over the earth. You will, however, no doubt, hear all that is to be said, and judge for yourself.

"My army is in fine order. You already have learned, by my courier to the queen, how the dark-visaged, barbaric King Occhoris entered Thebes the day of our arrival in the suburbs. Upon receiving intelligence that the van of my forces, which was cavalry, had just reached the sepulchres of the Pharaohs below the city, I pushed forward, joined them, and, at their head, entered the city; while the main body of the troops of the Ethiopian king was moving on from Edfu. But Occhoris had already been driven from his position in the palace of the Pharaohs, by an infuriated and insulted populace. The barbarian monarch, after entering the city without opposition, at the head of two hundred chariots, six hundred horse, and his gigantic body-guard of Bellardines, consisting of a thousand men in iron helmets, round shields, and heavy short-swords, in order to show his contempt of our national religion, here in what has been called both its cradle and its throne, commanded to be led into the temple of the sacred Bull, a wild African buffalo,—a bull of a species as ferocious as the lion,—and ordered him to be let loose against the god. The fierce animal charged upon him as he stood in the holy adytum with his curators, and, overthrowing him, gored him to death in a few moments. Thereupon the priests raised the wild cry of vengeance for sacrilege. It was caught up by the people, and borne from tongue to tongue through the city in a few moments of time. Fearless, indifferent to the arms of the soldiers, the three hundred and seventy priests of the temple, armed only with their sacrificial knives, rushed upon the barbarian and his guard. The Ethiopians rallied about their monarch, and for ten priests they slew, ten score filled their places. The floor of the temple became a battle-field. Occhoris, and the sixty men who entered the temple with him, formed themselves into a solid phalanx, facing their furious assailants, who seemed to think they could not die. Gaining at length the door, the king received reinforcements. But by this time the whole city was in an uproar and under arms, and the people, who feared Occhoris in the morning, and refused to oppose him, now knew no fear. The issue of this fearful combat was, that the sacrilegious king was forced to retire with the loss of two-thirds of his body-guard, and nearly every chariot and rider; for the avenging people with knives crept beneath the horses and stabbed them to death; while others, leaping upon horsemen and chariots, dragged them to the ground, and put them to death. Not less than four thousand of the citizens of Thebes perished in the act of pious vengeance. Before I entered the city I heard the cries, the shouts, the ringing of weapons, and the whole tumult of war; and, making my way over heaps of slain that lay in the great 'avenue of the gods,' I pursued the retiring monarch beyond the gates. He regained the head of his army, and came to a halt near the ancient temple of Amun on the Nile. My whole army are now in advance of Thebes, in order of battle, awaiting a threatened attack from the Ethiopian king. My head-quarters are at the palace of Amunophis I., from which he departed nearly a century ago to drive the foreign kings from Memphis. I felt a deep interest in being in the house of my great ancestor. I have also visited the palace of my father, the Prince of Thebes, who was slain, not long before my birth, in battle with the Ethiopians. I have paid a visit to his tomb; and as I stood gazing upon the reposing dead in the royal mausoleum hewn from the solid mountain, I wondered if his soul were cognizant that a son, whom he had never seen to bless with a father's benediction, was bending sorrowfully over the stone sarcophagus that held his remains.

"To-morrow we join battle with the barbaric king. From the tower of the pylon which looks towards the south, I see his vast army, with its battalion of elephants, its host of brazen chariots, its horsemen and footmen as numerous as the leaves. But I feel confident of victory. Prince Mœris has moved his galleys on the opposite side, in order to ascend secretly by night and gain the rear of the enemy, who are without boats. My chariots, some five hundred in number, have been crossed over in safety to this side, to co-operate with the Prince of Thebes. They are now drawn up in the wide, superb serpentine avenue, the 'sacred way' of Thebes, lined with sphinxes and statues which adorn this vast circle of temples to the gods.

"You shall hear from me after the battle. If we defeat and pursue Occhoris, we shall return to Memphis soon. If we are defeated and driven back upon Thebes—which the great God of battles forbid!—I know not how long the campaign will continue. I hope my mother, the queen, is well. Convey to her my most respectful and tender remembrances, and receive from me, beloved prince, the assurances of my personal regard and friendship.

"Remeses."

In the mean while, my dear mother, until I have further news from Prince Remeses, I will give you an account of the conversation I held with the papyrus-copier and decorator, Miriam, the Hebrewess.

"You are wonderfully skilled in the art." I said to her, as I surveyed the piece before her, which she said was the commencement of a copy of a funeral ritual for the priests of Athor.

"I have been many years engaged in transcribing," she answered, with modest dignity, without raising her eyes to my face.

"I have not seen you before in the palace, though I have often been in this hall," I said, feeling awakened in me an interest to learn more of the extraordinary people who toil for the crown of Egypt, and whose ancestors have been princes.

"I have been at Raamses for a few days. My mother was ill, and I hastened to her."

"I hope your return is a proof of her recovery," I said kindly.

"She raised her splendid eyes to my face, with a look in them of surprise. If I interpreted aright their meaning, it was, "Can this prince take any interest in the welfare of a Hebrew woman?" Seeing that my own eyes encountered hers with a look of friendly concern, she spoke, and said,—

"She is better."

Her voice had a mellow and rich cadence in it, wholly different from the low, silvery tones with which the Egyptian ladies speak.

"I rejoice with you," I said.

She slowly shook her superb head, about which the jet-black hair was bound in a profusion of braids. There were tones in her voice too, that again recalled Prince Remeses. Hence the secret of the interest that I took in conversing with her.

"Why do you shake your head?" I asked.

"Why should the Hebrew wish to prolong life?"

She said this in a tone of deep emotion, but continued her occupation, which was now copying a leaf of brilliantly-coloured hieroglyphic inscriptions into the sort of running-hand the Egyptians make use of in ordinary intercourse. There are three modes of tracing the characters of this system of writing; and scribes adopt one, which, while it takes the hieroglyph for its copy, represents it by a few strokes that often bear, to the uninitiated eye, no resemblance to the model. This mode the Hebrewess was making use of, writing it with ease and elegance.

"Life to you, in this palace, under such a gentle mistress as Osiria, cannot be bitter."

"I have no want. I am treated here as if I were not of the race of the Hebrews. But, my lord," she said, elevating slightly her noble-toned voice, though not raising her eyes, " I am not so selfish, believe me, as to have no thought beyond my own personal comfort. How can I be happy, even amid all the kindness I experience in this virtuous family, when my heart is oppressed with the bondage of my people? Thou art but a stranger in Egypt, O, prince,—for I have heard of thee and who thou art,—and yet thou hast seen and felt for my people!"

"I have, indeed, seen their misery and toil; but how didst thou know it?"

"From the venerable Ben Isaac, whose son Israel thou didst pity and relieve at the fountain of the shepherds." She said this gratefully and with feeling.

"Thou didst hear of this?"

"He was of my kinsfolk. They told me of your kindness with tears and blessings; for it is so unusual with our people to hear in Egypt the voice of pity, or behold a look of sympathy!"

"I hope the lad recovered," I said, feeling that her knowledge of that little incident had removed from between us the barrier which separates entire strangers. Besides, dear mother, it is impossible for me, a Syrian, to look upon the Hebrew people, who are also Syrians by descent from Abram, the Syrian prince, with Egyptian eyes and prejudices. They regard them as slaves, and look upon them from the position of the master. I never have known them as slaves, I am not their master, and I regard them, therefore, with interest and sympathy, as an unhappy Syrian people, who deserve a better fate, which I trust their gods have in store for them. Therefore, while an Egyptian would feel it a degradation, or at least infinite condescension, to converse familiarly with a Hebrew of either sex, I have no such inborn and inbred ideas. Miriam was in my eyes only a beautiful and dignified Syrian woman, in bondage. No doubt, if the proud and queenly Luxora had passed by, and discovered me in conversation with her, she would have marvelled at my taste; or have been displeased at an impropriety so unworthy of my position; for though, wheresoever I have seen Hebrews domesticated in families, I have observed the affability and kindness with which their faithful services are usually rewarded by those they serve, yet there cannot be a wider gulf between the realms of Osiris and Typhon, than between the Egyptian of rank and the Hebrew. The few thousand of the more refined and attractive of both sexes, who are to be found in palaces and the houses of nobles, are too limited in number to qualify the feeling of contempt with which the miserable millions of their brethren, who toil in the brick-fields south of On, between the Nile and the desert, and in other parts of Egypt, are universally regarded. Even the lowest Egyptian is deemed by himself above the best of the Ben Israels. What marvel, therefore, that the handsome, dark-eyed youths who serve as pages, and the beautiful brunettes who wait upon mistresses, have a sad and timid air, and wear a gentle, deprecating look, as if they were fully conscious of their degradation!

"He is well," Miriam answered, "and desires me to ask you (I pray you pardon the presumption!) if he may serve you?"

"I learn that a stranger cannot take a Hebrew into service," I answered.

"True. We are the servants of the Egyptians," she said sadly. "But the great Prince Remeses, son of Pharaoh's daughter, will suffer it if you ask him. Will you do this for the lad? Otherwise he will perish in the field for his spirit and strength are not equal to his tasks."

"The prince is absent, but I will ask the queen," I answered, happy to do so great a favour to the youthful Hebrew, in whom I felt a deep interest, inasmuch as it is our nature to feel kindly towards those for whom we have done offices of kindness.

"I thank you, and his father and he will bless you, O Prince of Tyre," she said, taking my hand and carrying it to her forehead, and then respectfully kissing it and as she did so, I saw a tear fall upon my signet finger.

"I feel much for your people," I said.

She continued her task in silence; but tears began so rapidly to rain down upon the papyrus, over which her head was bent, that she was compelled to turn her face away, lest she should spoil her work. After a few moments she raised her face, and said, with shining eyes,—

"Pardon me, my lord prince, but your few kind words, to which my ears are all unused, have broken up the sealed fountains of my heart. It is seldom that we children of Jacob hear the accents of sympathy, or find any one to manifest concern for us, when not personally interested in doing so."

At this moment, the sound of the sistrum before the sacred altar of the temple, fell upon my ears ; and, turning round to the east, I laid my hands across my breast, and bowed my head low in worship, it being the signal that the hierarch was offering incense and libations.

To my surprise, the Hebrew woman pursued her work, and remained with her head, as I thought, more proudly elevated than before.

" Do you not worship ? " I asked, with surprise.

" Yes, the One God," she answered, with dignity.

I started with surprise, that a bondwoman should declare so openly and familiarly, the mystery which even Remeses scarcely dared to receive, and which I had accepted with hesitation and awe.

" How knowest thou there is One God ? " I said, regarding her with deepening interest.

" From our fathers."

" Do all your people worship the One Unity ? "

" Not all," she answered, a shadow passing across her queenly brow. " The masses of our enslaved nation know only the gods of Egypt. They adore Apis with servility. They are the first to hail the new-found calf-god, if by chance he be found in the nome where they toil. They are ignorant of the True God, and degraded by their long servitude (for we are all born in bondage—*all !*); they worship the gods of their masters ; and pots of flesh which are sent from the sacrifices by the proselyting priests, as bribes to make our chief men bow down to Osiris and Apis, are temptations enough to cause these elders daily to deny the God of their father Abraham. Jacob and Joseph are become Egyptians, and the knowledge of the undivided God is preserved only by a few, who have kept sacred the traditions of our fathers."

This was said with deep feeling, and with an expression of anger mingled with sorrow.

" What do you worship ? " I asked.

" The God of Abraham."

" Abram was a Syrian prince," I said. " He must have worshipped fire, and the sun."

" In his youth he did. But the great Lord of heaven revealed Himself to him as One God, and thenceforth he knew and worshipped only the Lord of heaven and earth."

" How knowest thou mysteries which are approached with the greatest awe by the most sacred priests ? "

" Abraham, our father, gave to Isaac, his son, the knowledge of One God, God *of* gods !—above, beyond, higher, and over the fabulous Osiris, Apis, Thoth, Horus, and all other so-called deities. Isaac left the knowledge with his son Jacob. From Jacob it descended to his twelve sons princes by birth ; and we are their progeny ; and though in bondage, and tempted to bow down ourselves to the gods of Egypt, yet there remain a few in Israel who have never bowed the knee to the black statue of Apis, or crossed the breast before the golden image of Osiris."

" What is the name of the One God, you, and minds like yours, worship ? " I asked.

"He is called the One Lord; not only Lord of the sun, but Lord of the lords of the sun. He is One in His being, One in power, and yields not His glory and dominion to others. Such is the tradition of our faith."

"How hast thou resisted the worship of Egypt?" I asked. "Hast thou not from a child been an inmate of this palace?"

"Yes, my lord prince. But my mother taught me early the truths of the faith of Abraham, and I have held firmly to the worship of my fathers, amid temptations, trials, and menaces. But all the gods of Egypt have not turned me aside from the One God; and my heart tells me that in Him, and Him alone, I live, and move, and have my being!"

I regarded this noble-looking bondwoman with surprise and profound respect. Here, from the lips of a female, a slave, had I heard the mystery of God made known, by one who worshipped boldly the Divine Unity, which the wisdom of Remeses shrunk from certainly acknowledging; but felt after only with hope and desire.

"Prince," she said, looking up into my face, and speaking with feeling, "dost thou believe in these gods of Egypt?"

I confess, dear mother, I was startled by the question. But I replied smiling,—

"I worship the gods of my own land, Miriam."

"Are they idols?"

"What is an idol?"

"An image or figure in stone, or wood, or metal, or even painted with colours, to which divine homage is paid,—visible representations of the invisible."

"In Phœnicia we worship the sun, and also honour certain gods."

"Then thou art not above the Egyptians. I saw thee bend in attitude of prayer at the sound of the sistrum. Dost thou believe that the sacred bull is God,—who made thee, and me, and nature, and the sun and stars, and upholds the universe? Dost thou believe Apis or Mnevis at On, or Amun at Thebes, either or all of them, GOD?"

"Thou art a wonderful woman!" I exclaimed. "Art thou not a priestess of the Hebrew people?"

"Not a priestess. I simply believe in the unity of God, which you ought to believe in; for thou art open and ingenuous, and not afraid of truth. A priestess I am not, yet in my family and tribe is preserved sacredly the knowledge of the God who spake from heaven to our ancestor, the Syrian. Canst thou believe, O prince, that a bull is God?" she asked again, almost authoritatively.

"No, I do not," I answered without disguise.

"Dost thou believe that all minor deities will ultimately be lost in one God?"

"I do, most certainly."

"Then worship Him! Thou art a prince. I hear thou wilt become a king. What would be your opinion of your subjects, and ambassadors of other lands also, if, instead of presenting petitions to you, they should offer them to your grand-chamberlain, your royal scribe, your chief butler, or chief baker,—mistaking them ignorantly for you?"

I made no reply, dear mother. The argument was irresistible. It will be long, I feel, before I recognize in Apis, or in any statue of stone or any figure of a god, the One God, whose existence Remeses first hinted at to me, and which the Hebrew has made me believe in; for my own reason responds to the mighty truth! Do not fear, my dear mother, that I shall return to Tyre an iconoclast; for I cannot set up a faith in the One God in my realm, until I have His existence established by infallible proofs. In my own heart I may believe in Him and adore Him, whom my reason sees through and beyond all material images of Himself; but, with Remeses, I must secure a foundation for this new faith, before I overturn the ancient fabric of our mythology of many gods.

She resumed her work. It was colouring the wings of an image of the sun, which, encircled by an asp, his head projected, and with extended wings, adorned the beginning of one of the leaves. The sun was overlaid with gold; the asps were painted green, and brown, and gold, while the feathers of the wide wings were blue, orange, purple, silver, and gilt. It was an exquisitely beautiful picture.

"That is a god," I said, after watching for a time her skilful pencil; "and yet you design and colour it."

"The potter is not responsible for the use that his vases are put to. The slave must do her mistress's work. I fulfil my task and duty by obedience to the lords who are over me. Yet this is not a god. It is the emblem of Egypt. The eternal sunshine is symboled in this golden disk. The entwining asp is the winding Nile, and the two wings represent Upper and Lower Egypt, extending along the river. It is an emblem, not a god. In Egypt, no temple is erected to it. It is used only in sculpture and over pylons of temples. Yet," she added, "were it a god, I could not refuse to depict it. Commanded to do, I obey. The condition of my people is one of submission: if a king rules well, he is approved; if a slave obeys well, he also is approved."

At this point of our interesting conversation, I saw the noble-looking, grey-bearded Prince of Uz pass along the corridor, preceded by the page of the reception-room. Seeing me, he stopped and said with benignity and courtesy,—

"Prince of Tyre, it is a pleasure for me to meet with you here! I am about to leave Egypt for Damascus, and learn from her majesty, the good queen, that you have a galley which goes in a few days from Pelusium to Tyre. I have come hither, knowing you to be a guest of my friend the high-priest, to ask permission to sail in her. I have but a small retinue, as my caravan has already gone through Arabia Deserta, on its way to Upper Syria. I take with me but my secretary, scribe, cup-bearer, armour-bearer, courier, and ten servants."

I assured the venerable prince that it would give me the greatest pleasure to surrender to him the cabin and state-chamber of your galley, my dear mother. And he will be the bearer of a letter from me presenting him to you. I have already spoken of him in my account of my first banquet with the queen. He is a prince, wise, good, virtuous, and greatly honoured, not only for his wisdom, but for the patience, like a god's, with which he has endured the most wonderful sufferings. At one time he lost sons, daughters, servants, flocks, herds, houses, treasures, and health: yet he neither cursed the gods nor sought escape in death. In reward for his patience and endurance, the heavenly powers restored to him all things; and his name is now but another term for sacred submission to the divine decrees.

Having courteously thanked me for granting his wish, he looked closely at the Hebrew woman, and then said to her,—

"Is it true that thy people worship the One God?"

"It is true, O prince!" she answered modestly.

"This is the true wisdom of life, to know the Almighty, and be admitted into the secrets of the Holy One! Behold! happy is the man who attaineth to this knowledge. The world gropes in darkness in the daytime, and stumbles in the noon-day as in the night, not seeing the pathway to God. Blessed art thou, O daughter of the wise Abram, the princely Isaac, the good Jacob—the three great Syrian princes of the East—in that thou knowest, thou and thy people, the traditions of thy fathers! Can a man by searching find out God? Can the priests by their wisdom find out the Almighty to perfection? Their light is darkness! but the sons of Israel Ben Abram have the knowledge of the Most High, and are wiser than Egypt!"

Miriam regarded the majestic old man with eyes expressive of wonder and joy. They seemed to ask, "Who art thou?" He understood their interrogating expression, and said,—

"Daughter of Abram, offspring of wise kings, who walked with the One God, who found Him and came even unto His seat, when darkness covered the hearts of all men, I also worship GOD! I am of the family of the King Melchisedec, who knew Abram thy father! They both had knowledge of the mystery of the Divine Unity! They were friends, and worshipped God, the Almighty, when the understanding of men knew Him not and denied the God that is above, and the spirit of God who made them, and the breath of the Almighty that gave them life. Our God speaketh everywhere, yet man perceiveth it not, neither doth he know His voice! Touching the Almighty—who can find Him out? The world lacketh wisdom, and is devoid of understanding, to bow down to the work of their own hands, and see not Him who laid the foundations of the earth, who hath stretched His line upon the heavens, and to whom all the morning stars sang together at their creation, and all the sons of God shouted for joy!"

The venerable Syrian uttered these words with an air of inspiration. His eyes were fixed inquiringly upon my face, as if he directed his speech to me alone.

"I would know the God that you and the Hebrews know and worship," I said, with emotion. "I no longer recognize Deity in stone and metal, nor God in Osiris and Apis, nor the Creator of all in the sun, who is but a servant to light the world."

When I had thus spoken, the eyes of the Hebrew woman beamed with pleasure, and the Prince of Uz, whose name is Ra-Iub, or Job, took my hand in his and said with a smile of benignity,—

"Thou art not far from the house of Truth, O Prince of Tyre! May the Almighty instruct thee, and He who ordained the ordinances of heaven enlighten thee! He alone is the Almighty! Can Apis, or Io, or Adonis, the gods in whom you believe, give rain and dew, the ice and the hoary frost? Can they bind up the wintry seas of Colchis, so that men may walk upon the frozen face of the deep, as upon marble? Can Apis or Bel-Phegor bind the sweet influences of Pleiades, or loose the bands of Orion? Can they bring forth Mazzaroth in his season, guide Arcturus with his sons, and hang Aldebaran and Sirius in the firmament? Can they send forth the lightning, and give to thunder its voice? My son, there is a spirit in man, and the inspiration of the Almighty giveth understanding to them that seek it. Behold, God is great and we know Him not, neither can the number of His years be searched out; yet whosoever prayeth unto Him, He will be favourable unto, and will deliver his soul, and his life shall see the light of the living! Deny not, my son, the God that is above!

"But where, O wise man of God, is the Almighty to be found, and whither shall my understanding go out to find the place of His throne?" I asked, feeling like a child at his feet, under the power of his words. "I am weary of idols," I continued, catching the spirit of his speech, "and with worshipping myths born of the ignorance of man. Where shall the Maker be found? Show me His seat, O man of God, that I may fall down before His footstool!"

"God is everywhere, but His throne is in thy heart, His wisdom has no price, neither can it be gotten for gold. The depth says, It is not in me! The sea saith, It is not with me! It cannot be weighed in the balance; nor can it be valued with the gold of Ophir; and the exchange of it shall not be jewels of fine gold. The topaz of Ethiopia shall not purchase it, nor shall the coral and pearls of the isles of the sea equal it; for the price of the wisdom of God is above rubies! The fear of the Lord that is wisdom, and lo, the Almighty is found of them who humbly seek Him. An idol, my son, is a snare, and the false gods of the world lead to destruction; they have eyes but see not, ears but hear not, feet but walk not, hands which bless not, mouths that speak no wisdom! But God is the Maker and Father of His creatures, and concealeth His glory in the secret places of His heaven; yet the pure in heart shall find Him, and they that plead with Him shall not be mocked. He will come unto thee, and abide with thee, and thou shalt know the Almighty as a father. I have tried Him and He has proved me, and though He sorely afflicted me He did not forsake me, and in the end came to me with more abundant honour and blessing."

"Will God pardon transgression?" I asked, giving utterance in this brief question to a thought of my heart that no mythology could answer.

"There is no promise to man, that transgression against a sacred and sinless God can be forgiven. We must hope in His mercy at the end! I have prayed, in my affliction, O prince, for a Day's man—one to stand between me and the Almighty, to plead for me! My heart hath yearned for One; and I feel that the yearning of my heart is a prophecy."

"Dost thou believe a **Day's man, or** mediator, will be given by the great God to man, to intercede for transgressors against His holiness?" I asked, between sweet hope and trembling fear.

"We have a tradition that has overleaped the flood and come down to us, that One will yet stand between earth and heaven to plead with the Creator for His creatures, and that the Almighty will hear His voice."

"Is not this feebly typified in Horus, the son of Osiris, who presents the souls of the dead and acts as their friend?" I asked.

"Without doubt," answered the Prince of Uz. "This belief is found shadowed forth in all faiths of every land. But I must not detain you, my lord prince."

I then accompanied the white-haired Prince of Uz to the galley in which he had crossed the Nile, and, taking leave of him, promised to see him ere he sailed.

Believe me, dear mother, there is but One God, and that an idol is nothing on earth, not even the God-created sun. I have since had another long conversation with the Prince of Uz, and he has convinced me that in worshipping images and attributes we offend the High God, and degrade our own natures.

Farewell, dear mother.

Your devoted son,
SESOSTRIS.

LETTER XIX.

CITY OF ON.

MY DEAREST MOTHER,—

IT is many weeks since my last letter was written. The interval has been occupied by me in visiting all places of interest in Lower Egypt, previous to my voyage up the Nile, to the kingdom of the Thebaid. But the intelligence that your last letter contains, of the misunderstanding arising between you and the King of Cyprus, and your fear that war may ensue, will compel me to abandon my tour to the Cataracts, and return to Tyre, unless the next courier brings more pacific news. But I trust that the wisdom and personal influence of your ambassador, Isaphris, will result in an amicable termination of the difficulty. I have no doubt that the haughty King of the Isle will make due concessions for his treatment of your shipwrecked merchantmen, when your ambassador disclaims all intention, on the part of your majesty, of planting an invading colony in any part of his shores, and assures him that the vessels, which he supposed brought a company of Phœnicians to occupy his soil, were driven thither when bound for Carthage and distant Gades. But should he refuse to release your subjects and to restore their vessels and goods, war would inevitably ensue, and I will hasten home to conduct it in person. Do not delay sending me the earliest intelligence by a special galley. Until I hear from you, I shall linger in Lower Egypt.

Since writing the foregoing, dear mother, I have heard the most important intelligence from the seat of war in Ethiopia ; and what is more, that the Prince Remeses is even now on his return to Memphis, a conqueror ! The despatches brought by the courier state that four weeks ago the army of Egypt engaged Occhoris, beyond the gates of Thebes, and after a severe battle, in which the chariots and horse were engaged, he was forced to retreat ; that he gained a new position, and fortified himself, but was dislodged from it, and finally routed in the open plain, he himself being taken prisoner, with most of his chief captains ; while a great spoil in treasures, camp-equipage, elephants, camels, and horses, besides captives innumerable, enriched the victors. This news has gladdened the heart of Queen Amense, and relieved her mind from the great anxiety that has oppressed it ever since the departure of Remeses, lest he should lose his life in the campaign, as his father had done before him. But, without a wound, he returns triumphant, leading his enemy captive at the wheels of his war-chariot. The city is excited with joy, and in all the temples, ascending incense and bleeding sacrifices, together with libations and oblations, bear testimony to the universal gratitude of the nation at the defeat of the hereditary foe of the kingdom.

I will for a time delay this letter, that I may witness the scenes in the city and behold the rites for victory, which, I am told, will be most imposing, especially in the temples of Apis and of Vulcan

ISLAND AND PALACE OF RHODA.

Two weeks have elapsed since I laid down my pen, dearest mother. In the interval I have been too much occupied to resume it, but do so now with matter of the deepest interest to communicate. Remeses has returned. Two days ago he entered Memphis in warlike triumph. On hearing of his approach, I hastened to meet him three days' journey up the Nile. When we met, he embraced me as a brother, with expressions of joy ; but the first question he put to me was,—

"The queen—my mother, Sesostris, is she well?"

"Well, and happy at your victories," I answered.

"And your royal mother also, the Queen Epiphia, how fared she when last you heard from her ?"

"In good health, save her wish to see me," I answered.

Thus, dear mother, did this noble prince, amid all the splendour of his victories, first think of his mother and mine ! It is this filial piety which is one of the most eminent traits of his lofty and pure character ; and where love for a mother reigns supremely in the heart, all other virtues will cluster around it.

I found Remeses descending the river in a hundred-oared galley, to which I was conveyed by a barge which he sent for me on recognizing me. It was decorated with the insignia of all the divisions of his army. Behind it came two galleys containing the prisoners of rank, who were bound in chains upon the deck. The Ethiopian king was in the galley with Remeses, who courteously let him go free in the cabin, where he was served by his conqueror's own cup-bearer. Further in the rear came the fleet, their parti-coloured green, orange, blue, and scarlet sails, and the bronzed and gilded heads of hawks, eagles, wolves, lions, and ibises upon the topmasts, presenting a grand and brilliant spectacle. Ever and anon, a loud, wild shout would swell along the water from the victorious troops. One half of the fleet had been left in the Thebaid country with Prince Mœris, who intended to invade the interior of Ethiopia and menace its capital.

You may imagine, dear mother, that Remeses had many questions to ask and answer, as well as I. I drew from him a modest narrative of his battles; but he spoke more freely of the brilliant courage of Prince Mœris than of his own acts. After we had sat in the moonlight, upon the poop of his galley, conversing for several hours, I asked permission to see his royal captive, who I fancied was some wild savage chief, with the hairy head and neck of a lion, and the glaring eyes of a wolf. When I expressed my opinion to Remeses, he smiled and said,—

"I will send to him and ask if he will receive me and the Prince of Tyre; for he has heard me make mention of you."

"You Egyptians treat your captives with delicate courtesy," I said, "to send to know if they will receive you."

"I fear such is not our custom. Captives taken in war by our soldiers are, I fear, but little better off than those of other conquering armies; yet I have done all that is possible to alleviate their condition, and have forbidden unnecessary cruelty, such as tying their arms in unnatural positions, and dragging them in long lines at the rear of running chariots! If you see the army on shore, you will find that it is hard to teach the Egyptian soldier mercy towards a captive foe."

I regarded the prince with silent admiration. "How is it," I asked of myself, "that this man is in advance of all his predecessors and before his age in virtue?"

"His Majesty will see the Prince of Tyre and also his conqueror," were the words which the messenger brought to Remeses.

Descending a flight of steps, we advanced along a second deck, and then passing the door leading to the state-cabins, we descended again, and came to the range of apartments occupied by the governor of the rowers and the chief pilot. The latter had vacated his room to the royal captive. Upon entering, reclining on a couch of leopards' skins spread in the moonlight, which shone broadly in upon the floor through the columns that supported the deck, I beheld a young man, not more than my own age. His features were remarkable. His nose was slightly aquiline, his forehead high and commanding, his brows arched and delicate as a woman's, beneath which were the blackest and largest eyes I ever beheld, and which seemed to emit a burning splendour. His finely-formed mouth was almost voluptuous in its fulness and expression; yet I could perceive a slight nervous contraction of the under-lip, as if he were struggling between shame and haughty indifference, when he beheld us. His chin was without beard. His black locks were braided and bound up by a fillet of gold, studded with jewels. His helmet, which was of beaten gold, lay by his side, dented with many a stroke of sword and battle-axe; and I saw that a wound upon his left temple corresponded to one of these indentations. His hands were very small, and of a nut-brown colour (as was his complexion), and covered with massive rings. A collar, rich with emeralds, encircled his neck, from which was suspended an amulet of agate, and a little silver box containing a royal charm. He was dressed in a gaudy but rich robe of needlework, which was open in front, and displayed a corselet and breastplate of the finest steel, inlaid with gold. His small feet were bare, save a light sandal of gilded gazelle-leather. Altogether he was as elegant and fine-looking a barbaric prince as one would care to behold, dear mother, and not at all the monster in aspect I had pictured him : yet I am well convinced that in that splendid form lie powers of endurance which make him respected by the barbarians he commands ; and that within those fierce eyes blazes a soul, as fiery as any barbaric prince requires ; while the firm expression of his mouth, at times, betrayed a resolved and iron will, with which no one of his subjects would willingly come into antagonism.

He half rose gracefully from his recumbent attitude, and said with an indolent yet not undignified air, and in good Koptic, as it is spoken in the Thebaïd,—

"Welcome, Prince of Tyre ! I am sorry I cannot extend to you the hospitality you merit. You see my kingdom is somewhat limited ! As for you, O Prince of Egypt, you have a right to command ; I need not ask you to be seated or recline." Then, turning to me again, "I have heard of Tyre. You are a nation of merchants who cover the great sea with caravans of galleys, and plant your sandals in all lands. But you have not yet had Ethiopia beneath them."

"Our commerce embraces even your own country's productions, O king !" I answered. "I have seen in the mart of Tyre chœnixes of gold-dust, ostrich-feathers, dried fruits and skins, vermilion, ebony, ivory, and even baboons, apes, and leopards. In return we send you our purples."

"That is the name of Tyre, is it not,—the city of purple-cloth ?" he said interrogatively, and with a pointed sneer. "Ethiopia signifies the land of warriors—children of the sun."

I could not help smiling at his vanity. Remeses did not say anything. The king then added pleasantly,—

"I have no quarrel with thee, O Tyre ! Receive this ring—that is, if the great Remeses do not regard all I possess, as well as myself, his spoil—receive it in token that we are at peace."

As he spoke, he drew from his thumb a jewel of great price, and, taking my hand, placed it upon my thumb, without looking to see whether Remeses approved or no.

After a brief interview I left his presence, and soon retired to my state-room. Remeses insists upon my retaining the ring, which, in truth, the Ethiopian king, being a captive, had no right to dispose of. Remeses says that he displayed the most daring courage and marvellous generalship in battle ; and that, though young, and apparently effeminate, he inherits all the fierce, barbaric spirit of his ancestor, Sabaco I., and of his uncle, Bocchiris the Great, and third of the name.

At length arrived at the Island of Rhoda, Remeses hastened to embrace his mother, and to render to her an account of his expedition. The next day, preparations were made to receive the vast and victorious army, which had been slowly marching towards the capital, along the western bank of the river. They entered the plain of the pyramids on the same night, column succeeding column in a long line, attended by an interminable train of captives, and by waggons, cars, and chariots laden with spoils of arms, treasures, goods, and military stores. Having encamped on their former ground, they awaited the signal to move towards the city in triumphal procession.

The following morning the queen made her appearance at the head of the great square, in front of the temple of Apis. She was arrayed in her royal robes, and seated in a state-chariot of ivory, inlaid with gold, drawn by four white horses driven abreast, richly caparisoned, and with ostrich-plumes nodding on their heads. Attended by a splendid retinue of the lords of her palace, she took a position near the pylon, surrounded by her body-guard, in their glittering cuirasses of silver, and bearing slender lances in their right hands. The lords of the realm were ranged, in extended wings, on either side of her chariot —the whole presenting a strikingly beautiful spectacle.

When all was arranged, from the portals of the vast temple, headed by the hierarch in full dress, issued a procession of four hundred priests, a shining host, with golden tiaras, and censers of gold, and crimson vestments. Other sacred processions came advancing along all the streets, headed by their chiefs, each escorting the god of their temple in a gorgeous shrine, blazing with the radiance of precious stones.

Prince Remeses, attended by the governor of the city, the twenty one rulers of the departments thereof, and by all dignitaries, of whatever office, in their sumptuous robes and badges of rank, had already departed from the city to meet the army, which, headed by its generals, was in full motion. They came on in columns of battalions, as if marching through an enemy's country, and with all the pomp of war—their battle-banners waving, and their bands of music sounding. Instead of accompanying Remeses, I remained, by her request, near the queen. The towers of the pylones, the roofs of temples, the colonnades of palaces, terraces, house-tops—every vantage-point—were crowded thickly with spectators.

At length the voice of trumpets, faint and far off, broke the silence of expectation. Nearer and louder it was heard, now rising on the breeze, now gradually dying away; but soon other instruments were heard: the cymbals, the drum, the pipe and the cornet from a hundred bands poured upon the air a martial uproar of instruments, which made the blood bound quicker in every pulse. All eyes were now turned in the direction of the entrance to the grand causeway of the pyramids, and in a few moments, amid the answering clangour of the brazen trumpets of the queen's guards, a party of cavalry, shining like the sun, dashed into sight.

Their appearance was hailed by the vast assemblage of spectators with acclamations. Then came one hundred and seventy priests abreast, representing the male deities of Memphis, each attired like the image of his god—an imposing and wonderful spectacle; as in it Horus was not without his hawk-head, nor Thoth his horns and globe. Anubis displayed the head of a jackal, and Osiris held the emblems of his rank. These were followed by the high-priest of On, before whom was borne the shield of the sun, resting upon a car carried by twenty-four men, representing the hours. Following these were one thousand priests—a hundred in line—chanting, with mighty voice, the song of victory to the gods. They were succeeded by a battalion of cavalry, the front of which filled the whole breadth of the avenue. It advanced in solid column, till four thousand horsemen, in varied armour and arms, had entered the immense quadrangle. Now burst out afresh the clang of martial bands, and alone in his state-chariot, drawn by three black steeds, appeared the Prince of Egypt, standing erect upon the floor of his car. He was in full armour, and so splendid was his appearance, so majestic his aspect, that he was hailed with a thunder of voices as conqueror! Leaving the golden-hued reins loosely attached to the hilt of his sword, he suffered his proudly-stepping horses freely to prance and curvet, yet held them obedient to the slightest gesture of his hand. On each side of their heads walked three footmen. Behind him came his war-chariot of iron, from which he had fought in battle on the Theban plains. The horses were led by two lords of Egypt, and it was empty, save that it held his battered shield, emptied quiver, broken lances, the hilt of his sword, and his dented helmet—mute witnesses of his presence in the heat of battle. Behind the chariot was a guard of honour, consisting of a brave soldier out of every company in the army. But close to it, his wrists locked together with a massive chain of gold, which was attached to the axle of the war-chariot, walked the captive King of Ethiopia. His step was proud and defiant, and a constant smile of contempt curled his lip, as he saw the eyes of the spectators bent upon him, and heard their shouts of hostile joy on beholding him. He moved, the king in heart, though bound in hand. Over his shoulders hung a lion's skin as a royal mantle, but his feet were bare. Behind him came a solid front of chariots, which, line behind line, rolled into the square, until nearly three thousand war-cars had entered, and moved, with all the van of the vast warlike procession, towards the great pylon, before which, in chariot, stood the Queen of Egypt; for, as soon as the head of the column came in sight, she had risen to her feet to receive her returning army.

When Remeses came before her, he turned his horses towards her and remained at her side. Past them marched first the foot-soldiers. To the sound of drums and the tramp of ten thousand sandals, they wheeled into the arena of temples, elevating their war-hacked symbols, each man laden with his spoil. Then it was that a company of sacred virgins, issuing from the temple of Athor, each with a silver star upon her brow, all clad in white, and bearing branches of flowers, green palm-branches, ivy, and lotus leaves, cast them before the army, and sang with beautiful voices the hymn of the Conqueror. As they passed, the priests, with censers, waved incense towards them, and others sprinkled sacred water in the path of the battle-worn warriors. The soldiers responded to the hymn of the maidens with a loud chorus that rent the skies as they marched and sang.

When half the army had defiled, there came a procession of Ethiopian cars and waggons, drawn by captured oxen, and laden with trophies. Upon one was piled scores of shields, another was filled with helmets, a third bristled with spears, and a fourth was weighed down by cuirasses and swords. After many hundreds of these had passed —for the whole Ethiopian army was destroyed and their possessions captured—came chariots, heavy with chests containing gold, and silver, and bronze vessels; others glaring with ivory tusks; others full of blocks of ebony. Five royal elephants, with their castles and keepers, and a troop of camels, laden with treasures and mounted by their wild-looking guides, preceded a body of horse escorting the purple pavilion of the captive king—a gorgeous yet barbaric edifice of ivory frames, covered with silk and fringed with gold. Next came a painted car containing his wives, all of whom were closely veiled, and followed by a train of royal servants and slaves.

Bringing up the rear of the immense procession was another large body of horse, at the head of a long column of captives, twelve thousand in number—the disarmed and chained soldiers of the defeated monarch. Such a spectacle of human misery, such an embodiment of human woe!—how can I depict the scene, my mother? Perhaps when I am older, and have seen more of war than I have, I may feel less sympathy at a sight so painful, and be more indifferent to the necessary horrors of this dread evil.

Their features denoted them to be of a race very different from the Egyptian. They were slender and tall, with swarthy, but not black, faces like the Nubians—showing more of the Oriental than the African in their physiognomy. Their long hair hung half-way down the back, and they were dressed in costumes as various as the tribes which composed the army of Occhoris.

These captives marched in parties of from one to two hundred each —some linked by the wrists to a long connecting chain passing along the line; others chained two and two by the hands, and with shackled feet, were led by their captors. Many of them were confined to a long iron bar, by neck-collars, eight and ten abreast, each compelled to step together, and sit or rise at the same moment, or be subjected to dislocation of the neck. Several of the most unmanageable were tied with their hands high above their heads, in the most painful positions; while other wretches were so cruelly bound that their arms met behind in the most unnatural manner. There was a long chain of Nubian and Southern Arabian soldiers so bound, who writhed in agony as they were forced onward in the march. After these came hundreds of women and children, the latter naked and led by the hand, or carried by their mothers in baskets slung behind by a belt carried across the forehead. Finally, when these had passed the queen, who humanely ordered those so unnaturally bound to be relieved, the rear division of the army came tramping on, with symbols aloft, and drums beating, and trumpets blowing.

At length, this vast army of nearly one hundred thousand men, including chariots, horsemen, and foot-soldiers, had marched past before the queen, receiving her thanks and smiles, and the flowers that were showered upon them from thousands of fair hands. As they moved on, they wheeled in column, and gradually filled up the whole area of the vast quadrangle, save the space in front of the pyramidal gateway, where the queen and Remeses stood in their chariots.

At this juncture, the high-priest of On—a man of venerable aspect —amid the profoundest silence, advanced before them, and thus addressed Prince Remeses :—

"Mighty and excellent prince and lord of worlds, son of the queen, and upholder of the kingdoms of the earth, may the gods bless thee and grant thee honour and prosperity ! Thou hast led the armies of Misr to battle, and conquered. Thou hast brought down the pride of Ethiopia, and placed the crown of the South underneath thy foot. Thou hast fought, and overthrown, and taken captive the enemy of Egypt, and the scourge of the world. Lo, chained he walks at thy chariot-wheels ! his soldiers are captives to thy sword, and his spoil is in thy hand ! By thy courage in battle, thou hast saved Eygpt from desolation, filled her borders with peace, and covered her name with glory. Let thy power, henceforth, be exalted in the world like the sun in the heavens, and thy glory and virtues only be equalled by those of the sacred deities themselves ! "

Remeses, with the gentle dignity and modesty which characterize him, replied to this eulogistic address of the Egyptian pontiff. The queen then embraced him before the whole army, which cried, " Long live our queen ! Long live Remeses our general ! " All the while Oc- choris stood by the wheel of the chariot to which he was chained, his arms folded, and his bearing as proud as that of a caged lion. He did not even deign to look upon the queen, whom he had never before beheld ; and seemed to be above, or below, all manifestation of curiosity. Self-reliance, fearlessness, immobility, characterized him.

Preparations having already been made for a national thanksgiving, the queen and Remeses descended from their chariots, and led a procession consisting of the priest of On, the high-priest of Apis, the priest of Memphis, hierophants and chief priests from each of the thirty-eight or forty nomes, and several hundreds of ecclesiastics in magnificent dresses. This august procession entered the great temple of Pthah. Here, after an imposing invocation, offerings from the queen to the presiding deity, and also to Mars—whose statue was present—were made in recognition of their presence with the victorious army, and as an acknowledgment that it was by their special favour and intercession that the victory had been obtained.

This done, Remeses, in a formal manner, addressed the priest of the temple, presenting to the deity all the prisoners, and the spoil taken with them. As the vast army could not enter the temple, each captain of fifty and of a hundred was present for his own men. The high-priest then went forth upon the portico of the temple, and on an altar there, in the presence of the whole army, offered incense, meat-offerings, and libations.

All these customs and rites being ended, the army once more commenced its march and, passed through the city, and beyond the pyramid of Cheops' daughter to the plain of Libya, where Osirtasen used to review his armies. There they pitched their camp, prior to being posted and garrisoned in different parts of Egypt,—ready again to be summoned, at three days' notice, to go forth to war.

The captives, being delivered up to the authorities, were at once put to labour in the service of the queen, and are already engaged in building temples, cutting canals, raising dykes and embankments, and other public and state works. Some were purchased by the nobles; and the women, both Nubian and white, were distributed among the wealthy and noble families in the city. The Hebrew is the only captive or servant in Egypt who cannot be bought and sold. Those who have them in their houses do not own them, for, as a nation, they belong to the crown; but the queen's treasurer is paid a certain tribute or tax for their service, and must restore them whenever the queen commands them to do so.

The King of Ethiopia, himself, after having been led through the city at the chariot-wheel of his conqueror, was sent to the royal prison, there to await his fate, which hangs upon the word of the queen.

It is possible he may be redeemed by his own nation with a vast ransom-price; but if not, he will probably pass his days a captive, unless he consents to a proposition, which will be made to him by the prince, for recovering his liberty—namely, the surrender of the northern half of his kingdom to Egypt, in order that he may be permitted to reign over the remainder. As half a kingdom is far better than none, any other monarch would probably acquiesce; but the spirit of this king (whose looks and movements irresistibly make me think of a Nubian leopard) is so indomitable and proud, that I believe he would rather die a prisoner in a dungeon than live a king with half a sceptre.

This letter, dear mother, has been written at three or four different sittings, with a greater or less interval of time between them. It was my intention to have given you, before closing it, some account of a meeting which I had with a remarkable Hebrew, whose resemblance to Remeses is, if possible, more striking than that of Miriam the papyrus writer, or of Amram the royal gardener. But having quite filled it with a description of the triumphal entry of Remeses into the capital, I must defer doing so till another occasion.

With my most affectionate wishes for your happiness, I am, my beloved mother,

Your faithful son,
SESOSTRIS.

LETTER XX.

PALACE OF RHODA.

MY DEARLY BELOVED MOTHER,—

THE excitement, which the return of the triumphant army from its brilliant Ethiopian campaign created, has now subsided, and the cities of Memphis and On, and the thousand villages in the valley of the Nile, have returned to their ordinary quiet, interrupted only by religious processions, the music of a banquet, or the festivities of a marriage. In this delicious climate, where there is no particular incentive to action, the general state of the people is one of indolence and leisure. The chief business, at the marts and quays, is over before the sun is at meridian; and during the remainder of the day, shade and repose are coveted. But when the sun sinks westward, and hangs low over the brown hills of Libya, this inaction ceases, and all classes, in their best apparel and most cheerful looks, fill the streets, the groves, the gardens, the walks and avenues along the river; and the spirit of enjoyment and life reigns.

One evening, not long since, I strolled along the banks of the Nile, beneath a row of mimosa-trees, to enjoy the gay and attractive scenes upon the river. It was covered with gaily-painted barges, containing happy family parties, whose musicians played for them as the rowers slowly and idly propelled the boat; others, in sharp-prowed barisæ, darted in emulous races across the water; others were suspended upon the bosom of the stream, fishing for amusement; while others still moved about, with their beautifully pictured sails spread to the gentle breeze, as if enjoying the panorama of the shores they were gliding past.

I had rambled alone some distance up the river, without any vestige of my rank being apparent, in the plain Phœnician costume of a Tyrian merchant (which I often wear, to prevent constant interruption by the homage and prostrations of the deferent Egyptians), when I saw a small baris, containing a single person, coming close to the steps of the extensive terrace of one of the numerous temples of the image of Apis, which here faced the Nile, separated from it only by a double row of sphinxes. It was rowed by four Nubian slaves, clad in white linen vests and fringed loin-cloths, each having a red cap upon his head.

As the boat approached the marble steps, a decorated and unusually elegant galley, containing three young men of rank, as their dress and the emblems on their mast indicated, was coming swiftly down the stream, as if the owner strove to display the fleetness of his vessel before the eyes of the thousands who looked on. The pilot, at the lofty helm, called out to the baris to move quicker away from the line of his course; but either the rowers failed to hear or to comprehend, for they did not turn their heads. On like the wind came the galley. I called aloud to the person who sat in the stern of the baris, and who was intently engaged in reading a book, a portion of which lay unrolled at his feet.

He looked up quickly, and saw, first me, and then, by the direction of my finger, his danger. Before, however, he could give orders to his rowers, I heard one of the young men say to the pilot, who was changing his course a little,—

"Keep right on! It is but a Hebrew; and it would be a favour to the gods to drown a thousand a day."

The pilot obeyed his lord, and the bronze hawk-head of the gilded galley struck the boat near the stern, nearly capsizing it, and then the whole armament of twelve oars passed over it, striking overboard two of the slaves, as the twenty-four oarsmen swept the galley along at the height of its speed. I expected to see the priest, for such his costume betrayed him, also pressed down by the long oars, under which, like a low roof of inclined rafters, he was entangled; but stooping low until his forehead touched the book on his knee, the sweeps passed harmlessly over him, and when the galley had gone by, he recovered his sitting posture, maintaining, the while, a composure and dignity that made me marvel. His dark, handsome, oriental face betrayed scarcely any emotion at the danger or the indignity Seeing that one of the slaves was swimming ashore, and that the other rose no more, he waved his hand to the remaining two who had fallen into the bottom of the boat, and who, recovering their oars, pulled him to the steps.

"A Hebrew!" repeated I to myself. "Truly, and the very likeness of Remeses, save that his hair is of a browner hue, and his beard tinged with a golden light. A Hebrew! What philosophy under insult and peril! A Hebrew! What contempt of him and his life was evinced by the haughty Egyptian noble! A Hebrew and a *priest!*"

Such were the reflections to which I gave utterance in an undertone.

He debarked, and, giving an order to the slaves, placed his scroll of papyrus beneath his robe, and, ascending the steps, bowed low, and with singular courtesy (for the Hebrews, mother, are naturally the most polished and benignant people in the world), said in the Phœnician tongue,—

"I am indebted to you, sir merchant, for my life! Your timely voice enabled me to save myself, although I have lost one of the poor Nubian lads. Accept my gratitude!"

I could not remove my eyes from his face. It fascinated me! It seemed to be Remeses himself speaking to me; yet the hair of the prince is raven-black, and his beard also, while this man's is a rich brown, and his fine beard like a golden river. The eyes of Remeses are black, with a mild expression naturally, as if they were animated by a gentle spirit; while those of the priest are hazel, or rather a brilliant bronze, and full of the light of courage and of ardent fire. In person he is just the height of Remeses—carried his head in the same imperial manner, as if born to command; and the tones of his voice are marked by that rich emotional cadence—winning the ear and touching the heart—which characterizes the prince. His step is firm and commanding—his motion self-poised and dignified. He seems three or four years older than Remeses; but the likeness of the features, and the entire presence of the stranger, recalled my royal friend so forcibly to my mind, on the occasion of which I speak, that I said mentally, "Were the Prince Remeses a Hebrew, or were this Hebrew an Egyptian, I should think them cousins, if not brothers!"

Pardon me, dear mother, for thus speaking of a royal personage; but I only make use of the language to express to you how wonderful in every way, save in the colour of hair and eyes, is the resemblance of this man to the prince.

"I did but a common duty to a fellow-being," was my reply. "But why did you address me in Syriac?"

"Are you not a Syrian merchant?" he asked, looking at me more closely, after I had spoken.

"I am from Tyre," I answered. "You are a Hebrew?"

"Yes," was his reply, casting down his eyes and moving past me towards the temple.

"Stay one moment," I said. He turned and regarded me with a look of surprise; just such an one as the Hebrew woman Miriam,—to whom also, dear mother, he bore a very striking resemblance,—gave me when I irresistibly addressed her, in the courteous tone I would have used towards any of her sex: such was my tone in speaking to this Hebrew; for although his dress showed that he was only a neophyte, or attendant with secular duties, yet the man himself commanded my respect.

"May I inquire, without offence, why I see a Hebrew in the service of religion?"

"When we are only degraded slaves, and brick and clay workers, and worship not the gods of Egypt?" he answered interrogatively; and I imagined I detected a haughty light in his eyes, and a movement of his lip, caused by a keen sense of the degradation of which he spake.

"You have expressed my motives," I replied. "If you are proceeding along the avenue of sphinxes, I will accompany you, as I am merely loitering."

"Will you be seen walking with a Hebrew, my lord prince?" he said significantly.

"You know my rank, then?"

"Your language betrays you; merchants do not speak as you do. Besides, the signet of Prince Remeses, on your hand, designates your rank. I have, moreover, heard you described by one who will never forget that the first words of kindness he ever received, save from his kinsfolk, fell upon his ears from your lips, O Prince of Tyre!"

"Who is he?" I asked with interest.

"The lad Israel, whom you assisted in restoring to animation by the well of Jacob the shepherd!"

"At the strangers' fountain!" I repeated. "This little act seems to be known to all the Hebrews!"

"Not to all, but to a few," he answered; "yet it will be heard of by all of them; for kindness and sympathy from any one, especially from a foreign prince, is so strange an event that it will fly from lip to ear. Your name, O noble Sesostris, will be engraven in every memory, and the sound thereof warm hope in every heart!"

He spoke with deep feeling. We walked some distance side by side without speaking. After a few moments' silence I said,—

"Where is the youth Israel?"

"With his people near Raamses."

"I am to receive him into my service."

"He will faithfully serve you, my lord prince. He is of my kindred, and I shall be grateful to you for protecting his weakness. Every shoulder in Israel cannot bear the burden!"

"Are you, then, of the family of Miriam?" I asked, recollecting that the ritual transcriber, in the palace of the hierarch, had also claimed kindred with the son of the venerable Ben Isaac.

"Miriam the scribe?"

"In the service of Luxora and Osiria, of Memphis."

"She is my sister."

"I would have said it!" I answered. "Is your father living?"

"He is in charge of the queen's flower-garden in On."

"I know him," I answered.

"It is he who has spoken of you to me, as well as the aged Ben Isaac, young Israel, and Miriam. Therefore did I at once recognize you, when your polished words led me to see that you were in rank above chief pilots and governors of galleys."

"Will you reply to my inquiry? for, as we know each other's friends, we need not now discourse wholly as strangers. How came you, being a Hebrew, to become a priest? Do not you Hebrews worship the One Infinite Maker and Upholder of worlds?"

"There are a few who retain, unmixed with superstition and idol-worship, the knowledge of the one God of our ancestors Abraham, Jacob, and Joseph; but this knowledge is confined chiefly to the descendants of one man, Levi; and only to a few of these. The residue are little better than the Egyptians."

"Art thou of the family of this Levi?" I asked.

"I am. We are more given to study than our brethren, and seek knowledge and wisdom. Hence it is that some of our tribe are taken from the labour of the field to serve the priests. We are ready-writers, skilful with the stylus and the colouring pencil, and our lot is preferable to that of others who are more ignorant. Hence you behold me a servitor in an Egyptian temple!"

"Hast thou long been in this service?" I asked, as we stopped in the shade of the pyramidion of an obelisk, in front of the temple porch.

"From a child."

"So early! Then thou hast not borne the toils of thy people."

"I was discovered upon the banks of the Nile, in my fourth year, near the Island of Rhoda, weeping bitterly; for I had seen my mother commit my infant brother to a basket and launch it upon the river; and observing it borne down by the current, young as I was, I so felt all its danger, that I ran as well as I could along the shore crying piteously, when a priest (who has made known to me the incident) seeing me, took pity upon me, and, noticing that I was a Hebrew child, led me away, pacifying me by saying that I should see my brother. From that time I have been an inmate of the temple; for my mother, seeing him take me away, followed, and as he promised he would rear me as his own son, and that I should see her weekly, she yielded me up to him with reluctant gladness; for, my lord prince, in that day the children of Hebrew parents were not safe even at home, an edict having been published commanding all male infants to be strangled or drowned. Mothers held their children by a slight tenure, and seeing that the protection of a priest would insure my safety, and spare me the toils to which the little ones of our nation were early condemned, my parents readily acquiesced in the wishes of the priest."

"Was thy infant brother lost?" I asked with interest.

"Yes, without doubt. Like hundreds of other innocents, he perished."

"Might he not have been saved by some one as compassionate as your friendly priest?"

"Who would dare to save a child from the king's edict of death? Not one, unless it had been the king's daughter! All his subjects trembled at his power."

"I have heard of that cruel command of Pharaoh Amunophis," I answered. "What is your office in this noble temple?" I asked, surveying the majestic edifice, before which stood a black statue of Apis, the size of life.

"My office is not that of a priest, though it is priestly. I write books of papyrus for the dead. I cast images, in gold, of the young calf Apis. I interpret hieroglyphics, make copies of the tables of rituals, and keep a list of the sacred scrolls. I also study foreign tongues, and transcribe from their books the wisest codes and most solemn forms of worship."

"Yours is an office of trust and honour," I said.

"It is, through the favour of the venerable priest, who is my benefactor, and to whom I am as a son," he answered. "If you will now enter the temple with me, I will show you the casting-room of sacred images; for my duty is there, during the next four hours."

I thanked the courteous Hebrew, and, ascending the steps of the portico, entered the vestibule of the temple. By a side corridor, we reached a small court lined with alabastron, in which three priests were pacing up and down, reading and meditating.

Not being noticed at all by them, I was conducted by the stately Hebrew into a chamber, which was the vestibule to a large apartment, whither we descended by eight steps that led to a large brazen door with two leaves. This was secured; but a small side door admitted us into a vast subterranean room, which I saw was a place for casting. Numerous workmen were busy about heated furnaces: some blowing the fire beneath crucibles for melting gold, some weighing gold and delivering it to the smiths; and others washing gold. Some were casting small images of Apis in moulds, while a superintendent moved up and down, dressed in the close robes of vesture priests wear when not performing duties at the altar. It was a scene of busy toil and constant activity.

"This," said my guide, "is the casting-chamber of the temple. Each of us has his departments. It is mine to oversee the mixing of gold with the proper alloy, and I have a scribe who records the results. Here, you see, is a life-size image of Apis, when he was a calf. It is for the temple at Bubastis, of the Delta. There you behold a mould for one of larger size, ordered for the shrine at Osymandyes."

"Do you never cast any figures of the size of Apis?" I asked, looking about me in amazement at this extraordinary scene.

"Not of gold," he answered, conducting me through the vast room in which fourscore men were at work. "Those are cast of bronze, not here, but at a temple near the pyramid Dendara. The gods of this temple are in great repute throughout all Egypt. They are consecrated here before they are sent away, with ancient rites, known only to the priesthood of this shrine. Come with me into this side apartment."

I followed him through a passage having double-doors of brass, and found myself in a room full of vases, each one of which contained a quantity of jewellery, consisting of rings for the fingers and thumb, ear-rings, bracelets, flower-holders of gold, necklaces, and signets, all of gold.

"These are sent here from various temples in the different nomes, out of which, after melting them, we cast images of the size demanded."

In another room the intelligent Hebrew exhibited to me a great number of small figures of Apis, of gold of Havilah, which is remarkably beautiful from its deep orange-colour. These figures, though not a palm long, were valued at a talent. On all these images of the sacred calf I perceived that the mark of the crescent between the shoulders was distinctly imitated, as well as the other peculiarities. Upon the head of some of them was a sun enwreathed by the sacred uræus.

"Does your temple derive a revenue from all this?" I asked the Hebrew.

"There is a tithe retained from all the gold that is sent hither, for the expenses of the temple," he answered.

We now turned aside to see men grinding to powder an old image of Apis, of solid gold of Ophir. The image had been in the hands of the Ethiopians, and, being recaptured, was sent here to be ground to dust; for it was regarded as accursed until this were done. This process is effected by the free use of *natron*, and is an art known only to the Egyptians. The dust is then washed in consecrated water. In taste, I am told, it is exceeding bitter and nauseous. Thus gold, as a drink, would not be coveted by men.

We next came to a flight of stairs which led to a paved hall surrounded by columns, and thence a door led into a small garden, where three majestic palms towered high above the columns that enclosed it; while a fountain ceaselessly let fall its refreshing rain, in a vast shallow vase, wherein gold and silver fishes glanced in the light.

It was now near the close of day, and I began to thank him for his courtesy, when he said,—

"Do not leave now, O prince! This is my apartment, and the one opposite is that of the aged priest, my benefactor. Enter, and let me have water for thy feet and hands, and place before thee some refreshment; for it is a long walk back to the palace where thou art sojourning."

Willing to learn all I could of the remarkable Hebrew people, who seem to be a nation of princes as well as of bondmen, I accepted his invitation, and entered a cool porch, from which opened a handsome but simply furnished apartment, where he lodged. I seated myself upon a stone bench, when, at a signal made by him, two black slaves approached with ewers of water, one for the hands and the other with a silver basin for my feet. Each of them had thrown over his shoulder a napkin of the finest linen. But upon the vessels, the vestures, the slaves, and the napkins I saw the crescent, which showed that they were all the property of the temple.

At length, fruit, and wheaten bread and fish were laid before me. The Hebrew stood while I partook, declining to eat with me, saying that his nation never broke bread with any but their own people; adding, " and the Egyptians regard it as infamy to sit down with us.

"I have no such prejudices," I said, with a smile. When I had eaten, and laved my fingers in a crystal vase, which the priest placed before me, and the Nubians had retired, I said, " My meeting with you has been a source of great pleasure to me. I am deeply interested in your nation. As a Syrian we are not far from a kindred origin, and as a foreigner I have none of the feelings which, as masters, the Egyptians entertain towards a Hebrew. I have witnessed the working of the deep-seated prejudice in a variety of ways, and cannot but wonder at it. From all I can learn of your history, you have never been at war with them, nor wronged them."

"We are unfortunate, unarmed, and weak; and the greater ever oppress the helpless," he answered.

"Do you feel no resentment?"

"The bondage of one hundred and seventy years has graven the lines of patience deep in our hearts. Forbearance has become a second nature to the Hebrew. But, my lord prince, I feel that this will not always be," he added. "The time cannot be far off when Egypt, for her own safety, will give us our liberty and the privileges of citizens. We are not a race of bondmen, like Nubia's children. We were once free! Our fathers were princes in Syria; and was not Joseph the ruler of Egypt for sixty-one years, during the long reign of Pharaoh-Apophis? Not long after the Theban dynasty, which now rules the two Egypts, assumed the double crown did our degradation begin."

"Doubtless a change in your condition must ere long take place," I said. "There must be leaders among you. Not all the suffering of your oppression has destroyed the princely air among many of your people."

"But not one Hebrew is trained to war, or knows the use of any sort of weapon. For three generations we have been a labouring, patient, unarmed people. If, here and there, one rises above the masses, it is by accident, or favour, or from interest on the part of those who employ us. I have said that the family from which I spring is skilled in letters and art, and is ambitious of the learning of the Egyptians, and of becoming scribes and copyists to the priests. Others among us, of the sons of Dan, are skilful boatmen; others are builders; while others prefer the culture of the field, or the tending of flocks. We were twelve princes—brethren—in the ancient days, and the descendants of each are remarkable for some special skill; and the Egyptian taskmasters having discerned this aptitude, distribute them to their work accordingly. We are not all brick-makers, though four-fifths of the nation are reduced to that degraded toil—all, of every tribe or family, who are not skilful in some art, being driven into the field. Of late years, the Egyptian artificers have made such great outcries, to the effect that the Hebrews were filling the places of their own workmen, that the chief governor of the Hebrews in Lower Egypt has, in order to preserve peace, sent thousands into the brick-fields, who had never before encountered such heavy toil. The result is that hundreds perish, and that youths like Israel sink hourly under their unendurable sufferings."

"Have you no gods—no ear to hear your prayers?" I asked impulsively, as I am apt to do, dear mother, when my feelings are deeply moved. "Have you no worship? I hear of no altar or temple."

"A few among us have mysteries, such as the existence of One God; that He is a spirit; that all men are His offspring; and that we must be just in order to please Him. But I must confess, O prince," he said sadly, "that we have very little knowledge, even the best among us, of the God in whose existence we profess to believe. It is easier to serve and trust to the visible gods of Egypt; and our people, from the depths of their misery, stretch forth their clay-soiled hands to Osiris, to Pthah, to the images of Apis, and cry, 'Deliver us, O gods of Egypt, deliver us from our bondage!' They have cried to the invisible God of Abraham in vain, and they now cry in vain to the gods of the land, also. Neither hear—neither answer; and they sink into blank despair, without any hope left in a god—a nation of infidel slaves!"

"Can this be a true picture?" I said.

"Nearly so. Even I, O prince, under the ever-present power of the religion to which this temple is upreared,—I, from the influence of example, from ignorance of the worship of the Hebrew God of Isaac, from the education of my life, am half an Egyptian. The religion of Egypt appeals to the senses, and these, in most men, are far stronger than the imagination; and we Hebrews know nothing of a God, except that our fathers had one, but that He has deserted and left us, their miserable descendants, under the yoke of oppressors. Is it any wonder that the wisest of us turn to the gods of Egypt? If the Egyptians can be happy, and cherish hope and die in peace under their faith, let us also seek its shelter, and let their gods be our gods! Such is the prevailing language and growing feeling of our people."

This was all said in a tone of sadness and bitterness; while that despair of which he spoke, cast its shadow heavily over his noble countenance. I arose soon afterwards, and took my leave of him, more and more deeply interested, dear mother, in the history and condition of this singular people.

Your affectionate son,
SESOSTRIS.

LETTER XXI.

PALACE OF AMENSE, ISLAND OF RHODA.

MY DEAR MOTHER,—

It is with emotions I am unable to command, that I commence, after a silence of several weeks, another letter to you. I know not how properly to unfold and rightly to present before you the extraordinary events which have transpired since I last wrote to you. But I will endeavour to give a narrative of the unparalleled circumstances, in the order of their occurrence up to the present time, and will keep you advised of the progress of this remarkable and mysterious matter, as each day it develops itself.

I believe, in one of my letters to the Princess Thamonda, I spoke of the approaching birthday of Remeses—his thirty-fifth—and that the queen had resolved on that day, to confer upon him the crowns of Egypt, and resigning, with the sceptre, all dominion into his hand, retire to a beautiful palace, which she has recently completed on the eastern slope of the Libyan hills, west of the pyramids, and overlooking a charming lake, which, begun by former rulers, has been enlarged and beautified by each, and by none more than by herself.

This purpose of the queen was made known to Remeses, about three weeks after his return from Thebes with his victorious army. I was not present at the interview, but will repeat to you the conversation that passed, as it was made known to me by the prince, who extends towards me all the confidence of one beloved brother to another; and, indeed, keeps no secrets from me. This pleasing confidence is fully reciprocated on my part, and we are in all things as one.

I had been that morning on a visit to that part of Memphis which stretches away westward from the Nile in a succession of gardens, squares, palaces, and monuments, girdling the Lake of Amense with beautiful villas, and climbing with its terraces, grottoes, shrines, and marble pavilions, the very sides of the cliffs of Libya, two leagues from the river; for to the extent of Memphis there seems to be no limit measurable by the eye. Even the three great pyramids are almost central in the mighty embrace of the sacred city.

Upon landing from my galley upon the Island of Rhoda, my Hebrew page Israel, now become a bright and blooming youth, with a face always enriched by the light of gratitude, met me and said,—

"The prince, my lord, desires to see you in his private chamber. He bade me ask you not to delay."

I found Remeses walking to and fro in the apartment with a pale face and troubled brow. As soon as I entered, he approached me, and taking my hand between his, pressed it to his heart affectionately and said,—

"I am glad you have returned, Sesostris, my friend and brother! Come and sit by me on this seat by the window. I have much to say —much! I need your counsel."

"My noble friend," I answered, moved by his unusual emotion, "I am not able to counsel one so wise and great as you are."

"Nay, you are too modest, prince. I must tell you all. Strange events have occurred. Hear me, and you will then be able to strengthen my soul! You know that of late my dear mother has been given to melancholy; that she has appeared absent in thought, abrupt in speech, and ill at ease. Thou hast observed this; for we have spoken of it together, and marvelled at her mood, which neither the memory of our victories in Ethiopia, the prosperity of her kingdom, the peace in her borders, the love of her subjects, nor my own devotion could remove; nor the music of the harp, nor the happy songs of the chanters dissipate."

"Do you not think," I said, "that this state of mind is connected with her illness before you left, when the Viceroy Mœris dined with us?"

Remeses started, and fixed upon me his full gaze.

"Sesostris, what led you to connect the present with that event?"

"Because the queen has never been wholly well and cheerful since that day."

"What think you of Prince Mœris? Speak freely."

"He is a proud, ambitious, and unprincipled man."

"Do you think he loves me?"

"I fear not."

"You are right. But you shall hear what I have to relate. Three hours since my mother sent for me. I found her in the chapel where the shrine of Osiris receives her most private prayers. She was kneeling when I entered, her face towards the god; but her eyes, wet with tears, penetrated the heavens, and seemed to seek a living Power that could hear and answer prayer, Sesostris. She did not see me, and her voice was audible:—

"'Protect him! Guard him from his foe! Spare me the discovery of the secret, and place him upon the throne of Egypt, O immortal and pitying Osiris! O Isis, hear! O goddess of the sacred bow, and mother of Horus, hear! Give me strength to act, and wisdom in this my great perplexity!'

"I drew near, and kneeling by my mother's side, laid her head against my heart, and said,—

"'The God of all gods, the Father Infinite hear thee, O mother! What is it thou prayest for with such strong woe and fear?'

"'Hast thou heard me?' she exclaimed, rising and speaking wildly. '*What* didst thou hear? Nay, I have betrayed no secret?'

"'None, mother, none! Thou didst only speak of one which distressed thee,' I said soothingly; for, my dear Sesostris, I was inexpressibly moved by her agitated manner, unlike anything I have ever before witnessed in her usually calm, serene, and majestic demeanour.

"She leaned heavily upon me, and I led her to an alcove in which was the shrine of Athor.

"'Sit down, Remeses—my son Remeses,' she repeated, with a singular emphasis upon the words 'my son.' 'Hear what I wish to reveal to thee! I am now more composed. There is in my heart a great and ceaseless anxiety. Do not ask me what it is! The secret, I trust, will remain sealed for ever from thy ears! Ask not—seek not to know it. You may as successfully obtain an answer from the heart of the great pyramid, revealing what is buried there from human eyes, as obtain an answer from me of the mystery lying at my heart. It will be embalmed with me, and go with me to the lower world!'

"'Mother,' I said, alarmed at her depressed manner, 'thou art ill—let me send for thy physician—'

"'Nay, nay—I am not ill! I shall be better soon! *You*, Remeses have the key to my happiness and health,' she said tenderly, yet seriously.

"'Then I will yield it up to thee!' I answered pleasantly.

"'Hear my words, my son, for art thou not my son, my noble Remeses?' she asked, taking both my hands and holding them to her heart, and then pressing her lips upon them almost passionately; for I felt tears flow upon my hands.

"'Thy son, with undying love, my mother,' I answered, wondering in my heart, and deeply affected. She remained a few moments silent, and at length said,—

"'Remeses, hast thou ever doubted my love?'

"'Never, no never, my mother!' I replied, moved.

"'Have I not been a true and fond mother to thee?'

"'Why distress yourself, dear mother, with such useless interrogatories?' I asked. No longer agitated, and her nervous air having quite disappeared, she spoke calmly but earnestly,—

"'Have I neglected, in any way, a mother's duty to thee, O Remeses?'

"'Thou hast ever been all that a mother could be,' I answered her.

"'Do you think a mother could love a son more than I love thee?' she repeated.

"'No, O my mother!'

"'And *thou*, Remeses, dost thou love me?' she continued, with the same fixed, solemn, and painful earnestness.

"'Why shouldst thou doubt?' I asked.

"'I have no reason to doubt,' she replied; 'yet I would hear thee say, 'Mother, I love thee above all things beneath the sun!'

"I smiled, and repeated the words, distressed to perceive that something had taken hold upon her noble and strong mind, and was shaking it to its centre.

"Remeses, my son,' she said, answering my smile, and then immediately assuming an expression of singular majesty, 'I am now advancing in life. I have passed my fifty-first year, and am weary of the sceptre. I wish to see you king of Egypt while I live. I wish to see the grandeur and wisdom of your reign, and to rejoice in your power and glory. When I am laid in the sarcophagus, which I have caused to be hewn out in the chamber beneath the pyramidion of my obelisk, I shall know and behold nothing of thy dominion. It is my desire, therefore, to invest you with the sovereignty of Egypt; and after I see you crowned, robed, and sceptred as her king, I will retire to my Libyan palace and there contemplate thy greatness, and reign again in thee!'

"I rose to my feet in surprise, dear Sesostris, at this announcement from the lips of my mother, but listened with deference until she had concluded, and I then said,—

"'This intent and purpose be far from thee, O my mother and queen! Thou art in the meridian of life, and still in the possession of thy wonderful beauty. Scarcely a silver thread has stolen amid thy soft, dark hair; thou art yet young; and may the Lord of the kings of the earth long preserve thee upon thy throne, and lend thee strength and wisdom to wield thy sceptre. Far be it from me, therefore, my mother, to accept the crown, until Osiris himself transfers it from thy majestic brow to mine !'

"'Nay, Remeses,' she said firmly, yet sadly, 'my will is the law of Egypt. Thou hast never opposed it.'

"'But this is where my own elevation involves your depression,' I answered. 'It cannot be !'

"'I am firm and immovable, my son, in my purpose,' she replied. 'Your thirty-fifth birthday will soon arrive. That is the age at which Horus, the son of Isis, was crowned. It is a number of good omen, and I wish you to prepare for your coronation, by performing all the rites and sacrifices, that the religion and laws of Egypt require of a prince who is about to ascend the throne of the Pharaohs.'

"'Mother, my dearly honoured mother !' I said, kneeling to her, 'forgive me, but I must firmly decline the throne while you sit thereon. You are ill at ease in your mind to-day. Some deep grief, which you conceal from me, preys upon you. It is not because you are old that you would abdicate the throne to me, who am not yet old or wise enough to rule this mighty nation ; but you have some secret, painful reason, which I beg you to reveal to me.'

"My words seemed to inflict pain upon her. She rose to her feet, and paced the apartment twice across in troubled reflection. Then she came to my side, and said impressively, placing her trembling grasp upon my arm,—

"'Remeses, if I reveal to thee the secret of my heart, wilt thou then consent to be king?'

"'If I perceive, my mother,' I answered, 'that necessity demands my acceptance of the crown before my time, I will not refuse it.'

"'If your views of necessity do not influence you, O my son,' she said earnestly, and with a sudden gush of tears, 'let my affection, my happiness, my peace of mind, plead with you !'

"'Please, my beloved mother, to make known to me the circumstances under which you are moved to this unusual step,' I said.

"'Not unusual,' she replied. 'I have consulted the book of the reigns of Pharaohs, in the hall of books, in the temple of Thoth. Within two thousand years, not less than seven kings and three queens have resigned the sceptre of Egypt to children or adopted heirs. The Queen Nitocris resigned to her adopted son, Myrtæus ; Chomæphtha, after reigning eleven years, weary with the weight of the crown, resigned it to her nephew, Sœconiosochus. Did not Phruron-Nilus, the great monarch, decide to abdicate in favour of Amuthantæus, his son, when sudden death only prevented his retirement ? The crowns of Egypt are *mine*, my son, by the laws of the gods, and of the ancestral kings from whom I have inherited them. I will not wait for the god of death to remove them from my head ; but with my own hands I would put them upon thy brow ! It must be done soon,—*now !* or neither thou nor I will hold rule long in Egypt !'

"I begged my mother to explain her mysterious words.

"'Come, sit by me. Be calm, Remeses ! Listen with your usual meekness and reverence to me when I speak.' I obeyed her, and she thus began:—

"'Thou knowest thy cousin Mœris;—his lofty ambition; his impatience; his spirit of pride; his lust for dominion, which his viceroyship in the Thebaïd has only given him an unlimited thirst for;—his jealousy and hatred of you, Remeses! None of these things are concealed from you, my son.' My mother paused as if for my assent, which I signified by a respectful bow. She continued,—

"'This Prince Mœris, for whom I have done all in my power—whom I have made second only to me in the Thebaïd, I have reason to know seeks your ruin and my throne!'

"'What proof hast thou of this?' I cried, deeply moved.

"'Remeses,' said my mother, in ringing tones, 'I must unfold to thee all! I know how slow thou art to suspect or believe evil of any one; and that you fancy Mœris an honourable prince, overlooking his jealousy of you. You have confidence in my judgment and truth?'

"'I have, the most undoubted and deferential,' I answered the queen.

"'Then, my son, hear me!' she said with a face as pale as the fine linen of her vesture. 'Prince Mœris possesses a secret (ask me *not* what it is) which gives him a dangerous power over me. He obtained possession of it years ago, how I know not; but it has placed in his hands a power that I tremble beneath. Nay, ask not! My heart itself would as soon open to thine eyes, under the shield of my bosom, as reveal its secret! It will die with me! Yet Mœris, my nephew—a man of talents and ambition, in morals most unprincipled, and in disposition cruel and unjust—holds my happiness in his hand!'

"'My mother,' I cried, 'why then didst thou confer on him the principality of the Thebaïd and its enormous military power?'

"'To bribe him, when he menaced me with the betrayal of what he knew!' was the queen's almost fierce rejoinder.

"'But why make him the admiral of your fleet of the Nile?'

"'Another bribe when he renewed his threats to inform you—'

"'Me!' I exclaimed.

"'Did I say you? No! no!' she cried, checking herself; 'when he menaced me with the betrayal of the dreadful secret.'

"'And, my dear mother, who was interested to know it, whom would it benefit or injure?' I asked, lost in amazement.

"'Injure one whom—whom I love—destroy my happiness and hopes—benefit Mœris himself!' she answered, colouring with deepest confusion and alarm.

"'Why not crush such a dangerous subject when he menaces your peace?' I demanded, my whole spirit roused for my mother, and my indignation excited against this wicked man. 'If thy happiness is thus menaced, O my mother, if this prince is the cause of all your sorrow, say the word, and in thirty days hence, he shall be brought bound in chains to your feet.'

"'Nay, Remeses, I dare not. One word from his lips, though he were in chains, would reveal all it has been the study of my life to conceal, and give him all the revenge his bitter spirit would ask. No, no! Mœris must not be made angry. It is only his ambitious hopes that keep him quiet.'

"'What are these hopes?' I inquired, feeling that henceforth Mœris and I were mortal foes.

"Didst thou, O prince," said I, as he returned to his seat by me, which he had left, in the excitement of his narrative, to pace the floor, "suspect the secret?"

"No," he answered gloomily; "no, Sesostris; nor do I now know what it can be; neither have I the least idea, unless—" Here he coloured, and looked confused.

"Unless what?" I asked, painfully interested.

"Unless Mœris be the son of the Prince of the Thebaïd, and I the son of the brother of Pharaoh. In other words, that Mœris and Remeses have changed places, and that Mœris knows or suspects the fact."

"A most extraordinary idea!" I exclaimed; yet at the same time, I must confess that I was forcibly reminded of what I have before alluded to, dear mother, the total absence of all likeness between Remeses and his mother, Amense.

"What can possibly have suggested to your mind such a strange conjecture?" I added.

"A mystery, my dear Sesostris," he said, "calls into exercise the whole machinery of suspicion, and all the talent of investigation; and a hundred things, which before had only an ordinary signification, under its wand, take an importance and meaning wholly new. Irresistibly, my mother's anxiety to impress upon me that she had been 'all a mother could be to a son,' in connexion with her whole manner, and especially her uncalled-for reiterations of affection for me, and of appeals to my devotion to her;—all this rushed upon my memory, and with a dizzy brain, and a heart full of anguish, under the dreadful suspicion, I cried, 'Why must not Prince Mœris be made angry? Why may he not be prevented from doing thee harm?'

"'I have told you,' she replied, with a deadly pallor. 'Remeses, your roused spirit alarms me for us three.'

"'But I must oppose, and if necessary destroy him,' I said, in my emotion, 'who destroys my mother's peace.'

"'Yes, I am thy mother. Thou art a son to me. I know thou wilt protect me from this prince-nephew,' she said, in broken sentences. 'He shall not come between me and thee, and the throne.'

"'He has no claim to the throne. He does not aspire to it in your lifetime,' I said; 'and if I hold it after, I will take care of my own crown. My mother, fear not Prince Mœris. Let his secret perish with him.'

"'And thou, also, Remeses!' she said passionately.

"'I, my mother?' I repeated. A spirit of severe investigation then came upon me, strengthened by my suspicion.

"'My mother, Queen Amense,' I said, with the deepest emotion, and, O Sesostris, with fear and dread, 'a fearful suspicion has taken hold upon me! *Am* I thy SON?'

"No sooner had I given utterance to this interrogative doubt, which was wrung form my tortured heart, than shrieking aloud, she fell forward, and, but for my intervening arm, her form would have been prostrate at my feet. I caught her in my arms; I kissed her marble brow; I chafed her cold pulses; and breathed words of comfort, words praying her forgiveness, into her ears. At length she revived, as I supported her against my wildly beating heart; and, with stony eyes staring me in the face, gasped,—

"'Remeses? Who hath—who—who hath said this?'

"'No one, *no one*, my dearly loved mother,' I answered tenderly. And when I saw that she was more composed, I said, 'It was only a conjecture—a wild suspicion—for I could not comprehend the mystery between you and my cousin Mœris, except that (as has been done in former dynasties) he and I are in each other's places. Is Mœris thy son, and am I the son of the brother of Amunophis?'

"I had no sooner said this, than she raised her head from the gold-embroidered purple cushion of the ivory couch, on which she lay reclining against my arm, and with a strange laugh of joy and surprise, said,—

"'So this is *all*, Remeses! Then thou needest not fear. Mœris is not my son. He is nothing to me but my kinsman. Canst thou believe that that wicked prince is my offspring? I forgive thee, Remeses, because, perhaps, my words, and the necessity of guarding my secret, may have forced thee to this conclusion.' This she spoke with a mind evidently greatly relieved.

"'Then, dear mother, I *am* thy son in spite of Prince Mœris?'

"'In spite of Mœris,' she answered. 'Hast thou ever known any other mother? Remeses, let thy heart be at peace! Mœris is not my son! On that he does not found his hopes to grasp the reins of Egypt. Now hear me, my son,' she said solemnly. 'That prince once sought my life. When I was taken ill on the day that he dined with me, he had bribed my cup-bearer to drop a subtle poison in my cup. Dread of the prince forced him, under his eyes, to do it; but as the cup-bearer handed me the wine, he pressed my little finger, where it clasped the cup, so significantly, that I looked in his eyes, and saw them full of warning. I did not drink, but pleaded illness, and left the banquet-room. I sent for the cup-bearer, and he confessed what he had done. When I heard his confession, and was thereby acquainted with the purpose of Prince Mœris against my life, I was overwhelmed with despair. My future safety lay in sending for him the next day. He came. It was a brief but dreadful interview. He acknowledged that he sought my life, because I had the day before refused him the crown of Upper Egypt, declining to give him the half of my empire. He threatened to betray my secret, and I pleaded for silence. He demanded the white crown of the Thebaïd as his reward, but I put him off with evasions. He had command of the fleet, and I dared not anger him. I shrank from making known to you his demand, and the terror with which he inspired me. I promised that if he entered the Ethiopian capital within six months, he should reign in Thebes.'

"'My mother,' I cried, 'gave you such a promise to him? He is already marshalling his forces!'

"'And in order not so much to conquer Ethiopia, as to usurp one of the thrones of Egypt,' she answered.

"'And are you bound by this promise to him!' I demanded overwhelmed with amazement, both at the audacity of Mœris, and the power he held over my mother by means of this secret.

"'By all the vows that a mortal can make to the gods! Here, in this sacred chapel, before these shrines, he made me swear that in consideration he subdued the central capital of Ethiopia, and preserved my secret, I would transfer from my head to his the white-gold crown of Upper Egypt, the most ancient kingdom mortal ever ruled over on earth, after the demigods.'

"When, my dear Sesostris," said Remeses, after having related to me, with a dark countenance, the foregoing conversation, "I heard this, I was for some time confounded, and could not speak. At length I cried out,—

"'That mystery—that secret, known only to you and Mœris, and for the safe-keeping of which you part with one of your crowns, *what is it!* divulge it! Am I not worthy, O my mother, of the confidence which Prince Mœris, by foul means, shares with you? Will you not entrust me with the secret which he can extort by bribery?'

"The queen looked deadly pale, and her whole frame trembled. She essayed to reply, and then said, with an effort, as if a corpse had become vocal,—

"'Remeses—you must—must not know it! Do not ask—do not suspect evil. Do not doubt me, or you will kill me! Kiss me, Remeses! Kiss me, my son; Are you not my son? I love you, and know you love me. Let all else pass by. You shall be king! You shall wear the double tiara! You shall grasp both sceptres. Therefore is it, I would now make you king. Dost thou understand me? Mœris must not march into Ethiopia. That evil man must have a master. My power is failing! I would surrender it to thee. The only safety of Egypt, the only security for thy crown and dominion, is in taking the throne, and ruling all Egypt in thine own right.'

"'Is this so, my mother?' I demanded. 'Does Prince Mœris not only torture thy soul with a secret, which, as a just prince, he ought for ever to forget, if thou desirest it, but does he also aspire to sever Egypt, and rule in the Thebaïd, on the ancient throne of my ancestors, as the price of a secret held over thee with an unmanly advantage?'

"'He does, my son,' she answered. 'The only safety of the empire depends on my resignation of the crowns into your hands. Once Pharaoh, you have Mœris at your feet, and if he prate his secret, you will then be able to despise it, and put to silence his tongue.'

"'Mother, my dear mother,' I answered, after long reflection, 'what you have told me has brought me to a decision. I shall act blindly—not knowing the nature of the power of the prince over you; but I shall act from affection and sympathy for you, in obedience to your wishes, and for the preservation of the integrity of the united kingdom. I am ready to obey you. In order to defeat Prince Mœris, and relieve your mind, I will accept the sceptre which you are desirous of placing in my feeble and inexperienced hand. I am ready to enter upon the sacred rites of initiation, and in all things will be your dutiful and obedient son. The wickedness and ambition of Mœris must be crushed.'

"When I had thus said, my mother, with a cry of joy, cast herself into my arms. I bore her, almost fainting with happiness realized, to the apartments of her women, and again assuring her of my full compliance with her wishes, I took tender leave of her, and hastened to my room to reflect upon all that had passed in that extraordinary interview ; and then I sought you."

Thus the Prince Remeses ended his interesting and singular statement. I knew not what to respond to him when he had done. But be sure, dear mother, there must something grow out of this, of the greatest importance to this dynasty. Who can divine the secret?

But I must here close my letter, with assurances of my fondest attachment to you, my dear mother, whom the gods guard from all mysteries and secrets, and from ambitious princes like the lord Mœris.

Your ever faithful
SESOSTRIS.

LETTER XXII.

ISLAND OF RHODA, PALACE OF THE QUEEN.

MY VERY DEAR MOTHER,—

IN the preceding letter I have made known to you the extraordinary purpose of the queen to invest, with the dignity of royalty, her son, the Prince Remeses ; the singular scenes which passed between them ; the mystery which enveloped her motives ; and the final yielding of Remeses to her commands and earnest appeals.

It now became necessary that he should, according to the custom and laws of the realm, prepare himself for his coronation, by submitting to certain religious ceremonies, and a solemn initiation into the deeper mysteries of the temples : for though, as a prince, he was nominally, or by courtesy of the laws, the high-priest, yet not until he became king could he offer the supreme sacrifice on the altar of Osiris,—which is the highest religious act of the sacred priesthood; and it is only upon the shields of kings that the symbol of "priests" is sculptured. Thus, as chief priests, or pontiffs, the Pharaohs were the head of the hierarchy, which consolidated their political power, and gave them an influence over the minds of the people that the mere possession of the sceptre of Egypt could not have commanded ; for in their king, they also behold their mediator with the gods. Yet, although absolute over his subjects, he had no power over the priesthood, except by their own consent. As one of their body he was bound by certain most solemn and mystic vows, to the rules and regulations of their order ; and in all matters of state he was pledged to the hierarchy of prince-priests, who constituted a council of advice, to which he was by the laws (also made by a legislature composed of the hierarchs of each nome), compelled to submit his own will. All his duties are regulated by a code drawn up by the Priest of On, and subscribed by the king at his coronation. Thus the monarch is entirely under the influence and control of the priests. I will, by way of illustration, describe to you how the queen (who is also chief priestess, by virtue of her rank, and, as such, offered up a sacrifice on the altar of Osiris on the day of her coronation) has her daily duties and hours apportioned to her, by this august council of arch-hierophants :

When her Majesty arises in the morning, her royal scribe brings to her, in a shallow vase of gold, the letters that have come to her from all parts of her kingdom, and of the world. These she reads, and lays aside for reply after consultation with Remeses, and, if of great importance, with her council of state ; for she has also a cabinet of generals, lords of nomes, and high admirals, together with the lord of the nilometers, whom she calls together on matters exclusively of state, such as the affairs of the army or of the navy, the condition of the harvests and treasure-cities, and the state of the Nile ; on which two last matters the reign of prosperity or famine depends. She then receives, and at once attends to all reports or messages that are in writing, from any officers of her palace, such as the captain of her guard, the chief butler, chief gardener, her captain of chariots, and her master of horse. She then issues her orders to these and other servants of her household. All this time she reclines in a robe of white silk, elegantly embroidered with the leaves of the lotus and acanthus, and with flowers imitated to the full beauty of natural ones. Her hair is braided and confined by a rich turban ; and before her is an ivory table containing ink tablets, a stylus or two, and parcels of royal papyrus stamped with her signet, and beautifully gilded, upon which she inscribes her replies either with her own hand, or by her scribes, and sometimes only by impressing thereon her signet, upon which vermilion is rubbed from a small cushion by her side. For religious affairs the signet is different, having the sacred hawk's-head engraved upon it above the royal cartouch, and instead of red colour,—the sacred hue of the Memphitic realm,—it is bright blue, which is taken from a very small crystal bottle, held in readiness by a scribe's page, from whose thumb it is suspended by a ring of gold.

The queen having dismissed all these attendants, retires to her bathing room, which is hung with curtains of cloth of gold ; and having bathed, her handmaidens anoint her with costly perfumes, and arrange her hair with the highest art ; for in the style of the hair the Egyptian ladies of all ranks display great taste, and expend in dressing and beautifying it a large proportion of their time ; and I must acknowledge they display perfect skill in making most attractive this glorious adornment of your sex, dear mother. The young wear it in numerous braids, mingled with natural tresses ; others shape it into a sort of a helmet with a crest of curls falling around ; others fasten it behind in a rich knot, and let what is free flow upon the shoulders. Some cover the head with a braided tiara sparkling with gold and jewels; and others, especially at banquets, wear rich caps of embroidered cloth, of beautiful shape, terminating behind in a cape enriched with needlework, and ornamented with fringe of floss of gold,—a peculiar filament I have seen fabricated only in Egypt. Indeed, an Egyptian lady seems to regard her hair as her crown of beauty by nature, and she tries by art to make it also a diadem of glory. As if its natural brilliancy were not enough, after pouring upon it fragrant perfume, her maid, from a small ivory box, the convex lid of which is filled with minute perforations, sprinkles its smooth surface with powder of gold.

The dressing-room of the queen opens upon gardens, is furnished with luxury, and is encircled by columns of alabaster; its intercolumnar panels glitter with foreign marbles, and paintings of the highest art; the tables are resplendent with gold and silver, electrum, and variegated stones; while before its doors hang drapery of Tyrian purple wrought with gold, and representing scenes of the chase. More or less resembling this, are the dressing-rooms of all the ladies of rank. The lords of Egypt covet gorgeous and expensively adorned "halls of books" or libraries; but the ladies beautify and enrich their dressing-saloons, in which they spend so much of their time, and where they often receive their very intimate female acquaintances: and as a great favour, gentlemen, on familiar footing with the family, are sometimes admitted into this beautiful adytum, where the goddess of beauty is adored by homage the most religious.

The queen, after being attired by her ladies in magnificent robes, is adorned with jewels; and wearing over her shoulders the splendid leopard's skin of the sacrificer, and upon her head the insignia of sovereignty, she enters, with all her train, the private chapel of the palace, and there presents offerings to the gods, pours a libation of wine, and invokes Osiris. On certain high days her chief priest is present, who, after praying, sacrifices a snow-white fowl, and offers oblations of more or less magnitude. The queen then asks forgiveness of the gods for what she may have done wrong in ignorance, in administering her kingdom, and implores wisdom and guidance in the acts of the day. The priest now gently touches her crown and sceptre with his finger dipped in the vase of blood, pours the rest into a vessel upon the altar, and extending his hands over her as she kneels, blesses her in the name of Osiris, the lord of the worlds, and king of the rulers of earth. He also pronounces an imprecation against her enemies, exempts her from all accusation for things done in ignorance, and solemnly denounces those of her ministers who wrongfully have instructed her, or administered evil counsel.

Then the queen, coming forth from prayer, is met by pages who present her with flowers, and, at the sound of musical instruments, she is led to her breakfast apartment, where the choicest food is brought on golden dishes,—cakes of fine flour, steeped in milk or honey, the flesh of birds roasted or broiled, fruit of all kinds, mild wines of Palestine and Cyprus, and water of the Nile filtered with the paste of almonds, and flavoured with Arabian spices and Persian condiments.

The meal over, she goes forth to her throne-room, and seating herself, the doors are thrown open, and she receives all petitioners and comers who desire audience; but not official persons, such as ambassadors, who have certain hours for audience with her. She decides on all final appeals from the judges in the city, or in the nomes, and determines with wisdom and equity.

These duties over, she walks in her garden, or in the colonnades of her palace ; or rides out to visit her public works, or for air. At noon she dines, as do all other Egyptians. On these occasions she has her high officers, and strangers of rank, philosophers, and others, at her table. Whosoever she delights to honour, she invites to a banquet. If any of her subjects greatly distinguishes himself, so as to confer a benefit upon Egypt by any new art or improvement, she not only places him at her table, whatever his previous rank, but invests him with a robe of honour, throws a gold chain over his neck, puts a ring upon his finger, presents him with a chariot to ride in, and makes him a high officer over some of her works or departments. Thus, by her virtues and justice, has she won the esteem and love of her subjects.

The queen usually passes the afternoon with her maidens, in her embroidering rooms, where she always has a large number of handmaids at work with the needle or the loom, or engaged in the art of needlework, or embroidering for the use and decoration of the palace. She also, at evening, receives guests, and at that time Remeses is usually found in her company. She retires not long after the close of day, unless it be a moonlight night, when her players on instruments of music fill the gardens with harmony, while the queen and her friends, seated in the corridors, listen, or converse together. In conversation the queen never speaks evil of any one, and she frowns upon slander; hence this vice is scarcely known in Egypt, and the Egyptian ladies, when they hear one of their own sex spoken against, at once defend her, and find excuses for her. This is certainly a delightful trait, and should cause the world to concede to the dames of Egypt the foremost position in the rank of civilization.

I will now speak of the proposed succession of Prince Remeses to the throne. As I have before said, the king is the representative of the deity. His title, Ph'rah, or Pharaoh, signifies "the sun," "a king," the "lord of light." The head of the religion of the state, he is not only the judge and lawgiver, but commander of the army, and its leader in war. These latter duties have been delegated by his mother to Remeses, by the consent of her council, many years ago. The sceptre of Egypt is hereditary ; but in the event of there being no lineal heir, the monarch can adopt one, if taken from the priestly or military class ; as the army or the priesthood are the two professions followed by all men of rank, the navy not having been, until Prince Mœris, its admiral, demanded it, an exclusive service. Most of the Pharaohs have been from the military class, and younger princes, from the days of Osirtasen to Prince Remeses, have adopted the warlike profession ; but it is the universal belief, that no former Prince of Egypt has evinced such ability as Remeses to command vast armies, and lead the destinies of a mighty people.

When a prince is about to ascend the throne, the laws require that he should be instructed in all the mysteries of the religion of his empire, and initiated into the various offices of a sovereign pontiff. He is taught all that relates to the gods and other mysteries hitherto concealed from him, the services of the temple, the laws of the country, and the duties of a king, as inscribed in the ten sacerdotal books.

In order that in these things he may be properly instructed, he is enjoined to pass forty days in the temples of Osiris, Pthah, Isis, Athor, and other gods; and to remain one night, the last of all, in the temple of Thoth, before the pyramids, watching alone, praying for the blessings of the gods, and offering sacrifice and libations. This solemn vigil ended, and the sun risen, he is escorted by a grand procession of priests, who swing incense before him, and lead him to the temple of the Sun, to be crowned in the presence of all the nobles, high officers, and people of Egypt. This ceremony, as described in the royal books, is grand beyond conception.

In order, therefore, to enter upon this formal preparation, the Prince Remeses, on the third day after his interview with his mother, retired from the palace, and sought the holy solitudes of the temple of the Sun. A council of the hierarchy, assembled by the queen, had reluctantly given their consent to her abdication; but willingly yielded to the coronation of Remeses; for, however devoted a warlike nation may be to a reigning queen, the preference of the people's heart is for a king. While, therefore, the intelligence, which soon spread through Egypt, that Amense the Good was to lay down her sceptre in favour of her son, cast a shadow over their hearts, it was chased away by the light of the anticipated splendour, which the reign of a prince, a "Pharaoh," would shed upon the land of Egypt.

"As the good queen will still live, we need not grieve," said some of the artisans at work upon her obelisk; "we can rejoice in Remeses, and still honour his royal mother."

It was an affecting parting between the prince and his mother when he left the palace. I accompanied him to the vestibule of the temple. Here twelve priests, led by the high-priest, received him; and three others came forward to disrobe him of his vesture, his bonnet and sandals; while three more invested him with sacerdotal robes, a priestly tiara, and placed upon his feet the sacred sandals. Then enclosing him in their midst, as if to shut him out from the world, they moved forward into the gloomy cloisters of the temple, and disappeared with him from my gaze.

At his previous request, and at the earnest solicitation of the queen, who, in his absence, depressed in spirits, finds relief, as she kindly says, in my presence, I returned to the Island of Rhoda, and am now occupying the apartments of the prince; for when he is crowned king, he will remove to the superb old palace of the Pharaohs, on the banks of the Nile, between the river and the City of the Sun.

No one is permitted to speak with the royal novitiate until the forty days are ended; and when he proceeds from temple to temple, to go through in each certain rites and receive certain instructions, it is at midnight, and all persons are forbidden to appear in the streets through which the mysterious procession of priests passes.

It is now the thirty-fourth day since he entered upon his initiation. Since that time I have seen much more of Egypt and of the people. I have not, however, been far from the Island of Rhoda, as the queen constantly demands my society, and inquires of Acherres after me, if I am long away.

Yesterday afternoon, as I was engaged with a party of nobles fishing in the Lake Amense, which I have before described as almost a sea in extent, and bordered by palaces, a galley, rowed by twenty-four oars, was seen coming towards us at great speed. Upon seeing it, one said,—

"It is a royal barge!"

"Nay," said another, "it is that of the old Admiral Pathromenes. His sails are blue and white."

"I do not heed the colour of his sails," said the first lord. "Seest thou not that it is the queen's galley, by the golden hawk's-head at the mast, and the cartouch of the Pharaohs above the poop?"

"It *is* the queen's galley," I said, "for I have frequently been in it, and recognize its symbols."

Hereupon there was manifested a general curiosity to know why it was coming so swiftly towards us. In a few minutes I discovered my Hebrew page, Israelisis (for I have Egyptianized his name since he came into my service) upon the deck, and began to suspect the queen had sent him for me. I was not mistaken. The galley came sweeping round us with a roar of spray from its dashing oars, and the page, springing lightly upon the bulwarks of our vessel, with a low obeisance presented me the queen's signet, saying,—

"The queen has sent for thee, my lord!"

The party of nobles expressed great reluctance at parting with me, and one of them said,—

"You are in great favour with our royal house, O prince."

"Only as a guest and stranger," I answered, smiling.

They returned my parting bow with courtesy, and I went upon the galley, which was soon cleaving the shining surface of the beautiful lake, called by the Egyptians "the Celestial Sea." It is twenty stadia in circuit, and from it lead out canals in numerous directions, lined with verdure, and rich with harvests. It also communicates with the majestic Father of rivers by a winding artificial outlet, which is lined with gardens and palaces. Along this lovely serpentine stream, our galley, after leaving the broad lake, flew like the wind, all other vessels swiftly moving from its course and giving it the way. Shooting out into the swift Nile, between two colossal sea-dragons of red stone, which guarded the entrance to the canal, we crossed to the palace-covered Rhoda. As I was about to land at the stately quay, I saw, to my surprise, the war-galley of Prince Mœris riding near, her rowers still seated at their banks, as if ready to move at a moment's warning. I met Acherres, who has wholly recovered from his long illness, of which I wrote his father, at the gateway of the palace.

"My prince," he said, looking anxious, "I am glad you have come. Her Majesty is in some great distress."

"Is Prince Mœris here?" I quickly asked.

"No, my prince; but his galley has brought hither a courier with letters."

"Perhaps he has been defeated in the borders of Ethiopia," was my reflection; for I knew he had been contemplating an invasion of its capital, on account of the promise he had exacted from the queen, that he should rule alone on the ancient throne of the Theban kings in Upper Egypt.

Ushered from apartment to apartment, I was soon led into the immediate presence of the queen. In the ante-chamber, before I entered, I had seen a stranger, whose features and costume showed that he was a Theban lord or high officer. He bowed haughtily to me, as I acknowledged his presence in the usual way when strangers meet.

I found the queen alone. She was walking to and fro with a quick, nervous step. In her hand she held a letter with the seal broken. Upon seeing me, she came towards me, and said,—

"O Prince Sesostris, who art to me next to my son, I am glad you have come! Pardon me for sending for you!" Her eyes were bright with tears, and her voice was tremulous.

"You ought to have done so, O noble queen," I answered, "since you are in trouble."

"In trouble, Sesostris! It is more than trouble; it is a weight greater than I can bear!"

"Has Mœris been defeated?" I asked, with earnest sympathy.

"Mœris defeated! No, oh no; but rather conqueror. But I speak an enigma!"

"Has aught happened to Remeses in his sacred duties?"

"No, oh no! It is Mœris! He will break my heart!"

"What has he done? What can I do?" I asked, perplexed.

"Nothing—that is, *you* can do nothing! As for Mœris, he has done everything! But why do I talk to you? You understand me not! There is a fearful secret, O Sesostris! I did not send for you to reveal it to you—but—but for sympathy;—for your company! I know you love me, for you are the friend of Remeses, and you have a mother whom you love and honour."

"And I also love and honour you, O my mother!" I said, taking her hand and conducting her to a chair. But she refused to sit down. She regarded me with eager eyes, as if she were penetrating my soul to its depths. Suddenly she said,—

"Has Remeses told you *all* the conversations I have had with him?"

"He has talked much with me of what has passed between you, O queen," I answered.

"Did he speak of a secret I held locked in my heart even from him?"

"He did. He said it was known, however, to Prince Mœris, who held it over you as a power of evil."

"Did Remeses suspect its nature?" she demanded.

"He informed me that he once had a suspicion which your Majesty removed."

"Yes," she said, with a strange, cold smile, "he fancied that Mœris's secret was, that he was the true heir of the throne—my son; and that Remeses was the nephew of Pharaoh, not himself! Was it not an extraordinary idea, prince?" she asked me, with the same icy irony that was unaccountable to me. "Who could ever doubt that Remeses is my own son?"

"No one, your majesty," I answered, seeing she looked to me for a reply.

"Surely no one! Dost thou not mark how like our eyes are? And then our voices are much on the same key, though his, as becomes a man, is deeper. His smile, is it not mine? Nay, no one could say we are not mother and son, could they, O Prince of Tyre? How strange, is it not, that Remeses should have conceived such an idea?"

"He had probably heard, your majesty, traditions of infant sons of kings having been interchanged; and as he could not account for the Prince of Thebes' influence over you by a secret, on any other reasonable grounds, he ventured this supposition."

"But he never will doubt again, O Sesostris!" she cried in an earnest manner; "no one now could make him suspect, a second time, he is not my son! Oh no, never! never! Could they, think you, my lord prince?"

"No, madam," I answered; her singular manner and language wholly surprising me, and leading me to fear that she was not at all well; that her nerves had been too severely tried by the intelligence, whatsoever its nature was, which she had received from Prince Mœris. "Your Majesty, I hope, has had no evil tidings," I added, glancing at the letter she still grasped.

"Oh, evil! All evil, all!" she cried, with anguish in her looks. "Prince Sesostris!" she all at once exclaimed, "you can be trusted! I need sympathy. I cannot have it unless I reveal to you my terrible secret! I know I can confide in you. My heart will break unless I rest the weight which oppresses it upon another heart!"

"Remeses will in a few days be with you, and—" I began; but she interrupted me with accents of terror.

"No—no! It is of him! *He* must never know my secret! It would kill him—he would fall to the earth a dead man, as if the lightnings of heaven had smitten him! No, *not* Remeses! With him silence—eternal silence!"

"If it will relieve your Majesty to confide in me, I will receive with gratitude your revelation, and extend you all the sympathy in my power," I said, with emotion.

"Noble, excellent, virtuous prince!" she exclaimed, lifting my hand to her lips. "My determination is fixed! You shall know my secret! It will be safe in your honourable breast. But will you, O prince, consent to receive a revelation affecting Remeses, your friend, which you are forbidden to make known to him?"

"For your sake, O queen, I will receive it, and conceal it from Remeses, and all men," I answered. "I would not wish to make known to him what would affect him, as you say."

"Come with me, then, O prince, into my private cabinet," she said, with a voice deep and full, as if she were greatly moved.

I was about to follow her, as she went with a quick resolved step, when her page without the door gave the usual sign, by tinkling a silver sistrum, which forms the handles of their ivory sticks, that he wished to enter. The queen said, almost sternly,—

"I can see no one, prince."

I approached the double door, and, opening one of the inlaid valves, saw behind the page the tall figure of the Theban.

"This lord waits for an answer," said the page.

"The queen will give you audience by and by," I said. "At present her Majesty is engaged. Await her leisure."

The Thisian courier bit his lip, and scowled impatiently. I perceived that the man had caught the spirit of the master; and could judge how defiant and haughty Mœris must be when his courier could play the impatient follower so well. Rejoining her Majesty, I said, in answer to her inquiring look, "The courier from the viceroy."

"Yes—he is restless. But I must have time!" She grew so deadly pale, as she spoke, that I supported her into the cabinet, when she sunk upon a lounge, and would have fainted away but for water at hand. When she recovered she said,—

"Sesostris, my son, my friend, when your hear all, you will find excuses for me. Read that letter first."

And she placed in my hand an epistle, written upon the silver leaves which the kings of Thebes have always made use of for their royal letters.

But, my dear mother, I will here close this epistle. My next will not be for your eye at present, if ever; unless circumstances transpire which will remove the seal from the secret revealed to me.

I feel that your warmest sympathies will be with the unhappy queen.

Farewell, dearest mother! May the gods preserve you from all sorrow, and the Lord of the Sun, the Great Invisible, defend your life and throne. I hope soon to hear the result of your embassy to the barbaric King of Cyprus.

Your dutiful son,

SESOSTRIS.

LETTER XXIII.

PALACE OF RHODA.

MY VERY DEAR MOTHER,—

I EMBRACE the first leisure I can command, since closing my last letter, to resume the subject which filled its pages.

This letter, however, I shall withhold, until I either have authority to send it to you, or circumstances render it expedient to destroy it; but in order to keep a record of the events now transpiring, I write them down in the shape of an epistle to my dear mother, so that hereafter, if it be necessary to refer to it for facts, there may be written evidence of them.

The letter of Prince Mœris, which the queen placed in my hands, was dated some years back, and, no doubt, on noticing **this, my** countenance betrayed surprise; for she said quickly,—

"Read that first. I conceal nothing from you. You shall know from the beginning."

By permission of her Majesty, I took a copy of the letter, and of **the** two that follow. It was dated—

"Castle of Bubastis, Pelusian Delta.

"To Amense, Queen,—

"Your Majesty,—I address my **letter to you** from this petty castle, though, albeit, the stronghold of your kingdom seaward, over which you have made me governor. For a subject, this would be a post of honour. For me, the son of your husband's brother, your royal nephew, it is but an honourable exile from a court where you fear my presence. Honourable, do I say?—rather, dishonourable; for am I not a prince of the blood of the Pharaohs? But let this pass, your majesty. I do not insist **upon** anything based upon **mere** lineage. *I feel that I was aggrieved by the birth of Remeses.* I see that **you** turn pale. Do not do so **yet**. **You** must read further **before the** blood wholly leaves your cheek. I repeat, I am aggrieved **by the** 'birth of Remeses.' You see I quote the last three words. **Ere** you close this letter, your Majesty will know why I mark them *thus*. Your husband, the vicegerent of the Thisitic kingdom of the South, after leaving his capital, Thebes, at the head of a great army, died like a soldier descended from a line of a thousand warrior kings, in combat with the Ethiopian. I was then, for your Majesty **was** without offspring, the heir to the throne of Egypt. I was the son of **your** husband's younger brother. Though but three years old when **your** lord was slain, I had learned the lesson that I **was** to **be king of** Egypt, when I became a man. But **to** the surprise of all **men**, of **your** council of priests, and your cabinet **of** statesmen, lo! you soon afterwards became a mother, when no evidences of this promise had been apparent! Nay, do not cast down this letter, O queen! Read it to the end! It is important you should know all.

"When I became of lawful maturity, it was whispered to me by a certain person, **that** there were suspicions that the queen had feigned maternity, and that she had adopted an infant of the wife of one of her lords, in order **to** prevent the son of her husband's brother from inheriting. It is **true**, your Majesty, that my father, your lord's brother, loved you, **as a** maiden, and would have borne you from the palace of Pharaoh, your father, as his own. Yet why should your revenge extend to his son, after **he** married another princess? Why **did you** deceive Egypt, and supplant his son (myself), by imposing upon Egypt the infant Remeses, the child of **a** lord of your palace, whom no one knows, for you took care to **send** him, with an ample bribe of gold, to Carthage, or some other distant country. Now, your Majesty knows whether this be true or not. I believe it to be so, and that the haughty, hypocritically meek Remeses, has no more right to be called the son of Pharaoh's daughter than one of the children of the base Hebrews, or of an Egyptian swineherd ; and, by the gods, judging from his features, he might be a Ben Israel!

"I demand, therefore, that you make me viceroy of the Thebaïd. Unless you do so, I swear to your Majesty, that I will agitate this suspicion, and fill all Egypt with the idea that your favourite Remeses is not your son. Whether I believe this or not, matters not. If there be any truth in it, *your majesty knows*, and will, no doubt, act accordingly.

"Your faithful nephew,
"MŒRIS, Prince."

When I had finished reading this extraordinary letter, I raised my eyes to the queen. She was intently observing its effect upon my countenance.

"Dared that man write thus to your Majesty?" I cried, with the profoundest emotions of indignation.

"You have read," answered the queen, with a tremulous voice.

"And did not your Majesty at once send and arrest the bold insulter and dangerous man?" I said.

She bit her lip, and said, in a hollow tone,—

"Prince of Tyre, is he not this day viceroy of the Thebaïd?"

"Does your Majesty mean that you yielded to his demand?"

"Yes."

"I marvel at it," said I, confounded at the acknowledgment. "If what he had said had been true—"

"Sesostris, falsehood often flies faster than truth. It can do as much mischief. The rumour of such a thing, false or true, would have shaken my throne, and destroyed the confidence of the mass of the people in Remeses when he came to the sceptre. I resolved to stifle it by giving Mœris what he asked."

I regarded the queen with sentiments of pity and sorrow. She said quickly,—

"Read another letter from him." I did so. It was dated three years later, and demanded the command of the fleet, and its separation from the control of the general-in-chief of the armies. This general-in-chief was Remeses, dear mother. To the demand the queen yielded, and thereby erected the maritime arm of her kingdom into an independent service, acknowledging no superior authority but that of the throne. When I had ended the perusal of the letter, the queen placed in my hand a third missive from this powerful man.

"This is what I received but now," she gasped. "Read it, Sesostris, and give me your sympathy."

It bore date—

"CAMP, OPPOSITE THE PALACES OF THE
MEMNONIA, THEBAÏD.

"TO THE QUEEN AMENSE:

"Your Majesty,—I write from my pavilion pitched at the foot of the Libyan mountains. I need not forewarn you of the subject of this letter, when I assure you that within the hour I have received intelligence from Memphis, that you are about to abdicate your throne in favour of Remeses, your supposititious son. This intelligence does not surprise me. When I was in Lower Egypt, I saw through you and your policy. I perceived that while you feared me, you resolved to defeat my power over you. This purpose, to surrender the sceptre of the two Egypts, I can penetrate. You design, thereby, securely to place Remeses beyond my power to harm him, for that, being king, if I lift a finger he can destroy me. I admire your policy, and bow in homage to your diplomacy. But, O Queen, both you and Remeses are in my power! Nay, do not flash your imperial eyes at this assertion. Hear me for a few moments.

"Your ready compliance with my demand, a few years ago, to create me viceroy of Thebes, led me to believe that my suspicions were true; that is, that Remeses was the son of one of your noble ladies, whom you had adopted. And when you made me admiral of your fleet, on my second demand, I was convinced that you feared the truth, and that it might be proven, with proper evidence, that Remeses was not your son. I sat to work to obtain this evidence. You know that I have something of the sleuth-hound in my composition, and that once upon a track I will follow it to its termination, were it under the pyramid of Noachis itself. I employed emissaries. I bribed even your own courtiers. I ascertained who were of your court when your husband was killed in Ethiopia, thirty-five years ago. Three old lords and ladies still live, and have good memories when gold and jewels, and promises of place dazzle their humid eyes. From them I learned that about the time of the supposed birth of Remeses, you sent away in one day, five of your ladies and maids of honour, to a distant country; yet not so quickly but that one of them dropped the secret that you were not a real mother, and that the infant you called your own was the son of another woman. This secret was told to her brother, who, in after years, was my master of horse. When, on one occasion, I was about to put him to death for cowardice in battle, he informed me that he held a great secret 'concerning the queen, Prince Remeses, and myself,' and that if I would pardon and restore him to his rank, he would divulge it, saying, that for fear it would be traced to him by your Majesty if he ever spoke of it, he had never made it known to any man.

"Curiosity and instinct led me to pardon him. He then stated what I have above written,—that you feigned maternity, and, obtaining a male child from the Hebrew nurse of one of your ladies, who had given birth to it a few weeks before, you shut yourself up three months, and then palmed it upon the priests and people, as the heir of your throne and of the sceptre of the Pharaohs. The mother, the nurse, and the ladies who were parties to the transaction were then all banished from Egypt.

"Instituting a thorough investigation, by despatching galleys to Tyre, Carthage, Gades, and the isles of the sea, at length I was rewarded by the discovery of the port to which your women were carried. Two of them only were found alive. Those two are now in the city of On! When I was in Lower Egypt I saw them, and will name them: Thebia, of Pythom, and Nilia, of On. Your Majesty perceives how exact I am, that I have my way clear as I advance. Methinks I can see you turn deadly white, and that with a shriek you let fall the papyrus! Take it up again, and resume the perusal. It is useless to shrink from the development of the truth. You may shut your eyes at noon, and say, 'it is night,' but you cannot by so doing, destroy the light of the sun. You may close your eyes—you may destroy this letter, or may read no further; but the truth will shine nevertheless, with a brightness which will drive night itself before it!

"These venerable women, examined apart told the same tale. It is as follows :—

"'That you had approached the river on the morning of the festival of Isis (you see I am particular), to bathe, as your custom was, in the marble crescent at the foot of the gardens of your palace of Rhoda, where you now are residing. You had descended the steps into the water, and your women had taken your necklace and other ornaments from you; and, robed in your bathing-dress, you were about to step into the river, when you descried a basket floating slowly past, close to the place where you stood. While you were looking at it, it lodged against a group of flags, near the statue of Nepth, just above you. Your maidens were lingering upon the bank, or walking near at hand, awaiting you, when, seeing Nilia not far off, you called to her, and said,—

"'Seest thou the little baris of basket-work, O Nilia. Draw it in to the shore, and look what it contains.'

"The handmaiden obeyed you, aided by her companion, Thebia, and when you drew near and opened the lid, you beheld a beautiful child lying within it. It looked up into your face and wept so piteously, that you took it up, deeply impressed by its beauty and helplessness, and the extraordinary manner in which it had come to you. You placed it in the arms of Thebia, and said to her :—

"'This child is sent to me by Nilus, the deity of this great river of Egypt. I will adopt it as my own, for it has no father but the river, no mother but this little ark of flags and bitumen in which it has floated to my feet.

"You then gave the lovely babe many kisses, tenderly soothed its cries, and was so happy with the prize, that you hastened to leave the river. But before you did so, the wind blew aside its mantle, and you discovered that it was a Hebrew male child, for the Egyptians do not circumcise their infants. This discovery was made also by the two women, Nilia and Thebia, and you said,—

"'It is one of the Hebrews' children.'

"It was at the time when your father's edict for the destruction of all the male children of this Syrian race was in existence. You deliberated what to do with it, when its wailing tones moved your heart, and you said to them,—

"'It shall still be mine! Let us keep the secret! I will raise it as my son! Its parents think it has perished, for they could not have hoped to save it by committing it to this frail bark, and it can never know its origin!'

'That child, O queen, is Remeses! Of this I have certain evidence.

The two women say you ordered the little ark to be taken in charge by your chief of the baths. In verification of the account, the ark still exists and I have seen it.

"It is not necessary for me to add more. I have written enough to show you the power I hold over you, and over this Remeses-Mosis. His very name signifies 'Taken out of the water,' and was given to him by yourself, as if the gods would make you the means of your own conviction.

"Now, O queen, who intendeth to place a degraded Hebrew upon the throne of Egypt, I Mœris, write this epistle warning you, that unless you revoke your purpose and publicly adopt me as your son, and convey to me the two crowns, I will proclaim through all Egypt your shame, and the true history of this Remeses! I could have excused you had he proved to be the son of one of your ladies, as the report was; but an Hebrew! *He* deserves death, and *you* to forfeit your crown! But I will make these terms with your Majesty :—if you will call a council of your hierarchy and adopt me as your son, that I may be your heir, and will abdicate in my favour, I will conceal what I know from the Egyptians; and more still, I will make Remeses governor over Goshen, and lord of all his people under my rule. Is not this liberal?

"If you refuse my terms, I will descend upon Lower Egypt with my fleet, declare your throne vacant, Remeses a slave, and seize the sceptre! Once in my power your favourite Remeses shall die an ignominious death, and you shall remain a prisoner for life in the castle of Bubastis.

"I despatch a special courier—my master of horse—*whose sister was your lady in waiting at the finding of Remeses.* Unless I have a reply in the affirmative, for which my courier will delay six hours, you shall hear me knocking at the gates of Rhoda with the head of my spear! "Mœris,

"Nephew and heir of Amense, Queen of Egypt."

When, my dear mother, I had finished reading this extraordinary letter, I held it unrolled in my hands for a few moments, stupefied, as it were, with amazement. My eyes sought the face of the queen. It was rigid as iron—white as alabaster; but her regards were riveted upon my countenance.

"Your Majesty," I said, hardly knowing what to say, "what fable is this of the daring and impious Prince of Thebes—?"

She interrupted me with—

"What dost thou think, O Sesostris? If it be a fable, is it not, in such a man's hands as dangerous as truth? Dare I let him circulate such a tale throughout Egypt? *Can* I let it reach the ears of Remeses?"

"Why not, O queen?" I asked. "If it is false, it can be shown to be so; and my friend Remeses is too great and wise to heed it. Is it by so improbable and artfully framed a story as this you are made unhappy? and for this you resign your crown and hasten to secure Remeses in power?"

"Is it not enough?"

"No, O wise and virtuous lady!" I answered, with indignant feelings against Mœris, and sympathy for her womanly fears; "my advice to you is, to defy the malice and wickedness of the viceroy, inform Remeses of these letters—nay, let him read them—assemble your army, and meet him with open war. A row of galleys sunk across the Nile will stop his fleet; and if he land, your soldiers, with Remeses at their head, will drive him back to his city of a hundred gates, and—"

Again the queen interrupted me,—

"No, no! I cannot tell Remeses! He must never know of these letters!" she almost shrieked.

"Has Remeses any suspicion of the tale they tell?" I asked.

"No. He knows no other mother. If he hears this story he will investigate it to the last, to show me that he would prove it false in the mouth of Mœris."

"And this he ought to do, your Majesty," I said firmly.

"Prince Sesostris, dost thou believe he could prove it false?" she demanded in a mysterious and strange tone.

"Undoubtedly," I answered; though my dear mother, I could not wholly resist the recollection, which forced itself upon me most sharply and painfully, of the resemblance I had noticed between Remeses and the Hebrew people. But I banished the idea it suggested, regarding it more probable for an Egyptian and Hebrew to look alike, than for Remeses to have been born a Hebrew, and adopted by Pharaoh's daughter. Nevertheless there was apparent to myself a want of fulness in my tones when I answered her "undoubtedly."

The queen came close up to me, and said in a deep terrible whisper, looking first wildly around her, to see if any one overheard her,—

"*He cannot prove it false!*"

"You mean, O queen," said I, "that though Remeses cannot prove it false, it nevertheless *is* false?"

"*No.* It cannot be proven *false*, because it is TRUE!" she answered as if her voice came from within a sarcophagus.

"True?" I repeated with horror.

"True, O prince! It is impossible for me to conceal or prevaricate. I promised to confide in you; but I have kept back till the last the *whole* truth! I can do so no longer!" She caught by my arm to sustain her tottering form.

"Is not Remeses, then, your son?" I cried.

"No."

"Is he a Hebrew?"

"Yes."

"Then this letter of Mœris is all true?"

"All as to the fact that Remeses is a Hebrew!"

Such was the rapid colloquy which followed. O my dear mother, no mortal can estimate the amount of agony which overwhelmed my soul at this intelligence! I sank upon the pedestal of a statue near me, and covering my face with my hands, burst into tears. The queen did not speak, but suffered my paroxysm of grief and mortification to exhaust itself. At length I raised my head. I felt for her— felt, oh how profoundly, for the unhappy Remeses—ignorant of his

THE FINDING OF MOSES.

calamity, and engaged even then, in the vigils and rites which were to prepare him to ascend the throne! I could now understand all that had been inexplicable in the queen's conduct, unravel her mysterious language, see the motive of all her acts. I no longer marvelled that, she, loving Remeses with all a mother's love, trembled before Mœris and his secret, and gave him all he demanded as the price of silence. But when he asked for her throne as the bribe for secrecy, it was more than her spirit could bear; and unable alone, unaided, to meet him in his demand, she sought counsel of me and sympathy; and little by little made known to me, as I have narrated, the secret she would have sacrificed her life to conceal, if she could thereby have concealed it for ever from Remeses.

"Poor, noble, unhappy Remeses!" I ejaculated.

"He must *never* know it!" she cried, passionately.

"It will be known to him," I answered sorrowfully. "If you refuse Prince Mœris's demand, he will write another such missive as this, and despatch it to Remeses. The Prince, if I may, from love, still call him so, will, as you have said, examine the matter. Mœris will refer him to the ladies Nilia and Thebia. He will then come to you—"

"To me?" she cried with a shudder.

"To you, O queen, and ask of you if Prince Mœris and these women relate the truth."

"He would not believe—he would not believe it—so far as to come to me. He would not insult me by making such a demand of me!"

"He may be forced to it. Circumstances may overcome him, so that he will feel that he must appeal to you. He would refuse to ascend the throne of Egypt, so high is his integrity, if there were a doubt as to his legitimate right to it."

"O prince, counsel me! What shall I do?" she cried, wringing her hands, and looking towards me in the most appealing and helpless manner.

"I know not how to counsel your Majesty," I replied, greatly distressed, my heart bleeding both for her and Remeses, who, I felt, sooner or later, must come to the truth of the dreadful rumour; and also from my knowledge of the perfect uprightness and justice of his character, as well as his firmness, that he would investigate it until he either disproved or verified it.

At length after a long and painful interval of embarrassment, the queen, of her own will said to me,—

"Sesostris, I meant no wrong. I loved the weeping babe, in its desolate state, and no sooner did I take it up than it smiled, and won my heart. You know the fine appearance of Remeses as a man; judge you therefore how lovely he was when an infant three months old. I was childless. My husband had been a few weeks dead, and this infant seemed to be sent to me in part to fill up the place made void in my affections. That it was a Hebrew child did not move me. I had always opposed the cruel edict of the king, my father; and felt that, to save this child of the oppressed Hebrews, would in some degree atone for the death of so many who were destroyed in obedience to his orders. Thus I was influenced by a threefold motive—to save the infant, to adopt a son, to atone for evil."

"Good and lawful motives, O queen," I said, interested in her narrative, so touchingly told as to deeply affect me.

"I did not believe I was doing evil. I at once, at the suggestion of one of my maids, sent a Hebrew girl, who was gazing upon us from afar, to call a nurse from the Hebrew women for the child. She brought one, comely and gentle in manner, whom I took with me to the palace; and, after instructing her to keep the matter a secret, suffered her to take the child home, for she lived in a garden, not far above the palace, upon the island, her father being a cultivator of flowers for the priests. The tenderness of this Hebrew woman towards the beautiful babe pleased me, and, after I had, in a public manner, acknowledged the child, even as Mœris's letter states, I let it remain with her until it grew to be three years old, when I commanded her to bring it to the palace to remain; for although I had seen it almost daily, I now desired to have it wholly in my possession. From that time he has been brought up in my own palace, as my son, and educated as prince of the empire and heir to the throne. For all my care and affection, he has repaid me with the profoundest devotion, and tenderest attachment. At first, seeing he was very fond of his Hebrew nurse, I jealously forbade her again to visit him, so that I might be the sole object of his attachment. He soon forgot her, and from his fourth year, has known no love but mine. When he came to manhood, I had him instructed in the art of war, and made him general of the army of the pyramids. By the greatest philosophers and sages he was taught geometry, astrology, architecture, physics, mythology, and the knowledge of all science. I have spared no care to educate him in all the learning of the Egyptians. With all his wisdom and vast knowledge, he is as docile and gentle in disposition as a child: ever dutifully submissive to my will, the voice which has led armies by its battle-cry, melts into tenderness in my presence. Ah, prince, never mother loved a son as I have loved him!"

"I pity you, O queen, with all my heart," said I, warmly.

"Oh, what shall I do? What shall I reply to Mœris?"

"I know not how to counsel you!" I said, embarrassed by this appeal.

"I will then act. His courier shall not go back unanswered. I will defy him!" A new spirit seemed all at once to animate her.

She clapped her hands. A page entered.

"Bid the Theban courier enter. His answer is ready."

The master of horse came haughtily in, a cloud of impatience yet upon his brow.

"Go back to thy master, and say to him, that Amense is still queen of Egypt, and wears both the crowns of her fathers, and that she will defend them. Say, that I defy him, and fear him not!"

The courier looked amazed, bowed with a slight gesture of obeisance, and left the presence.

No sooner had the valves of the door closed upon him, than she said—

"It is done! The arrow is drawn from the quiver, and set to the bowstring. There is nothing left but to defy him, and trust the gods to aid the just cause. Remeses will be crowned king, ere Mœris can get my message and return a letter to him. There are but five days more to the end of the forty. Three days afterwards is the coronation. That is nine from to-day. It will take twelve or more days for a message to go and come from the camp of Mœris. Three days! Time enough to make or mar an empire. Sesostris, this prince of Typhon, this haughty Mœris, shall yet be confounded!"

Thus speaking, the queen, whose whole powers were aroused by despair linked with affection, laid her hand in mine, bade me good-night—for it was now moonlight, so long had we discoursed—and begged me come in the morning and breakfast with her.

Here, in the quiet of my chamber, dear mother, I have made a record of this extraordinary interview. The letter I shall preserve unless it be necessary to destroy it; but I shall not send it to you until the seal of secrecy is removed.

What can I say? How can I realize that Remeses is a Hebrew? How little he suspects the truth! Will he hear it? If he does; but it is useless to speculate upon the consequences. I pray that he may be well crowned before Mœris can do him any mischief; for, son of Misr, or son of Abram, he is worthy of the throne of Egypt, and will wield its sceptre with wisdom and justice, beyond that of any of the proud Pharaohs. The attachment of the queen is natural. I deeply feel for her. The conduct of Mœris is also natural. What will be his course? Farewell, dear mother.

Your affectionate son,
SESOSTRIS.

LETTER XXIV.

PALACE OF REMESES, CITY OF ON.

MY DEAREST MOTHER,—

I COMMENCE this letter, as I did one written and addressed to you two days ago, with the probability, that circumstances may yet render the seal of secrecy, now placed upon it, unnecessary; at least I shall detain both this one and that, for a time, if not finally destroy them. But I have a feeling that you will yet read what I write.

If the incidents and scenes recorded in the preceding letter, were of an extraordinary kind, you must be prepared to read in this, of events still more strange, and painfully interesting. It is with an effort that I calm my pulse, and subdue my emotions sufficiently, to narrate equably what I desire to make known to you.

The morning after my interview with the queen, I arose early from a sleepless couch; for the events of the preceding evening, recalled by an excited mind, kept me awake with reflections of the most anxious and distressing nature. I mourned for Remeses, my noble, wise, and great friend and counsellor,—a prince by nature, and by the seal of all the gods, if not by inheritance from the Pharaohs. Not regarding the Hebrew race with the disdainful eye of those who have been masters over them, like the Egyptians, but looking upon them only as an unfortunate nation, descendants of the three patriarchal princes of Palestine, I, dear mother, felt no contempt for Remeses on account of his lineage and blood. To me, he was still as dear and as much honoured. It was not the "prince" I loved from the first, but the "*man*," and he remains. I tossed my head on my pillow, grieving for him; as I knew, should the tidings ever come to his ears, and be confirmed as a truth, that it would break his great heart—crush his mighty soul to the earth; for, educated as an Egyptian prince, he entertains towards the Hebrews, the haughty contempt (so far as this sentiment can repose in such a benevolent bosom), which characterizes the Egyptian nation. How will he be humbled, overwhelmed, confounded, dismayed!

Such were my wakeful reflections, when at length the morning dawned; and I arose, bathed, and prepared to obey the command of the queen to breakfast with her. Believing that she must have passed a sorrowful night, and would not awake early, I sat down to read in a roll of papyrus which lay upon my table, among other books that belonged to Remeses; for I was occupying his own suite of rooms during his absence, amid the sacred mysteries of his kingly initiation. It proved to be written in the Theban running character, which I am not familiar with, and laying it down, I took up a leaf of new papyrus, on which I recognized the bold and elegant script of Remeses. As he had given me free access to all upon the table, I examined the subject, and finding that it was a sacred poem, I read therein a few sentences, when I perceived that it was the history of a remarkable era in the life of the venerable Lord of Uz, to whom I have alluded. This aged and interesting Syrian has already taken his departure, but previously made known to Remeses, as he told me, all the events connected with an extraordinary period of his middle life.

I read, therefore, with interest what Remeses had commenced: for it was only a beginning. After giving the name of the Lord of Uz, and that of the land in which he dwelt, he spoke of his uprightness, his holiness, his riches, and his pious care over his children—who were seven sons and three daughters; and also of their happiness, festivities, and prosperity; and how, by the permission of the One God, Typhon, or the Spirit of Evil, tempted him.

Thus far had my friend got in the history, and I was about to replace the scroll, when the door opened, and lo! Prince Remeses himself stood before me! I started with an exclamation of joyful astonishment; but seeing his visage haggard and pallid with woe, I was alarmed. I approached him to embrace him, as he stood just within the door, regarding me with looks of doubt and solicitude.

"Wilt thou, O Prince of Tyre, embrace a Hebrew?" he surprised me by asking, in a voice deep and tremulous.

"Then thou knowest it all," I cried, "O my friend!" as I threw myself into his embrace.

For a few minutes we wept in each other's arms. At length he spoke and said—

"Yes, Sesostris, I have heard it all! Thou knowest the secret also, says my moth——nay—I forgot—I should have said—the queen!" Here his emotion overcame him. He leaned his noble head upon my shoulder and continued: "Yet she is my mother, prince! She has ever been a mother to me! I have known no other! I shall love her, while my life lasts, above all earthly things. Pardon my grief, Sesostris! Nature is mighty in sorrow, and will have her way! The heart, like our Nile, will sometimes overflow, if full."

In a few moments he was composed, and said sadly,—

"Knowing my history, can you regard me as before?"

"I love thee as ever, O prince—"

He interrupted me—"Call me not 'prince,' call me by my name—that, at least, is left me! But I am a slave!"

"No—not to me! You are a descendant of kings! Are not Prince Abraham, Isaac, and the great Prince Jacob your ancestors? I am not an Egyptian any more than thyself," I answered him.

"True, true! I must not forget that! I thank thee, O prince, for reminding me of this. A slave in Egypt may be a freeman in Tyre!"

"That is true also," I said. "May I ask, O Remeses, why you have left the temples and are here; and how you heard this intelligence, which you bear up under like a god?"

"I am calm now; but, Sesostris, I have passed through a sirocco of the soul! You shall hear all. Come and sit here."

I placed myself by the table opposite to him. He then began as follows:—

"I need not describe to you, O my friend, the nature of the rites and ceremonies, nor the character of the mysteries which I have been in contact with, for five-and-thirty days; let it be enough for your curiosity to know, that beneath all the splendour of our polytheism is hidden the mystery, known to the 'sons of the Lord of heaven, or One God. This truth is guarded by the mystics, as a mystery, not as a doctrine; and is of no value to them nor to the world: it is as if the sun were for ever shrouded in impenetrable clouds. I have learned it only darkly; but this is not to my purpose now, my friend: perhaps at another time we will discourse of these things. I had passed my decreed days and nights, at all the shrines which the laws for kings direct, when, last night, I was borne across the Nile by a company of the mystics, who left me at the entrance of the avenue leading to the sphinx that is before Cheops and Chephres. There twelve other ecclesiastical mystics took me in charge. We marched together, six on each side of me, in profound silence; till, on passing the lion facing the sphinx, their leader cried—

"'Let the king be as a lion in strength and majesty!'

"The rest answered with one voice,—

"'And may his enemies be as lambs beneath his paws!'

"At the small temple, between the feet of the sphinx, three priests stood, one of whom sprinkled my head with sacred water; the second, with his little finger that had been dipped in the blood of a cock which he had sacrificed, touched my forehead; and the third waved incense before me;—while from within came a low, plaintive chant of voices and instruments, invoking the gods in a hymn on my behalf. The whole scene was solemn and impressive.

"I was then conducted to the pylon of the great temple before the pyramids. As I passed beneath the gate, the twelve priests left me; and twenty-four others, dressed in white robes and bearing torches, took me in charge, and conducted me at a slow march across the great quadrangle, leading me to a dark portal which descended, as I was told, to the base of the pyramid, down to the 'hall of all the mysteries of the earth.'"

"Is not this the temple of the magicians?" I asked, gratified to see that Remeses could for a moment so far forget his great sorrow, as to enter into these details, for my gratification.

"Yes, the place where the sorcerers and soothsayers hold their mystic and fearful rites. For ages, this subterranean temple, under the earth between the two pyramids, but no part of the pyramidal structure itself, has been their place of solemn assembly. Into this region I descended, led by only two men, who received me at the head of the stairs of stone.

"But I may not describe, more particularly, the progress of my mysterious journey through subterranean passages, which I had no conception existed beneath the space between the two pyramids; although tradition has it, that the whole territory underneath both is a labyrinthine catacomb, which assertion I have now no reason to doubt. After traversing vast gloomy corridors of pillars hewn from the solid rock, and a succession of chambers dedicated to mysteries, I was ushered, by the sound of awful music, from an unseen source, into a great central temple, so large that the torches borne by my guides, could not penetrate its outer blackness. In the centre of this solemn hall stood an altar of black marble. We approached it, when suddenly from it soared aloft a bright flame which illumined the temple, to its remotest obscurities, with a light like the moon when it is full, revealing in the height above, a firmament with its thousands stars reflecting the light. I had already, my Sesostris, passed through such varied and surprising scenes, in the progress of my initiation, that I was not surprised at this, for the arts of the priestly magicians seem to embrace a knowledge of all the secret alchemy of nature; and they possess wisdom and skill to control her wonderful powers. While this brilliant flame burned from a brazen vase which stood upon the altar, a procession of figures entered by a distant door, and slowly made the circuit of the massive corridor. I perceived at once that they were attired symbolically, representing the powers of nature, and were preceded by five stately and imposing forms standing for fire, water earth, air, and the Nile; symbols of which were worn upon their heads, and carried in their hands. Behind these came seven persons, each crowned with a star, the whole representing the seven stars. Then advanced Orion, belted and armed; Arcturus, Aldebaran, Procyon, Rigel, and Antares, each with a blazing coronet above his brow, and carrying the symbols and wearing the dress of the god. These, with an interval of space between, were followed by the twelve constellations of the zodiac; each zodiac consisting of twelve bands of men, subdivided into twenty-four smaller companies, and so moving, each in a place assigned him, as to show the position of every star of the constellation, which he was appointed to aid in illustrating. Each individual carried above his head a starry light, enclosed in a crystal cup.

"This imposing and magnificent representation and illustration of the march of Time through the heavens, with all the movements of the heavenly orbs, presented a spectacle of splendour unsurpassed by any human display. Solemn as the march of the stars themselves, this procession of constellations moved once around the grand circuit of the temple, and then the five leaders advanced towards the altar, by which I stood alone, deserted by those who had led me thither. Every one of these symbolic persons in succession bent the knee before me, in token that the powers of the earth, air, fire, and water with the great Nile itself, were submissive to my will. Ah, Sesostris," interspoke Demeses here, "how little did they suspect, when paying me this customary homage, that I was a mere Hebrew slave, who could make use of the air, of fire, of water, of the earth, or of the Nile, only by the permission of my Egyptian masters!

"Other striking ceremonies passed thereafter, and by-and-by I was left alone beside the altar, the flame of which it was my duty to feed with naphtha until morning, this being the first vigil of the last five nights. I was not, however, long left alone. Seven magicians, in their gorgeous apparel, came from a door that seemed to be an outlet from beneath the second pyramid, and approached me, chanting a war-song. Each bore a piece of royal armour,—one a helmet, one a cuirass, one a spear, another a shield. As they passed me they presented, and I received from each, a piece of the armour, and invested myself therewith. I was told by the leader to be strong and fight valiantly, for I should be assailed by powers of evil. They then left me, and again I was alone, yet on my guard. Feeding the flame till it burned high, I sought to penetrate the gloom, at least expecting to behold a lion let into the temple for me to combat with, that I might prove my right to the sword of the Pharaohs which I held in my grasp.

"I know not, Sesostris, who or what would have been my assailant, if due time had elapsed for his coming; but I suddenly heard a step behind me, and behold, instead of a fierce beast or a warrior, a single magician, tall and commanding, who bore in one hand merely the sacred *crux* or emblem of life, and in the other his black wand tipped with an emerald. I challenged him, as I was directed to do by my instructors, and demanded whether he came for good or evil, with war or peace in his heart.

"He made no other reply than—

"'Follow me!'"

"I obeyed. Ah, how little did I suspect, O Sesostris, that I was about to encounter what was more fearful than a roaring lion,—more terrible than an armed host! But you shall hear.

"I crossed the echoing temple-floor to a small portal, which at first did not reveal its presence, being a slab in the wall, but which, at a slight pressure of the magician's wand, betrayed an opening through which we passed,—I, with my sword held in my hand to defend or attack. The stone door closed behind me, and I was conducted through a beautiful chamber, adorned with marbles, and sparkling with precious stones, that seemed to shine by a light of their own, as I could discover no source of reflection; though doubtless, however, that was in some part concealed by the art of these ingenious and wise magicians.

"There was an inner chamber, or adytum, entirely encased with panels of black marble, polished like a mirror. I was conducted into this room, and commanded, by a voice unknown, and from an invisible person, to seat myself upon a stone chair in the centre of the floor. I obeyed; for princes, during their initiation, are taught constantly, that 'he who would know how to command must learn how to obey;' and thus, in these rites, submission and obedience are inculcated, as necessary elements in the character of one who wishes to exact them from others. Indeed, Sesostris, the whole routine of the ceremonies, though sometimes vain and frivolous, sometimes extravagant, is calculated to impress upon the heart of the prince the wisest lessons in self-government, and the profoundest knowledge of himself. Every temptation is offered him, that he may resist it. Every condition of life, from hunger and thirst upward, he passes through in his progress. Three nights and days I fasted in the temple of Pthah, that I might pity the hungry: two days I suffered thirst, that I might feel for the thirsty; six hours I toiled with burdens, that I might know how my poorer subjects toiled; one hour I was a servant, another a prisoner, a third cup-bearer to the high priest. Every rite is a link in the practical education of a prince; and he who comes to the throne, has reached it through every grade of society, and through every condition of humanity; and thus the king centres and unites within his own person, from having been engaged in each, the pursuits of all his people, and knows by experience their joys and sorrows, toils and pleasures; and can say to every class of Egyptians, 'there is nothing which appertains to you that is foreign to me. The people of Egypt are represented in their king.'

"When I had taken my seat in this chamber of black marble, which was dimly lighted by a misty radiance before me, I saw that I was alone. Now, O Sesostris, came my trial!—such an one as no prince of the house of Pharaoh had ever passed through. It is said that Osirtasen, when he was brought to this chamber, had it revealed to him that he was the son of the god Hercules; but to me was revealed, alas! thou knowest what, and shalt hear how!

"'Remeses-Moses,' said a deep and stern voice from what, in the obscurity, seemed to me a shrine, 'thou art wise and virtuous, and strong of heart! Gird thyself with courage, and hear what is to be revealed to thee! Know that thou art not the son of Amense, queen of Egypt, as thou believest. She was never a mother!'

"'It is false, thou wicked magician!' I cried, starting to my feet. 'Art thou, then, the foe I am to meet and destroy?'

"'Silence, young man!' cried another voice, with a tone of power. 'What the mysterious oracle utters is true. Thou art not the son of Pharaoh's daughter! Thou hast no title to the throne of Egypt!'

"'Who am I, then?' I cried impressed and awed, yet full of anger at the words.

"'Thou art the son of a Hebrew mother and a Hebrew father!' said the voice.

"I advanced sword in hand to meet these invisible persons, believing that the insult was but another of the series of tests, and this one in particular, of my patience and temper; for, O Sesostris," added Remeses to me bitterly, "what greater insult could have been put upon a prince of Egypt than this! When I came forward, I saw the wall, as it were, open before me; and I beheld the Nile in bright sunshine; the Island of Rhoda, with its palaces and Gardens; the distant towers and obelisks of On, and all the scenery adjacent, but seemingly so near that I could lay my hand upon it all.

"At this surprising spectacle manifesting itself in the dark chambers of the pyramids, I stood amazed and arrested! I felt that it was supernatural, or produced by magic. As I gazed, perplexed, a third voice said, "Behold! Thou seest that the obelisk of Amense is wanting; that the palace of the governor of the Nile has only its foundations laid. The scene is, as Egypt was thirty-five years ago.'

"I looked again, and recognized the truth. I saw it was not the Nile of to-day. I saw also, that its stream was at a height, different from its present mark upon the nilometer. I was amazed, and awaited with intense expectation. Suddenly I saw a party of spearmen enter a hut, which I perceived was one of a group that was occupied by Hebrew workmen, who were engaged upon the governor's palace. Presently they came forth, two of them, each bearing an infant aloft upon a spear, which was thrust through it, and followed by shrieking women. I could hear and see all as if I were on the spot. I impulsively advanced to slay the men, for all seemed so real, but as I did so, saw at my feet a yawning gulf. Then the men cast the infants into the Nile. I saw three others go into another hut, whence they were driven forth by two desperate Hebrews, who, armed with strawcutters, slew two of them; but the other fled, and returning with his comrades, they set fire to the hut of rushes, and consumed the inmates within it. I now perceived that it seemed drawing towards the close of day. From a hut, near the water, a man and a young girl, both Hebrews, stole forth, and collecting bulrushes in their arms, returned to the hut. It was now night. I had seen the shades of evening fall over the scenery, and the stars come out. Yet, by a power incomprehensible to me, I could look into the closed and barred hut, and see that, by the light of a rush dipped in bitumen, three of its inmates were making, in secret haste, a large basket. I saw them finish it, and then beheld the man smear it within and without with pitch. From their conversation, I learned that they wished it to resist water, and that they were to commit some precious freight to its frail protection; what I could not learn; as, when they spoke of it, their colloquy was in low hushed tones, and with looks of fear, especially the two females, who wept very much. One of them, I learned by their words, was the daughter of the man by a former wife. There was another child, a boy apparently of the age of three years, lying in sweet sleep upon a bed of rushes, made up in a corner of the hut. When the little ark was done, I watched with the deepest interest their further proceedings. At length the three went out together, and to my surprise I saw, by the setting moon, that it was near dawn. They bent their steps, swiftly and silently, towards the ancient temple of Isis, which was then, as now, in ruins, and deserted by every Egyptian, for the sacrilege done therein under the reign of Bnon, the Phœnician Pharaoh. I could see them steal along the tangled avenue beneath the palm-trees, and through that of the broken sphinxes, until they came to the pyramidion of the obelisk of Sesostris I. Here a deep, ancient excavation, covered with vines and rushes, showed a flight of broken steps. After carefully looking all about, to see if they were observed, they descended. In a few minutes the three came forth, the elderly woman holding in her arms an infant, upon the beautiful face of which the waning moon shone for a moment, but instantly she hid it with her mantle, and hurried to the river-side. Here the man put the basket upon the shore, and extended his arms for the child. The poor mother, as I now perceived she must be, burst into tears, and clasped it closer and closer to her heart.

"'Nay, Jochebeda,' he said, with gentle firmness, 'thy cries will attract notice. The child cannot live if we delay. Hast thou not had warning from the kind Egyptian woman, who was with thee when it was born, and who aided thee in concealing it, that its hiding place is known, and that in the morning soldiers will be there? Bear up, heart! If we commit it to the Nile, the God of our fathers, in whom we trust, and who will yet return to redeem us, according to His promise to our father Abraham, may guide the frail baris to some secure haven and provide for the child a pitiful heart to save it.'

"I saw the mother give it its last nourishment at her breast, and then, with tears, lay it softly, sweetly sleeping the while, within the basket of bulrushes,—pillowing its head first upon her hand, until the daughter had placed beneath it a pillow of wild-flowers and lotus leaves, gathered on the spot in the dawning light. The father then covered it carefully over, and kissing it, with grief shaking his strong frame, was about to commit the frail boat to the water, when the poor mother arrested his arm, implored one more look, one more embrace of her child! She was a young and beautiful woman; and, the last kiss given, knelt by the shore praying to her God, as the father launched the ark into the stream. At this moment, I beheld, straying upon the bank, as if seeking its parents, the other child that I had seen in the house. I now saw the current take to its embrace the little ark, and upon its bosom bear it downward. In a few moments it lodged amid some rushes, which the mother seeing, she ran hastily, entered the water, passionately kissed her child, and would have offered it the breast again, but the more resolute father sent it once more upon its way. In the vision, I now saw that day had dawned, and that the stir of life on land and water was everywhere visible. The father watched the bark, until it could no longer be seen for the curve of the shore, and then drew near to his wife, and gently led her away to the hut,—her lingering looks ceaselessly stretched towards the Nile. The little maid, who was not more than twelve or thirteen years of age, having been previously instructed by her mother, followed along the shore to see what would become of the ark. But I weary you, Sesostris, with details, which to me had a sort of fascination, as they were enacted before me in the scenes I beheld."

"And they are deeply interesting to me, my dear Remeses," I said with emotion.

"I followed the bark also," continued Remeses, "until, after several escapes from imminent peril, it lodged against a group of flags, at the moment that a beautiful lady, accompanied by her maids, came to bathe, at the foot of the garden of Pharaoh's palace. At a glance, Sesostris, I recognized, as she was in her youth, my mother—I mean to say, the Queen Amense. I saw her attention drawn to the little ark, in the fate of which I had become intensely interested, little dreaming how much and intimately it concerned *me!* I heard her bid the maids take the basket out of the river, and her cry of surprise, on opening it and seeing the babe, which answered her with a sorrowful wail, as it were, of appeal. I saw her offer it to the bosoms of three Egyptian nurses in vain, when the little maid, its half sister, drew near with mingled curiosity and fear, and said,—

"'O princess, shall I call one of the Hebrew women, that she may nurse the child for thee?'

"The princess said, Go!'

"Immediately the maiden ran with the swiftness of a gazelle, until she came at length to her mother's house. The poor Hebrew woman was at her task, combing flax and weeping as she toiled, feeling that she had parted with her child for ever. At the height of her grief, the young maid flew in at the door, crying with a voice choked with joy,—

"'Mother, run quickly! make no stay! Pharaoh's daughter has found my little brother, taken it from the ark, and sent me for a Hebrew nurse! Come quickly, before any other is found!'

"With a cry of joy, and with hands clasped to heaven in gratitude, I saw the mother about to rush out, wild with happiness, when her daughter said, 'Be calm, mother, or the princess will suspect. Put on your coif! Arrange your dress! Seem quiet, as if you were not its mother!'

"'I will try to do so—oh, I will try to do so!' she said touchingly. I saw that, in her emotion, she did not think of her other boy, who, though hardly four years old, had followed the stream, as if he understood what the ark contained. Him I saw kindly taken pity upon by an Egyptian priest, who carried him away to his house."

Here I uttered an exclamation which attracted the notice of Remeses; for I recollected the story of the young Hebrew ecclesiastic and gold image-caster, dear mother, and saw now that he was this brother of Remeses, and the mystery of the resemblance was solved, I did not make any remark to Remeses, however, in reply to his inquiring look, and he resumed his wonderful narrative.

But I will continue the subject, dear mother, in a subsequent letter.

SESOSTRIS.

LETTER XXV.

PALACE OF REMESES, CITY OF ON.

MY DEAREST MOTHER,—

YOUR courier reached me yesterday with your important letter, advising me of the refusal of the King of Cyprus to receive your ambassador, or release your subjects; and that you only await my return to declare war. I shall not fail to respond to your call, and will next week leave Egypt for Syria. I have not yet visited the Thebaïd, and the superb temples of Upper Egypt, nor seen the wonderful Labyrinth, nor the Cataracts; but I hope at some future day to revisit this interesting land. I feel, indeed, rejoiced to go away now, as the painful and extraordinary events connected with Remeses have cast a gloom over all things here, and changed all my plans.

But I will resume the narrative, interrupted by the abrupt ending of my last letter. That, with the preceding, as well as this, I shall now send to you, as the seal of secrecy is removed from them, by the publicity which has been given to all the events by Remeses.

To return, dear mother, to the account of the scenes which the magicians presented to his vision, in the black marble chamber of the pyramid.

"I now," continued Remeses, "beheld the excited mother reach the presence of the princess, trying to calm the wild tumult of hope and fear in her maternal bosom; and to her, I saw the princess, after many inquiries, commit the charge of the infant.

"'I shall adopt this child, O nurse,' she said; 'bring it, therefore, to the palace daily that I may see it. Take as faithful care of it as if it were your own, and you shall be rewarded with my favour as well as with a nurse's wages.'

"The joyful Hebrew woman tried to repress her happiness, and trembled so, that the princess said,—

"'Thou art awkward. Carry it tenderly; and see that thou keep this secret closely, or I shall take the boy away from thee, woman, and also punish thee. What is thy name?

"'Jochebeda,' she answered.

"'And thy husband's?'

"'Amram, your Majesty,' she replied.

"I saw her, O Sesostris, when she had well got out of the princess's sight, clasp, by stealth, her recovered child to her bosom, while words of tenderness were in her mouth, and her eyes streaming with tears of gratitude and wonder.

"That child, O Sesostris, was myself!" suddenly exclaimed Remeses. "Of this you have already been convinced. I saw the scene before me, rapidly change from day to night, and months and years fly by like a cloud, or like a fleet of ships leaving no trace or their track on the closing waters. Through all I saw myself, from the infant of three years old, taken into the palace from my Hebrew mother, to the boy of twelve—to the youth of twenty! Like the cycle of fate, that scene rolled by before my eyes, until I saw myself, that is, the

Hebrew boy, in every scene of my life up to the very moment then present. Then, with a sound of mournful music, the Nile and its scenes slowly faded from before my vision, and I was alone! The whole fearful history had terminated in me, and left me standing there in solitude, to reflect upon what I had seen.

"Rousing myself from my stupor of amazement, I staggered back, and sank in horror upon the stone bench. I know not how long I lay there, but I was at length aroused by a hand upon my shoulder; I looked up and beheld the magician with the emblem of life, and the emerald-tipped wand. He said,—

"'My son, thou hast read the past of thy life! Wilt thou still be King of Egypt?'

"'By what power hast thou opened the gates of the past? How hast thou known all this?' I cried, with a heart of despair.

"'Dost thou believe?'

"'As if the open Book of Thoth lay before me! I doubt not,' I answered.

"'Wilt thou be King of Egypt?' again asked another voice. A third, in another direction, took it up, and every subterranean echo of the vaulted pyramid seemed to take up the cry. I rushed from the hall, not knowing whither I went. Doors seemed to open before me, as if by magic, and I at length found myself emerging, guided by the magician, into the open night. The granite valves of the gate closed behind me, and I was alone, in the quadrangle of the great temple of Thoth. The stars shone down upon me like mocking eyes, watching me. I fled onward, as if I would fly from myself. I feared to reflect. I passed the sphinx, the pylones, the obelisks; and ran along the avenue of the Lake of the Dead, until I reached the Nile. I crossed it in a boat that I found upon the shore, and without having formed any clear idea of what I ought to do, sought the palace, and gained my mother's ante-room. Did I say 'my mother,' Sesostris? I meant the good queen. I sent in a page to say I wished to see her. In surprise at my return, before the forty days were fulfilled, she came to the door hurriedly, in her night-robe, and opened it. I entered as calmly as I could, and did not refuse her kiss, though I knew I was but a Hebrew! One night's scenes, dreadful as they were, O Sesostris, could not wholly break the ties of a lifetime of filial love and reverence. I closed the door, secured it in silence, and then sat down, weary with what I had undergone; and, as she came near and knelt by me, and laid her hand against my forehead, and asked me 'if I were ill, and hence had left the temple,' I was overcome with her kindness; and when the reflection forced itself upon me that I could no more call her mother, or be entitled to these acts of maternal solicitude, I gave way to the strong current of emotion, and fell upon her shoulder, weeping as heartily as she had seen me weep when lying in the little ark a helpless infant.

"During this brief moment, a suspicion flashed across my mind, that the magicians might have produced this as a part of my trial as a prince;—that it was not real, but that by their wonderful arts of magic they had made it appear so to my vision. I seized upon this idea, as a man drowning in the Nile grasps at a floating flower.

"'Mother,' I said, 'I am ill. I am also very sorrowful!'

"'The tasks and toils of thy initiation, my son, have been too great for thee. Thy face is haggard and thy looks unnatural. What is thy sorrow?'

"'I have had a vision, or what was like a dream, my mother. I saw an infant, in this vision, before me, placed in an ark, and set adrift upon the Nile. Lo, after being borne by the current some ways, it was espied by a princess who was bathing, whose maids, at her command, brought it to her. It contained a circumcised Hebrew child. The princess, being childless, adopted it, and educated it, and declared it to be her son. She placed him next to her in the kingdom, and was about to resign to him the crown, when—'

"Here my mother, whose face I had earnestly regarded, became pale and trembled all over. She seized my hands and gasped,—

"'Tell me, Remeses, tell me, was this a dream, or hast thou heard it?'

"'I saw it, my mother, in a vision, in the subterranean chamber of the pyramids. It was one of those scenes of magic which the arts of the magi know how to produce.'

"'Dost thou believe it?' she cried.

"'Is it not thy *secret*, O my mother, which Prince Mœris shares with thee? Am I not right? Does not that Hebrew child,' I cried, rising, 'now stand before thee?'

"She shrieked, and fell insensible!

"At length I restored her to consciousness. I related all I have told you. Reluctantly, she confessed that all was true as I had seen it. I then, in a scene such as I hope never to pass through again, assured her I should refuse the throne and exile myself from Egypt. She implored me with strong appeals to keep the secret, and mount the throne. I firmly refused to do so, inasmuch as it would be an act of injustice, not only to Mœris, but to the Egyptians, to deceive them with a Hebrew ruler. She reminded me how, for sixty-one years, Prince Joseph had governed Egypt. 'Yes,' I said, but it was openly and without deceit; while my reign would be a gross deception and usurpation.' But, O Sesostris, I cannot revive the scene. It has passed!—I have yielded! She showed me the letters of Prince Mœris. She implored me for her sake to keep the secret, and aid her in resisting the conspiracy of the viceroy When I reflected that he had made my mother so long miserable, and now menaced her throne, I yielded to her entreaties to remain a few days at the head of the affairs that have been entrusted to my control, and to lead the army against Mœris, should he fulfil his menace to invade Lower Egypt. After that, I said, I shall refuse to be called the son of Pharoah's daughter, and will retire from the Court."

"Not among the Hebrews?" I exclaimed.

"No, perhaps not. I have nothing in common with them. I can do them no good: I cannot yet consent to share their bondage. I shall seek my own family, for the queen has told me who they are. My mother, my *own* mother, Sesostris, shall again fold her child to her heart! I recollect her beautiful, tearful face, as seen in the vision of the pyramids. I have a brother, too, and a sister!"

"I know them both!" I cried, almost joyfully; though, dear mother, it was a sad joy I felt, to know that Remeses was a brother to Miriam and the ecclesiastic gold-caster. He became at once interested, and I told him all I knew about them, as I have you. He listened with deep attention, and seemed pleased. I also told him how often I had conversed, in the garden of flowers, with the venerable Amram, the father of Miriam.

"And *my* father also, you should add," he said, with a melancholy smile. " I knew it not, Sesostris ; I believed him to be the husband of my nurse. Thinkest thou all this time he knew I was his son?"

"I doubt it not," I answered. "The eyes of your father and mother must naturally have been upon you from your childhood up. They must have witnessed all your career, and rejoiced in it, and kept the secret locked in their own humble hearts, lest you and the world should know it, and the glory they secretly saw you sharing, be taken away or resigned by you."

"I shall see them. They shall yet hear me say, mother, father, brother, sister, to each one of them. But, Sesostris, I must then bid them farewell for ever, and Egypt also,—if the queen will permit me to go," he suddenly added, with bitter irony unusual with him; "for slaves must have no will but their master's."

I laid my arm kindly and sympathizingly upon his shoulder, and silently embraced him.

"I feel for you, O Remeses, with all my heart," I said.

"I know you do, O prince : I am sure that you do. But let us terminate this subject. My mother's—I mean, alas ! the queen's desire shall be gratified.. I will, for a few days, continue as I am, but no more return to the temples. My initiation is over. Without doubt the priests of the hierarchy will seek to put me to death, when they learn that a Hebrew has been initiated into all their learning and mysteries. It will be necessary for me to leave Egypt."

"Then let Tyre, O prince, be thy asylum—thy future home!" I cried. "There the Hebrew is not in bondage, and is a Syrian among Syrians. There you shall have a palace and retinue, and be served as becomes your wisdom and greatness. My mother Epiphia will welcome you with pleasure, for she has already learned to honour you, from my letters. Our city is about to go to war with the King of Cyprus, and my mother has written, urging me to return. Twelve galleys will await me at Pelusium, in a fortnight hence, to escort my own to Tyre. Consent, O Remeses, to go with me."

" Noble prince," he exclaimed, deeply moved, "how can I thank you ! It is the greatest consolation, in this my sorrow and humiliation, to know that you do not withdraw from me your friendship ; that you can still esteem me as a man ! Sesostris, I thank you. I will accept your offer, if my—that is, the queen, will change her mind, and permit me to address a letter, by a swift courier, to Prince Mœris. In it I will briefly say that I am informed of my true lineage, and that if he will quietly wait the succession, and be submissive to the queen, and withhold his army from Memphis, I will, within three days after obtaining his affirmative reply, leave Egypt for a foreign land.

Such a course will prove the best in the end for him and Egypt, and I have no doubt he will consent to adopt it. How extraordinary that this wily man should so long have kept the secret with which he so terribly menanced my—the queen!"

I approved of the course suggested. Remeses soon afterwards sought the queen; and at the end of four hours he returned to me, looking very weary and pale, yet smiling, saying,—

"It is achieved! It was a fearful struggle! The queen has consented! Indeed, she seems heart-broken, spirit crushed! This discovery, against which her soul has so long battled, has left her prostrate, almost wrecked! For her sake I bore up and hid my own unfathomable sorrow. She has at my solicitation, consented that I shall not only write to Prince Mœris, inserting a clause enjoining silence as to my birth, but her own courier shall be its bearer, signifying her wish for conciliation. The letter was written in her presence, the clause for silence introduced, and the courier is already gone with it."

While Remeses was speaking, a page entered and informed him that the queen wished to see him. He found her ill with a feverish pulse. She called him to her and said,—

"My son, I am about to die! This blow is too heavy for me to bear! I shall never recover! It was my wish to leave you firmly seated upon my throne; but the gods have decreed otherwise. Call a council of the hierarchy. I must not be faithless to my ancestors and leave a vacant throne. You have advised me to adopt Prince Mœris. I can do no otherwise. For this act, assemble my councils, both of state and of the priesthood."

"I obeyed," said Remeses, when he subsequently related what passed. "The next day the councils met in one session, and the queen, supported upon her couch, presided. Briefly she announced her intention of adopting Mœris-Mento,—giving his full name,—as her son, and the next in succession to the throne, their consent being obtained. Then came up the question, 'Why Prince Remeses declined?' Being present I answered that it was my intention to retire from the court, visit foreign lands, and leave the government of Egypt in the hands of Mœris. At the earnest request of the queen I made no allusion to the secret. The united councils yielded their assent, and the royal secretary drew up the papers in due form, which the queen, supported by me, signed. A courier was then despatched with a copy of the instrument to the prince. The cabinet was soon afterwards dismissed, and I was left alone with the queen, who soon became very ill."

Thus far, my dearest mother, had I written in this letter five days ago, when the chief chamberlain came hastening to my room, in great terror, saying that the queen was dying! I lost not a moment in following him to her apartments. Ever since the meeting of the council she had been growing worse, and all the skill of her physicians could not abate the disease, which was pronounced inflammation of the brain. She had been for two days wildly delirious, calling upon Remeses not to leave her, and accusing the gods of seeking to put upon her a stranger for her own son! At length her ravings and her fever ceased and she rapidly failed. When I entered, I found Remeses kneeling by her side, his manly head bowed upon her couch, and tears falling upon her cold hand, held in his. Her mind was clear now, but I could see that the azure circle of death girdled her eyes, and that the light of the soul within was expiring. Her whole attention was fixed upon Remeses, to whom she kept saying in a faint whisper, and with a smile, "My son, my son, my own son! call me mother!"

"Mother, O my mother;" he exclaimed, in his strong anguish, "I cannot part with thee! Thou hast been a mother to me indeed!"

As I entered, her gaze turned towards me.

"It is the Prince of Tyre! I thought it was the others!"

"What others, my mother?" asked Remeses.

"They will soon come. I commanded him to bring them all. I must see them ere I die. But the Prince of Tyre is welcome!" and she smiled upon me and gave me her other hand to kiss. It was cold as ivory! I also knelt by her, and sorrowfully watched her sharpening features, which the chisel of death seemed shaping into the marble majesty of a god.

At this moment the door opened, and I saw, ushered in by a Hebrew page, the venerable head gardener, Amram; the young Hebrew ecclesiastic; Miriam the papyrus writer; and, leaning upon her arm, a dignified and still beautiful dame of fifty-five. I could not be mistaken —this last was the mother of Remeses.

"Cause all persons to go forth the chamber," cried the queen at the sight, her voice recovering in part its strength. She glanced at me to remain.

"Come hither, Amram," she said, "and lead to my bedside thy wife! Remeses, behold thy mother and father! Mother, embrace thy son. Since he can be no longer mine, I will return him to thee for ever!" Her voice was veiled with tears. Remeses rose, and turning to his mother, who looked worthy of him, said,—

"My mother, I acknowledge thee to be my mother! Give me thy blessing, as thou hast often done in my infancy."

He tenderly and respectfully embraced her, and then pressing his father's hand to his lips, he knelt before them. They were deeply moved, and instead of blessing him, wept upon him with silent joy.

"Are there not two more—a brother, a sister?" said Remeses, his fine face radiant with that ineffable beauty which shines from benevolence and the performance of a holy duty. I then led forward Miriam whom he regarded with admiring surprise (for she looked like a queen in her own right), and then tenderly embraced, saying to me, "Though I have lost a kingdom, O Sesostris, I have gained a sister, which no crown could bestow upon me." Then, when he saw the noble and princely looking priest, he cried as he folded him to his breast,—

"This is, indeed, my brother!"

The whole scene was touching and interesting beyond the power of my pen to describe, my dear mother. The dying queen smiled with serene pleasure, and waving her hand, Remeses led first his mother, and then his father, and in succession his sister and brother, to her couch. Upon the heads of each she laid her hand, but longest upon the mother's, saying,—

"Love him—be kind to him—he has no mother now but thee! Love him for my sake—you cannot but love him for his own! If I took thy babe, O mother, I return thee a man and a prince worthy to rule a nation, and in whom my eyes, closing upon the present, and seeing far into the future, behold a leader of thy people—a prince to thy nation. Born to a throne, he shall yet reign king of armies and leader of hosts, who I see follow him obedient to his will, and submissive to the rod of his power. Remeses, I die! Kiss me!"

The noble Hebrew reverently bent over her lips, as if in an act of worship; and when he lifted his face, there remained a statue of clay. The Queen of Egypt was no more!

SESOSTRIS.

I closed, dear mother, my account of the death of the great and good Queen Amense (which I wrote the day following that sad event), in order to accompany Remeses to the chief embalmers. As I passed through the streets I saw that the whole population was in mourning. Women went with dishevelled hair, men ceased to shave their heads and beards, and all the signs of woe for death, which I have before described, were visible. By the laws of Egypt, not even a king can be embalmed in his own palace. Remeses, on reaching the suburb of the embalmers, was received into the house of the chief, and here he gave directions as to the fashion of the case and sarcophagus, and the pattern of the funeral car, and of the baris in which it was to cross the Nile to the pyramid which, I have already said, she has been, since the first year of her reign, erecting for her burial place—placing a casing of vast stones, brought down from the quarries near Elephantis, each year.

I will not delay to describe the ceremonies of preparation, nor the embalment and burial of the august lady whose demise has cast a pall over Egypt. Your assurance that it would take you five months to get ready your war-fleet against Cyprus, and the desire of Remeses that I delay until the eighty days' mourning for the queen were over, induced me to remain. It is now four days since her burial in the centre of her stately pyramid, with the most imposing and gorgeous rites ever known at the entombment of a monarch. Prince Mœris was chief mourner! I have omitted to state that he readily acceded to the conditions proposed in the letter of Remeses, and when the courier followed, conveying to him the fact that he had been adopted and declared her heir by the queen, he addressed a frank and friendly letter to Remeses; for it is easy for him to assume any character his interest prompts. As soon as the intelligence of the death of the queen reached him, he hastened to Memphis. Here he had an interview with Remeses, whom he treated with courtesy, and offered the supervision of that part of Egypt where the Hebrew shepherds dwell; for I have learned that in a valley, which leads from Raamses to the Sea of Arabia, there are hundreds of Hebrews who, like their ancestors, keep vast flocks and herds belonging to the crown, but out of which they are allowed a tenth for their subsistence. Over this pastoral domain, embracing about twenty thousand shepherds, the prospective Pharaoh proposed to place Remeses. I felt that it was intended as an insult; but Remeses viewed it as an evidence of kindness on the part of one who knows not how to be noble or great.

The interment of the queen past, there is nothing to detain either Remeses or myself longer in Egypt. By her bounty he is rich, and has given to his parents a large treasure, which will enable them to be at ease; and besides, the queen gave to them and to Aaron (this is the name of the elder brother of Remeses) and his sister the right of citizenship. Mœris, the day of the queen's burial, virtually ascended the throne. His coronation however, will **not** take place until after he has passed through the forty days' noviitate.

And now, my dear mother, you will **be** surprised to learn that, the information of the Hebrew birth of Remeses (who has modestly dropped his first Egyptian name and adheres only to the second, which is Mosis or Moses, as the Hebrews pronounce it), was wickedly conveyed with large bribes to the magicians by Prince Mœris himself; and that, upon this information and influence, they recalled from the past, which, **like** the future is open to their magical art, the scenes of his life, and presented them before his vision.

Wonderful, incomprehensible, dear mother, above all things **I have** seen in Egypt, is the mysterious power of these magicians and sorcerers. Originally of the priestly order, they have advanced into deeper and deeper mysteries, until the hierarchy, of the regular temple worship fear them, and deny their ecclesiastical character, saying, "that they have climbed so high the mountains of Osiris, that they have fallen headlong over their summits into the dark realms of Typhon, and owe their dread power to his auspices."

Whatever be the source of their powerful art, dear mother, **there is no** doubt of its reality. Not even all the invocations, sacrifices, oblations, prayers, libations and exercises of the regular priesthood can compete with these magicians and sorcerers. They can convert day into night! destroy the shadow of an obelisk! fill the air with **a** shower of sand, **or** of flowers! convert their rods into **vines** that bear grapes! and walk with **living** asps as if they were almond or acacia rods! They can present **before** the inquirer, the face or scene in a distant land that is desired to **be** beheld! They can remove blocks of porphyry by a touch of the finger, and make a feather heavy as gold! They can cause invisible **music** in the air, and foretell the rain! And when extra**ordinary** motives and rewards are brought to bear upon them, they can by **their** united skill and necromantic art, aided by sorcery, reproduce the past, as in the case of Remeses!

These powerful, yet dreaded and hated men, have for ages been an appendage to the crown and call themselves the "servants of the Pharaohs." The kings of Egypt, who have protected, favoured, and sought their assistance, have also trembled at their power. Without question they are aided by the evil genii; and perform their works through the agency of the spirit of evil.

This, dear mother, will be the last letter I shall write you from Egypt.

Accompanied by Remeses, I shall to-morrow embark in my galley for Pelusium. My friend, the Admiral Pathromenes, will accompany us to the mouth of the Eastern Nile. I ought to say that King Mœris now Pharaoh-elect, has extended towards me marked civilities, and seeks for a continuance of friendly intercourse. I shall bear a royal letter from him to your Majesty, expressive of his respect for you, and his desire to perpetuate the alliance. But I have no love for the man! If I can I will raise an army in Phœnicia, after I see the King of Cyprus chained to the poop of my galley, and, placing Remeses at the head, invade Egypt, call the Hebrews to arms, and, overturning the throne of Mœris, place my friend in his seat. Did not the dying queen prophecy that he was born to rule? It is over Egypt he will yet wield the sceptre. I will do my part, dear mother, to fulfil the prophecy.

To the lovely Princess Thamonda convey my devotions, and assure her that I shall make war against Cyprus more successfully, with her heart wedded to mine, than alone. Warn her, dear mother, that I shall claim her hand as soon as I return, and that Remeses will be the groom-friend whom I shall honour with the high place of witness and chief guest at our nuptials.

Farewell, dear mother.

Remeses desires to unite with me in affectionate regards to you.

Your son,
SESOSTRIS.

[*Here the correspondence* of the Prince of Tyre *with the Queen Epiphia terminates.*]

THE RED SEA.

LETTERS

BETWEEN REMESES AND OTHER PERSONS,

COVERING A PERIOD OF FIVE YEARS.

LETTER I.

REMESES TO AARON THE HEBREW.

CITY OF TYRE, SYRIA, MONTH ATHYR

MY ELDER AND DEAR BROTHER,—

It is with emotions wholly new to me, awakened by those fratrnal ties to which I have been hitherto entirely a stranger, that I take up my pen to address you, inscribing at the commencement of my letter the endearing words, "my brother!" It is true I have lost much in many respects; but I have also gained much in the affection of my newly discovered kindred.

After you left us below Memphis, the galley of the Prince Sesostris sped swiftly down the Nile, and ere noon we had entered the Pelusian branch. As I passed the old city of Bubastis, and Pythom, the new treasure-city, which is rising upon its ruins, I groaned with heaviness of heart! Around and upon its walls, I beheld the thousands of my oppressed countrymen toiling, like Nubian slaves, under the lash of their task-masters! I could only groan in heart; for what was I now able to do for them,—myself an exile, and flying from the land? May the prophecy which exists among your people (*my* people), as you asserted in the last long and interesting conversation we held together, on the day I embarked, be soon fulfilled! This bondage can not continue many years! There is not room in Egypt for two nations.

At Pelusium we found the prince's fleet awaiting him. It set sail shortly after our arrival, and coasting by the shores of Arabia, and passing Askelon, in Philistia, in seven days we entered the port of Tyre; which is built upon a rocky isle and peninsula, and rises from the sea with imposing magnificence.

I was most kindly received by the mother of Sesostris, whose glad reception of her son made my eyes fill with tears; for I remembered my (I was going to say, mother)—the Queen Amense's tenderness, whenever she met me after the shortest absence.

But I must not refer to the past.

Prince Sesostris treats me in every respect as an equal. Were I still Prince Remeses of Egypt, he could not show me more kindness and regard. We have now been here one month; and in that time I have seen much of Tyre, but my continued grief for the death of the beloved queen,—my more than mother,—renders me quite indifferent to external objects. As the guest of the prince, I have endeavoured to interest myself in what concerns him. He is engaged earnestly in preparations for war. The port of Tyre is thronged with war-galleys; and reviews of troops take place daily, on a plain which is overhung by the mountain range of Libanus. The grandeur of this mountain, in which the earliest worship of men rose to the gods, deeply impressed me. The fleet will sail in about one month.

DAMASCUS, SYRO-PHŒNICIA.

Since writing the above I have come to this beautiful city, which lies in a lovely vale watered by two rivers, the Abana and Pharphar, that fertilize it and render it indeed "the garden of the earth" —as it is termed. I travelled hither with the prince, who has come to take to wife Thamonda, the fair princess of this city. She is amiable and sensible, and I rejoice that my princely friend has such happiness in store! How fortunate for me, my brother, that while I was prince of Egypt, I did not interest myself in any princess, who would be now humbled and wretched at my degradation! The nuptial ceremonies will take place soon, and occupy some days. I wish Sesostris every happiness in his alliance.

I met here the venerable Prince of Uz. He had travelled thus far on his return to his own land, which lies on the borders of Chaldea and Sabæa, and when informed of my present position was deeply moved. We have had long and interesting conversations together, upon the unity of God! which have so deeply absorbed my reflections, that I have accepted an invitation to visit him, after I return from Cyprus, whither I accompany the prince and his bride.

THE PALACE OF THE PRINCESS OF DAMASCUS.

My beloved Sesostris is married. The ceremonies were unusually magnificent; several kings of cities and princes of provinces being present, with their retinues. But I do not excel in descriptions of scenes and festivities, and leave them to the more graceful and easy pen of Sesostris. We depart in three days with a gala procession of horsemen, to return to Tyre.

ISLE OF TYRE.

Having kept this roll of papyrus with me, I now close my epistle here, where I commenced writing it, with the intelligence of our arrival; the happy reception of her new daughter-in-law, by Queen Epiphia; and with the announcement that the fleet will set sail within three days for the Levantine island-kingdom.

Commend me, my brother, with respectful affection, to my father Amram, to my honoured mother, and to my stately sister Miriam. Trusting you are all in health and safety, I am your brother, with profound fraternal regard,

MOSES, THE HEBREW.

LETTER II.

REMESES TO HIS BROTHER.

PHŒNICIA.

A YEAR has passed, my brother, since I last wrote to you. In the mean while I have received your very kind epistle. It reached me at Tyre, where I found it awaiting me, on my return from the expedition against Cyprus. You have probably learned the result of the war, and that Prince Sesostris landed his army, defeated the King of Cyprus in a pitched battle, taking his battalion of chariots, which were armed with scythes, and destroying his cavalry. The king implored peace, and surrendered his capital. Sesostris, after levying a tribute of two thousand talents of silver upon it for ten years, and demanding a portion of the island, on the north for a Phœnician colony, returned triumphant to his country.

I am now travelling through the whole of Syria. From this point I shall proceed to the province of Uz. I desire to know more fully this wisdom of the one God, the Almighty, as taught by the Sage of that land. When I saw him in Damascus, a year ago, I informed him that I had begun to write an account of the wonderful incidents of his life; but when I read to him what I had commenced, and afterwards heard his conversation upon the God he worshipped, I perceived that I was a child in ignorance, and had entered upon a task impossible for me to perform, by reason of my religious education as an Egyptian.

"My son," he said, "thou art not far from the knowledge of the Almighty, and thy soul aspires after the true God. Come with me to my own land, for thou sayest thou art a wanderer, and I will teach thee the knowledge of the Holy One. Then thou mayest write the acts of the Invisible to man, and justify Him in His ways to me, His servant. The gods of Egypt darken knowledge, and veil the understanding of those who trust in them, and say to an idol of gold, 'Thou art my god.'"

I am now journeying, O my brother, to sit at the feet of this man of God, whose simple wisdom has enlightened my soul more than all the learning of Egypt; nay, I would gladly forget all the knowledge I obtained in Egypt, to know, and fear, and love the "Holy One"—the Almighty God—of the Prince of Uz. What is particularly worthy of note is, that his views of the Invisible are the same as those which you taught me were held by the elders among our people; and of the truth of which you so eloquently and feelingly endeavoured to convince me, on the evening before my departure from Egypt, as we sat by the door of our mother's home, under the two palms. Dissatisfied with the gods of Egypt, and the emptiness and vanity of its worship, as not meeting the wants of man, I turn to any source which will pour the light of truth into my soul. We both, brother, are feeling after God, if haply we may find Him; for I perceive that your own soul is darkened and clouded as well as mine, by the dark myths of Egypt, in which we have been educated. But let us both take courage, my noble elder brother. There is light, there is truth, there is knowledge somewhere on earth! and I go to the aged Prince of Uz to learn of him. Sitting at his feet, I will empty myself of all the false and unsatisfying wisdom of Egypt, and meekly say, "I am ignorant—enlighten me! Teach me concerning thy God, for I know that He is the God my soul longs for, whom the nations know not!"

Your letter spoke of Pharaoh, and his cruelty and power, I am prepared to hear that he takes new measures to heap burdens upon our people. The Lake Amense, which you say he is enlarging to an inland sea, will destroy thousands of the Hebrews whom you tell me he is putting to the work: for unaccustomed to labour in the water, they must perish miserably. I trust he will suffer you and my father's family to dwell unmolested. Be prepared at any moment to escape, should he seek to destroy the prosperity in which the beloved queen left you, and those dear to me by the sacred and affectionate ties of nature.

Farewell,
                                Your brother,
                                                MOSES.

LETTER III.

REMESES-MOSES TO AARON.

THE PALACE OF THE LORD OF UZ.

MY DEAR AND HONOURED BROTHER,—

I HAVE been here now one year. The venerable prince honours me as a son, and I repay him, so far as I can, by instructing him in the history of Egypt, and other knowledge; for, so great is his wisdom, he seeks ever to know more. In astrology, physics, geometry, and all arts, he is deeply learned. But above all, is his knowledge of the Almighty. This man has the mysteries of God in his heart, and to the eyes of his divine piety, the Most High is visible as He is. He hath spoken to the Lord of heaven face to face, and he communicates with Him as a servant with his lord.

When I came hither, after visiting Baal-Phegor and other places, he received me with affection, and gave me rooms in his palace, and servants, and a place at his table. I found him dwelling in a city he himself had builded, and reigning the wealthiest, wisest, and yet humblest prince in all the East. Around it lay the cities of Shuh, Teman, and Naamath, the lesser princes of which are his bosom friends, and once a week meet at his hospitable board. They hang upon the words of his lips, and reverence him as a father. He also possesses vast herds of cattle and oxen, which cover his plains; fourteen thousand sheep are on his mountains; six thousand camels; and stores of silver and gold. He has seven sons, who are princes of as many provinces, and three daughters, the youngest of whom, Keren-happuch, is married to the Lord of Midian; for when the Prince of Uz, three years ago, travelled down into Egypt, with a large caravan of his merchants, he passed through Midian, having this daughter in company, who, being comely in person, was admired by the prince of that land, and by him asked in marriage of her father. Of the two daughters who remain, no women in all the land are found so fair. Such is the prosperity and power of this mighty and wise prince.

Now, at length, my dear brother, I have written the book of the life of this venerable man; not as I began it in Egypt, with imperfect ideas of the God of heaven, whose servant he is, but from his own lips have I received the narrative which I inclose to you. When you have read it, you will arrive at the knowledge of the Almighty, whose name, and glory, and being, and goodness, and justice, and love, are recognized in every page. As you read, reflect that the God of the Prince of Uz is also my God, and the God worshipped by our fathers when they were in Syria. Away, O Aaron! with all the gods of Egypt! They are brazen and golden lies, all! The myth of Osiris and Isis is an invention of the priests. The whole system of their mythology is hostile to true religion and the adorers of idols are the worshippers of Satan—for this is the name of that spirit of evil, antagonistic to the true God, hitherto represented to us under the title of Typhon.

It would take a score of papyri for me to convey to you the course of divine and sage instruction by which I arrived at that clear, luminous, and just notion of the Lord God of heaven and earth, which I now hold; the possession of which fills my soul with repose, my intellect with satisfaction, my heart with joy, peace and love to God and man. With this *certain* knowledge of the Almighty that has entered into my soul, is an apprehension of His omnipresence, His truth, holiness, majesty, and benevolence; and a consciousness that I have received his Divine Spirit, which last is, as it were, a witness vouchsafed of Himself to me. By the light of this new spirit within me I behold His glory, and recognize that He is my God, my Creator, my Benefactor, and Lawgiver. I feel that in Him I live, move, and have my being, and that besides Him there is no God. The realization of these majestic truths, O my brother, is a source to me of the profoundest happiness. Before their light the dark clouds of the myths of Egypt dissolve and fade away for ever!

When I speak of Him I find new language rise to my lips: when I write of Him my words seem to clothe themselves with sublimity and majesty. Henceforth, like the Holy Prince of Uz, I am a worshipper of One God, whose name is the Almighty, and the Holy One.

To Sesostris I have written of these great things, and to you also I will send a treatise, that you may, without obscurity, behold His unity and glory as they were known to our fathers, Abraham, Isaac, and Jacob, before the false worship of Egypt corrupted our hereditary faith. With this knowledge, O Aaron, our people, even in bondage, are superior to Pharaoh on his throne.

Your affectionate brother,
MOSES.

LETTER IV.

REMESES TO MIRIAM.

TYRE, PHŒNICIA.

MY DEAR SISTER,—

I RECEIVED your letter, written to me from Bubastis. I grieve to hear that King Mœris is increasing so heavily the burdens of our people, as to drive to the fields, and to the new lake to which he has given his name, all who were servants in houses. Unused to toil under the sun, they will suffer more than others. I read the copy of the edict you inclosed, forbidding the Egyptians to receive, as domestics, any of the Hebrew people, that so all might be driven to become toilers in the field. His motive is evident. He is alarmed at the increase of the Hebrews, and would oppress them to death by thousands. My heart bleeds for those he has sent to the mines in the Thebaïd. This is a new feature in the Hebrew bondage. But there is a just God on high, O my sister Miriam, the Holy One, whom our fathers worshipped. He will not forget his people for ever, but in due time will bring them out of their bondage. Has not Aaron, our learned brother, made known to you the words of tradition that are cherished among our people,—that they are to serve Pharaoh a certain number of years, forty-one of which are yet to come? He sent me the copy thereof, wherein I find it written, as the declaration of Abraham our father, that "his posterity should serve Pharaoh four hundred years." Aaron, who, since I left Egypt, has been giving all his time to collecting the traditions and laws of our fathers, is confident that ere another generation shall have perished, God will raise up a deliverer for the sons of Jacob, and lead them forth to some new and wonderful land. If such a promise, O my sister, was given by the Almighty, He will redeem it; for He is not a man that He should lie! Let us therefore wait, and hope, and pray to this mighty God of our ancestors, to remember His promise, and descend from Heaven with a stretched-out arm for our deliverance. I rejoice to hear that my dear mother is well, also my father. Commend me to them with reverential affection. Aaron reads to you my letters, and you will have learned from them how I arrived at the knowledge of the true God, in whom, O Miriam, both you and he believed, while I, considering myself an Egyptian, was a worshipper of the false gods of Egypt! Yet, lo! by the goodness of the true God, I have been enabled, at the feet of the sage of Uz, to arrive at such clear conceptions of His glory, and majesty, and government of the universe, as to teach even you. I speak this not boastingly, but with gratitude to Him who has made me the instrument of illumining your mind, and of giving you greater confidence and trust in the God, who is the God of Abraham, and the God of the Prince of Uz.

I have now been five years absent from Egypt, and my heart yearns for my brethren in bondage. I feel that it is not becoming in me to remain here, at ease in the court of Sesostris; for he has now been two years king, since his royal mother's death, of which I wrote to my mother at the time. I pant to make known to the elders of the

Hebrews, the clear and true knowledge of the God of our fathers, which has come down to them imperfectly, and mingled with superstitions, even when it is not corrupted by the idolatry of Egypt. I wish to learn the character and condition of my brethren in servitude, whom I formerly viewed from the proud height of an Egyptian prince. Now I feel a desire to mingle among them, to know them, and be one of them. All my Egyptian pride, dear sister, is long since gone, and I seek daily to cultivate that spirit of meekness, which better becomes one, who is of a race of bondmen. But, my sister, rather would I be a slave, chained at the chariot-wheel of Pharaoh-Mœris, with my present knowledge of the Holy and Almighty One,—compared with which all the wisdom of Egypt is foolishness,—than be that monarch himself with his ignorance of Him, and his worship of Osiris and Apis!

May the God of our fathers, by whose will we are in bonds, in His own time send us deliverance, to whom be glory and majesty, and dominion and power, in heaven and earth, to the end of ages.

Most affectionately, your younger brother,

MOSES.

LETTER V.

REMESES TO HIS MOTHER.

PALACE OF SESOSTRIS, KING OF TYRE.

MY MOTHER, REVERED AND LOVED,—

In a letter written a few days ago, and which went by a vessel that was to touch at Pelusium on its way to Carthage, I alluded to a feeling (which has been increasing in strength for many months) that prompted me to visit my brethren in bonds in Egypt. It is true, I have no power. I am but one, and Mœris would, no doubt, gladly seize upon me if he knew I was in his kingdom. I have, however, determined to yield to the desire; and next month shall sail in a galley that goes to Egypt for ebony and ivory. Not long, therefore, after you receive this letter, which the scholarly Aaron will read to you, will you embrace your younger and long-absent son. It is expedient that I go unknown. I wish to observe the Hebrew people, without awakening suspicion, as to who I am. Should Mœris hear of me, he would quickly suspect me of planning evil against him. If I can do no more, I can carry to the elders the certainty of the truth, as they received it, by tradition, of One God, Lord of heaven and earth, Infinite in holiness, and Almighty in power. From the holy Prince of Uz, I not only received this, but many other things of wonderful interest—which he seemed to know by the voice of God—concerning the creation of the world in six days, and the formation of man and woman, whom he placed in a garden of beauty, with dominion over all things. But I will not go further into these divine and wonderful things, at this time, O my mother, as I shall hereafter read to you, from the sacred leaves, the narrative of the acts of creation, as they were written by the Prince and Prophet of Uz: to whom, before all men, has been revealed the truth of the Most High, and the mysteries which have been secret from eternity. Lo! the pages of the book of his patience under God's trial show, that no man on earth ever before had such illumination of divine light! Such language as that of his which I have written in the book, when he speaks of God, could only have been suggested by the inspiration of the Almighty. He talks of God as if he had sat at His feet, and daily beheld His glorious majesty, or heard His voice shake the heavens. Of him have I learned the wisdom of the past; and there whispers in my heart, O mother, a solemn voice, which bids me hope that if I fear God, and walk uprightly, and seek His face, and trust in Him, He will also draw nigh to me, unveil His glory, and speak face to face with me, as He hath done to His holy servant, the Prince of Uz! It shall be the aspiration of my heart, to be received into the divine favour as He has been, and made the recipient of His will, and of His laws for men! Censure me not,—charge me not with pride, O my mother! In the spirit of meekness and lowliness do I cherish this hope. The path to the ear of God, and to His favour, the Prince of Uz hath taught me, is prayer. On bended knees, therefore, seven times a day, do I bow in supplication before the Holy One Almighty, the Lord God of Hosts; and more and more do I feel my spirit go forth to Him; and daily, the infinite distance between earth and His throne seems to lessen! Nor will I cease to pray to Him, O mother, until I hear His voice in my soul, and feel the intimate presence of His Being in union with my own! Then will I reach the height of humanity, which is the reunion of the creature with the Creator, the restoration in his soul of the divine image, and the reception into his own of a divine and immortal life!

My friend, King Sesostris, reluctantly consents to my departure. He has never ceased his affectionate regard for me, and he has called his beautiful son, now four years old, Remeses—after me. This child, I love as if he were mine own. He is intelligent and full of affection, and already understands that I am about to go away, and sweetly urges me not to leave him. The Queen Thamonda has prepared many gifts for you and my sister, whom she loves, though not having seen. Here, dear mother, the bondage and degradation of the Hebrew is not comprehended. We are not, in their eyes, crown-serfs. We are but a Syrian nation held in captivity; and other nations regard us with sympathy, and have no share in the contempt and scorn with which we are regarded by our Egyptian taskmasters.

Israelisis the Hebrew, whom Sesostris brought with him five years ago to Tyre, is now a fine young man, and assistant secretary to his royal scribe. All that our people want, my mother, is to be placed in positions favourable to the development of their intellect, and they will rise, side by side, with any other people on earth. If we were a nation, with a country of our own, we would give laws to the world.

Farewell, my dear mother. In a few days you will embrace me.

Your devoted son,
MOSES.

LETTER VI.

REMESES IN EGYPT TO SESOSTRIS IN PHŒNICIA.

TREASURE-CITY OF RAAMSES.

It is with gratitude to God, O Sesostris, that I inform you of my safe arrival in Egypt, after a perilous passage across the sea. Our chief pilot, finding, after we left the port of Tyre, that the wind was fair for the mouth of the Nile, and the weather seeming to be settled, signified to me his intention to leave the coast, and boldly steer from land to land. Having no knowledge of nautical affairs, I neither advised nor objected, leaving him to act according to his own experience and skill : he therefore laid the course of the ship as nearly straight for Pelusium, as he could ascertain it, by the position of the sun at noon.

Before night we were surrounded by a horizon of water and, this being the first time since I had lived on the earth, that I had been unable to behold it, the situation was wholly novel, not only to me but to other passengers,—some of whom manifested the liveliest fears, lest we should no more behold the land. My mind was impressed by the sublimity and vastness of the view ; and the majestic idea of eternity—boundless and infinite—filled my soul. It seemed as if, from our deck, I could survey the universe of space, for there was nothing terrestrial to arrest and confine the eye.

"Who," I reflected, "as he surveys the illimitable sky, and the measureless ocean over which it extends, can withhold the confession that there is One God only, the Upholder of worlds and the Governor of His creation? Who, with such a scene before him, as day with its splendour and vastness of space, and night with its stars presented above the sea, could give the glory of the Almighty to another, and put his trust in such myths as are the gods of Egypt and the deities of Phœnicia? I rejoice, O king, that you have listened to the truths it was my happiness to unfold to you, and that in your heart you acknowledge and secretly adore the Almighty. May the time soon come when you will have strength given you, from Himself, to establish His holy worship in your dominions! A king is God's representative on earth, and his power is great ; and if he exercise it,—not like the Pharaohs, who reign as if they were gods, but—with judgment, and fear, and humble recognition of the Infinite source of all power, then He who is King of kings and Lord of lords, will bless him and cause him to prosper. When a king acknowledges that his power is delegated, and that he must be accountable for its use or abuse to his God, he has gained the highest wisdom that earth can give! Seek, O king, that wisdom!

Pardon me, my dear Sesostris, for presuming to teach you. I am diffident in speech when present with you, but you perceive I am bold, perhaps too much so, when away from you.

We continued, for three days and nights, sailing upon the sea, without a shore in view, and in a few hours more hoped to find the mouth of the Nile; when the wind after a sudden lull, came round to the south, the air was darkened with clouds, and night came on, enveloping our ship in the profoundest gloom, amid which we drove, our pilot knew not whither! It was a night of painful suspense. The seas dashed over us; our banks of oars were broken or washed away; and not a cubit's breadth of sail could remain on the mast, while the air was filled with sharp sand, blown from the Arabian desert.

The passengers and crew were in despair, and believing that every succeeding billow would go over us and destroy us, they called frantically upon their gods! The Syrian cried to Hercules, and the Sabæan upon the sun and upon fire. The merchants of Tyre prayed to Adonis and Io, the Arabians to Ammon and the Egyptians vowed libations and offerings to Apis, Osiris, and Thoth. Our pilot finding all hope desert him, burned a cake of incense to the deity of the sea, and vowed an oblation to all the gods he could in his extremity call to mind.

Then it was, O Sesostris, that I felt the power and excellency of my faith in God! Then did the folly, the vanity, and degradation of the religions of those about me, deeply impress me, and move me to pity. Calm, serene, confident in the Almighty, who holdeth the sea in the hollow of His hand, and directeth the stormy winds and tempests of the skies, I lifted my heart and my voice to Him, whom, with the eye of instructed intelligence, I beheld seated above the darkness and the whirlwind, in the ineffable glory and peace of His own heaven, and directing all things by His will. I felt that He could protect and defend me, and those who sailed with me; that the night to Him was as clear as the day; and that even I was not too insignificant to be cared for by Him, who, in His love, gave voices of music to the little birds, who painted the lily, and perfumed the flower.

"O Lord God, Holy One, the Almighty, who art the Creator of all things, if I have found grace in Thy sight, hear my humble petition, which I now offer before Thee. Let Thy presence be here, and Thy power; save us who are tossed upon the great sea, and who have no hope but in Thee. These call upon their idols, but I, O Lord God, call upon Thee, the God of our fathers. Guard us in our danger, and bring us in safety to our haven! For Thou art the only true and living God, and besides Thee there is no God!"

All the people who heard my voice, as I thus invoked the Living God, and saw my hands outstretched heavenward, turned from their idols and amulets, and ceased their prayers and cries, to hear me. The lightnings flashed about us in a continual flame, so that the ship seemed on fire, and I could be seen by all.

Judge, O Sesostris, my surprise, when instantly the winds—which at the first words of my prayer softened—ceased to roar; the waves fell level with the sea; the clouds parted above us, and revealing a bright moon shining down from the starry sky, they rolled, on all sides, swiftly away towards the horizon.

This sudden and wondrous change, evidently in response to my prayer, as a proof that it was heard by the Ear to which I, in fear and hope, addressed it, amazed me. It was the power and act of my God! I felt it to be so, and lifting up my eyes and hands to the cloudless skies, I said—

"Thine, O Lord Almighty, thine be the praise and glory; for Thou art the hearer and answerer of prayer, and art loving to all Thy creatures. Thou hast power in heaven and on earth, and on the broad sea, nor is anything hid from Thee. Darkness is no darkness with Thee, and no power can resist Thine! Thanks be to Thee, O Lord, God on high, for this manifestation of Thy presence, and this confirmation of my faith. Let these idolaters likewise glorify Thee, for whose sakes Thou hast also done this."

When I ceased, I beheld a crowd, made up of all nations, prostrate around me. The captain turning away from his god, was burning incense before me, while the invocations of the crew and passengers were being offered to me. With horror I drew back and waved them away, saying, "Rise, men, stand upon your feet! Not unto me, not unto me, but unto God, the one invisible Creator, give thanks and praise for your mighty deliverance!

I then made known to them the mystery of the true God, whose power they and I had witnessed, and exhorted them to turn from their idols, and worship Him in spirit and in truth; for that He was their Maker, and besides Him there was no God. Nevertheless, but for my stern anger against it, they would have sacrificed a sheep to me, as if I were Hercules.

In a few hours we reached Pelusium, and to escape the adulations of the people on shore, to whom the crew made known this miracle of God, I withdrew privately, and went to Bubastis. After visiting, unknown to them, the tens of thousands of my brethren, who are engaged in extending the walls of that place, and increasing the number of treasure-houses therein, I took boat and came hither secretly, for fear that Mœris, if he knew me to be in Egypt, might watch my movements, if not banish or imprison me.

I have now been several days in the bosom of my family. My mother and father are well; but they, and Miriam with all the other women of our nation, have tasks of weaving put upon them, which are to be done each day before they are permitted to sleep. My heart is deeply wounded at all this. On every side I behold oppression and cruelty. Daily, scores of the Hebrews perish, and their dead bodies are thrown into ditches, dug for the purpose, and covered with earth. Often, the wretched men who dig them are the first to occupy them, for the work goes on day and night. An edict has been published throughout all Egypt, within the past month, that no Egyptian shall assist a Hebrew; and that no Hebrew who sinks down under his toil, shall be suffered to remain upon the ground, but must be placed upon his feet again, and driven to his task, until he sinks to rise no more ; and to such, neither bread nor water shall be offered, that they may die ! Such, O king, is the heart of this Mœris !

Yet, with all these extraordinary measures, inspired by his fear, to lessen the number of the Hebrews, they increase in the most unprecedented manner. The women bring forth without midwives, and are put to no inconvenience whatsoever afterwards. Such a state of things alarms the Egyptian king, and well it may ; for it seems to me to be a direct act of the Divinity, so to multiply the people, that Egypt will be compelled to liberate them and send them forth to find a country of their own.

There is a prophecy which, as I associate more with the elders—who are slow, however, to give me their confidence, regarding me still as an Egyptian in feeling and prejudices—I ascertain to be well preserved, that, at the end of about four hundred years from the days of Prince Abraham, his descendants shall come out of Egypt a great nation. This period is drawing to its close. God, who can deliver from the storm, can deliver from the hand of Pharaoh those who trust in Him, and call for His Almighty arm to aid them.

MEMPHIS, HOUSE OF AARON.

Since writing the foregoing my dear Sesostris—for such is the familiar title notwithstanding the present difference in our rank and position, that you condescendingly permit me to make use of in addressing you —since writing the foregoing, I say, I have been studying the traditions of my fathers, the Hebrews of old. In them I have found the following prophecies ; and you will observe how confidently God, the Almighty, is recognized and spoken of as the one true God :

" Our father Abram, the Syrian, having been born in the great kingdom of Chaldea, served idols, as did all other men—the knowledge of the one God, being yet veiled under the multiplicity of gods. Abram, being just, and possessing those virtues and excellencies which elevate man, it pleased the one great and mighty God, only and true—who made all things in heaven above, in the earth beneath, and in the seas that are thereunder—to make Himself known unto him, as he was one day uttering a prayer to the sun. Suddenly he beheld a hand across the disk of the sun, and the earth was instantly covered with night. While Abram wondered and trembled, the mighty hand was removed, and the day was restored. Then came a voice from above the sun—

" ' O man and son of man that is clay ! dost thou worship the creature, and know not the Creator ? I am the Creator of the sun, the heavens, the earth, and man upon the earth ! Worship me, who alone can create light, and who maketh darkness ! I am God, and will not give my glory to a creature ! The sun is but clay, and thou, O man, art clay also ! Give *Me* thine heart ; worship Me, the Maker both of thee and of the sun.''

Then Abram saw the hand again cover and extinguish the sun ; but lo, instead of night, the universe was lighted by the brightness of the hand, which shone with the splendour of a thousand suns, so that our father fell upon his face, as if dead, before its consuming splendour.

When he rose again, the sun shone as before, and he fell prostrate upon the ground and said :

"'Lord God of the sun, Creator of all things, what is man, that Thou displayest Thy glory and revealest Thyself to him? I am as a worm before Thee! Teach me what Thou wouldst have me to do!'

"Then a still, small voice answered :

"'Arise, go forth from this Chaldea, thy country, unto a land flowing with milk and honey, which I will show thee; and there I will make of thee a great nation, who shall bear thy name; for I will make thy name great, and a blessing to all men; and those who bless thee I will bless, and those who curse thee I will curse; and in thee shall all the families of the earth be blessed!'"

This remarkable tradition then goes on to say, O Sesostris, that the Chaldean hastened to obey God, and going into the city of Haran, where he dwelt, gathered his substance, and took his wife, and nephew, and all his servants, and departed from the land—being then five-and-seventy years old. By a sign, the Lord God went before him through many lands, until he crossed over the river of the king of Sodom into Palestine, when the Almighty, taking him into a high mountain, showed him all the land, from the lake and fair valley of Gomorrah and Sodom to the great sea westward, and from Libanus on the north to the desert of Arabia on the south, saying:

"'Lift up now thine eyes, and look from the place where thou art, northward and southward, and eastward and westward, for all the land which thou seest, to thee will I give it and to thy seed after thee! Arise, walk through the land, in the length of it and in the breadth of it, for I will give it to thee; for the whole earth is mine!'"

"Night fell upon them while they looked from the mountain, and the Lord God said to our father: 'Look now towards heaven, and tell the stars if thou art able to number them. So shall thy posterity be. But know thou,' said the Lord to him, 'that thou, and thy son, and thy son's son shall be strangers in this land, and thy seed after thee shall also be strangers in the land shadowing with wings, and shall serve its kings, and they shall afflict thee four hundred years; but grieve not, for the nation whom they shall serve will I judge, and afterwards shall thy posterity come out of that land a mighty people, with great substance; and he whom I will raise up as their deliverer, shall lead them unto this land, and they shall enter in and possess it, and shall become a great people, and be in number as the sands of the sea shore, and as the dust for multitude.'"

Then Abram believed God. We, O Sesostris, are his posterity. Are we not as the stars of heaven in number, and as the sands of the shore? The four hundred years are drawing to a close. Will not He who has brought about the fulfilment of one part of His prophecy, accomplish also the other? Therefore do I look with hope to our release, ere another generation passes away. Who shall live to behold it? Who shall be so blessed as to see this deliverer that is to lead them forth to the promised land? I may not live to see that day of joyful deliverance! Perhaps thy son Remeses may behold it. That land, according to our tradition, is Palestine, through which I journeyed when I visited the ruins, visible above and beneath the Lake of Bitumen; near which, also, I beheld that extraordinary statue of an incrusted woman, on whom the shower of salt fell until it had encased her alive, and transfixed her to the spot, as if hewn from a column of salt. The people of that region informed me, that she was a niece of Prince Abram, overtaken in her flight, when the five cities of the plain were overthrown by fire from heaven. How beautiful is all that land of Palestine! It is like a garden for fertility, and is filled with populous cities, and a cultivated and warlike people. I also visited the city of Salem, where, anciently, King Melchisedec, the wise sage, and friend of God and of Abram, dwelt. It is now but a rock covered with fortresses and the treasure-city of the land. Is this land yet to be given by God to our people? Is it, indeed, already ours by the title of God to our Abram, only waiting for us to go up and possess it? We are then not without a country, though in bondage. This idea elevates my heart; and I have sought to rouse the dormant feelings and hopes of our elders and people, with the faith that our nation has a country reserved for us, by the God of our fathers.

But they shake their heads. They have so long sat in the dust of despair, that they have ceased to hope. Still, my brother Aaron and I everywhere try to lift up their feeble hearts, and to encourage them with the bright future. But one of the old men answered—

"Thou sayest that it is a land filled with a warlike people; that they are the descendants of the old Phœnician shepherd-kings, who once conquered Egypt. How, O son of Pharaoh's daughter," he added, giving me this appellation in his anger, "how can we Hebrews, who know not an arrow from a lance, or a spear from a bow, who are crushed in spirit and dwarfed by toil, how are we to conquer such a land, even if the God of our fathers has given it to us?"

"Does not this foreign land of which the stranger-Hebrew speaks," arose and said another, by the name of Uri,—whose son is the most skilful in Egypt in devising curious works in gold, and in silver, and in precious stones, having served with the queen's royal artificer,— "does it not lie beyond Arabia, and are there not many and strong kings in the way, the armies of Edom, of the Hittites, of the Philistines, and of the sons of Ishmael! Even though Pharaoh were to bid us begone to-morrow, to the new country of our God that we boast of, could we traverse the desert, or do battle with the nations on the way, much more conquer the warlike people who hold it? Listen not to this Egyptian-Hebrew, who doubtless would tempt us to leave Egypt, that we may be destroyed by the warlike people, who will dispute our march. Doubtless, Pharaoh, his former friend, hath sent him to talk with us that he might thereby either get rid of us, or seek occasion to destroy us in a body."

Thus, my dear Sesostris, were my words turned against me. Yet I will not fear, but shall quietly strive to influence my brethren, and persuade them to look forward with hope, to deliverance by the arm of God.

Farewell, Sesostris! May the Almighty give you His divine Spirit, and fill you with wisdom and judgment, that you may honour Him as King of kings, and rule your people mercifully and prosperously. To the beloved queen, Thamonda, I send the most respectful greetings; and thank her from my heart for giving to your daughter the dear and honoured name, "Amense." May the virtues of the pure Queen of Egypt be transferred to her; but may her life be far happier! To my namesake, the bright and beautiful Remeses, give my cordial affection. Tell him that I hope, when he shall be a man, and like other princes, visit Egypt, he will not find the Hebrew nation there in bondage, and that, if he inquires after the people of his father's humble friend, he will be answered—

"Their God, with a mighty hand and an outstretched arm, **led** them forth **to** a land given to them for **an** inheritance, where they now dwell, free and happy!" Ah, Sesostris, shall this dream of hope thus be realized? Tell Remeses to lay a bunch of flowers for me upon the tomb of Queen Epiphia, whose memory and kindness I shall ever cherish deep in my heart.

I once more write, farewell.

REMESES.

LETTER VII.

AARON TO KING SESOSTRIS.

CITY OF RAAMSES, EGYPT.

TO SESOSTRIS, KING OF TYRE, AARON THE HEBREW, GREETING,—

PARDON, O king, thy servant, for addressing an epistle to thee; but when thou art informed of the reason which has led me to take this liberty, thou wilt, I feel, acquit me of too great boldness.

Know, O King Sesostris, that my brother, thy beloved friend, who wrote the letter which I send to thee with this epistle (and which he himself would have forwarded, but for what I am about to relate), has fled from Egypt, pursued by the vindictive power of Pharaoh. I will, as briefly as I can, make known to thee the painful circumstances which led to this result.

The morning after he had completed his letter to thee, O king, he said to me, "I will go forth and see my brethren who are at work on Lake Mœris, that I may talk also with the old and young men, and inspire their heavy hearts with hope." So he departed, and, crossing the river, disguised as an Egyptian,—for no Hebrew dare now be seen walking along for fear of being challenged by the soldiers, who garrison all the country, and stand guard at every corner, and at every gate,—he came to the shores of Lake Amense, the beauty of which, with its garden and palace-lined shores, so much pleased thee, O king, when, five years ago, thou wast in Egypt. There he saw King Mœris clothed in scarlet, a chain of gold across his breast, standing in his chariot, as he slowly drove around the lake, giving directions to the chief captains over the works. My brother was not recognized by him, however, and went on his way, observing the severe labours of his brethren. In the two hours that he was there, he saw three strong men lie down in the foul water and die ! At length, coming to a place where several young and old men were working together, he beheld such cruelty exercised upon them, that he groaned in spirit, and prayed the Almighty to shorten the days of the four hundred years, and come to their deliverance. Unable longer to behold sufferings that he could not relieve, he walked sadly away, deeply meditating upon the mysterious providence of the Almighty, in His dealings with the seed of His servant Abraham. After a little time he found himself in a narrow, sand-drifted lane, between two walls, when he was suddenly aroused from his reflections by a cry of pain, accompanied by sharp blows with a stick. He looked up, and spied an Egyptian taskmaster dragging by the hair Izhur, a youth whom he greatly loved. The Egyptian had pursued him, as he fled up the lane from his blows, and was now plainly intent, in his great wrath, upon putting him to death.

My brother, indignant and grieved, commanded him in a tone of authority to release him ; whereupon the Egyptian, cursing him by his gods, drew his knife from his sheath and would in revenge have driven it into the heart of Izhur, when Moses caught his arm, and bade the young man fly. The Egyptian, thereupon, would have slain my brother, who, looking this way and that, and seeing they were alone, struck him to the earth with one blow of his hand, in the name of the God of Abraham, the Avenger of his people, so that he died on the spot ! He then hid the body in the sand, and returned home, where he made known to me what he had done.

"Surely," I said, in amazement, "thou art the first Hebrew, my brother, who hath slain an Egyptian. A divine motion must have moved thee ! Peradventure it is by *thy arm* that He will yet deliver His people !"

"Thereupon my brother, with his characteristic modesty, said—

"Not mine ! not mine, my brother ! Breathe into my heart no such ambitious pride ! Yet I felt moved and animated by God to do this. Therefore do I justify the act to man and my own conscience."

The next day, my brother visited the lake again, intending to make its circuit, and see certain elders to whom he wished to make himself known,—men wise and good, who were superintending the work of others of their own people. On his way he perceived two Hebrews striving together, and as he came up, one of them struck the other with his working tool, so that he staggered from the blow.

"Sirs, ye are brethren," he said ; "why do ye strive together, seeing ye are brethren?"—and then added, sternly and sorrowfully, to the one who had struck the blow—

"Friend, why hast thou done this wrong? He whom thou hast stricken is a Hebrew. Do not your taskmasters beat you enough, that you must strike each other?"

Whereupon the man who did the injury to his fellow, said fiercely, looking narrowly upon my brother,—

"Thou art Remeses, the Hebrew 'son of Pharaoh's daughter !' I remember thee. Dost thou think that thou art still a Prince of Egypt ? Maris is now our king. Who hath made *thee* prince and judge over us? Thou forgettest that thou art now a slave like the rest of us. Intendest thou to kill me as thou killedst the Egyptian yesterday?"

No sooner had the man thus spoken, than Moses, alarmed, perceived that the thing was known, and beholding the eyes of the Egyptian officers, and many of the Hebrews fastened upon him, he hastened to escape, for he beheld several men run to a high officer of the king, as if with the news, who at once drove rapidly away in his chariot, probably seeking Mœris, whom my brother knew to be not far off, superintending the placing of a statue of Horus upon a new terrace. Several Hebrews would have interposed to arrest Moses, when they heard who he was, for they look upon him more as an Egyptian than as one of their brethren. But he succeeded in retiring unharmed, and at once hastened to recross the Nile. When he had told us that what he had done to the Egyptian was known, and that he was recognized, and that Mœris would surely hear of it, his mother and I advised his immediate flight.

He said that he had no doubt the king would seek his destruction, and that he ought to be cautious and consult his own preservation. "But," he added, "I do not fear the wrath of Pharaoh so far that, were I in his power, I would either deny, excuse, or ask pardon for my act. What I have done I will justify. The oppressor deserved to die! And so, one day will God, by the hand of a Hebrew, slay Pharaoh and all his hosts!" This was spoken with the light of prophecy in his noble face, as if his words were inspiration. When Amram, his father, came in and heard all, he said,—

"The God of Jacob be glorified! There is one man in Israel to whom He has given courage to smite the oppressor of His people! Fly, my son! Fly not for fear, for thou art a brave man and hast been a tried soldier; but fly to preserve a life which my spirit tells me will yet be dear to our people!"

"My father," said Moses sorrowfully, "I believed that my brethren would understand that God was with me, and would acknowledge me as sent to be their friend, instead of joining the Egyptians against me! I will fly! Mœris will rejoice to hold me in his power! But with the hope, that even in a foreign land I may serve my people, at least by prayer and supplication to God for them, I will keep my life out of Pharaoh's hand."

In the garb of an Egyptian, with a store of provisions, and taking gold in his purse, my brother embraced us all, and departed from the house, my mother weeping and saying—

"A second time have I given up my son from the sword of Pharaoh —once to the waters, and now to the desert sands!"

"And the waters, O woman," said my father, "gave him to be a prince of Egypt, and from the sands of the desert God can call him to be king over Israel!"

I looked into my venerable father's face, for often of late years he is gifted with prophetic inspirations, and I saw that his aged eyes shone with a supernatural lustre. My brother returned a few steps, again embraced his mother, bowed his head before his father for his blessing, arose and went on his way eastward. I accompanied him for an hour, when tenderly embracing, we parted—he taking the way towards Midian. Ru-el Jethro, the lord of that country, O king, which was settled by Midian, son of Abram, by Keturah, thou didst meet at the table of thy friend "Remeses," when thou wast in Egypt, at which time, thou mayest remember, he invited my brother to visit his kingdom in Arabia.

It was well for Moses that he so thoroughly knew the character of King Mœris; for when I returned, I learned from my mother, that a party of soldiers had been sent by Pharaoh to seize him. Another hour and he would have fallen into his hand.

At my mother's request, O king, I have written the foregoing, and now inclose his letter to you. I had no sooner entered my house, than I saw my parents and sister preparing to fly from the king, fearing his vengeance when he should learn of the escape of Moses! Not that Pharaoh cared for the life of the slain Egyptian, but he would gladly seize upon the occasion, as a pretext to destroy his former rival.

May God long preserve thy life, O king,
Written in Egypt by thy servant,
AARON THE HEBREW.

AFTER AN INTERVAL OF FORTY YEARS,

REMESES, PRINCE OF TYRE, AND OF DAMASCUS,

SON OF SESOSTRIS,

VISITS EGYPT, AND ADDRESSES THE FOLLOWING

Series of Letters to his Father.

LETTER I.

PALACE OF PHAROAH, LAKE MŒRIS.

MY DEAR FATHER AND KING,—

It is with emotions of no ordinary kind, that I find myself amid the scenes familiar to your eyes, when forty-six years ago, a young man, you visited Egypt. Every object upon which I gaze is invested with new interest as I reflect—" And this my father also saw. On this pylon he has stood and surveyed the landscape ; and along these corridors, his feet have awakened the echoes which respond to mine."

The letters which you wrote from Egypt, during the reign of the wise queen Amense, addressed to my royal grandmother, and which are now in my possession, early familiarized my mind with this wonderful land ; and I recognize every place of interest from your descriptions.

There are, however, some changes. Pharaoh-Mœris, who has been long dead, and his son Meiphra-Thothmes, Thothmeses his grandson, and Thothmeses IV., the present king, all inaugurated their reigns by laying the foundations of temples, palaces, and pyramids ; while the ruins of others have been repaired. Mœris restored the ancient temple of Thoth, in the island of Rhoda, where Prince Remeses was hidden three months, and also all other temples in Egypt. His reign, though tyrannical, was distinguished by improvements in arts, in letters, in astronomy, architecture, and arms. His pyramid is an imposing one, and singularly pre-eminent, by having an obelisk at each angle. His lake, however, is this Pharaoh's greatest monument, if I may so term it.

This lake was begun by former princes, and enlarged by Queen Amense, in order to receive the surplus waters of the Nile, when the inundations, as sometimes happen, arise and overflow the fields after the corn is up. The lake, however, was not large enough wholly to correct this evil, and King Mœris still further enlarged it, by means of the services of the Hebrews, three hundred thousand of whom, it is said perished in the work, before it was completed. It is ample enough in breadth and depth to contain the excess of the Nile. One of the wonders of the world, it is only paralleled in grandeur by the pyramids. In the midst of this magnificent inland sea—for such it seems—arise two pyramids, upon the summit of each of which, three hundred and eight feet in the air, stands upon a throne, shaped like a chariot, a statue, one being that of Thoth, the other of Mœris. Upon the former is inscribed—

"The god prospered;" on the other, "Pharaoh builded." Beneath this inscription is written—

"This lake is three hundred and forty miles in circumference, and one hundred and fifty feet in depth. Within its bounds it can contain all the rivers of the earth."

This sublime work, my dear father, has upon the east side a canal eighty feet broad, and four leagues in length. At its entrance are seated two colossi, figures of Apis and Mnevis; and along its shores are double rows of trees, bordering a terrace, upon which face palaces, villas, temples, gardens, and squares. At the Nile termination stands a single colossus, representing the god Nilus. He is astride the canal, his feet upon the bases of pyramids, and beneath him are great floodgates that let in or exclude the waters of the river. On the south of the lake, upon a plain of sand, Mœris erected a vast temple to Serapis, dedicated it with great pomp, and inclosed it by gardens a mile square, the earth of which was carried by Hebrews in baskets, from the excavations of the lake. He commenced a noble avenue of sphinxes, leading from the lake to the temple, and which has been recently completed by Thothmeses IV., who last week invited me to be present at its inauguration. It was a magnificent spectacle, first the procession of priests and soldiers, nobles and citizens, with the king and his court in a thousand galleys, sailing across the lake; then the landing at the majestic pylon, the march of the procession for a mile between the double row of sphinxes, the mighty temple terminating the vista, and the solemn invocations, libations, and sacrifices before the god.

I marvel, my dear father, at such splendour having no other object than a black bull; such glory leading to an enshrined brute, before whom all this magnificence, power, and rank fall prostrate, as to God! Happy am I, O my wise and good father, to have been early instructed in the knowledge of the true God. I pity while I admire what I see in Egypt. This king is an intelligent man, and I often feel like saying to him, "O king, dost thou believe in thy heart that this bull is God?"

The shores of this vast artificial sea are lined with groves, palaces, and waving fields. The sides of the Lybian hills are terraced and adorned with marble palaces and gardens. At one point, where the cliffs stretch into the lake, are four temples, facing four ways, respectively dedicated to Athor, Pthah, Apis, and Bubastis, the four deities of Memphis; and their sides are covered with golden bronze, so that, in the sunlight, nothing can be more gorgeous.

Upon a small island, opposite this gilded promontory, and left for the purpose, Thothmeses II. erected, during his brief reign, a temple of Syenite stone to the goddess Isis, before which is a recumbent figure of Osiris, seventy feet in length. Its vestibule is enriched with sculpture, and is the most splendid portico in Egypt. In the interior it is surrounded by a peristyle of statues representing the twelve constellations, each eighteen feet in height.

Besides all these, I have visited, my dear father, during the six weeks I have been in Egypt, the "Plain of the Mummies," the Catacombs, the Labyrinth—a marvel of mystery and perplexity to one not initiated into the intricacies of its mazes—the chief pyramids, and that also of Queen Amense, at the entrance of which I placed fresh flowers for your sake.

Pharaoh-Mœris greatly extended the bounds of Memphis. It is not less than twelve miles in circuit. He covered with it a large portion of the plain westward of the pyramids; and where once was a barren waste, are now streets, avenues, colonnades, temples, public edifices, aqueducts, causeways, and all the splendour of metropolitan magnificence. Avenues of sphinxes are almost innumerable; colossal statues obelisks, and pyramids meet the eye everywhere. Near the foot of the hills he formed a chariot-course, that extends three miles along the lake. In the rock of the cliff he caused to be hewn fourteen sarcophagi of black marble, and of gigantic dimensions. In these he entombed the bodies of as many tributary kings, when, in succession, they died; commanding their mummies to be brought into Egypt for the purpose. He has everywhere multiplied, with singular variety, his statues; and in front of this tomb of kings stands one of them upon a pedestal, the feet of which are fourteen sculptured crowns, representatives of their own.

But, my dear father, Egypt is so familiar to you, that I will not weary you with any more descriptions, unless, indeed, I should visit the City of a Hundred Gates, as you were not able to go thither. I will speak, however, of a visit that I paid yesterday to the sphinx that stands before Chephres, and near Cheops. I was impressed, as you were, with the grandeur of the whole. But the great ancient temple, which you spoke of as ruinous, has, in forty-five years, become still more defaced. Indeed, the reigning Pharaoh has expressed his intention of removing it altogether, so that the pyramids may stand forth in solitary majesty.

Among other events of the reign of Mœris, was the discovery, by him, that the tradition which represented the great sphinx as being hollowed into chambers was a true one. He found the entrance, which was beneath the small temple, between the fore-paws of the statue. What he discovered is known to no man; but it is certain that he suddenly displayed vast treasures of gold and silver, jewels and precious stones, with which he carried on his magnificent and expensive works.

You have not forgotten the Ethiopian captive king, Occhoris. He still exists, though his beard is snow-white and his form bent. He remains a captive, each monarch in succession retaining so important a personage in chains, annually to grace their processions to the temples of the gods.

The condition, my dear father, of the Hebrew people, in whom you are so deeply interested, has enlisted all my sympathies also. Forty years have multiplied their number, notwithstanding all the ingenious efforts of the Pharaohs to destroy them by deadly labours, until they amount to three millions and a half of souls. The population of Egypt is only seven millions ; and thus, for every two Egyptians there is one Hebrew. This alarming state of things fills the mind of Thothmeses IV. with ceaseless anxiety. He does not hesitate to confess to me, freely, his fears for the security of his crown.

I have not yet described this monarch to you. When I arrived and presented your letters, he received me with marked courtesy ; inquired after your welfare and the prosperity of your reign ; asked your age, and when I told him you were seventy-three, he said he knew of no king so aged, unless it was Jethro, king of Midian. He inquired why I had delayed coming to Egypt until I was forty-two (for I told him my age, which exactly corresponds with his own) ; and when I informed him that I had been engaged in improving and restoring my kingdom of Damascus, which I inherited from my mother, and which the Sabæans had thrice invaded and devastated before I came of age, he expressed his pleasure that peace was restored, and that I had come into Egypt, at last. He seems naturally superstitious, credulous, and irresolute. I think he possesses little or no stability of character, and that he is easily influenced to do evil. He is timid in his policy, yet rash ; vain of his wisdom, yet constantly guilty of follies ; a devout worshipper of his gods, yet a slave to the basest personal vices ; jealous of his rights, yet, from want of courage, suffering them continually to be invaded, both by his subjects and tributary princes ; a man whose word is kept, only so far as his present interest demands; who will pardon to-night a suppliant, from irresolution and morbid pity, and execute him in the morning when the coldness of his nature returns. Were he my friend, I should distrust him ; were he my foe, I would not delay to place the sea between me and his sword.

Under such a prince, you may imagine that the condition of the Hebrew people is not less pitiable than under his predecessors. Fearing them, he doubles their tasks, and resorts to every device of destruction, short of open and indiscriminate slaughter. Yet even this infernal idea has been suggested by him to his private council, but it was opposed, on the ground that the burial of so many millions would be impossible, and that a plague would result fatal to the population of Egypt.

So the Hebrews still exist, feared, suspected, and crushed by additional burdens. I have been among them, and, as you directed, have made many cautious inquiries after the learned Hebrew, Moses. They are more enlightened than when you saw them. The idea of God is less obscure in their minds, while their hope of a deliverer is bright and ever present. Few of the old men remember Remeses, or Moses ; and none of them know anything of his present abode, but seem sure he is long since dead. I have become deeply interested in some of these venerable men, in whose majestic features, set off by flowing beards, I recognize the lineaments of Abram, their ancestor, as sculptured on the mausoleum of his servant, "Eliezer of Damascus." The beauty of the children and young women, amid all their degradation, is wonderful. I was struck with the seeming good feeling which existed among these and the women of Egypt. The latter, either from pity, or because the Hebrew women are gentle and attractive, hold kind intercourse with them; and at a marriage, which I witnessed in one of their huts, the Hebrew females, especially the bride, were decked with jewels loaned to them by their friends, the Egyptian maidens. I have also been struck with the patient, uncomplaining, and gentle manner in which the Hebrews speak of the Egyptians, excepting their task-officers—who are brutal soldiers—and the king. Generations of oppression have made them forbearing and submissive; and, besides, the Egyptians and Hebrews, who now know one another, knew each other as children, before either could understand their different positions.

Here and there I have met a lord who recalled your visit, dear father, with pleasure; but were you now here you would feel a stranger indeed.

Farewell, my honoured and revered father. I will continue my inquiries after Prince Remeses. To my sister, Amense, and her husband, Sisiris, King of Sidon, give my kindest greetings.

Your affectionate son,
REMESES OF DAMASCUS.

MY DEAREST FATHER,—

I unseal this epistle to inform you that while it has been lying three days, waiting for the galley of the Lord of Sarepta to depart, I have had intelligence of your old friend Remeses. He lives, and is in Midian, as you suspected, and is well, though, of course, far advanced in years. This is all that I can now add to my letter, as the secretary of the Sareptan noble is in my reception-room, and lingers only to take this letter, the wind being now favourable.

Your faithful son,
REMESES.

LETTER II.

REMESES OF DAMASCUS, TO HIS FATHER, KING SESOSTRIS OF PHŒNICIA.

CITY OF ON, EGYPT.

HAVING an opportunity, my dearest father, to send letter the day after to-morrow, I will herewith make known to you, how I obtained the intelligence, that your ancient friend Remeses is still in the kingdom of Midian, whither he fled from King Mœris.

In obedience to your last instructions, I have diligently made all inquiries that were likely to obtain the information which your lively friendship prompts you to seek. There is something, dear father, very beautiful in this undying attachment, which has survived a period of forty years, and which still looks forward to behold the beloved face of thy cherished friend once more!

Learning yesterday that a caravan had arrived from Ezion-geber (by the Edomites called Ekkaba), which lies near the head of the orient arm of the Red or Arabian Sea, and not far from which are the borders of peninsular Midian, I crossed the Nile to the suburbs of the City of the Sun, where the caravan had found quarters in the quadrangle of the Serail.

Having found the governor of the company of merchants, I made myself know to him as a foreign prince, travelling for knowledge, and sight of men and scenes. He courteously received me, and I asked him many questions about his country, his journey, and the articles he brought, until he was at his ease with me, when I inquired if he had ever been in Midian. He answered that he himself was a Midianite, and that twenty days before he had left Midian to join the caravan, part of which belonged to Jethro, prince and priest of that country. Upon hearing this name, dear father, I was struck by its similarity to that mentioned in the last letter of Aaron the Hebrew, as being that of the king of the country who had invited Moses, while prince, to visit him.

"Dost thou know this Prince Jethro?" I asked.

"I have sat at his feet—his hand has often rested upon my head when I was a lad," he answered.

"You call him a priest," I said; "what is his religion?"

"That of our progenitor, Abram the Chaldean."

"The Hebrews sprang from Abram," I replied.

"Yes, by Sara, his first wife. The Midianites are the sons of Midian, a son of Abram by Keturah, the wife he took after Sara died. The cities of Epher, Ephah, and Hanoch, in Midian, were founded by princes who were this same Abram's grandsons, and sons of Midian."

"Do you worship the God of Abram—or Abraham as the Hebrews called their ancestor?" I asked.

"Hast thou ever heard, O prince," he said, with feeling, "that we were idolaters, or fire-worshippers, or that we pray to bulls, and beasts, and creeping things, as these Egyptians do? We worship one God —the Lord of Heaven—the Almighty Creator, who revealed Himself to our Father Abram."

"When I told him that I also worshipped the same God, he took my hand, kissed it reverently, and said solemnly,—

"There is but one God!"

"What is your form of worship, that your king is also your priest?" I inquired.

"By sacrifices. Morning and evening, the priests offer up to God incense, and oblations, and sacrifices of lambs. Hence we have large flocks and herds. On great days, the king himself officiates, lays his hand upon the head of the victim, and asks the Almighty to take the life of the sacrifice instead of that of the people, and to visit upon its head the wrath which the kingdom had incurred."

"Did Abram thus sacrifice?"

"Not only Abram, but Noah, the first father, and all the fathers of the old world. Our worship, therefore, O prince, consists in offering the life of a victim, to preserve our own!"

"Yes, if the great Lord of Heaven will so receive it! For who can weigh the life of a man with that of his lamb?" I said.

"None but God, who, in His goodness and glory, wills it so to be!" answered the Midianite.

"Hast thou ever heard, in Midian, of a Hebrew called Moses?"

"Dost thou mean Moses the Egyptian?" he asked, quickly.

"He was educated an Egyptian, and was supposed to be the son of Pharaoh's daughter, but was only adopted by her: and being discovered to be a Hebrew, he left Egypt."

"This same Moses, once Prince Remeses, is now in Midian, where he hath been these forty years," answered the venerable chief-captain of the caravan. "He is son-in-law to our prince, who has made him ruler over all the companies of shepherds in the region that lieth between the city of Keturah and the sea, and even to the back of the desert, where, on the sides of Horeb and the valleys thereof, he feeds his flocks. Moreover, there also he meditates, and writes in a cave—for he is a man of vast learning, and greatly revered in Midian as a wise sage. He is married to the daughter of the Prince Ru-el Jethro, and by her hath had many sons, but two only—mere lads—remain, the rest having died early. Surely, what man in Midian knoweth not Moses, the wise shepherd of Horeb?"

Upon hearing this good news, dear father, I rejoiced, in anticipation, at the pleasure you would receive, when you should read my letter containing the pleasing tidings. I now asked the good Midianite when he would return. He said that in seven days he should depart, and that it would take him eleven days to reach that part of the country where Moses dwelt. Upon this, my dear father, after making sundry other inquiries about the route, I determined to accompany him; for I knew you would value one letter from me, saying I had seen and spoken with your friend face to face, more highly than many from the hundred-gated Thebes. I shall be gone but one month, and shall be well repaid, not only by seeing Moses, whose noble countenance I can just recollect as a pleasant remembrance of my childhood, but by conferring upon him the unexpected pleasure of hearing from you by your son, his name-sake. Thus, for your sake, as well as for his, and also my own gratification in seeing a new and rarely visited country, I take my departure with the caravan. After I reach Midian, and have seen your old friend in the land of his long exile, I will write to you fully of all that may interest you.

May the God of Abraham and of Moses have you always in His sacred keeping.

Your loving son,
REMESES OF DAMASCUS.

LETTER III.

MOSES TO SESOSTRIS.

LAND OF MIDIAN.

MY VENERABLE AND BELOVED KING AND FRIEND,—

WITH what emotions of joy and gratitude I embraced your princely son, Remeses, I can feebly express! I give God thanks for this happiness, vouchsafed to me in my eighty-first year, of hearing from you again, and by the mouth of your son. I rejoice to hear of your welfare, and prosperous reign. The sight of the young Remeses revives all the past, and in his face I see, with delight, your features and smile. I also perceive that he possesses all your virtues, and, above all, that you have taught him the knowledge of the true God. His presence here, and his readiness to come across the desert to see me, gratifies me. It assures me that I am loved by you both! Although, my friend, I have not written to you—for, since my flight from Egypt, my life has been wholly without events—yet, from time to time, by foreign merchants who have been in Tyre, I have had news of you, and of your prosperity. Until I beheld your son, I believed that I was quite forgotten!

I shall keep Remeses with me as long as he will remain. My way of life, however, is humble. We are a pastoral people, and my occupation is that of a shepherd ; for, though I am chief shepherd of the land, yet do I not disdain to lead my own flocks to feed upon the mountains, —where, as they browse, I meditate in solitude upon God, and also think upon the sad condition of my brethren in bondage in Egypt. Four kings have reigned and perished, and yet the sons of Jacob toil on, exchanging only one oppressor for another, each more cruel than the last! But the day draws near for their deliverance, O Sesostris, my friend and brother ! The four hundred years of prophecy are drawing to a close ! On the arrival of every caravan from Egypt I look for intelligence, that a deliverer has arisen, who, lifting the standard of the God of Abraham, shall call on Israel to rally around it, exchange their spades for spears, assert their freedom, and defy Pharaoh and his power ! Who will be this hero of God? Who the favoured man, to whom shall be committed the happiness and glory of leading the mighty Hebrew nation out of Egypt ? Will they hear his voice ? Will they acknowledge his authority ? Will they have the courage to follow him ? or has the yoke of Egypt so long bound their necks down, that they have no hope nor desire to be free ? Thus I meditate upon their fate, and meanwhile pray earnestly to my God to send the deliverer of my people ; for the time has come when He will remember His promise to Abraham, and to our fathers !

From the painful accounts that your son Remeses gives me, the cup of their bondage is full to overflowing !—also the cup of Egypt !—for the same prophecy which foretells their deliverance after four hundred years, adds, "and the nation which they serve will I judge." Thus, O king, do I look forward to the overthrow of the power of Egypt, when God shall send His angel to deliver Israel from beneath Pharaoh's hand of iron.

What courage, wisdom, patience, meekness, faith, dignity of person, and ardent piety, must the **servent** of God have, who will lead Israel out of bondage! What man on earth is sufficient for this high office? What man in all Egypt, among the Hebrews, has God raised up and endowed with these attributes? Alas, I know none! They are all oppressed and broken in heart, and the spirit of manhood has died out within them! But He who wills can do! and He can arm with **power** the weakest instrument of His will! Let us trust in Him! for **by** *His* arm, whoever be the agent, they will be delivered.

During my exile I have re-written the book of the life of the Prince of Uz, with great care, and a larger share of the wisdom of God. At the same time I have instructed many, in Midian, in the truths of God. It has also seemed good to me, under the inspiration of the Almighty, to write, from our divine traditions, a narrative of the first acts of creation, from the beginning, when God created the heavens and the earth, down to the death of Prince Joseph. Of this **book, a** copy has been made by my wife Zipporah, which I will send to you **by** Prince Remeses for your acceptance.

With greetings of true **and** holy friendship, I am, O King Sesostris, **thy** servant and friend,

MOSES THE HEBREW.

LETTER IV.

REMESES OF DAMASCUS TO THE KING HIS FATHER.

CAVE IN HOREB, WILDERNESS OF MIDIAN.

MY DEAR AND ROYAL FATHER,—

I HAVE been two weeks a guest of your venerable friend, the Hebrew Moses. My journey across the desert was agreeable from its novelty, and my sensations upon the boundless waste, were combined emotions of solitude and sublimity, similar to those I experienced on the great sea. Our route, after leaving the land of Egypt, continued eastward for five days—most of the time in the Arabian desert, with the mountains of Etham on our right, far to the south. Having on the sixth day passed round the western horn of the Sea of Arabia, we turned southwardly into the desert of Shur, which terminated at the base of a low range of hills, of mingled cliff and pasture-land. A valley opened between, and after three days' journeying, amid vales filled with herds and Arabian villages, we entered a mountainous region, the sea being on our right. Every hour the scenery became more grand and rugged, until the ridges, constantly rising in altitude, stretched far southwardly, and terminated in a majestic twin-peaked mountain, midway between the two arms or horns of the sea.

"That is Horeb," said the chief of the caravan. "It is in the land of Midian, though remote from the town of the king. In that mountain the royal flocks are pastured, and there you will find your father's friend

Moses the Hebrew, either with his shepherds and flocks or in the retirement of his cave."

The same evening we entered the valley of Mount Horeb, which rose in sublime majesty, with its double crown, far into the skies above us. We had turned an angle of the mountain, which rose as abruptly as a pyramid from the plain, and were entering a gorge through which a road lay to the city of the king—a day's journey distant—when I beheld from my camel, a shepherd standing upon a rock and leaning upon his staff—his sheep reclining about him. He was a tall, venerable man, with dark locks mingled with white, and a beard, like snow for whiteness, that descended over his breast. There was a majesty, and yet simplicity, in his aspect and costume, which impressed me, as he stood—the evening sun lighting up his kingly visage—upon a rock, like the statue of the god of the mountain-pass.

My heart instinctively said, " This is Moses !"

" Lo ! there stands the son-in-law of Jethro !" said the merchant.

I immediately caused my camel to kneel, and descended to the ground with haste and joy. The next moment I was bending before thy friend, my dear father, crying, with reverent feelings of emotion,—

" I am Remeses, son of Sesostris, thy friend ! Venerable father, give me thy blessing, for I bear thy name!"

He regarded me for an instant with surprise, and then raising me, embraced me and said, a holy radiance of love and joy illumining his face,—

" I see thy father, and hear his voice, in thee ! Welcome, my son ! How fares the good king ? Hast thou ventured across the desert to see the exiled Hebrew?" he asked, with a smile of benignity and pleasure, as he gazed upon me. " The sight of thee brings up all the past !"

His voice was disturbed with emotion; though I perceived it had also a slight natural embarrassment of speech. I related why I had come, and gave him your messages of love. He took me to his cave or grotto, which is like those of the sacred priests in Lebanon. The caravan encamped, near by, that night, and I remained in the company of the wise and virtuous sage. We conversed, for many hours, of you, of Tyre, of my grandmother, of Queen Amense, of the Hebrews in bondage, and his certain hope of their speedy deliverance.

How happy the princely old man was to hear from you, my dear father ! What a venerable and holy friendship exists between you !—fresh and green at fourscore, as in the fire and impulse of youth !

The next day, I accompanied him to the chief city of Midian. There I beheld his matronly wife, Zipporah, and his two sons, beautiful and ingenuous youths of sixteen and eighteen. I was also presented to the venerable Ru-el Jethro, or the King Jethro, now one hundred and one years old, but retaining the full vigour of manhood. He described to me pleasantly, under what circumstances he first met Moses, forty years ago.

" My seven daughters," said the patriarchal Prince of Midian, " were with my shepherds at the well, near the city, drawing water for the flocks ; for the Prince of the mountain having no water, had thrice sent his shepherds to draw it from this well, when we had but little for our own herds. I sent my daughters, thinking that they would reverence their presence; but the mountain shepherds would have driven them away, when a stranger, who was seated by the well, rose up, and with great courage chastised the assailants. Though many in number, they fled from him in great fear, when he turned and bade my daughters remain and heed them not; and he helped them water the flocks.

"When they returned to me earlier than I looked for them, I inquired the cause, and they replied,—

"'An Egyptian, a mighty man of valour, delivered us out of the hand of the shepherds, and aided us also in drawing water for our flocks.' 'Where is he?' I asked. 'Why is it that ye have left this brave stranger at the well?' They answered 'He is an Egyptian;' for such from his dress, and speech, and looks, they believed him to be. I then sent my daughter Zipporah after him, to invite him to come and eat bread with me. From that day we became friends, and when I learned his story, that he was a Hebrew, and, like myself, a descendant of Abram, I gave him Zipporah to wife, and he was content to remain in the land, and is now the greatest and wisest man in it, for God is with him."

I was much interested in this brief account, my dear father, and believe that you will be, as it is a connecting link in the life of Moses, that has been hitherto wanting.

The following week, I retired with Moses to the mountains, and here I pass my days, listening to his sublime teachings. Not all the wisdom and learning of Egypt can compare with his sublime knowledge. The secrets of nature, the mysteries of creation, seem unveiled to his intellectual vision. It is his habit to pass an hour or two every night in prayer, upon the mountain, beneath the silent stars, communing alone with his God, as if he were the high-priest of the earth. Horeb his altar, the universe his temple, and his theme the Hebrew nation in Egypt. Ah! my dear father, if God is to deliver them from Egypt by the hand of man, my heart tells me that Moses will be appointed their deliverer; for who on earth has so at heart their misery, or supplicates Heaven so earnestly for aid in their behalf? It is true he is an old man, seven years your senior, but his step is as firm as mine, his eye clear and brave, his natural force not abated, and his looks those of a man in his prime—so healthful is this mountain life, and the simple routine of his days.

He has written to you. I shall be the bearer of his letter, as well as of this, which I write in the door of his grotto, facing the valley, with the sea beyond. There go the ships of Ezion-geber, and the galleys of Ind. Far to the west is the blue line of the shores of Arabian Egypt, and to the east the rocky land of Arabia, and Eastern Midian. The prospect is sublime, and, at this hour of sunset, while purple mists are upon the hills, and a golden light upon the sea, it is beautiful and serene.

I had almost neglected to inform you, that your learned and eloquent friend Aaron, the brother of Moses, was lately in Midian, and was, for a time, an assistant priest of the sacrifices in the city; but has

has now returned to Goshen, where he married many years ago. His sister Miriam is here with Moses, and is one of the most majestic women I ever beheld. She is in her ninety-fourth year, but is as erect and buoyant in her step as a young and resolute woman. With her snow-white hair, piercing black eyes, and queenly mien, she looks like the venerable priestess of the sun at Baal-Phegor. The mother of Moses also dwells at Midian; but I think their father died in Arabia Deserta; for thither they fled from Egypt, before coming finally into Midian. Aaron is spoken of here as a noble-looking and stately priest, when, in his flowing robes, he used to offer sacrifices according to the simple rites of the Midianites, in the plain temple hewn from the rock, in which they worship God.

Farewell, my dear father. I am not surprised that you love Moses. He has won *my* heart.

Your affectionate son,
REMESES OF DAMASCUS.

LETTER V.

REMESES OF DAMASCUS TO SESOSTRIS.

TREASURE-CITY OF RAAMSES, EGYPT.

MY HONOURED AND BELOVED FATHER,—

YOU will see by the date that I am once more in Egypt; and I am here under circumstances the most wonderful and amazing. Remeses —that is, Moses, the servant of the Most High God—is here also. My trembling fingers can scarce form the letters legibly, so great is the emotion under which I now write to you! But I will not delay to give you a history of the events.

I wrote to you last, from the grotto of the shepherd-sage of Horeb. The following day he led a portion of his own flock, from a distant plain, to the secluded valley on the rear of the mountain of Horeb, away from the sea. Expecting his return, I had gone forth to meet him, and was descending a steep path, when I beheld him advancing before his shepherds, and leading his flock up the valley. He preceded them some distance, and was quite alone, when I perceived a bright flame arise by the side of his path. It rose above the bushes, which it seemed to consume without smoke. At the same moment I observed that Moses turned aside and approached the dazzling fire. In an instant he was lost to my gaze, and enveloped in its flame. I hastened down the mountain-path, surprised and alarmed at what I had seen; and, as the way was winding, it was some minutes before I came to the valley, where I expected to find the venerable sage consumed by the flames, that appeared to have surrounded him.

Upon reaching the valley, lo! I beheld the shepherds fallen upon their faces, the man of God standing before the burning bush, his countenance like the sun, and his raiment shining with supernatural light! My soul was seized with an indescribable awe at the sight! His sandals were removed from his feet, and he seemed as if he were standing in the presence of his God, so awful was the majesty of his countenance. He appeared to be holding discourse with one in the flames. I was transfixed to the spot, and fell upon my face at the sight of this stupendous vision, feeling the presence of the Almighty there. Then I heard a voice utter these words from the midst of the fire, in which I had seen appear the form of a man, radiant with glory above the brightness of the sun:

"I am the God of thy father, the God of Abraham, the God of Isaac, and the God of Jacob."

While the calm, divine voice spake in still, soft tones, the earth seemed to tremble, as if its Creator stood upon it. I looked up with fear and trembling, and, lo! Moses was standing with his face covered by his shepherd's mantle, for he was afraid to look upon God; while my heart sank within me, and I became as a dead man.

When I returned to consciousness, I heard, without raising my face again, Moses talking with the mighty Angel in the flame, which I perceived rested upon the thorn-bush like dazzling sunbeams concentrated thereon, but without consuming or changing a leaf. It was the radiance alone of this celestial Person's glorious presence that constituted the wonderful flame of fire.

"I have surely seen," said the voice from the flaming glory, "the affliction of my people which are in Egypt, and have heard their cry by reason of their task-masters; for I know their sorrows, and I am come down to deliver them out of the hand of the Egyptians, and to bring them up out of that land unto a good land, and a large, unto a land flowing with milk and honey,—the land of the Canaanites and the Amorites.

"Now, therefore, behold, the cry of the children of Israel is come up before me: and I have also seen the oppression wherewith the Egyptians oppress them. Come now, therefore, and I will send thee unto Pharaoh, that thou mayest bring forth my people, the children of Israel, out of Egypt."

Here the holy and divine Voice ceased. How did its words thrill my heart! Had the mighty God of the Hebrews come down from heaven at last to deliver His people, fulfil His promise to Abram, and also make Moses the servant of His power? My soul was overpowered with the thought.

Then Moses spake, in accents of the profoundest humility and fear, and said,—

"Who am I that I should go unto Pharaoh, and that I should bring forth the children of Israel out of Egypt?"

And the Voice replied,—

"Certainly I will be with thee; and this shall be a token unto thee, that I have sent thee,—lo! when thou hast brought forth the people out of Egypt, ye and they shall serve God upon this mountain."

Then Moses answered the Angel of the flame, with that meekness and humbleness of heart which characterizes him,—

"Behold, when I come unto the children of Israel, and shall say unto them, 'The God of your fathers hath sent me unto you;' and they shall say unto me, 'What is His name?' what shall I say unto them?"

The inquiry was made by him with the profoundest homage in the tones of his reverent voice, not as if he doubted God, but his brethren. Moreover, he now beheld, as it were face to face, the Lord God, of heaven and earth, whom he had so long worshipped, and whose name to men, neither he nor any man knew. And I heard the Voice answer—with majesty inconceivable, so that my spirit failed before it —and say unto Moses,—

"I AM THAT I AM. Thus shalt thou say unto the children of Israel, 'I AM hath sent me unto you!'"

Then after a brief silence, during which Moses fell upon his face and worshipped, the Voice from the midst of the fire said,—

"Thus shalt thou say unto the children of Israel, 'The Lord God of your fathers, the God of Abraham, the God of Isaac, and the God of Jacob, hath sent me unto you. THIS is my NAME *for ever;* and this is my memorial unto all generations!' Go, and gather the elders of Israel together and say unto them, 'The Lord God of your fathers, the God of Abraham, of Isaac, and of Jacob, appeared unto me saying,—

"'I have surely visited you, and seen that which is done to you in Egypt; and I have said, I will bring you out of the affliction of Egypt, unto the land of the Canaanites, unto a land flowing with milk and honey!' And the children of Israel shall hearken to thy voice; and thou shalt come, thou and the elders of Israel, unto the King of Egypt, and ye shall say unto him,—

"'The Lord God of the Hebrews hath met with us; and now let us go, we beseech thee, three days' journey into the wilderness, that we may sacrifice to the Lord our God.' And I am sure that the king of Egypt will not let you go, no, not by a mighty hand; and I will stretch out My hand and smite Egypt with all My wonders which I will do in the midst thereof; and after that he will let you go: and when ye go, ye shall not go empty, but ye shall spoil the Egyptians."

When the Voice had ceased, I heard Moses answer, and say with modest diffidence,—

"But behold, the elders and people of my brethren, the Hebrews, will not believe me nor hearken to my voice; for they will say, 'The Lord hath not appeared unto thee.'"

How extraordinary, O my father, this humility of the wisest of men! How impiously vain some sages and seers would have been, at such an infinite honour as the appearance of God to them, to talk with them, face to face, as He did now to Moses,—veiling the ineffable splendour of His glory under the form of an angel enveloped in a mantle of dazzling sunbeams,—His presence a flame of fire! But see this great and holy man modestly declining the service, considering himself mean and powerless when compared with the mighty Pharaoh, and utterly unable to do any thing for the Hebrew nation. Forty years ago, he had, indeed, felt a divine motion in himself to deliver them, which he then believed was an indication that God would use him as an instrument for that purpose: but forty years an exile, for-

THE PYRAMIDS.

gotten by the children of Israel, and being only a ruler of shepherds, and guardian of the flocks of a small province, he felt the humility and insignificance of his position, as well as his total want of means and power to do what God now commanded him to do. But, lo! God condescends to inspire him with the confidence and resolution, the magnanimity and fortitude, that his sublime errand demanded.

The voice of the Lord spake and said,—

"What is that in thine hand?"

He answered, "A rod."

This was the staff with which he climbed the sides of Horeb, and guided his flock, and upon which he often leaned his head when he stood and worshipped.

And the Voice said, with authority,—

"Cast it on the ground."

As Moses obeyed, I heard first the rod strike the ground, then a sharp hissing, as of a serpent, and lastly, a cry of surprise from Moses; when, raising my face from the earth, upon which I had remained prostrate, fearing to look upon the glory before me, I perceived, with horror, a serpent rearing its head angrily into the air, and Moses flying from before it. Then the Voice from the ineffable light said to him, "Put forth thy hand and take it by the tail." Moses, with hesitating obedience, obeyed, put forth his hand and caught it, when, lo! it became a rod again in his hand.

"This shall be a sign to them, that they may believe that the Lord God of their fathers, the God of Abraham, the God of Isaac, and the God of Jacob, hath appeared unto thee," was again spoken.

I had risen, and stood upon my feet in terror, at beholding the serpent, and would have fled, but had no power to move. I now heard the Voice command Moses to thrust his hand into his bosom: and he put his hand into his bosom; and when he took it out, behold, it was as leprous as snow. Then the Voice said—for I heard only, not daring to behold the Angel more—"Put thy hand into thy bosom again." And he put his hand into his bosom again: and when he had plucked it out of his bosom, it was turned again as it was before, like his other flesh.

Then I heard the Angel of God, who was God Himself, say to him,—

"It shall come to pass, if they will not believe thee, neither hearken to the voice of the first sign, that they will believe the voice of the latter sign. If they will not believe, also, these two signs, neither hearken unto thy voice, then thou shalt take of the water of the river of Egypt and pour it upon the dry land, and it shall become blood."

Then Moses looked troubled in spirit, and said unto the Lord,—

"O my Lord, I am not eloquent, neither heretofore, nor since Thou hast spoken unto Thy servant; but I am slow of speech and of a slow tongue."

This embarrassment of speech, my dear father, which existed in a slight degree, as I have heard you say, when you knew him, and which proceeded from modesty and diffidence when expressing himself in intercourse with others (though with his pen he is powerful and eloquent beyond all men), has, no doubt, been increased by his long retirement as a shepherd, and his love of solitude; yet, nevertheless, he is the most interesting teacher of wisdom to whom I ever listened. But no one save himself would accuse him of being slow of speech and slow of tongue.

Then the voice of the Lord said, with a rebuke in its tones,—

"Who hath made man's mouth? Or who maketh the dumb, or the deaf, or the seeing, or the blind? Have not I the LORD? Now, therefore, go, and I will be with thy mouth, and teach thee what thou shalt say!"

Notwithstanding all this, the heart of Moses failed him. He trembled at being an ambassador of God to his people, and said, with great fear and dread visible in his countenance,—

"Send, I pray Thee; but not by me, but by the hand of him whom Thou wilt send."

Thus speaking, he fell prostrate before the Lord and covered his face.

Then the anger of the Angel of the Lord seemed to be kindled against Moses, for the flames were agitated and spread abroad, and shot forth fiery tongues, and I looked to see him consumed. But from their midst I heard the Voice demand,—

"Is not Aaron, the Levite, thy brother? I know that he can speak well; and also, he cometh forth to meet thee, and when he seeth thee he will be glad in his heart. And thou shalt speak unto him" (the dread Voice was no longer in anger), "and put words in his mouth; and I will be with thy mouth, and with his mouth, and will teach you what you shall do. And *he* shall be thy spokesman unto the people; and he shall be, even he shall be unto *thee* instead of a mouth, and thou shalt be to *him* instead of GOD. And thou shalt take this rod in thy hand, wherewith thou shalt do signs."

Then Moses rose from the ground, and bowed his head low in submission and obedience to the voice of the Lord. The flame had already begun to fade slowly, until it appeared like a golden cloud, which now rapidly melted away like a mist touched with the setting sun. The next moment it was invisible, leaving the sacred bush as before, green with leaves and brilliant with wild-flowers; and, as I gazed, a pair of snow-white doves lighted upon it.

Then Moses, lifting up his eyes to heaven said, "O Lord God, who is like unto Thee among the gods? Who is like unto Thee, glorious and fearful, doing wonders? The Lord shall reign for ever, great in power and holiness! He is my God, and I will praise Him; my fathers' God, and I will magnify His holy name for ever! He hath remembered His covenant with Abraham, and His vengeance against the nation that oppresseth His people."

At this moment I beheld Aaron advancing along the defile. When he beheld Moses, whose person yet seemed bright with the lingering glory of the divine Presence, he ran to him, and kissing him, said,—

"Thus did I behold thee in my vision, brother!"

"Hast thou also seen God face to face?" demanded Moses, regarding him with affectionate earnestness, "that thou art come hither from Egypt so soon?"

"I was at prayer fourteen days ago, in Goshen, when a vision stood before me!—such a form, doubtless, as our father Abraham beheld. It said to me, 'Go into the wilderness to meet Moses.' Then, in the vision I beheld thee standing in the mount of God, and the glory of the Lord shone upon thee, and thou wast talking with one who seemed like an angel of God, and I knew that thou wast ordained of Him, with authority to deliver Israel out of Egypt. Therefore, delaying not, I am come hither according to the command of the angel of the Lord. My heart is glad at beholding thee! Speak now, O my brother, for the angel said to me, 'He shall tell thee all the words of the Lord, and all the signs which He hath commanded him.'"

Moses then told Aaron all the words which God had spoken unto him, and how the Lord had sent him to deliver Israel, and had given him courage and power to obey, removing his fears and confirming his faith. Thereupon he showed Aaron the rod in his hand, and said, "If this rod becomes a serpent, as it did before the Lord, then wilt thou know that He hath sent me, and is with me! for this is His sign."

As he spoke, he cast the rod far from him upon the ground, which it no sooner struck than it became a serpent, and ran swiftly towards Moses, who reached forth, and grasping it by the head without fear, lo! it became again a rod of almond-wood, as before! The other sign also Moses showed to his brother, who then answered and said,—

"Thou shalt deliver Israel, and I will be thy servant, and bear thy rod before thee!"

I had already, by the invitation of Moses, drawn near to these holy and great men, and walked with them, feeling, prince that I am, the deepest sense of inferiority and humility. I felt that I could be the servant of both, and that I was honoured when taking up the sandals which Moses had put off his feet. I knelt before him to put them on; but, in his modesty, this prince appointed of God would not suffer me.

The two venerable brothers—one eighty years of age, and the other eighty-three—now walked together towards the shepherd's cave on the mountain-side, discoursing of the wonderful and joyful events which had just passed, of the promised deliverance of Israel, and how God would accomplish it, and by what sort of exercise of power and majesty.

The next day Moses returned to Jethro, and said to him,—

"I pray thee, let me go, and return unto my people which are in Egypt, and see how they fare, and if my brethren of the family of Levi be yet alive—for the Lord hath shown me that all the men are dead which sought my life." And his venerable father-in-law said,—

"Go in peace."

Therefore, my dear father, three days afterwards, Moses, accompanied by his brother and myself, took leave of Jethro, and taking his wife and son, and holding the "rod of God" in his hand, left Midian. The next day we fell in with a caravan from the East, and after many days I once more reached Egypt. In sight of On, I parted from Moses, who went with his family to that part of the land of Goshen where his tribe dwells, which is not far from the treasure-city of Raamses.

The first hours I could command, after reaching the palace of the Governor of On, with whom I dwell as a guest, I have devoted, my dear father, to a recital of these extraordinary events. Moses seems to be a different man ; calm majesty sits enthroned upon his brow, and he is profoundly impressed with the sublime mission which Heaven has entrusted to him.

Aaron, who has, from time to time, revisited Egypt, and is well known to the elders of his people, will be a great support and aid to Moses, in his intercourse with the Hebrews. The two mighty brothers are now assembling the elders together, though it is but two days since they returned to Egypt. Secretly, messengers have been going by night throughout the land of Goshen, calling an assembly in the name of the God of Abraham, to meet, two nights hence, at the ruined fountain of Jacob.

I shall also be present, dear father, by permission of the inspired Moses. What infinite issues will grow out of that midnight meeting of these "sons of God," for such, though in bondage, are these Hebrews shown to be! How little Thothmes-Amosis, who calls himself also, vainly, after Amunophis the Great, and assumes the style, "Upholder of worlds," " Lord of the Diadem of Heaven," and "Beloved of the Sun," upon his cartouch,—how little, I repeat, he dreams that One mightier than he, the Upholder of the universe, very Lord of heaven and earth, and Creator of the sun, is armed with vengeance against him, and will presently bring him into judgment for the bondage of the Hebrews ! I saw him this morning in his palace, for he is now in his palace at On, having hastened to pay him my homage after my absence. He was in gay humour, for news had reached him that his "lord of the mines" had opened a new vein of silver, in the southern mountains near Ethiopia.

" I will send one hundred thousand of these Hebrews to work it, O prince," he said. " I will, to-morrow, give orders to all the governors, and chief captains, and officers over them, to choose me the strongest and most dangerous, and assemble them in companies of thousands, and, under strong guard, march them to the Thebaïd. By the gods ! yesterday I was planning some new device to destroy their children, male and female ; but the mines come happily to my aid !"

Thus does this proud, weak, luxurious, and cruel monarch, confident of power, and sitting as a god upon his throne, acknowledging no power above his own, dream of wealth, and rejoice in dominion !

Did policy prompt me to give him warning ? I feared the God of Moses more than I sympathized with a contemporaneous prince, albeit Tyre was his ally.

Farewell, my dear father.

My next letter will, no doubt, convey to you startling tidings.

Your affectionate son,

REMESES OF DAMASCUS.

MOUNT HOREB.

LETTER VI.

REMESES OF DAMASCUS TO KING SESOSTRIS.

CITY OF ON, EGYPT.

MY DEAR FATHER,—

The secret assembly of the elders, called by Moses, met last night. It was in a solitary place, far from any of the garrisons of soldiers. In the disguise of a Hebrew, I also was present, standing by Aaron. It was after midnight before all the elders could elude the vigilance of their officers, and had assembled. The well of Jacob you recollect. It is where you had the conversation with Remeses (now Moses), upon the condition of the Hebrews. The Egyptian soldiers, who are very superstitious, will not venture near this desolate fountain by night; for the tradition is, that it leads to the realms of the lower world, and that there are evil beings who issue from it in the darkness, and drag under the earth all who walk past it. The Hebrews have no such superstition, or despised their fears on an occasion like the present. Aaron, in selecting the spot, knew it would be safe from intrusion on the part of the Egyptians.

It was a sublime spectacle to see no less than four hundred and eighty elders of the Hebrews, forty out of each tribe, met together beneath the aged palm-trees that overshadowed the fountain, and where Jacob had sat, with his sons about him, in peace, under the protecting sceptre of the king of that day.

The moon shone here and there upon a silvery head, while others were grouped in shadow. There was a deep, expecting silence. At length Aaron stood up in their midst, his venerable figure visible to all present, as the pale moonlight fell upon him,—

"Men and brethren, Hebrews of the house of Abraham our father, hear, while I make known to you why I have called this strange meeting—for when before has Israel met in such an assembly! Your presence, your readiness to come, your courage, and your success in reaching here, all show to me the hand of God, and the power of God."

Aaron then gave a history of the origin of their nation, of God's promise to Abraham, of His prophecy of their bondage and deliverance, and His promise to give them the land of the Canaanites. They listened with deep attention, for he spoke with remarkable eloquence. He then said, "The hour of our deliverance is at hand. God has remembered His promise, and come down to our deliverance." Then, with thrilling power, the venerable speaker described the scene at the burning bush of Horeb, and, in conclusion, presented Moses, his brother, to the elders. He was received with a murmur of satisfaction; but some doubted. Others remembered that he had been raised an Egyptian, and openly expressed their fear that it was a plan to betray them into a movement that would give Pharaoh an excuse to destroy them all.

"Let us see his miracles! If God sent him, let us see his red become a serpent before our faces," said an old man, brutally and tauntingly.

Moses took the rod from the hand of his brother, and said with sternness,—.

"Thou shalt see and believe!"

He then cast it upon the ground, when it not only became a serpent, but its scales glittered like fire. With fierce hissing it coiled itself about the form of the doubter, and lifting its head above his own, darted it every way with flashing eyes, so that there was a universal cry of horror. The wretched old man fell to the ground, the serpent uncoiled from his form, and Moses taking it by the tail, it became a rod again in his hand!

At this miracle, the whole assembly, save one man, became convinced that Moses had been sent by God to them. This one said,—

"It is the magician's art! he hath been an Egyptian priest, and knows their mysteries."

Upon this Moses said —

"Korah, I remember thee! I was educated as an Egyptian, but I know none of their magic: and to show thee that this is the power of God, thrust thy hand into thy bosom!"

The man obeyed.

"Take it forth!" said Moses in a tone of command.

He did so, and it was leprous as snow, and the moon glared upon it, as upon the alabaster hand of a statue. He uttered a cry of horror.

"Be not unbelieving," said Moses. "Replace thy hand in thy bosom." He did so, and took it out restored like the other. The man who had been entwined by the serpent also rose to his feet, and both acknowledged the power of God, and the authority of Moses. He now made known to them that God had sent him to demand their release from Pharaoh; and that the king would at first refuse, but that after he had seen the power of God, he would yield and let them go forth out of Egypt, to the good land promised to Abraham for his seed for ever.

"Return now, elders and brethren," he said to them, like one who spake by authority to those who recognized it, "return to your places of toil. Be quiet and patient and wait the hand of God. He will manifest His glory and display His power in your behalf, as was never done on earth before. Bear patiently your labours, and do not doubt that the time of your deliverance is at hand. Let all Israel know the glad tidings of God's visitation, and that He has surely stretched out His arm over Egypt, to break their yoke of bondage."

This extraordinary assembly then separated, each man to his place; and Moses and Aaron went to the house of one Naashon, a Levite, whose sister had become Aaron's wife many years before. Here I remained until morning; but no eye closed in sleep, for many had followed the brothers, and till dawn they were holding discourse with their friends, on the wonderful things about to happen.

Moses said he should go before Pharaoh the next day but one, when he held public audience in the throne-room, that great hall of Egyptian state, which, my dear father, you once described, and where you were presented to queen Amense, as she was seated upon the same throne.

Farewell, my dear father. In three days I will write you again.

REMESES OF DAMASCUS.

LETTER VII.

REMESES OF DAMASCUS TO SESOSTRIS.

CITY OF ON, EGYPT.

MY DEAR FATHER,—

Moses has met Pharaoh face to face, and demanded of him the liberty of the Hebrew nation ! The scene in the throne-room was deeply interesting and striking ; and I will endeavour briefly to convey to you a conception of it.

The king, on that day gave audience in the throne-room, when, according to custom, no one, however humble, was refused permission to lay his petition before his king. At the hour appointed, Moses the mighty Hebrew, and Aaron his brother, accompanied by seven of the chief men of their nation—a venerable company with their flowing beards and snow-white locks—entered the city from Raamses, and proceeded towards the palace. The captain of the guard, seeing they were Hebrews, looked amazed, and would have stopped them, but the majesty and authority with which the two brothers moved, side by side, awed him, and without speaking he suffered them to enter the palace, and they passed on, looking neither to the right nor the left. Knowing that they would appear at that hour, I stood near and beheld them. They traversed the corridor of the vestibule, and the courtiers and lords and servitors gave way before them, for they were clad in long robes like priests, and appeared to them to be some sacred procession ; but when they perceived that they were Hebrews, they looked with contempt on them, yet let them pass. So these chosen men advanced and stood before the ivory throne, where the king sat in robes of cloth of purple and vestments of gold, wearing the double crown. His high officers stood about him, his body-guard were stationed on each side of the throne, while before him kneeled a single petitioner. It was a woman, whose son had accidentally wounded an ibis with an arrow, and was condemned to die. She pleaded to the king for his life.

"Nay, woman, he must not live !" answered Pharaoh. "If he had slain a slave or a Hebrew, I might grant thy prayer ; but to wound a sacred bird is sacrilege. Retire ! But who come hither ? " he demanded of his grand-chamberlain beside his footstool, as he saw the Hebrew company advancing. "Who are these ? "

"They look like Hebrews, father," said the son of Thothmeses, a young prince twenty years of age, who lounged indolently against one of the ivory figures that adorned the throne.

"Hebrews ? " said the king. "What do they here ? And in robes !

Ah, Prince of Tyre, welcome!" he said, turning to me, as, at the moment, I appeared and made my obeisance before him. "You honour us by your presence in our hall of judgment."

While he spoke, Aaron and Moses had reached the foot of the throne. Their venerable and majestic aspect seemed to impress him. "Who are ye? Are ye not Hebrews?" he demanded, with a face expressing mingled surprise and doubt.

"We are Hebrews, O king," answered Aaron, with respectful homage. "We are two brethren. My name is Aaron the Levite, and this my brother is Moses the Midianite; and these others are the elders of Israel—chiefs of the Hebrew people." This was spoken with calmness and fearlessness.

"And wherefore are ye come hither?" the king cried. "Who of my govenors has let you from your work? Who is Israel?"

"Thus saith the Lord, the Governor of the universe," answered Aaron: "'Israel is my son, even my first-born. Let my son go, that he may serve me.' And if thou refuse to let Israel go, O king," continued Aaron with an air of inspiration, "behold our God will slay thy son, even thy first-born."

The king started, and became pale with anger and amazement; and his son, Amunophis, sprang forward a step, and laid his hand upon the jewelled scimitar he wore at the girdle of his vesture, crying,—

"Slay me! What menace is this, greybeard? A conspiracy, my father!"

"Who is the Lord," demanded the king, "that I should obey His voice, and let Israel go? I know not the Lord, neither will I let Israel go. What threats are these? Ho! captain of the guard, seize these Hebrews, and put them in prison!"

The captain of the guard prepared to obey, but not a soldier moved. The majesty of Moses, as he fixed his eyes upon them, as it were, paralyzed them. Then Aaron answered Pharaoh, and said,—

"He is the God of the Hebrews, O king; the Lord of the sun, and Upholder of worlds. He hath met with us and commanded us to go three days' journey out of Egypt into the desert, and sacrifice unto Him, as our fathers aforetime did: and if we disobey His voice, He will fall upon us, and destroy us with pestilence or with the sword; for what other people is there that do not their sacrifices, save our nation? Therefore, thus saith the Lord of the Hebrews to thee, O King of Egypt, 'Let My people go, that they may hold a holy feast to Me in the wilderness.'"

"By the gods of Egypt, ye Moses and Aaron," cried the king, rising from his throne in great wrath, "I defy the God of the Hebrews! Wherefore do ye hinder the people from their works? Get you, and these old men with you, unto your burdens! Ye seek to destroy Egypt; for if the Hebrews, which are now many in the land, be let three days from their burdens, they will do mischief, and make sedition. Get thee from my presence! But for thy grey head, O Aaron, you should be put to death! This is a new thing in Egypt. Let them forth!" he called to his servitors.

Moses answered, speaking for the first time,—

"O King Thothmeses, the God of the Hebrews, whose servant I am, will yet make thee know His power, and that there is none else— no other God but Him!"

The king made no reply. He sank back upon his throne overcome with surprise; and I could perceive a certain look of fear in his eyes. Prince Amunophis followed the retiring ambassadors of God, and, as they reached the vestibule, he gave orders to the outer guard to arrest the whole company. But with a gesture of his hand, Moses caused them to retire before him; and the prince, returning with amazement, said to the king,—

"These two men are gods, O king! They carry the aspect and majesty of demigods, and all men fear to lay hands on them!"

"If I hear more of them," answered Pharaoh, by this time recovered from his emotion, "I will know whether they are gods or men! They shall die, by the life of Osiris! Do these Hebrews want more work?"

The king then commanded to come before him his chief officers, governors, captains, and head task-masters, and said to them, "Ye shall no more give the Hebrew people straw to make brick as heretofore. Let them go and gather straw for themselves. And the number of bricks which they have made heretofore, shall ye bind them to. Ye shall not diminish aught thereof; for they are idle, and cry, 'Let us go and sacrifice to our God.' Let there be more work laid upon the men, that they may be so employed as not to have leisure to regard the vain words of this Moses and Aaron!"

Thus, my dear father, the first result of the interposition of Moses for his people, is to increase their oppression! Yet their God is above all, and will manifest His power for their deliverance.

Your affectionate son,
REMESES OF DAMASCUS.

LETTER VIII.

CITY OF ON.

MY DEAR AND VENERABLE FATHER,—

MANY days have passed since I wrote to you. You will wish to hear the ultimate issue of the command of Pharaoh, to increase the burdens of the Hebrews, and its effects upon them.

In obedience to this command, the task-masters and officers of this unhappy people went out and strictly fulfilled it. The poor Hebrew brick-makers, in whose work coarse straw of wheat cut fine is necessary to make the clay cohere, as they are only dried in the sun, are now distributed all over Egypt seeking straw, which hitherto the Egyptian labourers brought to them in carts and laden barges. Thus dispersed, they gather stubble, and dry bulrushes, and grass, and everything they can in their haste find on the surface of the ground: for if night comes and their tale of bricks falls short, they are beaten.

As, therefore, one half of the time of many is consumed in searching the highways and fields, instead of being all the time, as heretofore, engaged only in making brick, the task put upon them is an impossible one ; and everywhere the sound of the rod and whip, and the cry of sufferers, goes up from the land. At length the elders and officers of the Hebrews (for their own people are often made their task-masters, who also had to account to their Egyptian captains for their fulfilment of the king's command), got courage from despair, and meeting the king as he was abroad in his chariot, cast themselves before him, crying, " Wherefore hast thou dealt thus with us? It is not our fault that we cannot make up the number of bricks, as heretofore, seeing straw is not given us ; and thy servants are beaten ; but the fault is in thine own officers."

Pharaoh angrily answered, " Ye are idle ! Ye are idle ! Ye have not enough to do, or ye would not think ye had time to go into the desert to sacrifice to your God. Go, therefore, and do your task, for there shall no straw be given you."

" And shall we deliver the tale of bricks ? " they cried.

" To the last one of them ! " answered the king ; and with an impatient sign for them to stand aside from his chariot-wheels, he dashed forward on his way, attended by his brilliant retinue. The unhappy men then perceived " that they were in evil case," as one of them said to me in relating this interview ; and meeting Moses and Aaron in the fields not long afterwards, one of their number said, indignantly, and with grief,—

" The Lord look upon you, Moses and Aaron, and judge you, because by your interference with the king, thou hast put a sword into the hand of Pharaoh to slay us."

Moses looked sorrowfully and troubled, and raising his eyes heavenward as he left them without a reply, for he wot not how to answer, they heard him cry unto his God, and say,—

" Lord, wherefore hast Thou so evil entreated this Thy people? Why is it that Thou didst send me? For since I came to Pharaoh to speak in Thy name, he hath done evil to this people; neither, O Lord God, hast Thou delivered Thy people at all ! "

Then came a voice from heaven, which they heard, and said,—

" Thou shalt see what I will do to Pharaoh ; for he shall let you go, and drive you out of his land. I am the Lord who spake to thee in Horeb, out of the burning bush ; and I appeared unto Abraham, unto Isaac, and unto Jacob, by the name of God Almighty. But by my name JEHOVAH was I not known to them. I have heard the groaning of the children of Israel. Wherefore say unto them, ' I am the Lord, and I will bring you out from under the burdens of the Egyptians, and I will take you to Me for a people, and I will be to you a God ; and ye shall know that I am the Lord your God, which bringeth you out from under the burdens of the Egyptians. And I will bring you in unto the land which I did swear to give to Abraham, and to Isaac, and to Jacob, and I will give it to you for an heritage. I am the Lord ! ' "

With these words, Moses sought to comfort the Hebrews, his

brethren, going to them and proclaiming it to them in their ears; but for an anguish of spirit, and the great pressure of their cruel bondage upon their minds, they did not hearken unto him. Hope in their bosoms was utterly dead. Moreover, many of them looked on him with eyes of hatred, as the author of this increase of their wretchedness.

What a situation was this for the servant of God! Confident of the power and truth of Jehovah, he could not reconcile therewith this increase of the power of Pharaoh. Perhaps, at times, his own faith was severely tried.

Since then, a month has passed, during which period I saw Moses often in Goshen, where he passed his time in encouraging those of his brethren who would give heed to him.

In the mean while, Pharaoh, as if in contempt or defiance of the God of the Hebrews, has been engaged in extraordinary religious rites; and every day the streets have resounded with the music of instruments and choral songs of processions to the gods. I witnessed all of these ceremonies, and will describe some of them that are not mentioned by you in your letters from Egypt, my dear father.

On the seventh day after Moses and Aaron left him, Thothmeses went in state to the black marble temple of the sacred serpent, Uræus, to offer sacrifice and oblation to its great image of gold with jewelled eyes and hideous head. He addressed it as the god of wisdom and sagacity, and presented offerings of flowers, and a necklace of emeralds; while, for the living serpents, held sacred by the Egyptians, he left gifts of money to purchase food for their repletion.

The next day he proceeded, at the head of the priests and the most magnificent religious procession I have seen in Egypt, from his palace along the sphinx-lined avenue to the terrace of the Nile, opposite the Island of Rhoda, where stands a brazen statue of the god Nilus, with those of Osiris and Thoth on either side of its pedestal.

Descending from his chariot, he advanced to the river, and poured from a goblet, set with diamonds, a libation of wine into its waves, and invoked the river itself as a deity, concluding his prayer with a curse upon the God of the Hebrews. Then, at his command, the chief sacrificer advanced, leading a Hebrew boy four years old, whom he laid upon the altar before the statue of the god, and, at a stroke of his sacrificial knife, sacrificed there. I could scarcely refrain from a cry of horror. I knew that the Egyptians, on certain occasions, sacrificed human beings to the gods; but I never expected to behold an immolation like this. The palpitating form of the child was then taken up by two assistants, and the blood of its heart was poured forth into the Nile, as a libation to the god. The empurpled wave then received the inanimate form, amid a crash of instrumental music. This unusual libation of blood to the Nile was intended as an act of defiance to the Hebrew JEHOVAH.

The following day, Pharaoh made a procession to the temple of sacred frogs, on the borders of the canal of Amun. Here libations were poured out before a colossal sphinx having a frog's head, and offerings made. The frog is held sacred by the Egyptians, because it is supposed to purify the waters by feeding on poisons in the marshes and river.

The succeeding day Pharaoh, as if possessed with a religious infatuation, that now led him to seek the favour of gods hitherto neglected by him, in his dread of the God of the Hebrews, paid a visit, with all his court, to the temple of the scarabæus, or sacred beetle of Egypt. This is a marble edifice, adorned with a frieze of scarabæi, having heads of every variety of animal. The god himself is a gigantic beetle of black marble, with a human head. He is supposed to protect the temples from vermin, such as lice and fleas; for one of these seen in a temple, or upon the garments of a priest, causes ceremonial defilement, and neither priest nor temple may be made holy again but by purification.

The next day a procession was made by Pharaoh and his people to the little temple of Baal-Zebel, a deity that is reverenced as their protector from flies, which sometimes infest the land in ravenous swarms, and which, it is believed, this idol only can remove. Can Thothmeses be so superstitious? Or does he make all this show of piety merely to humour the superstitions of his people, and sustain the priests of these shrines? Does he fear Moses and his power, so as to desire to strengthen himself in the affections of the priesthood and people?

The day after the visit to the temple of the fly-god, he went in great state to the temple of the sacred ox of On, Mnevis. Here he sacrificed, prayed, poured libations, and offered oblations. It was an imposing scene, as he was attended by one thousand priests clad in rich vestments, and wearing shining crowns, the whole waving censers of gold. Of the god he asked protection to all the cattle of Egypt, and prosperity to the harvests; and then solemnly denounced the God of the Hebrews, as a God not known or honoured in Egypt, and who, if He existed, was but a God of slaves.

The next day of this ten days' ovation, Pharaoh proceeded to the gloomy temple of Typhon, on the edge of the desert. Here a Nubian slave was sacrificed to the Evil Principle, by being bound to the altar and burned alive. The officiating priests then gathered the ashes and cast them high into the air, calling on their god and praying him, that wheresoever an atom of the ashes was borne on the wind, evil might not visit the place.

Thothmeses has diligently revived the human sacrifices which Queen Amense forbade, and the act sufficiently illustrates the native cruelty and superstition of the man.

Two days afterwards, having crossed the Nile in great pomp, he proceeded, in grand procession, to the temple of Serapis. The god Apis, you are aware, my dear father, has the peculiar office, besides many others, of protecting the country from locusts; and at the seasons when these destructive insects visit Egypt, Apis is invoked to command them to retire from the land.

The rites performed by the king before the god were imposing and gorgeous. He invoked him, not against locusts, but against the God of Moses!

Does not all this show a secret dread of the God he defies? Yet he knows nothing of His power, and has witnessed no act of wonder performed by Him. Doubtless he felt, that a servant who dared to be so bold and confident, must have a divine Master, who is great and powerful. Perhaps he had heard of the God of the Hebrews in times past;—of the dream of Prince Joseph and the seven years' famine;—of the destruction of the vale of Sodom, with its cities, by fire from heaven at God's command;—of the dispersion of the nations at the pyramid of Babylon;—of the mighty deluge which He caused to overflow the mountains and drown the world! Perhaps, for he is learned and intelligent enough, when Aaron spoke to him of the God of the Hebrews, he remembered who He was in times of old, and trembled to hear His name again.

Three days afterwards the king visited the shrine of Isis, and poured libations, and made thanksgivings; and invoked her, as the moon, and controller of the seasons and weather, to send abundant rains upon the mountains of Ethiopia, and the sources of the Nile, so that the annual overflow, now near at hand, may not fail, nor the land be deprived of its fertility.

Two days later, with a procession of all the priests of all the temples, and with chariots, and horsemen, and footmen,—a vast array,—he visited the great temple of Osiris, or the sun: and, after august ceremonies, himself acting as high-priest, with the high-priest of On for his assistant, he presented the statue of the god with a new crown of gold, and a crook and flail of ivory inlaid with jewels. He invoked him, by the appellation of the god of light, the dispeller of darkness, the terror of clouds, and the foe of lightnings and storms. And he implored clear skies, and serene weather for the harvests, as heretofore.

Thus the piety of Thothmeses has been quickened into unwonted activity by the dread of the God of Israel, as if he would secure his gods' faithfulness should the God of Moses be too strong for him. In the mean while the children of Israel are groaning under the weight of their increased oppression. I have seen Aaron to-day. He informed me, with looks of holy faith in his God, that Moses and he were, to-morrow, by God's command, to appear again before Pharaoh, and demand the release of the Hebrews.

What a scene will be enacted! Will these two courageous men brave his anger, and escape? I tremble for the result. They are firm and resolved, being strong in the strength of their God. I shall be sure to be at the palace to-morrow, that I may behold these servants of Jehovah meet, once more, face to face, this cruel Pharaoh, and his gods

Your affectionate son,
REMESES OF DAMASCUS.

LETTER IX.

REMESES OF DAMASCUS TO SESOSTRIS.

CITY OF ON.

MY VERY DEAR FATHER,—

You will read what I am about to write, with the profoundest interest. The two mighty Hebrews again sought an audience of the king, and boldly demanded the freedom of Israel.

This meeting did not take place in the palace of On, but in that at Memphis, on the avenue of the pyramids. Pharaoh was seated in the court of the palace, giving audience to the governors of the thirty-nine nomes, which now constitute the number of his provinces. When he had ended his instructions to them, Moses and Aaron were announced. I stood near him conversing with the prince; for I knew that the two men of God purposed to seek the king's presence.

"How darest thou announce these Hebrews?" cried the king sharply, to his trembling grand-chamberlain.

"I could not forbid them, O king! I fled instinctively and without power of resistance before the majesty of their presence. Behold them advancing!"

Pharaoh turned pale. He essayed to give some fierce order to those about him, but his tongue failed him.

"Who will slay me these men?" cried the Prince Amunophis, seeing the king's troubled looks.

Not a man moved. Awe and curiosity took the place of all other feelings. Side by side the two brothers came unfalteringly forward till they stood before the monarch,—fixing their regards only upon him.

"What are ye come for, Moses and Aaron?" at length he uttered, in a thick voice. "Have I spared your lives, that you might come again to mock me in my palace?"

"We are come, O king," answered Moses with dignity, and looking far more kingly than he whom he addressed—"we are come in the name of the God of the Hebrews. He hath heard their cry from all the land of Egypt by reason of their task-masters, and I am sent to command thee, in His name, to send the children of Israel out of thy land!"

"Have I knowledge of your God? What is His power? Let Him make Himself known! Or, if He hath sent thee to me, where are thy credentials from His hand? I listen to no ambassadors from God or man, unless they show me that they are sent. By what sign wilt thou declare thy mission? If a king sent thee, show me his handwriting; if a god, show me a miracle!"

Aaron held the rod of Moses in his hand, and casting it upon the marble pavement of the court, it became a serpent, slowly gliding along the floor and flashing fire from its eyes. The servants of Pharaoh fled before it. The king upon his throne, at first, became alarmed, but seeing the monster inflate its throat and stretch lazily and innocuously along the lion-skin before his footstool, he smiled contemptuously and said,—

"Thy Arabian life has given thee great skill, O Moses. Ho! call my magicians! I have magi that can equal thy art!"

All was expectation, until at length two stately personages solemnly entered, each with his acacia rod. They were Jambres and Jannes, the royal and chief magicians of Egypt, of whose fame other lands have heard. They were dark-featured, Arabic-looking men, and dressed with great magnificence, wearing robes blazing with gold and jewels. Their bearing was haughty and imperious, and they looked about them with disdain, as if they were beings of a better order than the Egyptians, who stood awed, or prostrated themselves in their presence.

"Seest thou this serpent?" demanded Pharaoh, directing the attention of Jambres to the monster, which lay coiled upon the lion-skin before the steps of the throne; while several of the guard with spears stood near, to thrust it through, should it approach the king. The magicians regarded it with surprise, and then looked fixedly at Moses and Aaron. They had evidently heard by the messengers, what had passed. "Half an hour since, he was a rod in the hand of that Hebrew magician!" said the king. "Show him thy art, and that we have gods whose servants can do as great miracles as this!"

The magicians advanced and said,—

"O king, beloved of the sun, live for ever! Behold the power of thy own magicians!" Thus speaking, they cast their rods upon the ground, when they became serpents also, after a few moments had transpired. Pharaoh then said, addressing the Hebrew brothers,—

"Ye are but impostors, and have done your miracle by the gods of Egypt, as my magicians do."

"If the god of Egypt be strongest, let his serpents destroy my serpent: but if the God of the Hebrews be the greatest and the only God, let my serpent devour his!" Thus quietly spake Aaron.

"So be it," answered Pharaoh.

In a moment, the serpent of Moses uncoiled himself, and fiercely seizing, one after another, the two serpents of the magicians, swallowed them. At this there was an outcry among the people; and, greatly terrified, Pharaoh half rose from his throne; but Aaron catching up the serpent, it became a rod as before. Instead of acknowledging the God of Moses, the king became exceedingly enraged against his own magicians, and drove them from him, and ordered Moses and Aaron to depart, saying that they were only more skilful sorcerers than the others, and must show him greater signs than these ere he would let Israel go. I have since learned that these magicians brought with them real serpents, which they have the power of stiffening, and holding at arm's length by pressing upon their throats: that they came with these, which could not be detected in the obscurity of the shadows where they stood, and casting them down they resumed their natural motions. That the rod of Moses should devour them, and return to a rod again, ought to have shown Pharaoh that it was a miracle, and not sorcery. But his heart seems to be hardened against all impressions of this nature.

The following morning, the governor of the nilometer having reported to the king that the Nile had commenced to rise, Pharaoh, according to custom, proceeded to the river, where the statue of Nilus stands, and where he had caused the Hebrew boy to be sacrificed and his blood poured as a libation into the stream. Here, with great pomp, he was about to celebrate the festivities of the happy event, when, lo! Moses and Aaron stood before him by the river's brink,—the latter with the rod, which had been turned into a serpent, in his hand.

"The Lord God of the Hebrews," cried Moses in a loud voice, "hath sent me unto thee, saying, 'Let My people go.' Lo! hitherto thou wouldst not hear. Now thus saith the Lord—' In this thou shalt know that I am the Lord!' Behold, O king, at His command I will smite with the rod that is in mine hand upon the waters which are in the river, and they shall be turned into blood!"

"I defy you and your God, and both of ye shall die!" answered Pharaoh, pale with anger.

Then Moses, turning calmly to Aaron, his brother, said in my hearing, and in that of the king and all his people, "Take this rod of God, and stretch out thine hand upon the waters of Egypt, that there may be blood throughout all the land of Egypt, both in vessels of wood and vessels of stone."

Aaron, obeying, stretched forth his hand with the rod and smote the water at his feet, in the sight of Pharaoh, and in the sight of the thousands of Egyptians present, and in a moment the Nile ran blood instead of water; the fish in hundreds rose to the surface and died, and the smell of blood filled all the atmosphere. The people uttered a great cry, and Pharaoh looked petrified with horror. From the galleys on the river, from the women on the opposite shore, from avenues, terraces, and plains, from every side, rose a loud and terrible wail such as was never before heard. The king sought his chariot, and fled from the face of Moses and Aaron, and all was wild dismay. These two servants of the God, whose words had wrought this great wonder, then walked calmly away. I felt too much awed to come near them, and in my chariot sought my own palace. On the way I saw that the canals were red with blood, also the standing pools, the lakes, and every body of water. Men were running in every direction seeking for water; women wrung their hands, and despair and fear were impressed upon every countenance. As I passed the fountains in the court of Pharaoh's palace, I saw that they also spouted forth blood; and in the corridor and porticos, the water in the vases for guests, in the earthern jars for filtering, and in those which stood in the cisterns, was of the same crimson hue. When I reached my own apartments, lo! there also the water in the vases and ewers was of the colour of blood. The voice of Moses, empowered by his God, had indeed turned all the waters of Egypt into blood. Surely, I said, now will the king let Israel go. In the afternoon I went forth, and saw the Egyptians digging everywhere for fresh water, along the canals and river. I drove out of the city towards Goshen, and saw all the people in motion and terror, for but few knew the cause of the awful visitation. After an hour I reached Goshen, the fair plain where Prince Jacob once dwelt, and where now the children of Israel dwell by hundreds of thousands. With joyful surprise I beheld, as I entered the province, that the canal was free from blood, the pools sparkling with clear water, and the fountains bright as crystal. As I rode on in the direction of the dwelling of Moses, I perceived that the plague of blood had not fallen upon the land where the Hebrews dwelt—only upon the Egyptians. This was a twofold miracle.

When Pharaoh found that water could be obtained by digging shallow wells, and also that Goshen was free from the plague, he sent for Jambres and Jannes, and offered to pardon them if they could turn water into blood. They commenced their incantations upon water dug up from his gardens—for the miracle of the rod covered only the waters at the time on the surface, whether in the river or in the houses. After art had for some time been practised upon the water, to my surprise it was turned to the semblance of blood.

"See," cried Pharaoh with great joy, "the servants of Pharaoh are equal to the servants of the Hebrew God!"

"And O king," said Jambres vainly, "had the Hebrew juggler left us the Nile, we could have turned that also by our enchantments."

Then Pharaoh rewarded him with a chain of gold, and hardened his heart, and defied Moses and his God. But in three days afterwards all the fish died in the lakes, and river of Lower Egypt, and a stench of their flesh and of crocodiles and reptiles that perished by the blood in the river, and the difficulty of getting water, rendered Egypt almost uninhabitable. Thousands fled to the pure air and water of Goshen, where also I remained. Every hour I expected to behold a royal courier coming for Moses and Aaron, ordering them to appear before the king, to receive permission to lead the Hebrews out of Egypt. At the end of seven days the river and waters of Egypt resumed their natural colour and purity, by God's permission, lest all the people of Egypt should die for Pharaoh's hardness of heart.

Then God appeared again unto Moses, and commanded him to go before Pharaoh with the same message as before. But the king, in great fury, ordered them from his presence, when Aaron stretched forth his hand over the streams, the river, the canals, lakes, and fountains, and in a moment myriads of frogs appeared on the shores, in the fields, in the streets, squares, corridors, terraces, gardens, groves, and porticos of the temples. They leaped upon every place, upon the people, upon the stairways. They found their way by hundreds into the houses and bedchambers, and upon the beds, tables, chairs of palaces and huts; leaped into the ovens and kneading troughs, and occupied every place. In horror the priests closed all the temples, lest they should enter, and dying there, defile them. Even Pharaoh was obliged to shut himself up in the recesses of his palace to escape their loathsome presence.

In great alarm, he was about to send for Moses, when Jambres, his chief sorcerer, stood before him, and said,—

"O king, believe not that the God of this Hebrew is greater than the gods of Egypt. Thy servants also can do this enchantment."

"Do so, and thou shalt have a rod of gold," answered the king.

Then, descending into a fountain, enclosed by a high wall of the palace, where the frogs had not yet appeared, the magician caused frogs also to appear. "At first," said the chief butler, who spoke to me of this deed, "the king was greatly pleased, but suddenly said,—

"'What thou hast produced by thy enchantments, remove by thy enchantments. Command them to disappear from the fountain.'

"This the two magicians not being able to do, the next day, the frogs rendering every habitation uninhabitable, and the lords of Egypt appealing to Pharaoh, he sent for Moses and Aaron. It had become time to do so. Every part of my rooms was filled with these animals; they got into the plates and cups, and defiled every place—while by night their combined roar filled all Egypt with a deafening and terrible noise, so that if a bed could be found to sleep in, sleep was nowhere possible; and by day we could tread nowhere but upon frogs."

When the two Hebrew brothers again stood in the presence of Pharaoh, he said, with mingled shame and displeasure—

"Entreat your God to take away this plague of frogs from me, my people, and the land of Egypt; and if thou canst free the land from them, I will acknowledge that it is the power of the God of the Hebrews, and will let the people go to do sacrifice unto the Lord, who hath commanded and sent for them."

Then Moses answered the king,—

"The Lord shall be entreated as thou desirest; and thou, O king, shalt set the time, lest thou shouldst say I consulted a favourable aspect of the stars. Choose when I shall entreat for thee to remove this plague from the land, the people, and their houses."

"To-morrow," answered Thothmeses.

"Be it according to thy word," answered Moses; "and when thou seest the plague removed at the time appointed by thee, know it is God's gracious act, and not our sorcery. To-morrow the frogs in all the land of Egypt shall be found in the river only."

What a scene did Egypt present the next morning! The land was covered with dead frogs; and it took all the people of Egypt that day and night to gather them into heaps and cast them into the river: for they threatened a pestilence.

When Pharaoh saw that his wish was granted at the time he named, and that there was a respite, he said,—"This was by my voice and my power, and not by their God, that the frogs died on the morrow I named! The glory over Moses shall indeed be mine, as he hath said!" Ceasing to speak, he sent orders to the task-masters to increase the burdens of the Hebrews, refusing to keep his promise to Moses and Aaron.

Then the Lord again sent them before Pharaoh, and in his presence Aaron stretched forth his rod, and smote the dust of the earth, when all the dust of the earth became alive, and rested upon man and beast in the form of lice!

Then, in a rage, Pharaoh called his enchanters, but they could not perform this miracle, and said plainly to the king,—

"This is beyond our power. This is the finger of their God."

Upon hearing this, Pharaoh drove both his magicians, and Moses and Aaron forth from his palace. The next day no sacrifice was

KARNACK.

offered, no temple open in all Egypt; for on the priests were lice, and no one could perform an official act with any insect upon his person, being thereby made unclean. The Egyptians were enraged, both with the Hebrews and with their king—but, shut up in his palace, he refused to consent to the demands of Moses.

Three days afterwards, by the command of God, given at the well of Jacob,—where, in a bright cloud like a pillar of fire, He descended to speak with Moses, and seemed to be now every day present in Egypt, in communion with his holy servant,—the two brothers again sought the presence of the king, as he was entering his galley. Reiterating their usual demand, Moses continued,—

"The Lord hath said unto me, 'Stand before Pharaoh when he comes forth to the water, and say unto him, thus the saith Lord, 'Let My people go; else, if thou wilt not let My people go, I will send swarms of flies upon thee and thy servants, and upon thy people, and the houses of the Egyptians shall be filled with them, and also the ground; and I will sever in that day the land of Goshen, in which My people dwell, that no swarms of flies shall be there; to the end that thou mayest know that I am the Lord in the midst of the earth. And I will put a division between My people and thy people; and to-morrow shall this sign be!'"

Pharaoh, in fear and anger, commanded his galley to leave the shore, heeding none of the words spoken by Moses. The next day when I awoke, lo! the air was darkened with flies. They covered the city like a cloud, and their noise was like the roar of the sea after a storm. When the sun was well risen, they descended and alighted upon the dwellings, and soon filled the houses, and rooms, and every place they could penetrate. It was impossible to hear for their hum, or to see for their number, as they would alight upon the face, seek the corners of the eyes and the edges of the eyelids, and inflict their bite. In a few hours the Egyptians became frantic under the plague, as it was impossible to keep them off; and if driven away, they would pertinaciously return to the attack. All employment in Egypt ceased. Eating and sleeping were impracticable. I fled in my chariot towards Goshen! My horses, stung to madness, flew like the wind. Hundreds of women, and children, and men were pressing in the same direction, for safety and relief. I crossed the great canal which divides the province, and not a fly followed me nor my horses across the aerial and invisible barrier God had set as their bounds. All Goshen was free from the plague, and the Hebrews were extending favours to the Egyptians who sought shelter among them.

The next day, Pharaoh, unable to endure the plague, and finding his magicians could neither remove nor cause it, sent for Moses and Aaron, who immediately answered his summons.

"Go," he cried, when he beheld them,—"go, sacrifice to thy God in this land; for He is a mighty God, and may not be mocked!"

"It is not meet, O king," answered Moses, "that we should sacrifice to our God in the land of Egypt. We Hebrews sacrifice bulls and rams, sacrifices abominable to the Egyptians, who call them their gods! Lo! shall we sacrifice the gods of the Egyptians to our God, before their eyes, and will they not stone us? If we sacrifice, we will go three days' journey into the wilderness, and sacrifice to the Lord our God as He shall command us."

Seeing the resolute purpose of the terrible Hebrew, Pharaoh consented to his demand, only adding, "Ye shall not go very far away! Now go and entreat your God for me, for the removal of these flies!"

While this discourse was passing between them, the fan-bearers of the king, with all their diligence, could not protect his face from the stings of the flies, which plagued him sorely; while upon Aaron and Moses not one alighted.

"To-morrow," answered Moses, as he went out, "the Lord, whom I will entreat for thee, shall remove this plague also. But deal not deceitfully, O king, any more, in not letting the people go."

When, the next day, Pharaoh saw that the flies were removed, so that not one remained, he repented that he had given his promise, and resolved not to keep it with Moses.

Once more God sent his servants, the two Hebrews, to the king, demanding the release of the children of Jacob from their yoke of bondage, menacing him with murrain upon all the cattle, horses, camels, and beasts of Egypt, if he resolved to hold them still in the land. The king, however, who seemed after every demand to grow more obstinate when the evil had passed, refused, and sent them away with threats of vengeance. Indeed, it is surprising, my dear father, that he hath not slain them before this; and I have no doubt he is miraculously restrained from doing so, by the Almighty God, whose faithful and holy servants they are.

On the morrow, according to the word of Moses, a fatal pestilence seized upon the oxen, the bulls, and cows of Egypt, so that all the cattle in the land died. When the priest of the sacred ox, Mnevis, came rushing from their temple to the palace, crying that their god was dead with the murrain; when at midnight came before him the priest of Apis, exclaiming that the sacred bull was also dead, then Pharaoh began to know and feel that the God of the Hebrews was greater than the gods of Egypt. Early in the morning, when he rose, hearing that not one of the cattle of the Israelites was dead, instead of repenting and trembling, he became enraged, acting like a man blinded by the gods, when they would destroy him by his own acts.

Judge, my dear father, of the patience and forbearance of the God of the Hebrews towards him who still refused to acknowledge His power. Behold the firmness and steadiness of purpose of Moses and Aaron,—their courage and independence! What a sublime spectacle! —two private men contending successfully with the most powerful king on the earth! What a painful sight to see this most powerful king of the earth measuring the strength of his feeble will against the power of the God of the universe!

Upon the refusal of Pharaoh to let Jehovah have His people, that they might serve Him, God commanded Moses in a vision of the night, beside the fountain of Jacob, where He talked with him as in the burning bush, to take the ashes of a human sacrifice, to be immolated by Pharaoh the next day, and sprinkle it towards heaven upon the winds. He did so; and instead of protecting the places wheresoever its atoms were carried, they broke out in boils upon man and beast, breaking forth with painful blains. The magicians and sorcerers, essaying to recover their credit with the king, attempted to do the same miracle; but the boil broke forth upon them also so heavily, that they could not stand before Moses, and fled with pain and cries from his presence. Yet Pharaoh remained obdurate, and grew more hardened and defiant: for the boils touched not his own flesh.

That night, the Lord appeared unto Moses, and commanded him again to make his demand upon Pharaoh for His people. Then stood Moses and Aaron in the morning before the king, who was walking up and down in the corridor of his palace, ill at ease; for all his public works were stopped by the sufferings of the Egyptians; and his soldiers in the fourscore garrisons at On, and Memphis, and Bubastis, and Migdol, were unfit for military duty. There was not a well man in all Egypt, save in Goshen.

"What now, ye disturbers of Egypt and enemies of the gods?" he called aloud, as he saw them approach and stand before him.

"Thus saith the Lord God of the Hebrews," answered Moses: "'Let My people go, that they may serve Me.'"

"'The same words! Thou shalt never have thy wish,—thou nor thy God! Who is the Lord? Will no man rid me of this Moses and Aaron? Speak! What more?"

"Thus saith the Lord, 'If thou, O king, refusest to let Israel go, I will send all My plagues upon thy heart, and upon thy people, that thou mayest know that there is none like Me in all the earth! For this cause, O Pharaoh, have I created thee and raised thee up on the throne of Egypt, that in thee I may show My power; and that by My dealings with thee, My name may be declared throughout all the earth. All nations shall behold My works with thee, and My vengeance on thy gods, and shall know that I am the Lord, and God of all gods! Thou art My servant to show forth My glory! Thy proud heart exaltest thyself above Me, and against My people, and thou wouldst contend with Me! Thou shalt know I am God, ere thou shalt be cut off from the earth; and that the heavens are My throne, and the earth is My footstool, and none can say, What doest Thou? Behold, to-morrow I will darken the heavens with clouds, and send hail upon the earth, and every man and beast in the field shall die by the hail.' If thou regardest the life of thy servants," continued Moses, "send, therefore, for all thou hast in the field."

This threat was made known everywhere in a few hours, and those who fear the word of the Lord have made their servants and cattle flee into the houses prepared for them; but those who regard not the warning have left them in the field. What will to-morrow bring forth?

Farewell, dear father.

Warned by Aaron, I departed at once for the sheltering skies of Goshen.

Your loving son,
REMESES OF DAMASCUS.

LETTER X.

CITY OF THE SUN.

MY DEAR FATHER,—

SCARCELY had I reached the confines of Goshen, after the threatened judgment of God upon Pharaoh, when I heard, as it were, in the air, a voice speaking which I knew to be the voice of Moses; and behind me I heard instantly, loud thunders uttering their voices and the earth shook beneath my chariot wheels. To the right of me, at the same moment, I beheld Moses and Aaron standing side by side on the tower of the ruined fountain of Jacob, beneath which I was driving; the former stretching forth his hands and his rod therein, northward towards the city of Pharaoh, upon the obelisks of which the sun was then brilliantly shining, and was also reflected in splendour from the shield of gold upon the lofty tower of the temple of Osiris. Leaping from my chariot, and leaving it with my servants, whom I commanded to hasten further into the land of the Hebrews, I drew reverently near the men of God, feeling greatly awed by their presence, but assured that near them was safety,—though they were the visible sources of God's terrible wrath upon Egypt. I stood not afar off, and beheld with expectation. Moses, his rod extended, and waving eastward, and northward, and westward, stood with a majestic and fearful aspect, his eyes raised to the heavens, which were already answering his voice by far-off thunderings. He continued, as I drew near, in these words,—

"And let thunder and hail, and fire, O Egypt, descend out of heaven from God upon thee, and let the fire mingle with the hail, and smite throughout all the land of Egypt, all that is in the field, both man and beast, and every herb in the field, and break every tree! Only in the land of Goshen let there be no hail."

No language, my dear father, can convey to you any idea of the terrible power and godlike authority with which he spake. To his words Aaron pronounced a loud " A-men,"—the Hebrew word for expressing full assent and confirmation.

Then I looked, with expectant awe, towards the land of Egypt, over which the thunders rolled without a cloud; when, lo! from the north came rolling onward a black wall of darkness, which I perceived was a mighty cloud from the great sea. It advanced with the swiftness and roar of ten thousand war-chariots rushing to battle. Out of it shot forth lightnings, and its increasing thunders shook Egypt. In a moment it had filled half the heavens, and still onward it rolled. Beneath it moved its shadow, dark as itself, extinguishing the light upon obelisk, tower, and pylon. I am told that Pharaoh, from the top of his palace, witnessed this scene also. Directly the sun was blotted out, and the city of On became invisible. Then I saw fire pour down upon the earth out of the cloud, as if lightnings could not fast enough exhaust its angry power; and I heard the voice of falling hail like the voice of the sea when lashed by a storm. A million of Hebrews who had gathered in Goshen, stood and beheld what I did. The roads, the fields, the plain were covered with people flying from the terror towards Goshen.

Onward marched this awful servant of the Almighty, more terrible than an army with banners. Fire ran along the ground before it, and red forked lightnings shot far out beyond its advancing edge athwart the blue sky, while in a moment afterwards, the cloud of blackness rolled beneath, like the sulphurous smoke that the priests of Egypt say for ever rolls above the fiery regions of Typhon!

Each instant it enlarged its compass, until from east to west it enveloped Egypt, while fire, mingled with hail, ran along the earth beneath it. Now behold, my father, the power of God! The vast pall which Jehovah had thus begun to draw over Egypt, no sooner had reached in the height of heaven over the borders of Goshen, casting its very shadow and pouring its stones of hail, and sending its tongues of fire almost to the foot of the tower whereon Moses stood, than it ceased to move! It became stationary in the air a mile high, and there hung beetling over the verge of Goshen like a crag, its edge working and agitated by the wildest commotion, and shooting its lightnings into the blue calm sky over Goshen, but restrained from advancing further by the power of Him who commandeth the heavens, who maketh the clouds His chariot, and who keepeth the lightnings in His quiver!

At length the darkness became so dense, that it seemed a wall between Egypt and Goshen, from the ground up to the cloud. Over the latter the sun,—oh, what a sublime contrast!—shone with unclouded brightness, the winds slept peacefully, the fields waved with the ripened flax and full-eared barley, the birds sang their songs of gladness, and the children of God dwelt in security, under the protection of His gentle love and terrible power.

Surely Pharaoh must perish if he dare any longer madly to resist the God of the Hebrews, who has now shown that He is God of heaven as well as of the earth, and that He is God alone, and there is none else! If, my dear father, your early instructions had not made known to me the God of Noah, who is the God of the Hebrews, I should ere this last manifestation of His awful majesty and terror, have prostrated myself before Him and acknowledged Him as *my* God. Wonderful that He who dwells in heaven should stoop to behold things on the earth, and make such displays of His glory, and majesty and strength, for the sake of a poor, enslaved people like the Hebrews. But, as the holy Moses taught me the other day, when I was humbly sitting at his feet, and hearing him discourse on these mighty events (for which he takes to himself no honour or merit, but only seems the more meek and lowly the more he is entrusted with power by God), these displays of God's majesty have a three-fold end: first, to prove to the trembling and heart-crushed Israelites that He who is so terrible in power, doing wonders, is *their* God, as He was the God of Abraham, and has power to deliver them from Pharaoh; as well as to teach them that if He can so punish the Egyptians, He can punish them also, with equal judgments, if they rebel and do wickedly: secondly, to punish Pharaoh for the oppression of His people, to afflict the land upon which they have groaned so many generations, and to show the Egyptians that He alone is God, that their gods are as stubble in His hand, "that there is none like Him in all the earth;" and thus bring them to acknowledge Him, and to fear and worship Him : and, thirdly, that the word of His mighty deeds and wonders done in Egypt, going abroad to the ears of kings and princes, priests and lords, and people of all nations upon the earth, may give *them* the knowledge of the true God, prove to them the impotency of their idols, and the supremacy of the God of the Hebrews, in heaven, and on earth, and over kings and people. "Therefore, and for these ends," continued the divine Moses, "that He might not leave Himself without a witness before men, and that He might declare His power to all His creatures, and His care for the oppressed, and His judgment upon kings who reign by cruelty, has He permitted, not only the bondage of our nation, but raised up such a man as Pharaoh, in whom to show forth His power and judgments, as he said to this king, 'And in very deed, for this cause have I raised thee up, to show in thee My power, and that My Name may be declared throughout all the earth.' Therefore did the Lord God say to me in the beginning, when He sent me before Pharaoh, 'I am sure that the King of Egypt will not let you go, no not until I stretch out My hand with mighty power, and smite Egypt with all My wonders, which I will do; and after that he will let you go, I did not understand this all at the first," said Moses, "but now I perceive the mind of God, and that He will do His will upon Pharaoh, and send yet more terrible punishments ; after which, humbled, and acknowledging God to be the Lord, he will let the people go !"

What a wonderful mystery is passing before us, O my father ! How dreadful is this God ! How wonderful, how glorious is His majesty ! In His presence, and before Him, what is man but dust, breath, vanity ? I humble myself before Him, and feel that I am a worm, and no man ! Yet Thothmeses, like a madman, stands and defies this living God !

Not all the horror of the plague of hail and fire, of the lightnings and thunderings, moved him to let Israel depart. When the judgment of God was at its height, driven to the interior of his palace,—from the tower upon which he had ascended "to see what Moses and Aaron would do," as he said,—he remained there three days, until, unable longer to bear the terrors of the scene, and the cries of his people, he sent for Moses and Aaron. No messenger could be found to go but Israelisis, your former page, who, since he returned to Egypt, is a servant of the king, greatly devoted to him, and from whom I have obtained much interesting information of the effects of these divine judgments upon him. Three couriers, one after the other, had been struck down by the hail. But the Hebrew walked forth fearlessly and unharmed, and moved through the showers of ice, as if he bore a charmed life. This alone should have proved the power of God to be with the Hebrew servant, and against Pharaoh and his servants.

Moving through the darkness, amid the fire upon the ground, and the hail and scalding rain, the man arrived, and told Moses and Aaron that the king had repented, and prayed them both to hasten to him, for he knew their God would defend them from injury on the way.

The king is represented as having received the Hebrew brothers in his bath-room, with his physicians around him, his face ghastly with

fear, and anxiety, and an indefinable dread. It is also said that his manner was servile rather than humble, and that his speech was mingled with lamentations and accusations. When they entered, he said,—
"It is enough, O men of God, it is enough! Entreat the Lord your God for me, that there be no more mighty thunderings and hail, and I will let you go, and without any longer delay."

As he spoke, the palace shook to its foundations, and the water in the fountain swayed to and fro with violence, as in an earthquake, while the hail, descending with a great noise into the outer courts, was piled many cubits in height against the columns, the sculptured work of which, struck off in every exposed part, fell to the earth mingled with the hail-stones.

"As soon as I am gone out of the city I will spread abroad my hands unto the Lord," said Moses, "and the thunder shall cease, and the hail, that thou mayest know how that the earth is the Lord's. But, O king, as for thee and thy lords, I know that ye will not *yet* fear the Lord God. Has He not mocked the power of your pretended goddess, Isis, over the heavens, and seasons, and winds? Who hath known a rain and hail in Egypt in this month? or hath seen the winds blowing clouds from the sea? God is God, and Isis is no god; or if a god, where is her power? Entreat her to remove this *chamsin* of heaven, such as earth never before felt upon her bosom."

"God is God, and entreat Him for me," answered the king, with a feeble gesture of impatience, doubtless humbled, and yet angry at being compelled to consent to lose six hundred thousand working-men from the mines and great works he is carrying on; for though he fears the number of the Hebrews, he would rather retain them, keeping them under by increased oppression, than release them, and thereby be relieved from the apprehensions to which their unparalleled increase has given rise.

When Moses had left the city of On behind him, he spread abroad his hands towards heaven unto his God; and the thunders, and rain, and hail, and lightnings ceased.

Anticipating the removal of the judgment, I had been standing for some hours by the tower and fountain of Jacob. Suddenly the awful mass of ebony-black cloud, which, for three days, had never ceased to utter its voices of thunder, and send forth its lightnings, hail, and fire upon the earth beneath, began to roll itself up, like a scroll, towards the north. The thunder ceased. The lightnings were no more visible. The hail fell no more. And, as the cloud receded, the shadows upon the land—now smitten and desolate—moved with it. Gradually the whole landscape reappeared; first I saw the walls of On, then its towers, then the obelisks caught the light, and all at once the effulgent sun poured, from the clear sky above it, the splendour of his beams, which the shield of Osiris caught and again reflected with its former brilliancy. Slowly, but with awful majesty, the cloud of God's anger descended the horizon, and finally disappeared in the north. And I thought that mayhap its dark volume would be seen passing over the sea, even from Tyre, to your consternation and wonder.

What a scene of desolation the land presented when, the next day,

I returned to On! The fields of flax and barley were smittten and consumed; the trees were broken and stripped of their leaves, either by the fire or hail; the houses and villages of the plain were devastated; in all the fields were dead corpses; and cattle and horses which had escaped the former plague, or been purchased from the Hebrews, were lying dead everywhere with their herdsmen. Chariots and their riders, overtaken in flight from On, lay upon the highways; and death, desolation, and horror reigned!

Entering the city, I saw soldiers that had been struck dead at their posts by the hail, still lying where they fell; and the streets filled with the dead and wounded, and with heaps of hail; while the sun shone down upon a scene of universal wailing and woe!

I passed on to the palace of Pharaoh, my position and rank having at all times given me free access to his presence. I found him at a banquet, as for three days and nights he had scarcely tasted food for terror and confusion, neither he, nor his lords, nor servants. They were feasting, and drinking wine, and the king's face was flushed with strong drink; for, seizing the present moment of security, he revelled, striving to forget the past terrors. As I entered, his singers were singing a hymn to his gods; and when it was ended, Pharaoh, with his cup in his hand, cursed the God of the Hebrews who had sent such terrors upon his land, for hitherto he had said it was the gods of Egypt who had done these things, forced thereto by the powerful enchantments of the Hebrew brothers.

I turned away from his hall, refusing to go in, when Moses and Aaron passed me, and entered his presence. Upon seeing them, Pharaoh's heart was hardened against them and their God, and he and his lords rose up in fear and anger.

"Are ye come again before me, ye Hebrews?" he cried, in his wrath and wine. "I will not let Israel go! Not a foot nor hoof shall stir from the land! I have sworn it by the life of Pharaoh, and by the gods of Egypt!"

Then Moses answered the king, and said,—

"Thus saith the Lord God of the Hebrews, O Pharaoh: 'Let My people go! How long wilt thou refuse to humble thyself before Me? Let My people go, that they may serve Me; else on the morrow will I bring the locusts into thy coasts, and they shall cover the face of the earth, and devour what remaineth in the field, and shall fill thy houses, and the houses of all the Egyptians, even as hath not been upon the earth unto this day!'"

"We have seen locusts in Egypt, O Hebrew and fear them not," answered Pharaoh, with a laugh of derision. "Go tell your God that Pharaoh and his gods defy Him and His locusts!"

Then Moses turned himself, and went out from Pharaoh. But the lords of Egypt feared, and said unto their king,—

"How long shall this man be a snare unto us and the evil destiny of Egypt? Let the men of the Hebrews go, that they may serve their mighty and dreadful God, as He commandeth them. Knowest thou not, O king, that Egypt is destroyed; and the locusts will destroy the wheat and the rye which are just bursting out of the ground, and the leaves that are putting forth?"

Then Pharaoh sent for Moses and Aaron, who had not yet reached the gate of the palace, and when they again stood before him, he said,—

"For the sake of these, and for Egypt's sake, which thy sorcery has nearly destroyed, I yield to thy demand, not because I fear thy God. Go, serve the Lord your God ; but who are they that shall go ?"

And Moses answered, and said firmly and fearlessly,—

"We will go with our young and with our old, with our sons and with our daughters ; with our flocks and with our herds will we go ; for we must hold a feast unto the Lord, and a sacrifice unto our God."

Then Pharaoh answered in great anger,—

"Let the Lord look to you, not to me, for His sacrifices, as if I will let you go, and your little ones, that you may feast to Him ! Look to it, provoke not my wrath, for evil is before you ! Ask not so. Go now, ye that are men, and serve the Lord, since that is what ye ask ! Now leave my presence ! Ye are become the curse of Egypt. What ! Do ye linger to ask more ! Drive the men forth from the palace !"

The guards followed for some paces, but drew not near them for fear ; and with calm dignity of demeanour, the divine brothers went out of the palace, and left the city. When we had departed from the presence of Pharaoh—for I had joined their holy companionship—he stretched forth his rod over the land eastward, and invoked the new judgment of God that he had threatened. Immediately a strong east wind arose, and blew all that day, and all the night, each hour increasing ; and in the morning, when I waked at a great cry of the people, I looked forth, and beheld the heavens dark with a strange aspect, wholly unlike a cloud, yet moving like one, or, rather, like a great ocean-wave rolling along the sky. It was attended in its approach, which was from the direction of the Arabian Sea, by a confused humming, like the wind sweeping through the tall cedars on Libanus. As it drew near, it covered half the heavens, and appeared many hundred feet in thickness, the lower surface being not far from the earth. I soon perceived from the cries around me, that it was the threatened plague of locusts coming upon Egypt, loosed from the open palm of God's hand. My position was at a window in the house of Aaron, and not far from the line between Goshen and the rest of Egypt. I saw them, as they passed over the plains, and fields, and city, and villages, descend in showers like flakes of snow, hundreds and thousands at a time, until the whole earth was brown with them. Thus the flight continued all that day, and all night, and all the next day and next night,—an endless cloud, darkening the sun by day and the stars by night. The surface of Egypt seemed agitated and alive like the sea after a storm, restless, and in continual motion in every part ; while the noise made by the wings of the locusts was incessant,—a monotone awful to hear, without variation or diminution, till the ear became weary of hearing, and in vain sought relief from the deep, angry bass of this voice of vengeance of the Hebrews' God ! In crossing the Nile, myriads fell into it, and covered its surface,—galleys, barges, men, and sails ; and the water was defiled by their presence. At noon-day there was a dreadful twilight prevailing, for the beams of the sun could not penetrate this living cloud. They covered the whole face of Egypt, and their voracity left not a bud, or leaf, or any green thing on the trees, which were just putting out again; or in the herbs of the field, which had sprung up since the hail; for much seed was in the ground, which came up after the hail, only to be destroyed by the locusts.

Then the people, in despair, besieged the palace of Pharaoh with great cries. Though the Egyptians regard their king as their priest, and as a god, and are proverbially submissive to his will and power, they had now lost all fear, being driven to despair by this last plague. Nothing but famine and death were before them, and their wives, and little ones! Pharaoh also became alarmed at the endless power of the God of the Hebrews! He had long since given his magicians, Jambres and Jannes, to death, because they failed to keep pace with Moses and Aaron, and he evidently felt that this was the power of a God he could no longer compete with. He therefore sent for Moses and Aaron in haste. When they came into his presence they beheld him in a closed room, lighted by the seven golden lamps which Osirtasen captured from the king of Nineveh; for the locusts made it necessary to close every shutter, and turn day into night, in every house. He was reclining upon a lounge covered with Tyrian purple, and adorned with needle-work; and was surrounded by the ladies of his palace, who were imploring him, as the Hebrew brothers entered, to let Israel go! Even his son, the careless and gay Prince Amunophis, was kneeling before him, and urging him to abide by his resolution, to grant the demand of the God of the Hebrews. When he beheld the tall and majestic persons of Moses and Aaron enter, he rose from his couch, and cried,—

"I have sinned against the Lord your God, and against you. Now, therefore, O Moses and Aaron, forgive, I pray thee, my sin only this once, and entreat the Lord your God that He may take away from me this death only!"

This confession seemed to be made with a certain frankness and sincerity, and a show of deep humility; and Moses answered,—

"The Lord forgive thee, acording to what is in thy heart. I will entreat the Lord for thee, and the plague shall be removed from thee and thy people."

Then Moses went out from the presence of Pharaoh; and when he had come into Goshen he ascended the tower of Jacob, and entreated the Lord for Pharaoh. Immediately the cloud of locusts became tossed as with a whirlwind; and the wind, changing from the east to the west, blew strongly, and pressed back the mass of locust-clouds, sweeping those that were on the earth into the air, and rolling the whole body of winged creatures eastward. This wind blew all night, and all the next day, and the next night, a mighty wind, and on the following morning not a living locust was visible in all the coasts of Egypt.

Moses now sent messengers all through Egypt, calling upon the children of Israel to leave whatever they might be occupied in, and assemble themselves in the land of Goshen, with their wives, and children, and flocks, and all that they had. He had previously sent men into Upper Egypt and to the mines; and, what is wonderful, the Hebrews in the mines were permitted to go forth from thence by their keepers, for the fear of Moses had reached their ears and they gladly let them go! The messengers whom Moses now sent everywhere, from Migdol to Syene, were Hebrews, and were nowhere molested as they went; for a fear and reverence of them, as the people of the mighty God of Moses, had taken the place, in the minds of the great body of the Egyptians, of their former contempt: nay, every one was willing to do them a kindness.

Now, my dear father, you are prepared to read that Pharaoh, according to his word, permitted the children of Israel to depart from his dominions. But Thothmeses IV. is no ordinary man! Probably such a character as his is unknown in the history of kings. Such a union of opposite qualities is rarely encountered in one individual. Superstitious, yet sacrilegious! cowardly, yet braving death! faithful to his oath to his gods, yet a perjurer of himself to men! tender-hearted as a woman to his own children and family, yet cruel as a tiger and relentless as a lion to the Hebrews and their little ones! Treacherous, sycophantic, malicious, and ironical, he is twofold in speech, and double-minded in secret intention; he promises when in danger, and revokes his word in security! Despising his foes, yet fearing them, he flatters, smiles upon, and deceives them! Trembling under judgment, he denies his terrors when they are past! convinced of the truth, yet opposing it! confessing the power of God, yet defying it! These qualities, God, who reads the character in the heart, saw in Pharaoh, and knew from the beginning what he would do, and how he would receive Moses, far better than we can know how our well-known friends would act under supposed circumstances. It was perhaps, therefore, on account of the peculiar character of this Pharaoh, that God chose the time and the man for showing His power, glory, majesty, and terror to Egypt, to Israel, and to the world! Under such a queen as Amense, or such a prince as the mild Thothmeses II., the first miracle of the serpent swallowing the rods of the magicians, would have drawn their consent to let Israel go. Where then would have been the manifestation of the power of God, that the earth is now witnessing with awe and fear? God, therefore, knowing what was in the man, chose this Pharaoh as the person in whom, through the natural agency of his obdurate heart, He might make manifest His name as the God of heaven and earth, whose power neither man nor gods can resist. Thus Pharaoh, unwittingly, through the perversity of his own will, and the instability of his character, is actually carrying out God's ultimate designs, glorifying Him in His greatness, and drawing forth these stupendous manifestations of His Almighty power over earth, and air, and skies! Yet is he no less guilty before God; for he does not intend His glory, but, on the contrary, denies and defies Him in its every successive manifestation.

Pharaoh, therefore, did not stand to his word now, dear father. When left to himself, he forgot all that had gone before, and sent word to Moses and Aaron not to attempt to remove the Hebrews, as he would not let them go; for Egypt was devastated, and nearly ruined in every part, and he must first have the labours of the Hebrews to restore the dikes and canals, and the terraces and gardens of the lakes, and then he would let them go.

Then Moses and Aaron went at noonday and sought the Lord as aforetime, in the silence and loneliness of the well of Jacob, where they ever prayed unto Him, and where He spake unto them all the words He commanded them to speak before Pharaoh. And when they had ended their prayers and supplications before their great and terrible God, whose name they never spake but with the profoundest awe, the Lord said unto Moses,—

"Stretch forth thine hand towards heaven, that there may be darkness over the land of Egypt, even darkness that may be felt."

Obeying the command, Moses ascended the tower of Jacob, and stretched forth his hand towards heaven.

Then followed a scene, my dear father, of solemn terror. The atmosphere became the colour of blood. The sun disappeared as if extinguished. A thick and instant darkness fell upon the earth. The birds ceased their songs; the cattle lowed; the wail of Egypt went up in one great cry! Though On is several miles distant, the cry of the city reached the ears of the children of Israel in Goshen. But with them all was light, and joy, and beauty. The sun shone; there was light in every dwelling; the birds sang; the green harvest waved in the joyous sunshine; the verdant fields and leafy trees danced in the soft breeze; for no plague had come nigh the Hebrews, their fields, foliage, or dwellings. The darkness stood, like a great wall of black mist rising high as heaven, between Goshen and Egypt.

Its sudden descent upon Egypt caught the Egyptians on the road, in the fields, upon the Nile, in the streets, temples, and palaces, as they chanced to be; and where it fell upon them, there they were compelled to remain. No flame could burn in the thick, black fog, which felt slimy to the touch. I would have entered it for a moment after touching it, but Aaron warned me not to tempt God; that safety was alone in the sunlight of Goshen. Out from the black abyss came, now and then, a fearful cry of some desolate wayfarer, and the Hebrews answered kindly back, and so by their shouts directed the wanderer in the darkness how to move towards the light. During this darkness, the Hebrews, by the command of Moses, were collecting their flocks, and preparing to depart to sacrifice to their God: also, those who had not been circumcised now received the rite.

This horrible night continued without change—without moon or star to lend it a ray—until the third day, when Pharaoh, unable longer to hold out in this unequal combat against God, sent two Hebrews, born in his house, to Moses; for only the Hebrew could walk through this night of God as in the light. Without a word of impatience or doubt, Moses and Aaron rose up and disappeared in the awful veil of darkness, in response to the summons of the king. No sooner did Pharaoh behold them, than he cried out, in a voice of mingled complaint and condescension,—

"Go ye, Moses and Aaron, ye and yours, only let your flocks and herds stay in the land; for hast thou not destroyed," he added with bitterness, "whatsoever parteth the hoof in all the land of Egypt? Your little ones may also go with you." This was spoken in a tone of condescension.

And Moses answered and said,—

"Thou must suffer our flocks and **herds** to go with us, O king, that we may have sacrifices and burnt-offerings wherewith to sacrifice unto the Lord our God. **Our** cattle, therefore, must also go with **us**. There shall not a hoof be left behind."

When Pharaoh heard Moses speak **thus** firmly and boldly to him, abating nothing from his first demand, he seemed to lose his reason with rage. Casting his sceptre from his hand at the two brothers, he cried,—

"Get ye from me, ye destroyers and curse of Egypt! Take heed to thyself, O Moses, and see my face no more, for in that day thou seest my face thou shalt die!"

Then Moses answered, with calm and severe majesty,—

"Thou hast spoken well, O Pharaoh. I will see thy face no more. But hear thou the word of the Lord, which, knowing thy heart, He hath spoken unto me to say now before thee: 'I will bring yet one plague more upon Pharaoh and upon Egypt. About midnight will I go out into the midst of Egypt, and all the first-born in the land of Egypt shall die, from the first-born of Pharaoh that sitteth upon his throne, even unto the first-born of the maid-servant that is behind the **mill**; **and** all the first-born of beasts: and all these thy servants shall **bow** down themselves unto me, saying—" Get thee out, and all the **people** that follow thee; and thy lords, and high captains, and governors, and great men, and all who **serve** thee, shall come down to me, to urge me to go forth out of Egypt: after that I will go out."' These, O king, **are the** words of the Lord against thee. Thou hast cast thy sceptre **at** my feet. As I step my foot upon it, so shall **the** Lord place His foot upon Egypt!"

Thus speaking, Moses went out from Pharaoh in great anger. **As** he left the palace, the Egyptians prostrated themselves before him, and sought his favour, and some cried, "He is a god! Let this god, who is mightier than Osiris and greater than Serapis, be our god!"

"But Moses sternly rebuked them," said Aaron, who related **to me all** that had passed, "and felt deeply grieved and humbled at so great a sin, and called upon them to worship God in heaven, whose servant only he was, with no power in himself to do these wonders which they had witnessed."

Farewell, my dear father. My next letter, without doubt, will convey to you the victory of the Lord God over Pharaoh and his gods, and the deliverance of the Hebrews from their bondage.

Your affectionate son,
REMESES OF DAMASCUS.

LETTER XI.

REMESES OF DAMASCUS TO SESOSTRIS.

WRITTEN IN THE WILDERNESS OF ARABIA BY THE SEA.

MY DEAR FATHER,—

THE events which have transpired since I last wrote to you, mock my pen by their sublimity and infinite grandeur. Upon a rock for a tablet, the desert around me, the Sea of Edom before me, I desire to record, while they are vivid in my memory, the stupendous scenes of the past six days. The millions of Israel have come forth out of Egypt! The Sea of Suphim is between them and the land of their bondage! But I have so much to write, such wonders to relate, that I will not anticipate your curiosity, but proceed to send you a narrative of each event in due order. Let all the earth say that the Lord God of the Hebrews is the only God: besides Him there is no God!

The day that Moses and Aaron departed from the presence of Pharaoh-Thothmeses, in truth to see his face no more, the Lord commanded them to call together the elders and people of the Hebrews, and instruct them to take a male lamb, or a kid without blemish, one to each household, keep it till the fourteenth day of the month, which day was just at hand, and kill it on the evening thereof, sprinkling, with a bunch of hyssop, the lintel and door-posts of their houses dipped in its blood, and roasting the flesh, eat it at night, leaving none until morning. "And ye shall eat it," said the Lord, "in haste, with your loins girded, your shoes on your feet, and your staff in your hand; for it is the Lord's passover, who will the same night pass through the land of Egypt, and smite all the first-born of the land of Egypt, both man and beast; and against all the gods of Egypt I will execute judgment! I am the Lord: and this day shall be a memorial to you for ever."

Then Moses did as the Lord commanded. Moreover, on the day of the night on which the lamb, that had been selected from the flocks three days before, was to be slain, he said to the elders of Israel, whom he called together, "Thus saith the Lord your God, 'Let none of you go out at the door of his house until the morning; for this night the Lord will pass through to smite the Egyptians; and when He seeth the blood upon the lintel, and on the two side-posts, the Lord will *pass over* the door, and will not suffer the destroyer to come in unto your houses to smite you.'" There were also other ordinances of bread unleavened established, which bread they were commanded to eat for seven days, at the "feast of unleavened bread."

And when Moses had proclaimed these and other ordinances, the people bowed their heads and worshipped God, and said they would do all that the Lord had commanded Moses and Aaron to say unto them.

Then, my dear father, followed a scene of the deepest interest! It was three millions of people preparing to break their bondage of generations, and to go forth from under the cruel sceptre of the king of Egypt for ever. The mighty miracles of Moses had, long since, silenced the murmurs and doubts of the elders, openly uttered at the beginning, when Pharaoh in revenge against Moses and Aaron, increased their burdens, and denied them straw for their bricks. At each successive miracle they had gained confidence in their powerful advocate before Pharaoh; and when they saw that he could not be equalled by the magicians, they became vain and proud of him, whom before they had condemned; and waited, with wonder and expectation, their mighty deliverance. At the occurrence of the sixth miracle they threw up all work, and no Egyptian had the heart to say, "Go to your tasks!" for they saw that God was with them. Thus from all parts of Egypt, drawn by curiosity, hope, wonder, and a desire to behold this mighty leader whom God had raised up, they flocked to Goshen, until the land was filled with their vast numbers! The houses and huts could not contain them, and they slept by thousands in the fields, and by the wayside. When they perceived that the darkness, and the locusts, and the hail approached not their land, the most timid and desponding took courage, and lifted their voices to the God of their fathers, in hope and gratitude. Indeed, after the awful plague of darkness, thousands of the most ignorant Hebrews shouted that he was a god, and the Egyptians of all classes were ready to acknowledge him as Osiris or Thoth! And in some of the temples, the day after the darkness passed, the priests waved incense to Osiris by the name of Musæusiris, or Osiris-Moses: and, I doubt not, divine honours will be paid him in Egypt for generations to come! Yet this mighty servant of God moves among the people, as unassuming and self-forgetful as the humblest of his brethren, quietly giving his directions for the greatest movement earth was ever to behold—a nation marching in one day from bondage to freedom!

I moved in and out, everywhere among them. There was a strange joy lighting up every face. Old men looked calm and happy; young men were noisy with hope; maidens were full of joy; mothers smiled with delight, as they clasped their babes to their bosoms, in the certainty that they would not grow up in servitude to Pharaoh. All eyes were turned to Moses and Aaron, as they passed to and fro, and many fell on their knees, and worshipped them: while others shouted, as the only way they could express their emotions. How must the heart of the servant of God have swelled with gratitude to his Creator, as he beheld the happiness around him! And how deeply he must have realized his responsibility, as he reflected that the hopes of three millions of people, whom he had assembled in Goshen, with the promise of deliverance from the sceptre of Pharaoh, hung upon his single arm, but which was, for the time, the arm of God!

With what emotions of awe and expectation did the children of Israel, each at the door of his house, prepare to slay the chosen lamb, and sprinkle its blood on the side-posts and lintel! To them it was the command of Moses simply, and beyond that none knew the significance. It was a beautiful and serene evening. The sun had filled the skies with golden atoms, and the horizon was tinged with commingled emerald, blue, and orange colours, fused into an atmosphere of ineffable glory. It seemed as if the presence of the God of the Hebrews was in His skies, beholding His people! At the given hour, being the ninth of the day, a hundred thousand sacrificial knives —held in the hands of the men of a whole nation, which became, for the moment, a nation of priests to God—flashed in the sun, and the blood of the victims, pouring upon the land of Goshen, consecrated it as the altar where the God of the Hebrews first received the national worship of His people, and their recognition of Him as their God.

Then, with hyssop dipped in a basin of the blood, each man sprinkled the door-posts, and cross-piece of the entrance of his house, in behalf of all who either should dwell in it, or who, being stranger-brethren, came from other parts of Egypt, and could enter no house for the throngs, yet were numbered with some one household: as, for instance, the house of Aaron's father-in-law, which could hold but thirty people, had on its list three hundred and seventy names, as its household,—all brethren from other provinces; for Goshen was now like a mighty camp. There were besides, hovering about the confines of Goshen, and even mingling with the Hebrews, thousands of Egyptian families, who, flying from the terror of the Lord in Egypt, had sought safety near the Hebrews, and under the wing of the God who had protected them,—hoping to share their safety. Many of these brought their substance with them—their rich apparel, their gold, and jewels, and silver—hoping, therewith, to purchase the favour of their once despised, and now dreaded, bondmen.

How, my dear father, shall I record the events of the night that followed the death of the lambs! As the sun went down, the Hebrews, with awe, retired within their dwellings, and closed the doors. Mothers, with anxious haste, drew in their first-born. Even many of the hapless Egyptians, who had heard the command to the Hebrews, chose a lamb and slew it—their hands trembling, and hearts sinking between hope and fear—and sprinkled the door-posts of their wretched places of shelter, if, peradventure, the great and terrible God of the Hebrews would, in the coming night of His vengeance upon Pharaoh, seeing the blood, pass them by, and spare their first-born also.

At length a silence, like that which for ever reigns in the heart of the pyramids, reigned throughout Goshen. Not an eye was closed in all Israel, during those first hours of dread watching for the first sound abroad of God's coming down upon Egypt. I remained up, in the house of the venerable Aminadab, the father-in-law of Aaron. Elisiba, the wife of Aaron, with her arm around her eldest son Nadab, a fine young man, held him firmly by her side. Aaron and Moses were apart, in a room by themselves, engaged in low conversation, or in solemn prayer. No other sound was heard, but the voice of this wonderful man talking, as if face to face with his God.

Suddenly, at midnight, a bright light from heaven shone above the dwelling, and from it went forth a glory which filled the land of Goshen with its beams. I stood, at the moment, in the court, and fell with my face to the earth; for I knew that it was the presence of God. At length Moses touched me, and said,—

"Fear not! Rise and behold the glory of God, that when thou shalt return and sit upon thy throne, thou mayest teach thy people that the God of the Hebrews is the God of heaven and earth! For thy sake, as well as for Israel, and Pharaoh, and the Egyptians, and all the nations who shall hear of this, are these wonders and judgments done; that Pharaoh, and all kings, and the whole earth, may know who is the Lord, and worship only Him!"

I arose, and lo! in the height of heaven I beheld a column, or pillar of fire, the base of which was above the roof of the house, and the summit thereof in the region of clouds. It was in the form of a Hebrew staff, with a bar of light across it near its top, upon which seemed to be a crown of glory, shooting forth thorns of light and splendour. In this cloud, or pillar of light, there seemed to stand a form like that of a man, but resplendent with ineffable radiance, and I covered my face and worshipped. When I looked again, the dazzling vision, if such it were, was in motion towards Egypt, and the city of On. As it moved, it lighted up the whole earth. When it came over the city of the Sun, a sword seemed to be drawn by the man who stood in the pillar of fire, and I beheld it sweep over the palace of Pharaoh, and strike. Then, with the swiftness and dazzling gleam of lightning, it turned every way over Egypt, till I could not, dared not behold longer, and bowed my head, veiling my eyes, and adoring.

Then we heard, even in Goshen, a cry as from the living heart of Egypt, as if every mother in the vast cities of On and Memphis, and the hundred surrounding villages, had lifted her voice in one prolonged, dreadful wail of woe.

I knew what that cry meant, and trembled in silent awe. I prostrated myself before God and cried for mercy!

At length the sword was drawn back by the hand of the man in the pillar of cloud, and the shining column returned and stood over the house where Moses and Aaron remained; a calm, lambent light, soft as moonbeams, being now emitted from it, instead of the angry splendour with which it shone before.

One or more hours passed, and two horsemen, riding like the wind, entered Goshen and cast themselves upon the ground at the feet of Moses and Aaron. They were couriers from Pharaoh.

"My lords," cried one of them, pale and trembling with fear and haste, after he had risen from his prostration, "the king hath sent us to thee, and these are the words he hath commanded us to say: 'Rise up, Moses and Aaron, and get you forth from among my people, and from Egypt, both ye and the children of Israel, and go and serve the Lord as ye have said. Take your flocks, and your herds, and all that ye have, and be gone; and pray your dreadful God for me, that He may bless me also, for He hath slain my son!'"

Then came, while he was yet speaking, a large company of lords, and high officers, and great men of Egypt, whose sons the wrath of God had slain (for there was not a house in Egypt where there was not one dead, from the first-born of Pharaoh that sat upon the throne, to the first-born of the captive that was in the dungeon), and they were urgent upon Moses and Aaron, and the Hebrew people, imploring them, with tears and supplications, to hasten from the land, with all they had, and to make all haste.

Then Moses, as soon as it was day, sent word throughout all Israel to prepare to go forth out of Egypt that day. He directed the people to take all the jewels, and gold, and silver, and raiment, which the Egyptians were forcing upon them to bribe them to hasten; "for," he said, "it is yours, as the Lord hath commanded you to spoil the Egyptians, for whom ye have laboured without wages. It is the Lord's gift to you from those whom He would spoil, and whose lives He has spared to them."

Now followed a spectacle of wonderful interest and sublimity. As if moved by one spirit, Israel marshalled itself into companies of hundreds, and these into bands of thousands, and these into mighty divisions of tribes, so that by noon there were twelve separate armies of God, ready to march at the voice of Moses. The whole plain of Goshen, as far as the eye could see from the tower of Jacob, was covered with their mighty hosts. Each tribe had its women, and little ones, and flocks and herds within its own square. They waited now for the signal to move forward, every man with his loins girded, his shoes on his feet, and his staff in his hand, their bread unbaked in their kneading-troughs, and their persons laden with the jewels and gifts which the urgent Egyptians had forced upon them, either that they might see their faces no more, or from fear, or in the hope to be blessed by their Lord God for these favours: for so the Lord, to whom the gold and silver of the earth belong, had disposed their hearts towards the Hebrews.

Then, at the going down of the sun, Moses gave the signal for this mighty march. There were no trumpets sounding, no military display of banners and spears; but they moved to their own tread, which seemed to shake the earth. They came on in columns, a thousand men abreast, and marched past the tower of Jacob, on which Moses stood, with Aaron by his side, the miraculous rod in his hand. When the van of this army of Jehovah, terrible in its strength, came up with the tower, the white cloud of the Presence of Jehovah (which, all day, had stood in the air like a snow-white cloud, immovable and wonderful to behold), advanced, as if borne upon a gentle wind, and placed itself before the host. Night came on ere half the divisions had passed by where Moes stood; and, as the sun went down, never more to rise upon Israel in Egypt, the Pillar of Cloud became a Pillar of Fire, and shed a glory over the innumerable armies of Israel equal to the splendour of day. It was midnight ere the last tribe had passed by with its face to the desert. Then Moses and Aaron descended, and I kneeled before them, and asked if I might be permitted to go out of Egypt with the Lord's people, and continue to behold the power of God. Moses answered me with benignity, and said I should be with him as a son, that I might see the wonders of Jehovah, and make known in Phœnicia His glory and power.

While he was speaking, a mixed multitude of Egyptians, Nubians, slaves, captives of Egypt, and of all those persons who hoped to be blessed and benefited with Israel, fell to the ground before Moses, and entreated him to suffer them to go up to the new land to which he was going. Moses granted them, without hesitation, their prayer.

Then I learned that those among the Egyptians who had, in obedience to the command of Moses, sprinkled their **own** door-posts, escaped like the Israelites, for it was the sign of the blood of obedience alone, that the angel of the Lord regarded; on the other hand, several Israelitish families saw their first-born perish, they having neglected to obey the command of Moses, from avarice or indifference, or doubt of the intention of God, or supposing that being **Israelites** would save their households.

And here, my dear father, let me make known to you that I have learned from Aaron the significance of this sign; for God having made known to him that "he is to become the high-priest, as Moses is the leader, of His people, has revealed to him that the slaying of the lamb is a type of a divine and innocent Person, who shall come down from God, and one day be sacrificed. Earth, as the antitype of Egypt, is to be the altar of this future stupendous sacrifice. And as by the blood of a lamb, and the death of the first-born, Israel is delivered from Egypt, so by the blood of the Lamb, the first-born of God, shall the whole of mankind who look to His blood be finally delivered from this earth, and from Satan its Pharaoh, and be led by God into a heaven above the skies, a land of eternal happiness and peace, to dwell there till the end of ages."

Is not this a sublime doctrine? Is God, then, making with Israel, an outline of what He is to perform with the whole earth? Shall we escape this world-broad Egypt, and under a divine leader like Moses, by the blood of the mysterious Lamb of God, be led to another world? I have but indistinct knowledge, my dear father, of all this; but have learned enough to make my heart bound with joy. For in this enlarged conception of the wonderful theme, you and I, and all in the whole earth,—who shall look to the God of Israel, and by foresight of faith trust in the sprinkling of the blood of the Lamb upon the threshold of our hearts,—are also of Israel; their God is our God; their land of heaven our land of promise also! Oh, who can fathom the wisdom, and goodness, and love, and power of God. To His name be glory, majesty, dominion, and worship from all nations! Before Him let kings fall down, and princes prostrate themselves, and every knee of all people, nations, kindred, and tongues, be bent; for He is the Lord of heaven and earth, and besides Him there is no God!

Also, my dear father, Moses, whose lips ever distil celestial wisdom, was graciously pleased, on the night before the death of the first-born, as he walked to and fro in the court of the house of Aminadab, to reveal to me the divine aim in sending such miracles as He did upon Egypt, instead of any others. I listened with wonder and increased awe, and, if I may so express it, redoubled admiration of the wisdom and justice of God.

Said the holy Hebrew and sage, "The Egyptians have ever believed, that the jugglery and magic arts, in which their magicians and priests of mysteries display such astonishing proficiency, are actual miracles, exhibiting the power of their deities, and their co-operation with their priests to enable them to do these deceptions. Miracles, therefore (or magic), were regarded by them as acts of their idols. It became necessary that the Lord God of the Hebrews should manifest Himself and His power by miracles also; and not only this, but that the miracles which He performed should be of such a character as to distinguish them from the jugglery of the magicians, and at once convince the Egyptians that they proceeded from a Being omnipotent over their idols, and show the Israelites themselves, who had almost forgotten God, that the author of such mighty miracles as they beheld, must be the only living and true God of the

T

earth and skies. Now, my dear Remeses," he continued, " if you will give heed to my words for a few moments, you will perceive how perfectly fitted the ten miracles which God performed in the sight of Pharaoh, Egypt, and Israel, were to destroy their faith in the gods of Egypt, and make known the true God as the only Deity to be feared and worshipped by men.

"At first, in conformity with the Divine purpose, the strength of the magicians was brought out and fairly measured with my own, as God's servant, inspired by Him, for of myself I did nothing. Unless this trial of skill had been made, both the Egyptians and doubting Israelites would have said that I derived my power from their gods (for they would not forget I had been an Egyptian and knew their mysteries), and God would not have been honoured. But when the royal magicians appeared in the name of the gods of Egypt, lo! the God of heaven was shown not only to be superior to their sorcerers by His miracles, but, as you will perceive, hostile to their idolatrous worship. The observers of both sides were permitted not only to distinguish the power of God from the inferior arts of the magicians of Egypt, but are led to withdraw with us, as is the case with tens of thousands who seek to follow us from Goshen,—their confidence in the protection and power of their gods being utterly destroyed. Observe now, my dear prince, the direction taken by the miracles.

"The first one, which confirmed my authority and mission to Pharaoh, destroyed the serpents. This was the first assault of the Almighty upon the gods and sacred animals and things of Egypt; for you are aware of the temple of the sacred Uræus, where the serpent is worshipped. The serpent of the rod of God destroying the serpents of the Egyptians, showed Pharaoh that his gods could not live, or save themselves in the presence of the servant of the true God. Thus the serpent form taken by the rod was not merely an arbitrary shape; there was profound design concealed thereunder.

" The Nile is held sacred, revered as a god by the Egyptians, and the fish they regard as holy. Its waters supply all Egypt with a drink which they quaff with reverence and pleasure, believing that a healing virtue dwells in its waves. Changed to blood, and its fish becoming putrid, they loathed their god and fled from his banks with horror.

"The next miracle—of frogs—was also directed against a god of the Egyptians and the worship of these unclean animals. He was made to become their curse; and as they dared not kill them, being sacred, they became to them a terror and a disgust unspeakable.

" The miracle which followed was directed against their priests and temples; for, by the laws of the forty-two books, no one could approach the altars upon which so impure an insect harboured; and the priests, to guard against such an accident, wore white linen and shaved their heads and bodies every other day. The severe nature of this miracle, as aimed against the religious rites and altar-services of the Egyptians, you will perceive. So keenly did the magicians feel this, and foresee how it would close every temple in Egypt, that they were forced to exclaim, in my presence,—

"'This is the finger of God!'

"The succeeding and fifth miracle was designed to destroy the confidence of the Egyptians in their god of flies, Baal-zebul. This god had the reputation of protecting Egypt from the swarms of flies which, at certain seasons, infest the air throughout all Egypt. The inability of the magicians who were sent for by Pharaoh to remove them, showed that the Lord God was more powerful than their fly-god, and thus led them to look upon their own idol with contempt.

"The miracle which destroyed their cattle was aimed at Apis, and Mnevis, and Amun, the ram-headed god of Thebes, and at the entire system of their worship of animals. Thus, by this one act of power, the Lord Jehovah vindicated His own honour, and destroyed their confidence in their idols, and the very existence of their gods.

"When, by the command of God, I took ashes from the altar of human sacrifices, and sprinkled it towards heaven, as did their priests, to avert evil, and evil came in the shape of the boil, God taught them, that what they trusted to, He could make against them, and out of their idolatrous rites bring a curse upon them and upon Egypt.

"The eighth miracle," continued Moses, while I gave ear to his words with wondering attention, "was directed at the worship of Isis, as the moon, and controller of the seasons, and clouds, and weather. When the hail and the rain, the lightning and thunder, was brought by God upon the land, and all the prayers to Isis failed to stay the fearful tempest of His wrath, it should have convinced Pharaoh of the folly of his idolatry, and taught the people not to put their trust in an idol that could not help them against the power of the God of the Hebrews.

"The miracle which followed, was directed against the adoration and rites of Serapis, and his whole gorgeous system of worship; for the Egyptians saw that the god who was regarded as their peculiar protector against the destructive power of locusts, was impotent to remove the cloud of these voracious insects, which God brought upon them from the sea; and that only when Pharaoh entreated God, were they removed.

"The last miracle was aimed at the universal worship of Osiris, or the Sun. It was intended to teach Pharaoh and the Egyptians, and also Israel, that the God of the Hebrews was superior to their 'lord of the sun,' and that He could veil His splendour when, and for any length of time, it pleased Him! And also that they were called by the exhibition of this mighty miracle to worship Him who made the sun, and moon, and stars, and all the glory of them—Jehovah is His name!"

When, my dear father, the man of God had ceased speaking, I remained for some time silent with awe, meditating upon what I had heard; worshipping, and adoring, and praising God, whose wisdom, and power, and judgments, are over all His works, who will not give His glory to another, nor leave Himself without a witness of His existence upon earth.

Thus you see, my dearest father, that the miracles were not arbitrary displays of power, but grand divine lessons, mingled with judgments. It was JEHOVAH vindicating His own worship, and showing the impotency of false gods, by the manifestation of His supreme power and majesty, as the destroyer of gods, and the only potentate,—God of gods, King of kings, and Ruler over all, blessed for evermore!

Having now revealed to you the mystery, veiled under the miracles of Moses, I will close my long letter, leaving you to reflect, my father, upon the wonders of God, and to contemplate His wisdom. In one or two more letters, I shall close my correspondence; as travelling in the desert, I shall have no opportunity to communicate with you. I shall proceed into Syria by the caravan route in a few days, and by the way of Palestine and the valley of the Jordan, return to Damascus, and thence, as soon as my affairs will permit, shall hasten to see you at your palace in Tyre.

Farewell, my dear father.

Your affectionate son,

REMESES OF DAMASCUS.

LETTER XII.

PRINCE REMESES OF DAMASCUS TO KING SESOSTRIS.

HOREB IN THE DESERT.

MY DEAR FATHER,—

I WILL now resume the subject which occupied the foregoing portion of my last letter, namely, the departure of the twelve armies of the Hebrews from the land of Egypt.

When the last division had passed the tower, after midnight, Moses and Aaron went forward and travelled all night, along the column of march, addressing the leaders of tribes, divisions, thousands, and hundreds, as they went, giving them words of courage, and commanding them to keep in view the Pillar of Fire.

This Divine Glory, which the whole people of the Hebrews, and even the Egyptian followers, were permitted to behold and gaze at with wonder, as if it were the moon or sun, moved onward, far in advance of the last division, and seemingly directly over the head of the column. When I reached, with Moses, the van of the mighty slowly-moving host, I perceived that a sort of sarcophagus on wheels was drawn by twelve oxen in front of all; and that over this, the "shekinah," as Aaron termed the presence of God in the cloud of light, was suspended. I had not seen this before, but knew that it must contain the embalmed body of Prince Joseph, which the children of Israel had jealousy guarded and concealed from the Pharaohs of the present dynasty, waiting the time of the deliverance; for the venerable Joseph, on his death, had taken an oath from his brethren, the children of Israel, that they would carry up his bones out of Egypt, when God should send the deliverer to bring them forth.

Faithfully were this wonderful people now fulfilling the oath of their fathers to Joseph, after more than two hundred years had passed. Thus their going out of Egypt bore a resemblance to a national funeral. At the side of the sarcophagus Moses and Aaron walked, and thus the solemn march advanced towards the wilderness. All that night they journeyed from the plain of Raamses, and came to the verge of a rocky valley where the way was rough, compared with the fertile and level plains of Egypt. When the sun arose, the Pillar of Fire faded, as it were, into a columnar cloud which still advanced miraculously and wonderfully before us. When the heat of the day increased, the cloud descended and rested over a place called Succoth. Here Moses ordered the people to encamp, and bake their unleavened bread which they brought with them in their kneading-troughs from Egypt. The next night they travelled up the valley to a place called Etham, a short journey; and thence, after a rest, turning back a little, they traversed the valley between rocks eastward, and encamped at a well of water called Pi-hahiroth, where there were many palm-trees. Here they remained to rest, with the hills on either hand, wondering why God should not have let them pass into the desert at Etham, instead of bringing them into that defile, which seemed to have no outlet but at the shore of the sea. Passing Pi-hahiroth, with its castle and garrison, the latter of which fled at our advance, as also the garrison of the tower of Migdol, which guarded the way to Egypt from the Arabian Sea, and so up the cliffs of the valley-sides, Moses encamped between Migdol and the sea, which spread far away eastward in front, with the towers and fortified city of Baal-zephon visible on the opposite side. The Pillar of Cloud had indicated this place of encampment, by resting above it near the shore.

When I surveyed the place, I marvelled to know how Moses would move forward the next day; for the mountainous ridges of the rocky valley, along which we had come, continued close to the shore of the sea on the right hand, and on the left, and I could perceive, as I walked to the place, no room for a single man, much less an army, to go either south or north between the mountains and the water; for the sea broke with its waves against its perpendicular sides. I concluded, therefore, that on the morrow the whole host would have to retrace its steps, and enter the desert by the way of Etham, where it had before encamped, and so make a sweep around the head of the sea to the northward and eastward. But I did not express to any one my thoughts. The calm majesty and repose of Moses awed me. Upon his expansive brow was stamped confidence in his God, who, if need were, could make a road across the sea for His people, for whose deliverance He had done such wonders. I reflected, too, that the leader was God Himself, and that He had gone before, and led them to the place were they were. I therefore waited the will of God, to see what in His wisdom He would do.

How little did I anticipate the end! How far was I from understanding that God had led His people into this defile, which had no outlet but that by which they entered, in order to display His glory, and present to the world the final exhibition of His power, and His judgments upon Pharaoh and the Egyptians!

The divinely inspired Moses seemed to understand my thoughts when I returned to the camp.

"My son," he said, "this is done to try Pharaoh; for, when he heareth that we are in the valley of Pi-hahiroth, before Migdol, he will say, 'They are entangled in the land—the wilderness hath shut them in.' 'Then,' saith the Lord to me, 'Pharaoh will repent that he let you and My people go, and he will follow after you, and when he shall come after you, I will be honoured upon Pharaoh and upon all his host; that the Egyptians may know that I am the Lord.' God will yet avenge Himself upon this wicked king, and reward him for all his wickedness that he hath done against Him and His people Israel! Wait, and thou shalt see the power of God, indeed!"

With what expectation, and with what confidence in God I waited the result, my dear father, you may conceive. How wonderful is this God, and His ways how past finding out! "It was just four hundred and thirty years from the day Israel left Egypt," said Aaron to me, "to the day their father Abram left Chaldea for Canaan; and that, their book say, is the exact time prophesied for their deliverance. Their actual residence in Egypt, from the Syrian Prince Jacob's coming to settle in Goshen, to the day they left, was two hundred and fifteen years. The existence of their *bondage* began at the death of Joseph, who died sixty-five years, not seventy, as you supposed, before the birth of Moses. This servant of God is now eighty years old; therefore, the number of years *that they were in servitude* is one hundred and forty-five, or equal to five generations. Thus, were the descendants of Abraham, and Abraham himself, wanderers without any country of their own for four hundred and thirty years, according to the word of the Lord to Abraham; not all this time in bondage, indeed, but under kings of another language. Now, at length behold them returning a mighty nation, to claim from the Canaanites and Philistines the land so long ago promised to their remote ancestor, Abram. God is not forgetful of His promise, as this vast multitude proclaims to the world, though He seems to wait; but His purposes must ripen, and with the Almighty a day is as a thousand years, and a thousand years as one day.

Now behold, my dear father, a new manifestation of His glory and power, and the awful majesty of His judgments, before whom no man can stand and live! The next day, being the seventh, whereon a divine tradition ordains rest, but which in their bondage could not be regarded, Moses and Aaron commanded the whole host to repose. Thus time was given Pharaoh, not only to hear the report,—as he did by some Egyptians who, in dread of the wilderness, went back,—of their being shut in by the craggy mountains, with the sea before them,—but to arm and to pursue and destroy them or compel them to submit again to his yoke.

I have learned from an officer of Pharaoh, who, fearing God, escaped from the palace, and came and informed Moses of the king's purposes, that when the news reached the king, who had been three days bitterly repenting his compliance with the demands of Moses, he sprang from the table at which he sat, and, with a great oath by his gods, cried,—

"They are entangled between Pi-hahiroth and the sea! They

have played me false, and are not gone by Etham into the desert to sacrifice! Their God has bewildered them in the Valley of Rocks by the sea! Now, by the life of Osiris, I will up and pursue them!" He called all his lords and officers, and gave commands to send couriers to the army already assembled at Bubastis, and expecting to march against the king of Edom, who had long menaced Egypt. He ordered this army to hasten, by forced marches, to the plain before On. He then sent to the city, where he kept his six hundred chosen chariots of war, for them to be harnessed, and meet him the next day before Raamses. Couriers on fleet horses were sent to every garrison, and all the chariots in other cities, and in the three treasure cities, to the number of four thousand charioteers, each with his armed soldier, gathered on the plain which the Israelites had left four days before. The forty-seven fortresses of the provinces sent forth their garrisons, of three and four hundred men each, to swell the Egyptian hosts.

All this intelligence reached Moses; but he remained immovable in his camp, the Pillar of Fire also standing in the air above the tent of Aaron, in which was the sarcophagus of Prince Joseph. Messenger after messenger, sometimes an Egyptian friendly to the Israelites, sometimes an Israelite who had been detained and did not leave Egypt with his brethren, came to Moses, and as they passed through the camp, gave up their news to the people.

One man said Pharaoh had left his palace, armed in full battle-armour, and at the head of his body-guard of six hundred chariots of gold and ivory, was driving to the plain of Raamses. A second messenger brought tidings, that the king's great army, from the vicinity of Bubastis and Pelusium, had passed On in full march,— seventy thousand foot, ten thousand horsemen, and two thousand chariots of iron! A third came, reporting that four thousand chariots had also assembled from all parts of Lower Egypt, and that every man was rallying to the standard of the king, to pursue the Hebrews and destroy them by the edge of the sword. By and by, a fourth came, an escaped Hebrew, who told that the king had marshalled his vast hosts of one hundred thousand foot, twenty thousand horsemen, nine thousand chariots of iron, besides his six hundred chosen chariots of his body-guard, and was in full pursuit of the Israelites by the way of Succoth. These tidings filled the bosoms of the Hebrews with dismay. They were in no condition to do battle, there being among them all, one only who knew the use of arms, which one was Moses; who, with God on his side, was an army in himself.

The Egyptian army, marched all night, without rest to hoof or sandal. Before the sun was up, their approach was made known by the distant thunder of their chariot-wheels, and the tramp of their horses. At length, when the Pillar of Fire was fading into a white cloud, and the sun rose brilliantly over the Sea of Arabia, the van of the Egyptian army became visible, advancing down the enclosed valley. When the Israelites beheld its warlike front, and heard the clangor of war-trumpets and the deep roll of the drums, they fled with fear. The elders then hastened, and, pale with terror and anger, came before Moses, and cried to him,—

"Because there were no graves in Egypt, hast thou taken us away to die here in the wilderness? Wherefore hast thou dealt thus with us to carry us forth out of Egypt? Did we not, at the first, tell thee in Egypt, 'Let us alone, that we may serve the Egyptians?' for it had been better for us to serve the Egyptians, than that we should die in the wilderness.'

Then Moses answered their tumult, and said, without displeasure visible in his godlike countenance,—

"Fear ye not! Stand still, and see the salvation of the Lord, which He will show you to-day! for the Egyptians whom ye have seen to-day, ye shall see them again no more for ever! The Lord shall fight for you, and ye shall hold your peace. Wait to see what He will do."

Then Moses with a troubled face, entered his tent, and his voice was heard by those near by, calling upon God.

And the Lord answered him from the cloud above the tent,—

"Why criest thou unto Me? Speak unto the children of Israel *that they go forward!* But lift thou up thy rod and stretch out thy hand over the sea, and divide it; and the children of Israel shall go on dry ground through the midst of the sea. And behold Pharaoh, (whom I withhold from nothing which he chooseth in his hard heart to do, leaving him to his own devices to reap the fruit of his own ways), he shall follow you with the Egyptians into the sea! and I will get Me honour upon Pharaoh, and upon all his host, upon his chariots and upon his horsemen. And the Egyptians shall know that I am the Lord!"

Then Moses came forth from the tent, whence the voice of the Lord had been heard by all, both near and afar off. Now, lo! the angel of God in the Pillar of Cloud, as soon as the armies of Israel began to move forward to the sea, removed from the front, and went to the rear of the Hebrew host, and stood behind them in the Pillar of Cloud! Thus, it stood between the camp of the Israelites and the camp of the Egyptians, so that when night came, the Israelites, lying encamped on the shore, had the full splendour of its light; while the Egyptians, to whom it presented a wall of impenetrable darkness, also encamped, fearing to go forward in the unnatural night which enveloped them. So the two hosts remained all night, neither moving—the Pillar of Fire and the Pillar of Cloud between them, creating day on one side of it, and tenfold night on the other.

Now, at the going down of the sun, on that day when the Egyptians encamped because of the cloud, Moses had stretched forth his hand over the sea by God's command, and lo! there arose a mighty wind upon the sea, rising from the south and east; and all that night we heard the sea and waves roaring, and the hearts of Israel sunk within them for fear. The Pillar of Fire cast upon the sea a radiance like moonlight, so that we could perceive that it was in a great commotion, and that God was doing some great wonder in the deep. It is said that the noise of the waves reached the ears of Pharaoh, and that he at first believed it was the sound of the tramping of the whole host of the Israelites, advancing with their God to give him battle in the darkness. He called his men to arms, and tried to show front of war; but the shadow of the cloud between him and the Hebrews, rendered it impossible for any man to move from one place to another, or to see his fellow.

At length morning came to us, but not to the Egyptians, whose night still continued. But what a spectacle of sublimity and power we beheld! Before us, an avenue, broad enough for two hundred men to march abreast, had been cut by the rod of God through the deep sea, the water of which stood as a wall on the one side and on the other, glittering like ice on the sides of the rocks of Libanus, when capped with his snows. At this sight, the Hebrew hosts raised a shout of joy to God, for they could see that the sacred avenue reached as far as the eye could extend across the sea; but so great was the distance, that its sides converged to a point far out from the shore, and seemed but a hair line. Then Moses, lifting up his voice, commanded the children of Israel to form into companies and columns of one hundred and eighty men abreast, and enter the sea by the way God had opened for them. First went Aaron and the twelve elders, being one of each tribe, who guarded the body of Prince Joseph. Then followed the sarcophagus, drawn by twelve oxen, one also furnished by each tribe. Then came a hundred Levites, carrying all the sacred things which the Hebrews had preserved in their generations. Now came Moses, leading the van of the people in column. I also walked near him. As we descended the shore and entered the crystalline road, I marvelled, yet had no fear, to see the walls of water, as if congealed to ice, rise thirty cubits above our heads, firm as if hewn from marble, with sharp edges at the top catching and reflecting the sunlight. The bed of the sea was hard and dry sand, smooth as the paved avenue from Memphis to the pyramids. All day the Israelites marched in, and when night came, not half their vast column had left the land. All the while the Pillar of Cloud stood behind, in the defile between the Israelites and the Egyptians. At length, in the first watch of the night, it removed, and came and went before the Israelites, throwing its beams forward along our path in the sea. Its disappearance from the rear removed also the supernatural darkness that enveloped the Egyptians; and when, by the light of the skies, Pharaoh beheld the Israelites in motion, he pursued with all his host, leading with his chariots his eager army. It was just light enough for him to see that his enemy was escaping, but not enough to see by what way; but, doubtless, he suspected that they were wading around the mountains; for great east winds have from time to time, swept the sea here outward, so that the water has been shallow enough for persons to make a circuitous ford around the northern cliff, and come in again upon the same shore into the desert above. Pharaoh knew that the wind had been blowing heavily, which he at first mistook for the Israelites in motion, and there is no doubt that he pursued with the idea that the sea had been shoaled by the wind, and that they would come out a mile or two on the north side, and gain the desert by Etham, and so double the head of the sea into the peninsula of Horeb. There can be no other reason assigned for his pursuit into such a road of God's power, unless it was judicial madness,—a hardening of his heart by God, in punishment for his contumacy and opposition to His will.

Doubtless this is one way in which God punishes men, by making their peculiar sin the instrument of their destruction.

Pharaoh and his chariots, and horsemen, and host pursued, and came close upon the rear-guard of the Israelites, against whom they pressed with shouts of battle. The sea was faintly lighted, and the king of the Egyptians did not see the walls of water which enclosed them, as they rushed madly and blindly after their prey, urged on by the loud voice of Pharaoh. At length, when they were in the midst of the sea, the Lord, in the Pillar of Cloud, suddenly turned and displayed its side of dazzling light towards the astonished Egyptians! By its sun-like splendour, Pharaoh and his captains perceived their peril, and the nature of the dreadful road in which they were entangled. The walls of water on each side of them, say the Israelites who were in the rear and saw, moved and swelled, and hung above them in stupendous scrolls of living water, upheld only by the word of God! The vivid light of the shekinah blinded their eyes, and bewildered their horses, and troubled the whole host. All the horrors of his situation were presented to the mind of the king. With frantic shouts to his charioteers to turn back, he gave wild orders for his army to retreat, saying,—

"Let us flee from the face of Israel! for the Lord their God fighteth for them against us!"

Then followed a scene of the most horrible confusion. The steady gaze upon them of the Angel of the Lord, in the cloud of fire, discomfited them! They turned to fly! Their chariot-wheels sank in the deep clay which the waggons of the Hebrews had cut up, and came off! The king leaped from his car, and, mounting a horse held by his armour-bearer, attempted to escape, when the Lord said unto Moses, who now stood upon the Arabian side of the sea,—

"Stretch out thine hand over the sea, that the waters may come again upon the Egyptians, upon their chariots, and upon their horsemen."

Then Moses stretched forth his hand upon the sea, in the deep defile of which, cleaved by God for His own people, the Egyptian hosts, chariots, horse and foot, were struggling to retrace their course to the Egyptian shore, each man battling with his comrade for preference in advance. The whole scene, for several miles in the midst of the sea, was a spectacle of terror and despair such as no war, no battle, nothing under the skies, ever before presented. The shouts and cries of the Egyptians reached our ears upon the shore with appalling distinctness.

Now Moses stretched forth his hand over the sea, out of the path through which the last of the Israelites were coming forth, when the billows that had been cloven by the rod of God, and made to stand in two walls like adamant, began to swell and heave, and all at once both edges of this sea-wall fell over like two mighty cataracts plunging and meeting, roaring and rushing together each into the chasm wherein the whole host of Pharaoh—his captains, chariots, and horsemen—with their faces towards Egypt, were struggling to escape from the snare that God, in His just vengeance, had laid for them. The returning waters covered the whole host of them before our eyes, and, while we looked, the wild sea rolled its huge waves, laden with death, above the abyss;

and then subsiding, the great sea once more flowed calmly over the spot, and Pharaoh, who had been erecting for years a majestic pyramid to receive his embalmed body, was buried by the God whom he defied, beneath the chariots and **horses in which he trusted for victory** over the sons of God.

This spectacle of God's power and judgment filled all **Israel with** awe. Those who had murmured against Moses sought his presence, and prostrated themselves before him, acknowledging their fault, and asking him to **entreat God to** pardon their iniquity, declaring that henceforth they would receive the voice of Moses as the voice of God.

That day the Israelites encamped on **the shore**; and all night the waves cast upon the **coast the** dead **bodies of** Pharaoh's host, **and** chariots innumerable, **with their stores of quivers of arrows**, lances, swords, and spears; **so that the men of Israel, to the number** of one hundred thousand chosen out of each **tribe, save that of Aaron**, were armed from the spoils of the dead soldiers **and chariots.** Was not this, **also, the** finger of God, O my father? **The** impression made upon the minds of the children of Israel, by this wonderful exhibition of the power of God,—of His goodness to them and **His** vengeance **upon** Pharaoh,—was such that they believed God, **and** feared Him, **and** professed themselves ready henceforth to be obedient to His voice.

When Moses and the children of Israel saw that their enemies were dead, they chanted a sublime hymn of praise and triumph to God upon the shore. Then came Miriam, the sister of Aaron, the aged prophetess of God, bearing a timbrel in her hand, **and** followed by an innumerable company of maidens and daughters **of** Israel, each with her timbrel in her hand, and singing songs **of** joy and triumph, while the virgins danced before the Lord.

Now, my dear father, I have brought my letters nearly to a **close.** I have recorded the most wonderful events earth ever saw, and displays of Divine power which man has never before witnessed. In contemplating these wonders, you will be impressed with the terrible majesty of God, and overwhelmed by His greatness. You will be struck with His unwavering devotion and care for His people whom He hath chosen, and with His unceasing vengeance upon His enemies, and such as oppress those **whom** He protects. You will be awed and humbled with a sublime perception of His limitless power in the heavens, on earth, and in the sea; and feel deeply your own insignificance as a mere worm of the dust in His sight; and you will cry with me, as I beheld all these manifestations of His glorious power,—

"What is man that Thou art mindful of him, O God, **who fillest the** heavens with the immensity of Thy presence, and in Thine own fulness art all in all?"

From the Sea of Arabia, Moses led the **armies** of Israel, for three encampments, into the wilderness towards Horeb. Here was no water but that which was bitter; and the people murmuring, Moses pacified them by a miracle. Thence they came to Elim, where were twelve wells of water, and seventy palm-trees, and here we encamped for some days. After certain further wanderings we came to a wilderness, just one month after departing from Egypt, God, in all that time taking not away the Pillar of Cloud by day nor the Pillar of Fire by night from before the people. Indeed, the whole journey was a miracle, and attended by miracles ; for in this wilderness, Sinn, their provisions failed, and the people (who are a perverse and stiff-necked people, forgetful of favours past, and rebellious—as is perhaps natural to those who have been so long in bondage, and find themselves now free), murmured, and again blamed Moses for bringing them from their fare of flesh and bread in Egypt, to die of hunger in the wilderness. God, instead of raining fire upon them, mercifully and graciously rained bread from heaven to feed them, returning their want of faith in Him with loving-kindness and pardon. And not only did God send bread from heaven—which continues to fall every morning—but sent quails upon the camp, so that they covered the whole plain. The taste of this heavenly bread is like coriander-seed in wafers made with honey. It is white, is called by the people manna, and is in quantities sufficient for the whole of them. The camp thence moved forward and came into the vale of Horeb, where I had first beheld Moses standing by his flock. Here there was no water, and the people murmured in their thirst, and again blamed Moses for bringing them out of Egypt into that wilderness, not remembering the mighty deliverance at the Sea of Arabia, nor the manna, nor the quails. At the first obstacle or privation, they would ever cry out against Moses, who, one day, exclaimed to his God, in his perplexity,—

"What shall I do to this people? They are almost ready to stone me!"

Then the Lord commanded him to take his rod and strike the rock in Horeb. He did so, and the water gushed forth in a mighty torrent, cool and clear, and ran like a river, winding through all the camp.

We are now encamped before Horeb. From this mountain God has given, amid thunders, and lightnings, and earthquakes, His laws to His people, by which they are to walk in order to please Him. They are ten in number : four relating to their duty to Him, and the remaining six to their duty to one another. It would be impossible, my dear father, for me to describe to you the awful aspect of Horeb, when God came down upon it, hidden from the eye of Israel in a thick cloud, with the thunders, and lightnings, and the voice of the trumpet of God exceeding loud, so that all the camp trembled for dread and fear. Nor could I give you any idea of the aspect of the Mount of God, from which went up a smoke, as the smoke of a furnace, for seven days and nights, and how the voice of the trumpet waxed louder and louder, sounding long and with awful grandeur along the skies, calling Moses to come up into the mount to receive His laws, while the light of the glory of the Lord was like devouring fire. In obedience to the terrible voice, Moses left Israel in the plain and ascended the mount. Aaron and others of the elders accompanied him so near, that they saw the pavement on which the God of Israel stood. It was, under His feet, as a sapphire stone, and as it were the body of heaven in its clearness.[1] He was absent forty days. When twenty days were passed

---

[1] Exodus xxiv. 10.

and they saw him not, nor knew what had happened to him, the whole people murmured, became alarmed, believed that they would never see him again, and resolved to return to Egypt if they could find a leader. Aaron refused to go back with them; but at length they compelled him to consent, if in seven days Moses returned not. At the end of this period they called Aaron and shouted,—

"Up! Choose us a captain to lead us back to Egypt."

But Aaron answered that he would not hearken to them, and bade them wait for Moses.

Then came a company of a thousand men, all armed, and said,—

"Up! make us gods which shall go before us! As for this Moses, we wot not has become of him."

At length Aaron, no longer able to refuse, said,—

"What god will ye have to lead you?"

"Apis! the god of Pharaoh and the Egyptians, whom we and our fathers worshipped in Egypt."

Then Aaron received from them the jewels of gold they had taken from the Egyptians, and cast them into a furnace, and made an image of the calf Serapis, and said, in grief, irony, and anger,—

"This, and like this, is thy god, O Israel, that brought thee up out of the land of Egypt!"

And erecting an altar before this image, these Israelites, not yet weaned from Egyptian idolatry, burned incense and sacrificed before it, and made a feast to the god, with music and dancing, as the Egyptians do. At length Moses reappeared, sent down from the mount by an indignant God, who beheld this extraordinary return to idolatry. When the holy prophet saw what was done, he sternly rebuked Aaron, who excused himself by pleading that he was compelled to yield, and that he did so to show them the folly of trusting to such an idol, after they had the knowledge of the true God. Moses took the calf they had made, and made Aaron burn it in the fire, and he ground it to powder, and made the idolatrous children of Israel drink of the bitter and nauseous draught. Again he rebuked Aaron, and called for all who were on the Lord's side, when several hundreds of the young men came and stood by him. He commanded them to slay all who had bowed the knee or danced before the calf; and in one hour three thousand men were slain by the sword, in expiation of their sin against God.

Now, my dear father, my last letter must be brought to a close. Moses informs me that the Lord, in punishment of this sin of Israel, will cause them to wander many years in the wilderness ere He bring them to the land promised to their fathers, and will subject them to be harassed by enemies on all sides, some of whom have already attacked them, but were discomfited by the courage of a Hebrew youth, called Joshua, who promises to become a mighty warrior and leader in Israel, and whom Moses loves as an own son.

In view, therefore, of this long abode of the children of Israel in the desert, I shall to-morrow join a caravan which will then pass to the northward, on its way into Syria from Egypt. It will be with profound regret that I shall bid adieu to Moses, to Aaron, to Miriam, and all the friends I have found among this wonderful people. Will not the world watch from afar the progress of this army of God, which has beheld the wonders by which He brought them out of Egypt? Doubtless, ere this you have heard, by ships of Egypt, of some of the mighty miracles which have devastated her cities and plains; and you will hear, ere this letter reaches you, of the destruction of the whole army of Egypt, with their king Pharaoh-Thothmeses, in the Arabian Sea.

Farewell, my.dear father; in a few weeks I shall embrace you. We will then talk of the majesty, and power, and glory of the God of Israel, and learn to fear Him; to love, obey, and serve Him,—remembering His judgments upon Pharaoh, and also upon His chosen people Israel when they forgot Him; and, that as He dealt with nations, so will He deal with individuals! Obedience, with unquestioned submission in awe and love to this great and holy God, our august Creator, is the only path of peace and happiness for kings or subjects; and the only security for admission, after death, into His divine heaven above, "whither," saith His holy servant Moses, "all men will ultimately ascend, who faithfully serve Him on earth; while those who, like Pharaoh-Thothmeses, despise Him and His power, will be banished for ever from His celestial presence into the shades below, doomed there to endure woes that know no termination, through the cycles of the everlasting ages."

Farewell, my dear father; may the Pillar of Cloud be our guide by day, and the Pillar of Fire by night, in the wilderness of this world! With prayer to God to bring me in safety to you, and to guard you in health until I see your face again,

    I am your ever affectionate son,
       REMESES, PRINCE OF DAMASCUS.

APPENDIX.

A FEW WORDS TO THE EGYPTIAN STUDENT AND TO THE CRITIC.

THERE are necessary, perhaps, a few words to show that the author of the preceding book has not arbitrarily employed facts, and made use of traditions to suit a certain series of hypothetical events; but has been controlled strictly by authorities.

Scholars, versed in Egyptian archæology, will do the author justice in the plan and execution of his work; for minds, enriched with true erudition, upon the history of the land where his scenes are placed, will not only understand the difficulties which a writer has to contend with, but appreciate what he has done. Captious criticism will, of course, hold itself wholly independent of facts; while hypercriticism must be suffered to show its *quasi* erudition. To fair and manly scholastic criticism, whether from theological scholars, or students in the "learning of the Egyptians," the work is open; and the author will be grateful to any judicious and respectable scholar who will kindly point out errors—proving them to be such.

The reader of Egyptian history is aware that but little reliance can be placed on the assigned length of periods, which furnish us with neither names nor facts, nor reliable monuments; because at this day we have no control over the fictions and errors of historians. To carry up to the first century of history a connected chain of authentic chronology is not yet possible.

We have given due credit to MANETHO'S statements, but have little confidence in many of his alleged facts, vouched as they are by JOSEPHUS and HERODOTUS. The late discoveries by CHAMPOLLION *le Jeune*, BUNSEN, Dr. YOUNG, LEPSIUS, and others, with the revelations of actual historical inscriptions, have rendered the books of these hitherto universally quoted writers nearly obsolete. The traveller of to-day, who visits Egypt and can read hieroglyph, knows more of the history of Egypt than MANETHO, JOSEPHUS, DIODORUS, HERODOTUS, STRABO, or any of the cis-Pharaoic writers thereupon. As revelations are made from time to time, we have to change our dates, revise our "facts," and reform our whole history of the past of Egypt, both in its chronology and dynasties. In this work we have availed ourselves of the latest discoveries, down to those of last year, by the celebrated French *savant*, M. AUGUSTE MARIETTE, whose discoveries have, until recently, been made known only to the Academy of Sciences, France, in modest and unpretending reports of his scientific researches.

As we have very thoroughly gone over the ground of Egyptian archæology, both in its scientific and theological relations, we are aware from what quarters attacks will be likely to come, if this book is honoured by the notice of scholars. But to such, we beg leave to say that, while we may not have formed our work on the plan *their* views would have suggested, we have done so on a plan which is defensible ; for there are several schools of interpretation of chronology and dynasty; and as we have chosen to abide by one of them alone, we are ready to defend our position, so far as may be necessary to prove that we are not ignorant of the subject we have attempted to illustrate.

The impartial scholar will see that we have endeavoured to combine the different, and often conflicting statements and opinions of the mythology of Egypt, and to present a system which should represent the belief of the Egyptian people at the time ; and out of confusion to create order.

In writing a book, the *time* of which is placed anterior to the language in which it is written, and even to the Greek and Roman, there is of necessity the use of terms, which in one sense are anachronisms, unless one actually makes use of the vernacular of the Egyptians. For instance, the Greek form of names of gods and men, is often adopted instead of the Misric, the use of which would be unintelligible pedantry: therefore, Apollo, Hercules, Venus, Isis, and Mars, are often written in our pages instead of the Egyptian names.

In order to show the general reader the variety allowable in Egyptian names and dynasties, as well as chronology, we will append a few examples :—

According to one writer on Egypt, it was Amenophis who was lost in the Red Sea. According to another, it was Thothmes III.; to another, Thothmes IV. ; and to still another, Amos I.; and to another, Osis !

Amuthosis is called by KENRICK (ii. p. 154), Misphragmuthosis. Thothmes is also called Thothmeses and other variations. Osiris has many titles and many legends, but we have adopted the popular one in Egypt.

Sesostris is called Ositasen, Osokron, Remeses, and other names, according to the interpretation of his cartouches, and other inscriptions.

The pyramid of Chephren is called also Chafre, Chephres, Cephren, and other designations, while Cheops has half a dozen appellations. A writer, therefore, who seeks to present an intelligible view of the manners, customs, religion, and polity of the ancient Egyptians must decide what authority and what path he will follow ; and having chosen each, he should pursue it undeviatingly to its close. This we have tried to do : and while those who might have selected a different one may, perhaps, not coincide with our judgment, they will at least have the candour to acknowledge that we are as much entitled, as scholars, to respect in the choice we have made, as if we had made one in harmony with their own peculiar views.

APPENDIX.

The question of "dynasty" has presented singular difficulties; but we have mainly followed NOLAN and SEYFFARTH, leaving their guidance, however, when our own judgment dictated a deviation from their views. When some chronologers of the highest character place the birth of Moses 1572 B.C. (vide Nolan), others 1947 (vide SEYFFARTH), others 2100 years, others 1460, it is necessary that a writer, whose book requires a fixed date, should make a decision. We have, after careful consideration of the whole ground, adopted the era which we believe to be the true one. The confusion attending the adjustment of the Pharaoic dynasties to their true time, is well known to scholars, and admitted by all except those who have advanced figures of their own, and expect Egyptian Chronology henceforth to be construed by them alone. NOLAN (vide Book IV., Sect. iv.), has presented to our minds the clearest exposition of the question; and we have followed, very closely, his table of the dynasty of the Pharaohs between the eras of Joseph and the Exodus.

The Biblical scholar need not be informed that Moses was forty years of age before he interested himself openly in the Hebrews. Egyptian history (see NOLAN) shows that in his thirty-fifth year, the queen-mother, Pharaoh's daughter, died, and was succeeded by Mœris; and as the Scriptures are silent, as to the occupation and place of Moses in the interval, we are justifiable in placing him out of Egypt, during the six years that followed, as we have done.

We desire here to acknowledge our indebtedness to the following authors, whose works, either directly or indirectly, we have consulted, and from which we have made use of such parts as served our purpose; and not wishing to burden our pages with notes and references, we here make our grateful acknowledgments to them, and recognition of their works:—

G. SEYFFARTH, A.M., Ph.D., D.D., seriatim, especially, "Observationes Egyptiorum Astronomicæ, et Hiæroglyphice descriptæ in Zodiaco," &c., &c.—Leipz.

"The Egyptian Chronology Analyzed;" by FREDERICK NOLAN, LL.D., F.R.S.—London.

"The Monuments of Egypt and Voyage up the Nile;" edited by FRANCIS L. HAWKS, D.D., LL.D.

"Ancient Egypt under the Pharaohs;" by JOHN KENRICK, M.A. A work which presents at one view the most complete illustrations of Egypt extant.

To SIR GARDINER WILKINSON, D.C.L., F.R.S., &c., the writer is indebted for much information respecting details of art, society, and customs.

"The Philosophy of the Plan of Salvation;" edited by Professor C. E. STOWE, D.D., by an anonymous author.

Dr. MAX UHLEMANN'S writings on Egyptian antiquities.

Rt. Rev. BISHOP WAINWRIGHT'S "Land of Bondage."

MILLS' "Ancient Hebrews."

LEPSIUS' "Discoveries in Egypt, Ethiopia," &c., and this eminent author's other valuable writings upon Egyptian archæology and antiquities.

STANLEY'S " Sinai and Palestine."
HENGSTENBERG'S " Egypt and the Books of Moses illustrated by the Monuments of Egypt."
Col. HOWARD VISE on the Pyramids.
J. A. ST. JOHN'S " Egypt and Nubia ; " London, 1845.
" Antiquities of Egypt ; " London, Rel. Tr. Soc., 1841.
ROSSELLINI'S works.
BURTON'S " Excerpta Hierogl."
J. C. NOTT, M.D., Mobile, to whose courtesy the author is indebted for several valuable works illustrating ancient Egypt.
VON BOHLEN (Petrus).
BIRCH, Roy-Soc. Lit.
" Description de l'Egypte," pendant l'Expedition de l'Armée Française, 1826.
LESUEUR, " Chron. des Rois d'Egypte."
Dr. ROBINSON'S very valuable researches.
BUNSEN'S " Egypten " and other writings, seriatim.
" DENON'S Voyage."
HERODOTUS, SOCRATES, DIODORUS, STRABO, PLINY, PTOLEMY, ERATOSTHENES, PLUTARCH, and other Greek and classic authors who have written upon Egypt, have been made use of by the author as sources of information, and adopted as authorities so far as subsequent monumental revelations have not lessened the weight of their testimony.

We are also under obligations to Professor HENRY S. OSBORN, for the aid afforded in the Phœnician portion of our book, by his recently published work, " Palestine, Past and Present," with " Biblical, Literary, and Scientific Notes ; " one of the most valuable and interesting books of travel and research which has appeared for many years, on the East : Challen and Son, Phil. 1859.

Besides the above, we have availed ourselves of numerous sources of information accessible to the Egyptian student, to enumerate which would extend this note to a catalogue.

We have sought in the foregoing work, to illustrate and delineate events of the Old Testament, as in the " Prince of the House of David," the New, so that they should " come home with a new power," to make use of the language of another, " to those who by long familiarity have lost, as it were, the vividness of the reality," and bring out their outlines so as to convey to the mind of the reader a more complete realization of scenes which seem to be but imperfectly apprehended by the general reader of the historical parts of the Old Testament. The work is written, not for scholars nor men learned in Egyptian lore ; it advances nothing new ; but simply offers in a new dress that which is old. The writer will have accomplished his object, " if his book," to quote the words of Mr. STANLEY, in his preface to " Sinai and Palestine," " brings any one with fresh interest to the threshold of the divine story ' of the Exodus,' which has many approaches, and which, the more it is explored, the more it reveals of poetry, life, and instruction, such as has fallen to the lot of no other history in the world."

The intention of the author in writing these works on Scripture narratives is to draw the attention of those persons who do not read the Bible, or who read it carelessly, to the wonderful events it records, as well as the divine doctrines it teaches ; and to tempt them to seek the inspired sources from which he mainly draws his facts.

The author's plan embraces three works of equal size. They cover the three great eras of Hebrew history, viz. : its beginning, at the Exodus ; its culmination, as in the reigns of David and Solomon ; its decline, as in the day of Our Lord's incarnation.

J. H. I.

www.ingramcontent.com/pod-product-compliance
Lightning Source LLC
Chambersburg PA
CBHW030018240426
43672CB00007B/1005